# Counter-Terroris
# Political Violenc



This edited volume aims to deepen our understanding of state power through a series of case studies of political violence arising from state 'counter-terrorism' strategies.

The book examines how state counter-terrorism strategies are invariably underpinned by terror, in the form of state political violence. It seeks to answer three key questions:

- To what extent can counter-terror strategies be read as a form of state terror?
- How fundamental is state terror to the maintenance of a neo-liberal social order?
- What are the features of counter-terrorism that render it so easily reducible to state terror?

In order to explore these issues, and to reach an understanding of what it means to say that the 'war on terror' is terror, the contributing authors draw upon case studies from a range of geographical contexts including the UK and Northern Ireland, the US and Colombia, and Sri Lanka and Tamil Eelam. Analysing these case studies from a psychological warfare and hegemonic perspective, the book also includes chapters by Noam Chomsky and John Pilger, which provide a global and historical context.

This book will be of great interest to students of critical terrorism studies, political violence, war and conflict studies, sociology, international security and international relations.

**Scott Poynting** is Professor of Sociology at Manchester Metropolitan University. He is co-author of, among other books, *Bin Laden in the Suburbs: Criminalising the Arab Other* (Sydney Institute of Criminology, 2004) and *Kebabs, Kids, Cops and Crime: Youth, Ethnicity and Crime* (Pluto Press, 2000).

**David Whyte** is Reader in Sociology at the University of Liverpool. He is co-author of *Safety Crimes* (Willan, 2007), co-editor of *Unmasking the Crimes of the Powerful* (Peter Lang, 2003) and author of *State, Crime, Power* (Sage, 2009).

**Series: Critical Terrorism Studies**
Series Editors: Richard Jackson, Marie Breen Smyth and Jeroen Gunning
*Aberystwyth University, UK*

This book series will publish rigorous and innovative studies on all aspects of terrorism, counter-terrorism and state terror. It seeks to advance a new generation of thinking on traditional subjects and investigate topics frequently overlooked in orthodox accounts of terrorism. Books in this series will typically adopt approaches informed by critical-normative theory, post-positivist methodologies and non-Western perspectives, as well as rigorous and reflective orthodox terrorism studies.

**Terrorism and the Politics of Response**
*Edited by Angharad Closs Stephens and Nick Vaughan-Williams*

**Critical Terrorism Studies**
Framing a New Research Agenda
*Edited by Richard Jackson, Marie Breen Smyth and Jeroen Gunning*

**State Terrorism and Neoliberalism**
The North in the South
*Ruth Blakeley*

**Contemporary State Terrorism**
Theory and Practice
*Edited by Richard Jackson, Eamon Murphy and Scott Poynting*

**State Violence and Genocide in Latin America**
The Cold War Years
*Edited by Marcia Esparza, Henry R. Huttenbach and Daniel Feierstein*

**Discourses and Practices of Terrorism**
Interrogating Terror
*Edited by Bob Brecher, Mark Devenney and Aaron Winter*

**An Intellectual History of Terror**
War, Violence and the State
*Mikkel Thorup*

**Women Suicide Bombers**
Narratives of Violence
*V.G. Julie Rajan*

**Terrorism, Talking and Transformation**
A Critical Approach
*Harmonie Toros*

**Counter-Terrorism and State Political Violence**
The 'War on Terror' as Terror
*Edited by Scott Poynting and David Whyte*

# Counter-Terrorism and State Political Violence

## The 'war on terror' as terror

**Edited by Scott Poynting and David Whyte**

Routledge
Taylor & Francis Group
LONDON AND NEW YORK

First published 2012
by Routledge
2 Park Square, Milton Park, Abingdon, Oxon OX14 4RN

Simultaneously published in the USA and Canada
by Routledge
711 Third Avenue, New York, NY 10017

First issued in paperback in 2013
*Routledge is an imprint of the Taylor & Francis Group, an informa business*



*British Library Cataloguing in Publication Data*
A catalogue record for this book is available from the British Library

*Library of Congress Cataloging in Publication Data*
Counter-terrorism and state political violence: the 'war on terror' as terror/edited by Scott Poynting and David Whyte.
p. cm. – (Critical terrorism studies)
Includes bibliographical references and index.
1. Terrorism–Prevention–Political aspects. 2. Political violence. 3. State-sponsored terrorism. I. Poynting, Scott. II. Whyte, David.
HV6431.C69125 2012
363.325'17–dc23
2011049080

ISBN: 978-0-415-74809-4 (pbk)
ISBN: 978-0-415-60720-9 (hbk)
ISBN: 978-0-203-11633-3 (ebk)
Typeset in Baskerville
by Wearset Ltd, Boldon, Tyne and Wear

# Contents

# Contributors

**José M. Atiles-Osoria** is a Ph.D. candidate in Sociology of Law and Political Philosophy at the University of Coimbra, Portugal, and the University of the Basque Country.

**Alan Brecknell**, from South Armagh, has been a caseworker at the Pat Finucane Centre since 2001. He specialises in investigating claims of RUC/UDR collusion with loyalist paramilitaries. In 1975, his father, Trevor, was shot dead by a paramilitary gang that included police officers and British soldiers.

**Noam Chomsky** is an American linguist, philosopher, cognitive scientist and activist. He is an Institute Professor and Professor (Emeritus) in the Department of Linguistics and Philosophy at Massachusetts Institute of Technology, where he has worked for over 50 years.

**Pablo Ciocchini** is a Ph.D. candidate at the University of the Basque Country EHU/UPV. He has been a visiting Research Fellow at the University of Liverpool and the Max Planck Institute for Foreign and International Criminal Law.

**Jeremy H. Keenan** is Professorial Research Fellow at the School of Oriental and African Studies, Universtiy of London. He is an anthropologist with some 40 years' experience of Africa, especially the Sahara on which he has written six books, including *The Dark Sahara: America's War on Terror in Africa* (Pluto, 2009) and *The Dying Sahara: US Imperialism and Terror in Africa* (Pluto, 2012).

**Stéfanie Khoury** is a Ph.D. candidate at the University of Milan and the University of the Basque Country. She has worked as a Researcher at the Centre for International Sustainable Development Law, McGill University, and at the University of Liverpool.

**Victoria Mason** is a Lecturer in the School of Politics and International Relations/Centre for Arab and Islamic Studies at the Australian National University. Her broad research areas focus on Middle East politics and human rights issues and debates.

**David Miller** is Professor of Sociology at the University of Bath, UK. His recent books include *Neoliberal Scotland: Class and Society in a Stateless Nation* (co-editor, Cambridge Scholars, 2010); and *A Century of Spin – How Public Relations Became the Cutting Edge of Corporate Power* (co-author, Pluto, 2008).

**Paul O'Connor** lives in Derry city and has been involved in the Pat Finucane Centre and the Bloody Sunday Campaign since 1993. He has a degree in Peace and Conflict Studies from the University of Ulster and has spent time in the US, Nicaragua, Spain and Germany.

**John Pilger** has been a war correspondent, author and documentary film-maker. He has won many awards for his journalism, including Britain's Journalist of the Year Award, twice, and for his documentary films of which he has made 58. He is the author of numerous best-selling books, the latest of which is *Freedom Next Time* (Bantam, 2006).

**Rizwaan Sabir** is a Ph.D. student at the University of Bath, where he is researching UK government policy towards Muslims. He regularly appears on UK media to discuss counter-terrorism issues and was one of the two men falsely imprisoned under the Terrorism Act while conducting academic research at the University of Nottingham in 2008.

**Vicki Sentas** researches the criminalisation of racialised communities. She is currently working on a project comparing the effects of terrorism laws on self-determination for Kurds and Tamils. Vicki Sentas is the Newton International Postdoctoral Fellow at the School of Law, King's College London.

**Graham Smith** is a Senior Lecturer in Regulation at the School of Law, University of Manchester, and member of ManReg (Manchester Centre for Regulation, Governance and Security). He has written extensively on remedies to police misconduct and is the police complaints consultant to the Council of Europe Commissioner for Human Rights.

**Elizabeth Stanley** is Senior Lecturer in Criminology at Victoria University of Wellington, New Zealand, where she teaches and researches on the issues of state crimes, human rights, transitional justice, social justice and imprisonment. Her book *Torture, Truth and Justice: The Case of Timor-Leste* is published by Routledge (2009).

**Oliver Villar** is a Lecturer in Politics at Charles Sturt University. His forthcoming co-authored book, *Cocaine, Death Squads, and the War on Terror,* is a study of the political economy of Colombia, cocaine and the US imperial state and the class war which underpins the politics of the Colombian cocaine trade.

# Introduction

## Counter-terrorism and the terrorist state

*Scott Poynting and David Whyte*

An established body of research has noted that the mainstream of terrorism studies, in restricting its vision of terrorism to that committed by non-state actors, or by otherwise ignoring or overlooking state terrorism, develops a way of thinking about terrorism that effectively constructs states, particularly Western states, always as the victims and never the perpetrators of 'terrorism' (Herman and O'Sullivan, 1989; Chomsky and Herman, 1979; Herman, 1982; Schlesinger, 1978; George, 1991). This book is firmly located in this critical tradition of 'bringing the state back in' to the study of terrorism, and is likewise building upon a more recent body of work which revives and updates this literature (Blakeley, 2007, 2009; Jackson *et al.*, 2009, 2010).

This book, however, is not merely part of a growing critical mass, but it also sets out to make a distinctive contribution to this literature. The chapters collected in this volume address a particular form of state terrorism: one that results directly from 'counter-insurgency' and 'counter-terrorist' operations. As the contributions herein testify, there is always a hidden solidarity between the terrorism of the state and the techniques states use under the broad rubric of the 'war on terror'.

### State and sub-state political violence

It is now almost beyond controversy in the academic literature to point out that the violence perpetrated by 'state' institutions – measured in terms of the numbers of people killed and maimed – entails a far more significant social impact than the terrorism of 'sub-state' or 'non-state' groups. However, the point of bringing together the chapters in this book is not merely to set state terrorism against its sub-state counterpart in some kind of quantitative or qualitative exercise in comparison. We are not interested in contrasting these forms of political violence as opposites. This book is, rather, concerned with what *connects* those forms of political violence.

At the level of the empirical, we can make an observation about the phenomena described in this text: that state terror arises out of strategies aimed at eliminating or alleviating subversion or opposition from sub-state political forces. As the chapters in the book collectively demonstrate, counter-terrorist strategies can be connected directly to a range of forms of state terror: genocide and cultural genocide; mass killings of civilians by state-sponsored militias and paramilitaries; military raids on and carpet bombing of civilians; mass rape as a weapon of terror; 'ethnic cleansing'; assassinations; torture; abduction and indefinite detention; demolitions of homes and obliterations of villages and neighbourhoods; deliberate and politically motivated destruction of civilian infrastructure, schools, universities, hospitals, and so on and on.

Of course, in deploying these strategies, states routinely depict the sub-state forces that challenge their monopoly of violence as 'terrorist'. Now, the most obvious question to be asked in interrogating this connection between state and sub-state political violence is whether what is described as counter-terrorism is always what it purports to be. Can we take this claim at face value? Can we accept that counter-terrorism is indeed always conducted with the aim of eliminating or mitigating terrorism? Or is it deployed for another purpose – or a range of other purposes? To take those questions a step further, we might question whether state terror, rather than being some kind of unintended consequence of counter-terrorism, might indeed be its originary purpose. This is a question that is too rarely asked directly, even in the more critical and analytical studies of terrorism. Yet it is a question that arises unavoidably when we begin to connect state political violence to sub-state political violence.

A further connection is illustrated well by interrogating the widely used cliché that one person's freedom fighter is another person's terrorist. This observation is often made in the context of scenarios in which yesterday's 'terrorists' (Nelson Mandela, Gerry Adams, Xanana Gusmao...) become embedded in today's political institutions. Their transformation is typically put down to a decision made at some Damascene moment to reject violence in favour of politics. But this is always an oversimplification. Established in the political systems of their respective countries they may have become, but this should not imply that their struggle was at any point outside the realm of politics. These former freedom fighters (as we can now name them) have not 'gone into' politics after winning that right in their liberation struggle; rather, their struggle has always been a political one.

This is certainly not how the relationship between politics and terrorism is conventionally presented to us. Politics and violent struggle in public discourse are kept strictly apart. Sub-state actors (including pro-state and proto-state paramilitaries and national liberation groups) engaging in political violence against states are generally portrayed as irrational, motivated by fanaticism, blind fury, blood-lust, inherent violence and criminality, greed and self-interest, racism, hatred, envy and other manifestations of 'evil'. In other words, they are portrayed in ways that blind us to the politics of those struggles, ways that eliminate the possibility that their violence may be a human response to objective political conditions. That is, the political violence of the oppressed is always represented as pathological and inhuman; it may be understood in rational terms, but can never be conceded to be rationally explicable, let alone conceded as a rational response to the historically transmitted, material context of conflict.

Similarly, where politics is discussed in the context of state terrorism, it is presented in a pathological way, as a result of an 'abnormal' political system (e.g. Apartheid as a 'criminal' state) or as a result of 'abnormalities' within the political system (e.g. as in the crimes and human rights abuses of the Indonesian military regime or the British in Northern Ireland) or exceptional circumstances, well beyond the normal. The pathological point of view, which envisages the crimes and human rights abuses perpetrated by states always resulting from flawed or abnormal politics, as opposed to being a routine and almost universal consequence of the politics that we can find across a broad spectrum of different state forms, has enabled debates on state terror to be marginalised or erased altogether. Yet in each of the cases noted above (in Apartheid South Africa, in British-occupied Northern Ireland and in Indonesia), extreme political violence, torture and the eradication of civil and political liberties (both formally and informally) were implemented explicitly as part of a strategy of *political* domination. Indeed, the argument that state terror is always related in some way to a planned political strategy seems to us to be irrefutable. If we see the political violence of the state as routine, and as a common and predictable consequence of the political strategies of those cases, then we have to consider political violence always as a central element in the politics of state-building and maintaining. State terror – and the threat of state violence – is, in every case, a strategy of reasoned political domination.

It may seem too obvious to mention, but the political violence perpetrated by both state and non-state actors is always deeply *political*; yet their construction in popular discourse proposes the opposite.

Wendy Brown (2006, p. 15) has noted how a process of 'depoliticisation' has become particularly virulent in the current period of late capitalism. She defines this process as:

> removing a political phenomenon from comprehension of its historical emergence and from a recognition of the powers that produce and contour it. No matter its particular form and mechanics, depoliticization always eschews power and history in the representation of its subject. When these two constitutive sources of social relations and political conflict are elided, an ontological naturalness or essentialism almost inevitably takes up residence in our understandings and explanations.

In the late twentieth century/early twenty-first century, governments, particularly in the neo-liberal era, have sought a more technocratic mode of politics in which there are, it is claimed, fewer political choices, and decision-making is increasingly reduced to judgements of national interest removed from the social and economic relations of power that underpin those judgements (Harvey, 2005; Burnham, 2001; Flinders and Buller, 2006; Hay, 2004). The argument in its most basic form is that in the elevation of particular market 'experts' and institutions above structures of democratic accountability, neo-liberal policies and practices erode the prospects for political intervention and restrict the scope of political decision-making (Whyte, 2008).

## The hegemonic eradication of politics

This process of 'depoliticisation' or what we would describe as a *hegemonic eradication of politics* is concretised by the organising concepts that are used to describe political violence. Sub-state political violence is no longer called political violence, but terrorism. And the political violence of the state is described by its fiercest critics using language which, though denunciatory, can obscure its political content.

Labelling state political violence as 'state terrorism' of course has a useful condemnatory function in hoisting the Western liberal state with its own petard, so to speak, echoing the declamatory language used by states. Yet as an exercise in counter-hegemony, this labelling process also runs the risk, through its resort to the same scandalising language, of implying, at least semantically, that state terror is an exceptional, rather than a routine, condition. This is not *merely* a semantic point, for, as we have argued, the term 'terrorism' as a hegemonic device is powerful precisely because it is able to eradicate politics from sub-state political violence. We need to consider that this might also be the effect when we fix the term 'terrorist' onto terrorist states.

Whatever semantic or lingustic strategy we deploy, however, to reintroduce politics into state and sub-state 'terror' amounts to an exercise in redefining the material basis for violence. If we are to understand adequately the origins and the motivations for political violence, and indeed if we are to appraise realistically the chance of its reduction, the imperative task for any genuine counter-terror strategy is to bring the political back into our analysis and response to 'terrorism'.

It seems undeniable that in order to 'bring politics back in' to the study of terrorism and indeed so-called counter-terrorism, we need to rethink our organising concepts. At the level of the state, this task has become both clearer and more muddy in recent years. The constant entreaty on the part of governments and their experts to think about security as apolitical has added to the muddiness as the language and practice of counter-terrorism have spread through domestic and foreign policy. This is perhaps most apparent in the key set of theoretical claims that stand behind the current 'war on terror': the 'new terrorism' thesis.

The dominant set of ideas that has shaped both hegemonic claims around terrorism and political and military responses can be described in shorthand as the new terrorism thesis. This thesis has its origins generally in the counter-terror strategies in Latin America in the late 1980s/early 1990s, supported by a number of key academic experts who are embedded in the US and British military establishment (Burnett and Whyte, 2005).

According to this thesis, the structure of the new terrorist organisation has changed fundamentally. Where the terrorist organisations of 'old' are said to have had structures that were tangible and amenable to negotiation on the one hand, or infiltration on the other, the new terrorists are assumed to depart from this 'traditional' model. Thus, such organisations no longer have clearly identifiable chains of hierarchy and command and tend to be networked globally. The new terrorist networks are said to have access to more potentially destructive weapons and technologies than the terrorists of old. Finally, the new terrorism is said to be much less discriminating in its targets – more likely to target civilian populations – and has more ability to strike from remote distances without warning. A hallmark of the new terrorism from this perspective is therefore that it has much greater lethality, and it poses a greater threat to a more diverse array of targets.

What is being conjured up here is a terrorist threat as a force that cannot be politically bargained with. Access to new technology and weapons of mass destruction – opened up by a crudely imagined process of globalisation – indicates a rupture with previous forms of terrorism. The new terrorism therefore constitutes a potential threat against which a robust response is justified and proportionate. Those features are used to argue for burgeoning resources, expanded police and military powers, and even responses outside the norms of domestic and international law in order to deal with a potentially catastrophic threat. The new terrorism thesis sets up an understanding of an enemy that is both more apocalyptic and dangerous, and at the same time less amenable to traditional forms of control. The 'new terrorism' has no political demands like the terrorism of old, for example because it is concerned with jihad – seen as the global war for an Islamic order – rather than the national liberation type wars of 'terrorists' of old: the Palestine Liberation Organisation (PLO), Irish Republican Army (IRA), African National Congress (ANC), Revolutionary Front for an Independent East Timor (Fretilin) and so on. In fact, the new terrorist theorists appear almost nostalgic about the old, political, terrorism. This nostalgic terrorology has a vision of new terrorist 'groups' as ideologically (as opposed to politically) driven organisations, supplemented with an assumption that they are beyond the boundaries of negotiation or reasoning, and that they therefore exist in a space which is beyond politics.

When violent resistance is abstracted from its formative conditions in this crude way, only then can the terrorist be known and recreated in a form that enables the Palestinian intifada, the Chechen resistance, and various armed groups in Afghanistan and Iraq to be understood as part of the same threat to order. Since the very particular historical and political conditions that enable us to understand political violence are abstracted from their specific location, our capacity for understanding the political and historical context for this violence is lost.

The new terrorism thesis therefore decontextualises the formative conditions of violence and eradicates its socio-economic and political content. This is the most useful effect of the 'new terrorism' to Western states as they hide their own political violence. For when the socio-economic and political roots of political violence are discussed and understood, too many awkward questions about Western state violence rise to the surface.

## Counter-terrorism as state political violence

The depoliticisation of political violence makes it more difficult to imagine 'terrorism' as a response to state political violence. Depoliticisation is the means by which state and sub-state political violence can be represented as occupying entirely different moral universes, connected only by a particular mode of violence. The material connections between those forms of violence are thus merely expressed in the mode of 'terror' that both may or may not deploy, rather than being understood through the political struggles that sustain them.

And this is where we can begin to see a feature common to how we are encouraged to think about sub-state political violence and counter-terrorism. For, just as the former type of political violence must be depoliticised and decontextualised, so state political violence must be represented in apolitical and asocial terms; as a technical response to a problem seen in both technocratic and Manichaean moral terms. Ultimately the representation of the 'war on terror' by protagonist states masks political and socio-economic context. In doing so, it legitimises the idea of a 'proportionate' response to an infinite evil.

State discourses around 'terrorism' are thereby able to present some highly complex, value-laden decisions as a matter of a simple value-neutral choice between opposing terrorism on the one hand and allowing terrorism to go unchecked on the other. Any political or ethical dilemma around the violence of state responses to terrorism is diminished since this is a violence that is discussed principally as a technical problem; counter-terrorism seeks only to control the threat of terrorism and is devoid of any content other than security or protection. The point of representing 'terrorism' and 'counter-terrorism' in those terms is to remove the political content from political violence. Once this is achieved, there can be no political counter-argument to counter-terrorism.

This process occurs even in some of the most directly political acts of state violence. Consider the case of Abu Zubaidah, the tortured inmate of Guantánamo Bay who is the subject at the centre of the infamous 'Torture

Memos'. There is compelling evidence from the testimonies of interrogators at the Senate Armed Services Committee hearings that Abu Zubaidah was caught up in a political charade in which US military personnel were given the task of torturing people to establish a link between al Qaeda and Iraq (US Senate Committee on Armed Services, 2008; see also Cockburn, 2007). Torture in this context can be understood only as an overtly political act: committed to provide material that could guarantee international support for the US-led invasion of Iraq. And yet the 'Torture Memos' present the acts of extreme violence by state personnel in highly technicist, operational and utilitarian terms – in terms which eradicate the political purpose of the torture.

## Empire terrorism

The hegemonic eradication of politics in this context is, of course, nothing new. Counter-insurgency theory (its post-war British colonial variant and its variants in post-war US imperial domination of Latin America) has always been less concerned with the socio-economic and political roots of violence and insurgency than with the operational or technical aspects of military strategy.

The patterns of state terror that are described in this book have a long tradition in British and American foreign policy. A case that continues as we write involves claims for compensation by the communities affected by the use of assassination and torture by British military officials, allegedly sanctioned by the British government, as a central tactic of terrorising anti-colonial opposition in Kenya in the 1950s. Indeed, there is more than enough documented evidence on public record to show how the use of torture by British officials was woven into the very fabric of British colonial rule in the twentieth century (Curtis, 2004), not least in Northern Ireland (Bunyan, 1976; McEvoy, 2001; O'Connor and Brecknell, this volume, Chapter 3).

The repertoire of state counter-insurgency measures clearly developed in the context of empire. Concentration camps, for example, with all the terror and atrocity towards civilians that they entail, were employed by the British at the turn of the last century, in the second Anglo-Boer War. They were used again in the dying days of the British empire in Kenya and Malaya, the places where today's counter-insurgency methods were widely developed (Curtis, 2003). Contemporaneously, the same counter-insurgency methods were used by France in Algeria. In the Vietnam War, US imperialism coined the sanitised term 'hamletisation' for similar practices. As Pilger's contribution to this volume asserts (Chapter 5), the post-9/11 'war on terror' must be situated in relation to the Vietnam War. In 'imperialism's return journey to respectability', the rhetoric of civilisation and morality continues to provide a cover for state terrorism.

It has been traditional for states to call their own terrorism 'counter-terror', a tradition that perhaps most famously pertains to the Third

Reich. The US national security doctrine from the 1970s onwards was founded upon a principle of counter-terrorism/state terror: the same national security doctrine that has established the basic co-ordinates for the current war on terror. It is a doctrine that not only overshadows any prospects of a 'victory' over 'terrorism', but one which can only guarantee the ongoing escalation of political violence.

The sub-contracting of terror to client states and friendly agents has long been part of the repertoire of the US and British states. The practice now widely known as extraordinary rendition (Poynting, 2010a, 2010b) has long historical antecedents. Sub-contracting terror has also been an ever-present technique in the strategies of US imperialism, perhaps most clearly in the work of the School of the Americas (renamed as the Western Hemisphere Institute for Security Cooperation; Blakeley, 2006; Gill, 2004).

As well as the officially recognised counter-insurgency functions of state political violence oriented outside the nation-state or towards (real or perceived) insurrections within, we must consider the important social control function of 'war without end' (Meiksins Wood, 2003). The Cold War allowed the US to maintain many aspects of its highly profitable 'war footing' political economy for most of the second half of the twentieth century. The suppression of class struggle within could be ideologically linked to the communist enemy without – and very successfully so – just as neo-imperialist interventions around the globe could be similarly rationalised. The politics of fear played an important part. As the Cold War ground to its conclusion, and the Soviet Union declined and disintegrated, the organic intellectuals of capital in the US and its allies turned their attention to a new enemy that would replace the 'evil empire'. For well over a decade leading up to 9/11, right-wing commentators could be frequently read and heard in the media raising the spectre of global terrorism as the new evil to be confronted. We should recognise that the new 'axis of evil' (ever expanding or reconstituted, according to expediency) has a similar function to the old enemy in disciplining populations internally, as well as mobilising 'war footings' for adventures abroad.

## From counter-terrorism to state political violence

The process of depoliticisation that we describe here is not merely a source of justification for counter-terrorism but has sustained the enduring presence of state political violence under the guise of 'counter-terrorism'. This source of justification is equally important for domestic ordering strategies as it is for legitimising occupations and invasions of foreign territories. The targets of so-called counter-insurgency and counter-terrorism are labelled in ways that diminish the legitimacy of their political claims to self-determination or to an alternative form of government. The Israeli state, for instance, claimed that its unlawful military incursion into Gaza in December 2008 was 'an attack against the Hamas terror infrastructure in the Gaza strip' (Israeli Ministry of Foreign Affairs, 2009). Similarly, Sri Lanka's President Rajapaksa, in a triumphalist address to parliament after that state's military rout and genocidal mass murder of separatist Tamils, proclaimed that 'the hopes and expectations of ... all people of our country for several decades, to see a Sri Lanka that is free of murderous terrorism, have been realized' (Permanent Mission of Sri Lanka, 2009).

To recapitulate: if there is a core rationale or logic at the heart of contemporary counter-terrorism policies it is the eradication of political and socio-economic content from both state and sub-state political violence. In this logic, sub-state political violence in opposition to the state appears ideologically as irrational and driven by fanaticism. State political violence is presented as defensive, responsible, rational and unavoidable, rather than being motivated by a particular ideological bias or political choice. As each of the chapters in this book attests in different ways, the logic of political violence is always *political*. Of course this seems axiomatic, even tautological. But it is a point that is missed in many contemporary accounts of 'state terrorism' and 'sub-state terrorism'. More specifically, the chapters in this collection seek to uncover the hidden solidarity between the terrorism of the state and the techniques states use under the broad rubric of what is today represented as a 'war on terror'. They do this in a range of contexts, including: Spain and the Basque Country; the UK and Northern Ireland; the US and Colombia; the US and Puerto Rico; Israel and Gaza; the US and European powers in the Sahara; Indonesia and Timor-Leste and West Papua; Sri Lanka and Tamil Eelam; the UK and immigrants (especially from 'suspect communities'), political dissidents and asylum seekers. All of these contributions explore what it means to say that the 'war on terror' *is* terrorism.

## References


Blakeley, R. (2006) 'Still Training to Torture? US Training of Military Forces from Latin America', *Third World Quarterly*, vol. 13, no. 27/8: 1439–61.

Blakeley, R. (2007) 'Bringing the State Back into Terrorism Studies', *European Political Science* vol. 6, no. 3: 228–35.

Blakeley, R. (2009) *State Terrorism and Neoliberalism. The North in the South*, London and New York: Routledge.

Blakeley, R. (2010) 'State Terrorism in the Social Sciences: Theories, Methods and Concepts'. In R. Jackson, E. Murphy and S. Poynting (eds), *Contemporary State Terrorism: Theory and Practice*, Abingdon: Routledge, pp. 12–27.

Bowring, B. (2008) *The Degradation of the International Legal Order: the Rehabilitation of Law and the Possibility of Politics*, London: Cavendish.

Brown, W. (2006) *Regulating Aversion: Tolerance in the Age of Identity and Empire*, Princeton, NJ: Princeton University Press.

Bunyan, T. (1976) *The Political Police in Britain*, London: Julian Friedmann.

Burnett, J. and Whyte, D. (2005) 'Embedded Expertise and the New Terrorism Thesis', *Journal of Crime, Conflict and Media Culture*, vol. 1, no. 4: 1–18.

Burnham, P. (2001) 'New Labour and the Politics of Depoliticisation', *British Journal of Politics and International Relations*, vol. 3, no. 2: 127–49.

Chomsky, N. and Herman, E. (1979) *The Washington Connection*, New York: South End Press.

Cockburn, A. (2007) *Rumsfeld: His Rise, Fall, and Catastrophic Legacy*, New York: Scribner.

Curtis, M. (2003) *Web of Deceit: Britain's Real Role in the World*, London: Vintage.

Curtis, M. (2004) *Unpeople: Britain's Secret Human Rights Abuses*, London: Verso.

Flinders, M. and Buller, J. (2006) 'Depoliticisation: Principles, Tactics and Tools', *British Politics*, vol. 1, no. 3: 293–318.

Fouskas, V. and Gokay, B. (2005) *The New American Imperialism*, London: Praeger.

George, A. (ed.) (1991) *Western State Terrorism*, London: Polity.

Gill, L. (2004) *The School of the Americas – Military Training and Political Violence in the Americas*, Durham, NC: Duke University Press.

Harvey, D. (2005) *A Brief History of Neo-liberalism*, Oxford: Oxford University Press.

Hay, C. (2004) 'The Normalising Role of Rationalist Assumptions in the Institutional Embedding of Neo-liberalism', *Economy and Society*, vol. 33, no. 4: 500–27.

Herman, E. (1982) *The Real Terror Network: Terrorism in Fact and Propaganda*, Boston: South End Press.

Herman, E. and O'Sullivan, G. (1989) *The Terrorism Industry: the Experts and Institutions that Shape Our View of Terror*, New York: Pantheon.

Israeli Ministry of Foreign Affairs (2009) 'Operation Cast Lead: Israel Strikes Back against Hamas Terror in Gaza', www.mfa.gov.il/MFA/Terrorism-+Obstacle+to+Peace/Hamas+war+against+Israel/Israel_strikes_back_against_Hamas_terror_infrastructure_Gaza_27-Dec-2008.htm, accessed 19 August 2011.

Jackson, R., Breen Smith, M. and Gunning, J. (2009) 'Introduction: the Case for Critical Terrorism Studies'. In *Critical Terrorism Studies: A New Research Agenda* Abingdon: Routledge, pp. 1–9.

Jackson, R., Murphy, E. and Poynting, S. (eds) (2010) *Contemporary State Terrorism: Theory and Practice*, London: Routledge.

Kagan, R. (2003) *Paradise and Power: America and Europe in the New World Order*, London: Altantic.

Kolko, G. (2002) *Another Century of War?*, New York: The New Press.

McEvoy, K. (2001) *Paramilitary Imprisonment in Northern Ireland: Resistance, Management and Release*, Oxford: Oxford University Press.

Meiksins Wood, E. (2003) *Empire of Capital*, London and New York: Verso.

Pape, R. (2005) *Dying to Win: the Strategic Logic of Suicide Terrorism*, New York: Random House.

Permanent Mission of Sri Lanka to the United Nations at Geneva (2009) 'President Rajapaksa Declares Sri Lanka's Victory over Tiger Terrorism', 19 May, www.lankamission.org/content/view/2170/1/, accessed 19 August 2011.

Petras, J. and Veltmeyer, H. with Vasapollo, L. and Casadio, M. (2005) *Empire with Imperialism: the Globalizing Dynamics of Neo-liberal Capitalism*, London: Zed.

Poynting, S. (2010a) '"We Are All in Guantanamo": State Terror and the Case of Mamdouh Habib'. In R. Jackson, E. Murphy and S. Poynting (eds), *Contemporary State Terrorism: Theory and Practice*, London: Routledge, pp. 181–95.

Poynting, S. (2010b) 'Render unto Caesar', *Criminal Justice Matters,* December, vol. 82: 14–15.

Schlesinger, P. (1978) 'On the Shape and Scope of Counter-Insurgency Thought'. In G. Littlejohn, B. Smart, J. Wakeford and N. Yuval-Davis (eds), *Power and the State,* London: Croom Helm, pp. 98–127.

US Senate Committee on Armed Services (2008) Inquiry into the Treatment of Detainees in US Custody: Report of the US Senate Committee on Armed Services, Washington, 110th Congress, 2nd Session, 20 November, available online at: http://armed-services.senate.gov/Publications/Detainee%20Report%20Final_April%2022%202009.pdf, accessed 26 February 2010.

Whyte, D. (2008) 'Market Patriotism and the War on Terror', *Social Justice,* vol. 35, nos 2–3: 111–31.

Whyte, D. (2010) 'Dismantling the Reasons of State', *Criminal Justice Matters,* December, vol. 82: 4–5.

# 1 Counter-terrorism as counterinsurgency in the UK 'war on terror'

*David Miller and Rizwaan Sabir*

## Introduction

1 In this Act 'terrorism' means the use or threat of action where –
  a the action falls within subsection (2),
  b the use or threat is designed to influence the government or an international governmental organisation or to intimidate the public or a section of the public, and
  c the use or threat is made for the purpose of advancing a political, religious, racial or ideological cause.
2 Action falls within this subsection if it –
  a involves serious violence against a person,
  b involves serious damage to property,
  c endangers a person's life, other than that of the person committing the action,
  d creates a serious risk to the health or safety of the public or a section of the public, or
  e is designed seriously to interfere with or seriously to disrupt an electronic system.

(HM Government 2000)

This definition of terrorism is taken from the UK Terrorism Act 2000 and is the definition currently in force, being referred to explicitly in both the Terrorism Act 2006 (where it was slightly augmented) and the Counter-Terrorism Act 2008. We use this definition to analyse counter-terrorism in the UK and its relationship to counterinsurgency. We focus on the extent to which UK government action in this area might be said to meet the definition.

While the UK government has provided troops and logistical support for the US-led wars in Afghanistan and Iraq it has also focused significant effort on the UK itself to combat what it says is a significant internal 'terrorist threat'. Rather than treat the threat as a matter of policing, successive governments have opted to treat it as a matter that requires exceptional powers which integrate the theory and practice of counterinsurgency. This is noteworthy because counterinsurgency embodies a series of techniques for targeting 'insurgents' and the population within which they move as the enemy, undermining liberal democratic rhetoric about the existence of democratic politics. We argue that, in fact, the adoption of counterinsurgency doctrine and practice in counter-terrorism by the British state results in a series of measures and practices that bear more than a passing resemblance to 'terrorism' as officially defined by the UK government.

Since 9/11 and especially since the attacks in London in 2005 (7/7), the British government has introduced a series of counter-terrorism programmes and initiatives through its CONTEST strategy, which aims to '[r]educe the risk of international terrorism to the UK and its interests' (HM Government 2009: 12). CONTEST has been divided into four workstreams, or the 4 Ps as they are commonly known – *Pursue, Prevent, Protect and Prepare.*[1]

We focus here on the domestic components of Pursue and Prevent – the latter of which was under review by the coalition government at the time of writing – as the main coercive and communicative elements of the policy. The Pursue workstream aims to confront the threat posed by terrorism through counter-terrorism initiatives including intelligence and investigation (HM Government 2009: 63), while Prevent aims to stop terrorism from taking place by 'winning the hearts and minds' of the Muslim community (Department for Communities and Local Government 2007b: 1).

Both these strands have faced intense criticism for practices that repress and discriminate against Muslims, and label them as 'suspect' (Pantazis and Pemberton 2008; Fekete 2001; Liberty 2004; Kundnani 2009). Notable examples include exceptional legislative measures being created specifically to target Islamic terrorism, extended pre-charge detention periods, intrusive surveillance programmes, newer and broader terrorism offences, securitised community projects and policies that legitimate the use of deadly force such as 'Operation Kratos' that, in certain circumstances, authorises the use of a 'head shot' – otherwise known as a policy of 'shoot-to-kill' (Metropolitan Police Authority 2005a, 2005b).

These measures, however, rather than successfully targeting terrorists have largely affected Muslims indiscriminately, meaning many innocent Muslims have been disproportionately affected. This is not an unpleasant by-product of mistakes, ignorance or arrogance, we argue: the laws and programmes that underpin these strategies have been created intentionally and purposefully to coerce and instil fear within the Muslim community and those who stand with it. This is because key components of the Pursue and Prevent strands are based on the theory and practice of counterinsurgency, which involve both 'coercion' (in the sense of using physical or 'kinetic' power, i.e. violence), and 'propaganda' and 'communication' (in the sense of using psychological warfare against a perceived enemy).

We use an investigative research approach to uncover the intellectual and practical antecedents of the policy and examine the way in which it has been put into practice. The chapter uncovers the hitherto little-known development of counterinsurgency doctrine in the UK, using documents released to the authors under the Freedom of Information Act; it examines how the doctrine utilises coercion and 'propaganda' and looks at the involvement of military officers in formulating key parts of the CONTEST strategy and their specific expertise in counterinsurgency and information operations (I-Ops). The practical implementation of the strategy is then examined by analysing the governmental bodies involved, namely the Civil Contingencies Secretariat in the Cabinet Office and the Home Office-based Office of Security and Counter Terrorism (OSCT) and its key offshoot, the Research, Information and Communications Unit (RICU). We also look at one of the key civil society bodies set up and funded by the OSCT – the 'anti-extremist' Quilliam Foundation. But, before turning to analyse the role of those bodies, we commence our analysis by looking at the three fundamental counterinsurgency measures that have become deeply entrenched within Pursue and Prevent – exceptional legislation, pre-emptive incapacitation measures and intelligence and surveillance structures.

## Counterinsurgency

Counterinsurgency is a military doctrine developed in Western states, and mainly intended to deal with small wars and insurgency or guerrilla campaigns abroad. According to historical accounts of the development of British counterinsurgency, the important elements of the doctrine have – since the mid-1950s – consistently been the integration of civil and military power, the use of intelligence and the increasing role of communicative activities.

The main doctrinal publications have emphasised 'civil–military co-operation'. Most notably, *Keeping the Peace* (British Army 1963) drew on the experience of the British role in Malaya, and contained 'some new wisdom: an awareness of the increasing role of the mass media and public opinion' (Mockaitis 1995, 135). These two themes have been present ever since. The next major doctrinal publication was the *Land Operations* series, first issued in three parts in 1969 and 1970, or just after British troops were deployed in Northern Ireland. It was revised in 1995, in July 2001 (before 9/11) and in 2009 (Ministry of Defence 1969a, 1969b, 1970, 1995, 2001, 2009). All versions emphasised the two central themes of civil–military co-operation and the importance of communications, and also the 'vital role of intelligence' (Mockaitis 1995, 136). In addition, exceptional and emergency legislation and pre-emptive controls are considered essential (Hocking 1988).

This integrated conception of counterinsurgency is endorsed by today's most influential counterinsurgency thinkers such as David Kilcullen, the Australian counterinsurgency writer who has served as an official adviser to the US State Department, and David Petraeus, the architect of the 'Surge' in Iraq in 2007. This has brought the advocates of a 'hearts and minds' approach, specifically Kilcullen in the position of 'Senior Counterinsurgency Adviser, Multi-National Force – Iraq', to the centre of policy-making (Kilcullen 2007b; Miller and Mills 2010: 207). Kilcullen advocates a military strategy that draws on insights from the social sciences and is attentive to particular cultures and societies. 'War is a form of armed politics', he has written 'and politics is about influencing and controlling people and perceptions' (Kilcullen 2004a). Kilcullen has also been influential in the UK, being cited by both Gordon Brown (as Prime Minister) and David Miliband (as Foreign Secretary) (D'Ancona 2007). For example, in 2009, Miliband wrote in his Foreign Office blog, 'I think that some of the best thinking about terrorism has been done by David Kilcullen' (Miliband 2009).

In Kilcullen's view, the United States and its allies are involved in a global war which demands that they use an updated model of counterinsurgency theory rather than the conventional counter-terrorism paradigm. In an article in 2004, Kilcullen writes that 'the present conflict is actually a campaign to counter a globalised Islamist insurgency. Therefore, counterinsurgency theory is more relevant to this War than is traditional counter-terrorism'. A key aspect of this approach is 'improved cultural capability' (2004b: 1).

In other words, Kilcullen, seeks a more advanced understanding of particular cultures and societies to ensure that America and its allies can 'influence and control' them more efficiently. In another article (2006: 122) he writes: 'in modern counterinsurgency, where there is no single insurgent network to be penetrated but rather a cultural and demographic jungle of population groups to be navigated'. That being the case, 'the counterinsurgent must control the overall environment rather than defeat a specific enemy'. The overall environment, however, does not stop at the borders of the country in which the insurgency operates or indeed where the insurgency stops. Thus Kilcullen (2007a: 647) argues that 'Europe is both a source and a target of terrorist activity, and faces threats including Al Qaeda-inspired terrorism, extremist political parties, insurgent sympathizer networks, subversive movements, and the overlap between crime and terrorism'. The global war on terror is, therefore, just that – a global war that focuses on the territory of the West as well as that of the occupied or developing world. The 'primary threat', writes Kilcullen, is 'terrorist-linked subversion, which seeks to manipulate and exploit the sociological and ethnographic features of immigrant communities'. Counter-terrorism needs, therefore, to combine counterinsurgency and 'countersubversion' (Kilcullen 2007a: 647).

As Mockaitis notes, the tendency over the forty years from the mid-1950s has been 'the increasing emphasis on psychological operations, media briefing and propaganda in the official literature' (1995: 146). But it is more than that. The 2009 revision of British counterinsurgency doctrine makes this clear by opening its section on 'Information Operations' with a quote from David Kilcullen (Ministry of Defence 2009: 6-2): 'Traditionally in the course of conventional operations we use information operations to explain what we are doing, but in COIN we should design operations to enact our influence campaign,' This distinction between explaining and enacting is absolutely critical to understanding the counterinsurgency approach to information. Information is seen as a weapon of war as opposed to a means of supporting weapons of war (Miller 2003). It is worth emphasising that this erodes the distinction between 'physical' or 'kinetic' operations (coercion and violence) and information operations (PSYOPS or strategic communication). It suggests that information operations are viewed as part of 'kinetic' operations. This impression is reinforced by the discussion of what is included in I-Ops: 'Information operations will on occasions require an aggressive and manipulative approach to delivering messages (usually through the PSYOPS tool). This is essential in order to attack, undermine and defeat the will, understanding and capability of insurgents' (Ministry of Defence 2009: 6-5).

I-Ops are also said to include 'PSYOPS, electronic warfare, presence posture profile, computer network operations, deception, physical destruction, information security, Key Leader Engagement (KLE) and the handling of visitors' (Ministry of Defence 2009: 6-3). KLE is a strategy which suggests cultivating and/or managing the 'leaders' in local communities. A US manual (also distributed by the UK government's Stabilisation Unit) notes that KLE is a long-term means of 'building relationships to the point of effective engagement and influence' that 'usually takes time'. 'KLE is not', it notes, 'about engaging key leaders when a crisis arises', but over time with 'enough strength and depth', so that 'they can then support our interests during times of crisis' (Joint Forces Command Joint Warfighting Center 2010: iii–8).

The Ministry of Defence *Manual* (2009: 5-11) notes that there is a 'requirement for intelligence staffs to support KLE'. 'At battlegroup level', it says, 'the commander should focus on KLE and the use of tactical PSYOPS to influence the local population and affect the will and understanding of the insurgent' (Ministry of Defence 2009: 6-3). This is accomplished by a variety of means including 'deception'. 'The primary aim of deception', the *Manual* notes, 'is to mislead the adversary, guard our real intentions and thus persuade him to adopt a disadvantageous course of action. Deception has great utility in tactical counterinsurgency operations and requires effective OPSEC in order to succeed' (Ministry of Defence 2009: 6-5).

The integration of all material on 'influence activities' (Ministry of Defence 2009: iii) into a single chapter in 2009 is one key indication of the move towards a model of strategic communication in counterinsurgency thinking. The move is not without its dangers for the military as it might lead critics to imagine that media, information and psychological operations are simply differing elements of an overall 'propaganda machine'. This possibility is specifically raised in the *Manual* especially in relation to the 'aggressive and manipulative' approach noted above.

> When this is the information operations focus, great care must be taken to maintain the integrity and credibility of the media operations organisation. At other times, the activities conducted by formation information operations cells will require more delicate approaches to influencing target audiences in different ways, such as through neutral or uncommitted groups (third parties).... To avoid giving the impression that the media are being manipulated in any way, which would undermine media operations activity, a distinction must be maintained between the two. Essentially, they must remain separate but closely related activities. For example the information operations officer cannot be double-hatted as the media operations officer/spokesman. However, they both serve the commander in his attempt to dominate the information and cognitive domain by being proactive and staying 'on message'. The headquarters layout needs to reflect this rather complicated arrangement and encourage close cooperation.
>
> (Ministry of Defence 2009: 6-5)

Sceptical observers may conclude that the 'impression' of media manipulation is unlikely to be expunged by taking 'great care' to suggest that differing elements of a unified influence operations strategy are actually separate.

Though the phrase 'strategic communication' is not used in the 2009 *Manual*, it is apparent that strategic communication has evidently been influential. The Ministry of Defence 'lead' on strategic communication is Steve Tatham, an experienced military media handler. He was a public spokesman for the British Military in Sierra Leone (2000), Afghanistan (2001–2) and Iraq (2003) (Powerbase 2011a). From 2007 to 2009 he was the Director of 'Communication Research' at the UK Defence Academy's Advanced Research and Assessment Group (ARAG).

Tatham argues that the term 'strategic communication' is widely misunderstood and misconstrued because it is understood as a replacement term for 'spin', media and information operations, or propaganda. Tatham describes these as 'emotive and often inaccurate terms'. This is, he writes, 'unhelpful and mires understanding' (Tatham 2008: 5). Strategic communication is, he argues, 'an extremely powerful tool that may hold the key to the dilemma of 21st century conflict, the power of information and opinion and its ability to enable behavioural change' (Tatham 2008: 20).

He suggests that any definition of the concept must 'recognise that the success of non-kinetic effect is amplified by threats of kinetic activity' (Tatham 2008, 15). In other words, strategic communication is integrated with an overall kinetic strategy and is itself part of a coercive strategy. As Tatham himself puts it: 'Influence does not mean the exclusion of hard power', nor is it only directed at 'external' audiences or at an 'enemy' (Tatham 2008: 15), but it is also directed at 'internal' audiences, meaning sections, or all, of the general public (Tatham, 2008: 4).

Lastly, we should note that just as Kilcullen has supported counter-subversion in combating terrorism, so too has Tatham. His argument undermines his own suggestion that strategic communication is new and perhaps puts it closer to the classic definitions of propaganda than he would like. He notes that:

> for all the sophistication of the current information environment, paradoxically these are not new skills, merely ones that we must relearn. The Political Warfare Executive (PWE) of World War 2 employed academics, journalists, scientists, housewives, misfits and reprobates – all possessing a common thread of innovation and an ability to think – to harness their eclectic skills and personalities to fight the Allies' information battle against Nazi Germany. Was it because it was a war of national survival that PWE was accepted, even congratulated, whilst the 2007 announcement by the British government of the establishment of the Research, Information and Communications Unit (RICU) was met with such public derision and scorn?
>
> (Tatham 2008: 20)

The fact of a war of national survival certainly has something to do with it, but Tatham appears to forget that the UK is not 'at war' in any similar way with 'radical Islam'.

To summarise, the ideas set out in counterinsurgency theory emphasise four key elements:

1. the integrated nature of strategy and co-ordination between civil and military powers;
2. the key role of intelligence and surveillance;
3. exceptional legislation, allowing for pre-emptive controls;
4. the crucial importance of strategic communication.

Our characterisation draws on previous research in this area (Hocking 1988, 1993), but it is important to note several differences. The first is the closer integration of counterinsurgency and counter-terrorism in theory and practice since 2001, the second is the closer strategic integration of the various elements. The integration is such that 'the correct balance of kinetic and non-kinetic effect' is used 'to influence the will and ultimately positively affect the behaviour of a target group' (Tatham 2008: 15). Finally, we should note that Hocking in 1988 listed 'media management' as a key element. This was characterised by the integration of the news media into a national security model and 'voluntary' self-restraint by the news media. Since then, as we saw above, the development of the doctrine of strategic communication has moved some considerable way in treating communication and media as instruments of war fighting.

Taken together, these four elements form a highly coercive strategy intended to manage the consciousness and behaviour of the British public. It is a declaration of war on the public mind and on the will to dissent or resist. This does not sit well with liberal notions that the government is accountable to the people. Nor does it seem to easily fit with official pronouncements such as the following:

> This is not about a clash of civilisations or a struggle between Islam and 'the West'. It is about standing up to a small fringe of terrorists and their extremist supporters. Indeed, Government is committed to working in partnership with the vast majority of Muslims who reject violence and who share core British values in doing this.
>
> (Department for Communities and Local Government 2007b)

So it is to explicating the parallels between counterinsurgency and counter-terrorism in the UK that we now turn.

## Pursue: hard power

The counterinsurgency theorists Robert Thompson (1966: 52–5) and Frank Kitson (1971: 69) wrote after the end of British and French counterinsurgency campaigns in Malaya, Cyprus and Algeria that the state's response to terrorism and insurgencies must be 'in accordance with the law' but emergency legislation should be carefully drafted to ensure simplicity. It should also, they argued, favour 'preventive detention' of suspected insurgents or terrorists. During the Northern Ireland 'Troubles', this was the exact approach taken by the UK under the auspices of emergency legislation that was enacted, notably through the use of internment.

The Prevention of Terrorism Act 1974 (PTA) lasted for twenty-six years and was replaced (prior to the attacks of 9/11) with the Terrorism Act 2000. The 'temporary' status of the Prevention of Terrorism Act meant that it was considered exceptional legislation and was thus subjected to regular parliamentary scrutiny and debate. However, as Walker (2009: 23) notes, although the 2000 Act is very similar to the PTA, it differs in the sense of its permanent status, which means that it is not subjected to the same oversight or scrutiny as its predecessor. 'There is [no] ... serious chance', writes Walker, 'that any part of the legislation will be struck down or seriously analysed in an hour and a half of [a parliamentary] debate' (2009, 25).

Thompson's and Kitson's prescriptions also fed into the Anti-Terrorism Crime and Security Act 2001, which was passed in the immediate aftermath of the 9/11 attacks. This law was fundamentally based on the use of pre-emptive action to incapacitate foreign nationals suspected of being terrorists by the state. It was, essentially, the first manifestation of a counterinsurgency approach in the post-9/11 world because it was based on using 'exceptional legislation' to legitimise the use of 'pre-emptive' measures before any 'terrorist' act had occurred.

In 2004, the House of Lords ruled that internment of foreign nationals contravened human rights, was discriminatory and thus had to be repealed (BBC News 2004). However, it was immediately replaced with the equally illiberal Prevention of Terrorism Act 2005.

The PTA 2005 replaced internment with indefinite house arrest, in what became known as 'control orders'. Under a control order, the Home Secretary makes an executive order (i.e. not subject to judicial review) to place an unlimited range of restrictions on any 'suspected' terrorist where the 'evidence' is held but considered too sensitive and thus kept secret (Liberty 2009). Secrecy is of the essence because the evidence may have been acquired by foreign intelligence services that employ torture, with the connivance of MI5 (Hewitt 2008: 38). 'Controlees' are denied the right to see the evidence against them and are therefore unable to mount a defence in court. These powers use 'exceptional legislation' to legitimise the use of 'pre-emptive' measures – principles that are highly consistent with counterinsurgency approaches.

It was in the aftermath of the 7/7 bombings that the biggest change to the UK's counter-terrorism apparatus emerged, notably when Tony Blair declared that in the war against terrorism, 'the rules of the game are changing' (Brown and Woolfe 2005). The 'new rules' meant the adoption of further policies drawing on counterinsurgency theory and practice.

A campaign to increase the pre-charge detention to ninety days was launched, allegedly to equip the police to investigate complex, often internationally connected, terror cases. It also permitted the police to investigate any person who was considered by them to be involved in terrorism. The government, however, failed to secure the ninety-day extension and settled, instead, for twenty-eight days. The current pre-charge detention limit has, at the time of writing, reverted to fourteen days after the coalition government refused to renew the clause that authorised twenty-eight days.

Other examples of the adoption of counterinsurgency practice came through the 2006 Terrorism Act, notably through the 'new' offences of 'encouragement of terrorism' and 'dissemination of terrorist publications', which essentially criminalise certain types of free speech, but without any test for actual incitement. This is because the law outlaws both direct and indirect encouragement. For example, if a person fails to realise that their words or dissemination may 'indirectly' encourage another person to commit terrorism through their 'recklessness', they could be guilty of an offence (Sabir 2010a, 2010b).

This power is exceptionally, but purposefully, broad because it has been founded on the counterinsurgency principle of taking pre-emptive and premeditated action against potential insurgents and their alleged supporters. Schlesinger (1978: 115) notes that a key concept within counterinsurgency theory is based on premeditating, anticipating and taking pre-emptive action against those who may perpetrate violence before it is undertaken.

One of the consequences of counterinsurgency-infused counter-terrorism is the feeling of siege and of suspicion within the 'suspect' community (Sabir 2010a, 2010b; House of Commons 2007: 15; Muslim Council of Britain 2005; Kundnani 2006).

These are the predictable consequence of official policy, whether or not they are deliberate. But rather than take measures to mitigate such problems by curtailing such approaches, the official policy has been to adopt the Prevent programme – a 'hearts and minds' campaign directed at the Muslim community – which was launched in 2006. However, as the next section now discusses, the fundamental premise of this programme is also seated deep in counterinsurgency assumptions and practice.

## Prevent: hearts and minds

The Prevent programme is the second strand of CONTEST and aims to win the 'hearts and minds' of British Muslims who 'reject violence' and 'share core British values' by equipping them with the ability to 'stand up to terrorists and their extremist supporters' (Department for Communities and Local Government 2007a: 4). The overarching objectives of Prevent are to stop 'radicalisation', reduce support for terrorism and discourage people from becoming terrorists (HM Government 2009: 14). In other words, the counterinsurgency principles of pre-emption, prevention and communication are at the core of this strategy. In a bid to ensure that prevention work is successful, 'intelligence gathering', another of the key counterinsurgency components, forms an essential part of Prevent.

The Prevent strategy can be traced back to 2003, the year when CONTEST was launched. At this time, Prevent was the least developed component of CONTEST, but after the 7/7 attacks, in a bid to prevent similar attacks, the Prevent strand aimed to win the 'hearts and minds' of the Muslim community (Department for Communities and Local Government 2007a: 4). The Prevent policy essentially became a focal point of UK counter-terrorism (HM Government 2009: 82–3).

The bulk of the practical responsibility for this programme fell to the Home Office's OSCT, its strategic communications wing RICU and the Department for Communities and Local Government (CLG).

The CLG was responsible for delivering the Prevent strategy on a local level through community-based projects and local partnerships. The OSCT was created specially in 2007 as an overarching body that was responsible for co-ordinating the entire cross-governmental approach to CONTEST (HM Government 2009: 9) whilst its key off-shoot, RICU, became responsible for offering communication advice to governmental and local agencies involved in counter-terrorism work (House of Commons 2010: Ev. 203). It also works towards 'exposing the weaknesses of violent extremist ideologies and brands' (House of Commons 2010: Ev. 203).

Muslim community and human rights organisations have claimed that Prevent targets Muslims in general and reinforces their image as a fifth column or an enemy within (House of Commons 2010: Ev. 91). But such criticisms only add up if they are viewed through the lens of counterinsurgency which intends to take 'collective preventive action' against the community that allegedly 'hosts' the 'insurgent', or 'terrorist', or in this case, the Muslim community and those who stand with it.

This approach was best summarised by the head of the OSCT, Charles Farr, when he said that because 'al-Qaeda tends to focus its recruitment operations on people in Muslim communities ... [therefore] it would be best to look at ... Muslim communities' (House of Commons 2010: Ev. 72). This claim explains why the government in 2006–7 compelled all local authorities with 2,000 or more Muslims to accept funding under Prevent (Kundnani 2009: 12). This suggests that Muslims as a whole have been targeted under Prevent (i.e. they are viewed as the problem). Targeting Muslims has also been undertaken via intelligence gathering, another core component of Prevent and counterinsurgency.

In 2009, a series of allegations were made by the *Guardian* and the Institute of Race Relations, arguing that Prevent was collating information on the (non-violent) political opinions of Muslims within the UK, and other personal and private information, such as health, sexual behaviours and theological outlooks (Kundnani 2009; Dodd 2009a, 2009b; Sabir 2009).

Agencies and ministers involved have constantly denied that Prevent is, or has ever been, about spying or intelligence gathering (Hanson and Malik 2010; Johnson *et al.* 2010), but the CONTEST strategy categorically states that one of the overarching objectives of Prevent is to develop 'intelligence, analysis and information' (HM Government 2009: 84). Indeed, CONTEST states that this objective 'supports' the five primary objectives of Prevent (HM Government 2009: 84).

A leaked 'restricted' police document seems to confirm such an approach. The document categorically states that the police, through the Prevent programme, are collating intelligence and information on 'all members of the [Muslim] community', 'priority groups' and those who are have not perpetrated violence but are 'moving toward extremism' (Association of Chief Police Officers (TAM) 2008: 11).

The collation of low-grade information that may not be particularly accurate or useful is a counterinsurgency technique that Kitson (1971: 131) recommends. He writes that 'the system for developing background information only works if there is a lot of [information] to develop. It is not important that [the information] should be immensely reliable because all that is needed is something on which to build' (Kitson 1971: 131).

In the context of Prevent, this information is collated through a range of different avenues such as neighbourhood policing (HM Government 2009: 85), 'community intelligence' (Powerbase 2011f) or, as is the case in the West Midlands for example, through Security and Partnership Officers (SPOs). SPOs are a series of specially selected uniformed counter-terrorism police officers who liaise with the Muslim community and develop information (i.e. local intelligence) regarding it in 'key community locations' such as 'mosques' and 'community centres' (West Midlands Police Authority 2010: 1). This, along with community intelligence and neighbourhood policing information, is then fed into a collaborative MI5 and police programme entitled 'Rich Picture' (West Midlands Police Authority 2010: 1) which processes it to 'provide a wider understanding of … terrorist activity and radicalisation in this country' (HM Government 2009: 65; Powerbase 2011e). Developing a 'Rich Picture' understanding of the 'enemy' and its 'supporting community' is one of the fundamental connections that Prevent has with counterinsurgency theory. Such a 'picture' is essentially what Kitson calls 'background information', that is, information which is irrelevant in isolation, but useful when accompanied with supporting information.

Further connections with counterinsurgency can be seen in the institutions set up to take CONTEST forward, in the personnel involved and in the activities they undertake. We examine these next.

## Counterinsurgents in government

The main new organisations set up to tackle the alleged terrorist threat are the OSCT and, within that, RICU. The Cabinet Office's Civil Contingencies Secretariat (CCS) and Strategic Horizons Unit (SHU) are also heavily involved in the domestic counter-terrorism field. Former military officers or individuals linked to the military establishment have played a significant role in devising domestic counter-terror strategies. Ideas derived from counterinsurgency have, in this way, been applied to domestic counter-terror policy. Two of the key figures who have been involved in this have been Commander Steve Tatham, whose ideas we have already discussed, and Dr Jamie Macintosh.

Tatham, a military officer, was, in 2009, seconded to the SHU – a unit created in September 2008 and housed in the Cabinet Office (Powerbase 2011a; Maude 2009). This fact reinforces our case on the influence of counterinsurgency theorists in the domestic counter-terrorism arena. The fact that the SHU is part of the Joint Intelligence Organisation (which fits with the counterinsurgency priority of close intelligence co-operation) also displays a deeper level of military involvement.

Tatham was previously situated at the Defence Academy, where his boss was Dr Jamie Macintosh. Prior to becoming Ministry of Defence research scientist, Macintosh 'served in the British Army for ten years. His final operational tour was in Bosnia during most of 1993' (Powerbase 2011d). Macintosh joined the Defence Evaluation and Research Agency in 1993, moving on to the Defence Science and Technology Laboratory (DSTL) which replaced it in 2001. During his time there, he made 'strategic and operational contributions in the emerging fields of Information Superiority and Information Operations (IS-IO)' (Defence Academy 2009).

Macintosh collaborated with the head of the Government Information and Communication Service, Mike Granatt, in co-authoring the White Paper 'and conceptual research design' 'at the direction of the Prime Minister' that led to the creation of the CCS in 2001. The CCS was the body involved in issuing information about the alleged threat to Heathrow Airport and on the 'ricin plot', which turned out not to involve any ricin (Miller 2004). Indeed, according to Archer and Bawdon (2010), the jurors in the ricin trial, there was never any so-called ricin 'plot'. In this case, as in others, official information can seem as if it embodies the tactics described in UK counterinsurgency doctrine as 'manipulation' and 'deception' (Ministry of Defence 2009: 6-5, 6-E-1).

Macintosh spent over a year as the personal adviser on 'Transformation and National Security' to Home Secretary John Reid. A biographical note claims that 'he catalysed the use of a "war room" facility to begin building the capacity needed to transform the Home Office'. His advice, the Ministry of Defence claims, 'was instrumental' in the creation of the OSCT and its strategic communications division, RICU (Defence Academy 2009), more evidence of military involvement in domestic counter-terrorism.

## Research, Information and Communications Unit

RICU is a 'strategic communications unit' within the OSCT. Based in the Home Office, it is also funded by and answerable to the Foreign Office and the Department for Communities and Local Government. Latterly the Ministry of Defence has also become involved in funding RICU. In 2009/10, RICU's budget was £5.7 million (Powerbase 2011c). On its launch, the *Sunday Times* reported that 'officials deny this is in any way a propaganda department, although one conceded: "It does sound horribly cold war"' (Correra 2007).

RICU's history suggests that it does more than propaganda in the sense that strategic communications must be strongly integrated with the wider elements of CONTEST, in particular integration with repressive measures by the state and a close connection with intelligence – both cardinal principles of counterinsurgency. Indeed, it is clear that RICU is itself an intelligence-connected body, notably because of its connections with the OSCT which is currently led by Charles Farr, a former career MI6 officer. The *Guardian* recently reported that the OSCT was 'widely regarded in Whitehall as being an intelligence agency' (Dodd 2009a).

Furthermore, the role of Prevent in gathering intelligence on Muslim communities is complemented by RICU's focus on commissioning research on Muslim communities. Between 2007 and 2010, for example, RICU concentrated on research projects relating to how 'young British Muslims felt about their identity and sense of belonging', 'how young British Muslims use the internet', 'media consumption among British Muslims', 'how Government messages are perceived by Muslim communities', 'Islamic Blogs', 'The Language of Terrorism', 'why some voices are more credible than others to Muslim communities, understandings of "Britishness" and terrorism and where these feelings come from within the British population' (Home Office 2009).

The basic details of some of the research conducted by RICU has had to be dragged out of the Home Office through a series of repeated freedom of information requests, though significant details, including copies of research, even the titles of some projects, remain secret. Nevertheless, we can take one project to examine the type of material it has been responsible for producing.

The report was the product of an Economic and Social Research Council (ESRC) grant given to Dr David Stevens of the University of Nottingham to study 'radical blogs' in a secondment to RICU (see Powerbase 2011b). This is, of course, what RICU was interested in. However, when the research came to be published after a two-year delay, the title referred only to 'Islamic' blogs. The lack of differentiation between 'radical' and 'Islamic' is carried all the way through the report. 'The purpose of this project', writes Stevens, 'is to study the link patterns and discussions of Islamic bloggers with particular reference to the UK' (Powerbase 2011b).

The report published a list of the top twenty 'Islamic' blogs with the inference that these were in some sense 'radical'. Among those on the list were a number of blogs which can be described as 'radical', as 'Islamic' or even as 'blogs' only tenuously or by distortion. The *Guardian* noted a number of examples:

> the man identified in the report as Britain's third most influential 'pro-Islamic' blogger is actually an atheist based in the United States. As'ad Abukhalil, a Lebanese-American professor of political science at California State University who blogs as 'The Angry Arab' is furious

> about it. 'How ignorant are the researchers of the Home Office?' he writes. 'How many times does one have to espouse atheist, anarchist, and secular principles before they realise that their categorisation is screwed up?'
>
> ...Top spot in the league table of Britain's most influential 'pro-Islamic' bloggers goes to Ali Eteraz, a Cif ['Comment is free', *Guardian*] contributor. Back in 2007, he wrote a series of articles for Cif, from a liberal perspective, about reforming Islam.
>
> (Whitaker 2010)

At least five of the top ten 'Islamic' blogs are questionable (Powerbase 2011b). To describe these blogs and websites as in some way related to 'radicalisation' suggests a sleight of hand that smears opponents of UK government foreign policy as supporters of terrorism. If the evidence of this report – published by the Home Office – is anything to go by, the notion that the government carefully targets the terrorist threat as opposed to targeting critics or indeed all Muslims or even perceived Muslims is at least open to question.

For this brief overview of its activities, it is clear that RICU is more than a simple 'propaganda' body in that it is closely integrated with the overall strategy (including the coercive elements), is intelligence-linked, and engages in a form of propaganda which is simply part of a wider coercive strategy directed at managing behaviour and activity as opposed to being solely focused on 'winning hearts and minds'.

## Quilliam Foundation

Another key element of Prevent that is closely modelled on counterinsurgency and strategic communication theory is the Quilliam Foundation, the London-based think-tank that claims to challenge Islamic extremism in the UK. We noted that earlier counterinsurgency doctrine emphasises 'Key Leader Engagement' (KLE) in the wider management of populations. Quilliam is arguably an attempt by government to use an ostensibly unofficial think-tank to engage with the Muslim community in a bid to win influence. KLE is intended to operate alongside PSYOPS 'to influence the local population and affect the will and understanding of the insurgent' (Ministry of Defence 2009: 6-3). Quilliam functions as a classic 'front group' for government, appearing to be an independent Muslim-led initiative. It was set up by self-styled ex-extremists Maajid Nawaaz and Ed Husain, both former members of the political Islamic group, Hizb ut-Tahrir. It was launched on 22 April 2008, and between 2008 and 2011 received almost £2 million from the government in funding (Fanshaw 2010; Hughes 2010). The Quilliam Foundation does not disclose the extent of its government funding on its website, but a comparison of our data from freedom of information requests with funding disclosures that have been made public through its progress report (Quilliam Foundation 2010b: 21) shows that government funding accounted for over 92 per cent of its entire income for 2009/10. This suggests that it is little more than a semi-covert element of government strategy.

The organisation says it aims to 'counter the Islamist ideology behind terrorism, whilst simultaneously providing evidence-based recommendations to governments for related policy measures' (Quilliam Foundation 2010a) and provides 'a counter narrative to the al-Qaeda mindset' (Fanshaw 2010). Quilliam, in other words, is a key part of the strategic communication component of Prevent. Since its establishment, the think-tank has been embroiled in several controversies for encouraging domestic spying and preparing secret blacklists of citizens and groups that it alleges share the 'ideology of terrorists' (Dodd 2009b, 2010).

What seems to be clear from the work carried out by RICU and the Quilliam Foundation is that they are both integral elements of a highly coercive counter-terrorism strategy. Viewed in isolation, their activities may appear to be simply about the management of information and communicative strategy. Viewed from the point of view of the counterinsurgency theorists, they are essential to the efficacy of coercion and the generation of fear. They are thus core to coercive counter-terrorism, having the aim of curtailing dissent, sometimes using direct force and sometimes maintain the legal scope of civil liberties – in other words, indirect force. As evidence for this we would point to the words of the British government leader on strategic communication: Commander Tatham insists that any definition of the concept must 'recognise that the success of non-kinetic effect is amplified by threats of kinetic activity' (Tatham 2008: 15).

## Conclusions

British counter-terrorist policy draws heavily on counterinsurgency doctrine. This has been developed mostly in circumstances where 'normal' liberal democratic rules did not apply and thus higher levels of coercion, violence and discrimination were possible. In fact, we can see that in order for such policies and strategies to be implemented in the UK, many of these defining liberal democratic rules have had to be suspended, especially under the 'Pursue' strand of CONTEST. The ideas and practices promoted by counterinsurgency theorists are profoundly inimical to liberal democratic principles such as the free circulation of information and the importance of the democratic role of information and media in creating the possibility of a democratic polis. The denizens of strategic communication are profoundly opposed to such notions, seeing information and communication as part of the armoury of coercion leading to 'behaviour change'. PSYOPS, information operations and especially strategic communication are means to subvert the possibility of any kind of free and open debate and indeed are conceived directly as coercive.

This is why information collection, for example, plays a key role in the Prevent strategy. This is also why, for example, possession and distribution of so-called 'terrorist' information is unlawful, even though such offences undermine the historic principles of the common law. The use of direct coercion through highly militarised policing programmes such as shoot-to-kill and detention of 'suspected' terrorists for what was until recently twenty-eight days, has led to the dissemination of systematic fear and mistrust within the 'suspect' community. Such policies, viewed through the lens of counterinsurgency theory, amount to the conscious planning of a campaign of coercion against dissent in general and Muslims in particular.

It is our argument that because of counterinsurgency influences on domestic counter-terrorism, mistrust, intimidation and fear have been deliberately implemented under the CONTEST strategy. In other words, because counterinsurgency doctrine explicitly attempts to coerce populations (indirectly) by intimidating and spreading fear among a section of the population as well as (directly) by the use of 'kinetic force', the policies adopted under CONTEST fit neatly within the official definition of 'terrorism'.

## Note

1 The latter two Ps are premised on increasing resilience of the UK through enhanced protective security measures (Protect) and working towards mitigating the effects of a terrorist attack, lest it cannot be thwarted (Prepare).

## References

Archer, Lawrence and Bawdon, Fiona (2010) *Ricin! The Inside Story of the Terror Plot That Never Was*, London: Pluto Books.

Association of Chief Police Officers (Terrorism Allied Matters) (2008) Business Area, Police PREVENT Strategy – Partners Briefing, 'Restricted', 27 March 2008, Version 1.7, p. 11, www.scribd.com/doc/35833660/ACPO-Police-Prevent-Strategy accessed 12 August 2010.

BBC News (2004) 'Terror Detainees Win Lords Appeal', 16 December, http://news.bbc.co.uk/1/hi/uk/4100481.stm, accessed 12 May 2010.

British Army (1963) *Keeping the Peace, Part I: Doctine*, London.

Brown, Colin and Woolfe, Marie (2005) 'Rights Law to Be Overhauled as Blair Says "the Game Has Changed"', *Independent*, 6 August, www.independent.co.uk/news/uk/politics/rights-laws-to-be-overhauled-as-blair-says-the-game-has-changed-501649.html, accessed 20 February 2011.

Correra, Gordon (2007) 'Don't Look Now, Britain's Real Spooks Are Behind You', *Sunday Times*, 2 December.

D'Ancona, Matthew (2007) 'Brown Is Leading the Way in Counter-terrorist Thinking', *Guardian*, 2 August 2007, www.guardian.co.uk/commentisfree/2007/aug/02/comment.politics1, accessed 9 December 2010.

Defence Academy (2009) 'Dr. J. P. Macintosh', www.da.mod.uk/our-work/governance/board-biogs/dr-j-p-macintosh, accessed 6 May 2009.

Department for Communities and Local Government (2007a) 'Preventing Violent Extremism: Winning Hearts and Minds', London: Department for Communities and Local Government, www.communities.gov.uk/documents/communities/pdf/320752.pdf, accessed 12 December 2010.

Department for Communities and Local Government (2007b) 'Preventing Violent Extremism Pathfinder Fund: Guidance Notes for Government Offices and Local Authorities in England', February, London: Department for Communities and Local Government, www.communities.gov.uk/documents/communities/pdf/320330.pdf, accessed 16 January 2011.

Dodd, Vikram (2009a) 'Government Anti-terrorism Strategy Spies on Innocent', *Guardian*, 16 October, www.guardian.co.uk/uk/2009/oct/16/anti-terrorism-strategy-spies-innocents, accessed 7 May 2010.

Dodd, Vikram (2009b) 'Spying Morally Right Says Think-tank', *Guardian*, 16 October, www.guardian.co.uk/uk/2009/oct/16/spying-morally-right-says-thinktank, accessed 22 December 2010.

Dodd, Vikram (2010) 'List Sent to Terror Chief Aligns Peaceful Muslim Groups with Terrorist Ideology', *Guardian*, 5 August 2010, www.guardian.co.uk/uk/2010/aug/04/quilliam-foundation-list-alleged-extremism, accessed 22 December 2010.

Fanshaw, J. (2010) 'Freedom of Information Requests – Quilliam, Ref 14890', Letter to Rizwaan Sabir from Office for Security and Counter-Terrorism, Home Office, 24 September 2010.

Fekete, Liz (2001) 'The Terrorism Act 2000: An Interview with Gareth Pierce', *Race & Class*, Vol. 43 No. 2: 95–103.

Hanson, David and Malik, Shahid (2010) 'Prevent Is Here to Protect, not Spy', *Guardian*, 2 November, www.guardian.co.uk/commentisfree/belief/2009/nov/02/prevent-extremism-protect-not-spy, accessed 3 March 2011.

Hewitt, Steve (2008) *The British War on Terror: Terrorism and Counter-Terrorism on the Home Front Since 9/11*, London: Continuum.

HM Government (2000) *Terrorism Act 2000*, Section 1, Part 1. www.legislation.gov.uk/ukpga/2000/11/section/1, accessed 8 April 2011.

HM Government (2009) *Pursue, Prevent, Protect, Prepare: The United Kingdom's Strategy for Countering International Terrorism*, CM 7547, London: Stationery Office.

Hocking, Jenny (1988) 'Counterterrorism as Counterinsurgency: The British Experience', *Social Justice*, Vol. 15, No. 1: 83–97.

Hocking, Jenny (1993) *Beyond Terrorism: The Development of the Australian Security State*, St Leonards: Allen & Unwin.

Home Office (2009) Freedom of Information Response (email correspondence from R. Stokes to D. Miller), 8 April 2009. Received 20 April 2009, 16:51.

House of Commons (2007) 'Counter-Terrorism Policy and Human Rights: 28 Days, Intercept and Post-Charge Questioning', *Joint Committee on Human Rights*, Nineteenth Report, Session 2006–7, 16 July, www.publications.parliament.uk/pa/jt200607/jtselect/jtrights/157/157.pdf, accessed 3 May 2010.

House of Commons (2010) 'Preventing Violent Extremism', Sixth Report of Session 2009–10, *Communities and Local Government*, 30 March www.statewatch.org/news/2010/mar/uk-hoc-preventing-violent-extremism-report.pdf, accessed 13 June 2010.

Hughes, Lucy (2010) 'Internal Review – Freedom of Information Act 2000 Request Ref 0185–10 and 0186–10', Letter to Rizwaan Sabir from Directorate for Defence and Strategic Threats, Foreign and Commonwealth Office, 17 August 2010.

Johnson, Alan, Desai, Unmesh, Whitworth, Andrew and Turner, Jackie (2010) 'Preventing Radicalisation in the UK', *Guardian*, 20 October, www.guardian.co.uk/politics/2009/oct/20/prevent-terrorism-muslims-radicalisation, accessed 3 March 2011.

Joint Forces Command Joint Warfighting Center (2010) 'Commander's Handbook for Strategic Communication and Communication Strategy Version 3.0 US Joint Forces Command Joint Warfighting Center', 24 June, www.carlisle.army.mil/DIME/documents/Strategic%20Communication%20Handbook%20Ver%203%20-%20June%202010%20JFCOM.pdf, accessed 7 April 2011.

Kilcullen, David (2004a) *Complex Warfighting. Australian Army's Future Land Operational Manual*, www.quantico.usmc.mil/download.aspx?Path=./Uploads/Files/SVG_complex_warfighting.pdf, accessed 14 January 2011.

Kilcullen, David (2004b) 'Countering Global Insurgency', *Small Wars Journal*, 30 November, http://smallwarsjournal.com/documents/kilcullen.pdf, accessed 8 December 2010.

Kilcullen, David (2006) 'Counter-insurgency Redux', *Survival*, Vol. 48, No. 4, 111–30, http://smallwarsjournal.com/documents/kilcullen1.pdf, accessed 4 December 2009.

Kilcullen, David (2007a) 'Subversion and Countersubversion in the Campaign against Terrorism in Europe', *Studies in Conflict & Terrorism*, Vol. 30, No. 8: 647–66.

Kilcullen, David (2007b) 'Understanding Current Operations in Iraq', *Small Wars Journal* Posted by Dave Kilcullen on 26 June 2007 7:11 a.m. http://smallwarsjournal.com/blog/2007/06/understanding-current-operatio/, accessed 8 April 2011.

Kitson, Frank (1971) *Low Intensity Operations: Subversion, Insurgency and Peacekeeping*, London: Faber and Faber.

Kundnani, Arun (2006) 'Criminalising Dissent in the "War on Terror"', London: Institute of Race Relations, 2 May, www.irr.org.uk/2006/may/ak000006.html, accessed 14 May 2010.

Kundnani, Arun (2009) 'Spooked: How Not to Prevent Violent Extremism', London: Institute of Race Relations, www.irr.org.uk/pdf2/spooked.pdf, accessed 13 October 2010.

Liberty (2004) 'The Impact of Anti Terrorism Powers on the British Muslim Population', London: Liberty, www.liberty-human-rights.org.uk/policy/reports/impact-of-anti-terror-measures-on-british-muslims-june-2004.pdf, accessed 13 December 2010.

Liberty (2009) 'Summary of the Prevention of Terrorism Act 2005', www.liberty-human-rights.org.uk/materials/what-are-control-orders-short-introduction-july-2009.pdf, accessed 13 December 2010.

Maude, Francis (2009) 'Strategic Horizons Unit: Manpower Cabinet Office', Written answers, to Tessa Jowell, 26 June 2009, www.theyworkforyou.com/wrans/?id=2009–06–26c.249902.h, accessed 17 January 2011.

Metropolitan Police Authority (2005a) 'Operation Kratos', www.met.police.uk/communities_together/docs/v_05–11–08_srb_anna_de_vries_1_.pdf, accessed 13 December 2010.

Metropolitan Police Authority (2005b) 'Re: Counter Suicide Terrorism', Memo to All Members cc: SMT, Nick Baker, Keith Dickinson, 8 August 2005, released under the Freedom of Information Act, www.mpa.gov.uk/downloads/foi/log/kratos-attach.pdf, accessed 7 April 2011.

Miliband, David (2009) 'Accidental Terrorists', *FCO Bloggers: Global Conversations,* 31 March, www.powerbase.info/images/a/aa/Milband_blog_screengrab.jpg, accessed 4 December 2009.

Miller, David (2003) 'Information Dominance: The Philosophy of Total Propaganda Control?', *Scoop,* 29 December, 3:17 p.m., www.scoop.co.nz/mason/stories/HL0312/S00216.htm, accessed 4 January 2011.

Miller, David (2004) 'The Propaganda Machine', in David Miller (ed.) *Tell Me Lies,* London: Pluto.

Miller, David and Mills, T. (2010) 'Counterinsurgency and Terror Expertise: the Integration of Social Scientists into the War Effort', *Cambridge Review of International Affairs,* Vol. 23, No. 2: 203–21.

Ministry of Defence (1969a) *Land Operations Volume III – Counter Revolutionary Operations: Part 1 – Principles and General Aspects,* Army code No. 70516 (Part 1) A/26/GS Trg Publications/3011, London: Ministry of Defence, 29 August, www.scribd.com/doc/28437160/15355-Land-Ops-Vol-3-Part-1?in_collection=2383030, accessed 12 January 2011.

Ministry of Defence (1969b) *Land Operations Volume III – Counter Revolutionary Operations: Part 2 – Internal Security,* Army code No. 70516 (Part 2) A/26/GS Trg Publications/3028, London: Ministry of Defence, 26 November, www.scribd.com/doc/28437430/15356-Land-Ops-Vol-3-Part-2?in_collection=2383030, accessed 12 January 2011.

Ministry of Defence (1970) *Land Operations Volume III – Counter Revolutionary Operations: Part 3 – Counter Insurgency,* Army code No. 70516 (Part 3) A/26/GS Trg Publications/3039, London: Ministry of Defence, 29 August, www.scribd.com/doc/28436846/15858-Land-Operations-Volume-III-Part-3?in_collection=2383030, accessed 12 January 2011.

Ministry of Defence (1995) *Army Field Manual – Volume V – Operations Other Than War – Section B Counter Insurgency Operations,* Army code No. 71596 (Part 1) DGD&D18/34/56, 1995, released under the Freedom of Information Act, www.scribd.com/doc/28438057/11709-AFM-Vol-v-Operations-Other-Than-War?in_collection=2383030, accessed 12 January 2011.

Ministry of Defence (2001) *Army Field Manual–Volume 1–Combined Arms Operations: Part 10–Counter Insurgency Operations (Strategic and Operational Guidelines),* Army Code 71749, Issue 1.0, July 2001. www.scribd.com/doc/28440249/15974-COIN?in_collection=2383030>, accessed 12 January 2011.

Ministry of Defence (2009) *British Army Field Manual–Volume 1–Part 10 Countering Insurgency,* Army Code 71876, October, www.scribd.com/doc/28411813/British-Army-Field-Manual-Counterinsurgency-2009?in_collection=2383030, accessed 12 January 2011.

Mockaitis, Thomas (1995) *British Counterinsurgency in the Post-imperial Era,* Manchester: Manchester University Press.

Muslim Council of Britain (2005) 'Muslim Council of Britain Calls on MP's to Reject Anti-terror Bill', 9 November, www.mcb.org.uk/media/presstext.php?ann_id=171, accessed 14 May 2010.

Pantazis, Christina and Pemberton, Simon (2008) 'Trading Civil Liberties for Greater Security: The Impact on Minority Communities', *Criminal Justice Matters,* Vol. 73, No. 1: 12–14.

Powerbase (2011a) 'Steve Tatham', www.powerbase.info/index.php/Steve_Tatham, accessed 6 January 2011.
Powerbase (2011b) 'Estimating Network Size and Tracking Information Dissemination amongst Islamic Blogs', www.powerbase.info/index.php/Estimating_network_size_and_tracking_information_dissemination_amongst_Islamic_blogs, accessed 6 January 2011.
Powerbase (2011c) 'Research, Information and Communications Unit', www.powerbase.info/index.php/Research,_Information_and_Communications_Unit#cite_note-4, accessed 16 January 2011.
Powerbase (2011d) 'Jamie Macintosh', www.powerbase.info/index.php/Jamie_Macintosh#cite_note-2, accessed 17 January 2011.
Powerbase (2011e) 'Project Rich Picture', www.powerbase.info/index.php/Rich_Picture, accessed 1 March 2011.
Powerbase (2011f) 'Community Intelligence', www.powerbase.info/index.php/Community_Intelligence, accessed 3 March 2011.
Quilliam Foundation (2010a) 'About Us', www.quilliamfoundation.org/about-us.html, accessed 16 December 2010.
Quilliam Foundation (2010b) 'Progress Report 2009–2010: Making Our Country Better, Safer and Prouder', 23 March, www.quilliamfoundation.org/images/stories/Annual-Report-2009–2010-V13.pdf, accessed 9 April 2011.
Sabir, Rizwaan (2009) 'Linking Islam and Terrorism Is Wrong', *Guardian*, 19 October, www.guardian.co.uk/commentisfree/libertycentral/2009/oct/19/uk-prevent-muslim-terrorism, accessed 3 December 2010.
Sabir, Rizwaan (2010a) 'Keeping Britain Unsafe: The Stubborn Myths of "Effective" Counter-terror', *Ceasefire*, 24 September, http://ceasefiremagazine.co.uk/columns/on-security-3/, accessed 20 February 2011.
Sabir, Rizwaan (2010b) 'Victims to Villains: De-Radicalising the Anti-Terror Stance', *The Platform*, 16 February, www.the-platform.org.uk/2010/02/16/victims-to-villains-de-radicalising-the-anti-terror-stance/, accessed 20 February 2011.
Schlesinger, Phillip (1978) 'On the Shape and Scope of Counter Insurgency Thought', in Gary Littlejohn, Barry Smart, John Waterford and Niva Yuval-Davis, eds, *Power and the State*, London: Croom Helm.
Tatham, Steve A. (2008) *Strategic Communication: A Primer*, Advanced Research and Assessment Group, Defence Academy of the United Kingdom, Special Series: 08(02), December, www.carlisle.army.mil/dime/documents/DAUKARAG08(28)Strategic%20Communication.pdf, accessed 8 February 2010.
Thompson, Robert (1966) *Defeating Communist Insurgency; The Lessons of Malaya and Vietnam*, London: Chatto and Windus.
Walker, Clive (2009) *Blackstone's Guide to the Anti-Terrorism Legislation* 2nd edn, Oxford: Oxford University Press.
West Midlands Police Authority (2010) 'Security and Partnership Officers: Report to the Chief Constable', Community and Security Committee, 28 January, www.west-midlands-pa.gov.uk/documents/committees/public/2010/07_ComSecurity_28Jan2010_Securityand_Partnership_Officers.pdf, accessed 2 March 2011.
Whitaker, Brian (2010) 'Not Much Blog for Your Buck: Home Office Research Has Thrown up Some Blindingly Obvious Insights into the Muslim Blogosphere. Why Did They Bother?', *Guardian*, 25 March, www.guardian.co.uk/commentisfree/belief/2010/mar/25/blogs-islamic-home-office-report, accessed 15 January 2011.

# 2 Shoot-to-kill counter-suicide terrorism

## Anatomy of undemocratic policing

*Graham Smith*[1]

In this chapter a shoot-to-kill counter-suicide terrorism strategy, code-named Operation Kratos, developed and implemented by the police in the United Kingdom, is examined as an example of state violence. In this case, the use of state violence, ostensibly to protect the public and combat terrorism, was sustained by a state campaign of secrecy and cover-up. Such has been the secrecy surrounding the strategy that full details have never been placed on public record despite police acknowledgement of its existence after an operation in London in July 2005 ended with the fatal shooting of an innocent man, Jean Charles de Menezes. Neither this recourse to lethal state violence in the pursuit of counter-terrorism, nor the secrecy by which it is guarded, can be understood in isolation from their political contexts.

Whether in the form of military action or police force, the question of what constitutes political state violence is always dependent on standpoint. It is a question of perception whether operations conducted to prevent crime, protect the public or combat terrorism amount to harassment of the dispossessed, suppression of a just cause or perhaps even state terrorism. As conceptualised by Jackson *et al.* (2009: 3), state terrorism involves 'the intentional use or threat of violence by state agents or their proxies against individuals or groups who are victimized for the purpose of intimidating or frightening a broader audience'. The killing of Jean Charles de Menezes, and the carefully protected state strategy that led to it, may not demonstrably have had this purpose. Nevertheless, a close analysis of this state strategy and the de Menezes case is indispensable for understanding the form that counter-terrorism has taken in contemporary Britain.

### Secret development of a shoot-to-kill policy

Jean Charles de Menezes, mistakenly believed to be a suicide bomber by two Metropolitan police officers, was shot dead at Stockwell underground station, London, on 22 July 2005 when they fired seven 124-grain hollow-point bullets into his head at point-blank range. Authorised firearms officers with a combined experience of more than twenty years, the two officers gave evidence to the coroner's inquest into the cause of de Menezes's death more than three years later (Her Majesty's Coroner 2008: 24, 27 and 28 October). Engaged in a joint surveillance, firearms and anti-terrorist operation (codenamed Operation Theseus 2) to apprehend a suspected suicide bomber whose device had failed to detonate the previous day, the two officers were issued with firearms and irregular ammunition shortly before the shooting and briefed that colleagues were observing premises where the suspect was thought to be living. They were informed that a Designated Senior Officer was co-ordinating the operation from a control room in Scotland Yard, unusual tactics might be used and to trust the information communicated to them. The counter-suicide terrorism-trained officers understood that they might be directed to fire a critical shot to the brain stem of a suicide bomber to prevent the detonation of an explosive device in accordance with a shoot-to-kill policy that was referred to in the Metropolitan Police Service at that time as Operation Kratos.

Prior to the Stockwell shooting the police had not publicly acknowledged the existence of Operation Kratos. Since then the shooting has been subjected to thorough public scrutiny in the form of wide coverage in the international news media, Metropolitan Police Authority (2008) meetings and reports, two investigations by the Independent Police Complaints Commission (IPCC 2007a, 2007b) and legal proceedings in administrative, criminal and coronial courts. A relative of de Menezes unsuccessfully challenged the Crown Prosecution Service's decision not to commence criminal proceedings against individual officers in the Administrative Court (*R (on the application of da Silva)* v. *Director of Public Prosecutions and another* (2006) EWHC 3204 (Admin)); the Office of the Metropolitan Police Commissioner was fined £174,000 and ordered to pay £350,000 costs following a one-month trial at the Central Criminal Court for breach of the Health and Safety at Work Act 1974 (Metropolitan Police Authority 2008); and, after a sixteen-week inquest, a jury in the Inner South London Coroner's Court declined to accept that de Menezes had been lawfully killed and returned an open verdict[2] into the cause of his death (Her Majesty's Coroner 2008). More than five years after the shooting, the shoot-to-kill counter-suicide terrorism strategy has not been subjected to anything remotely similar to the thorough examination into de Menezes's death. Calls for a full public debate by senior practitioners, including the Commissioner of the Metropolitan Police Service, Sir Ian Blair (British Broadcasting Corporation 2005b), and the Chair of the IPCC, Nick Hardwick (IPCC 2008), have not been accepted. This is primarily due to the fact that, despite publication of operational reviews by the Metropolitan Police Service, and a series of other reports presented to the Metropolitan Police Authority (2005c, 2006a, 2007, 2008, 2009), the Association of Chief Police Officers of England, Wales and Northern Ireland (ACPO 2006) and Her Majesty's Inspectorate of Constabulary (2007, 2009), information has not been forthcoming from the police on the details of the shoot-to-kill counter-suicide terrorism strategy as it was before or after the de Menezes shooting.

There are two principal reasons for this lack of openness and transparency. Clandestine development of the policy is attributable to the convention of constabulary independence. This doctrine was developed in English common law ostensibly for the purpose of ensuring independent and impartial law enforcement and protecting police services from political interference. The doctrine grants chief officers wide discretion when discharging their law enforcement responsibilities, and police operational independence has not been successfully challenged in the courts since the 1960s (Lustgarten 1986; Dixon and Smith 1998). This convention empowered the Metropolitan Police Service and ACPO to develop a counter-suicide terrorism policy following the al Qaeda attack on the USA on 11 September 2001, with minimal involvement by politicians or public scrutiny (Smith 2009). A second reason, closely connected to the first, is the strongly held belief among police and politicians that public dissemination of police policy and methods will alert terrorists to the types of operation suicide bombers may face and weaken the effectiveness of the UK's counter-terrorism strategy.

There was much speculation about police shoot-to-kill immediately after the Stockwell shooting. The next day ACPO (2005) issued a Briefing Note in which it acknowledged the development of a shoot-to-kill counter-suicide terrorism strategy and declined to provide detailed information on operational grounds. Answering questions at a full meeting of the Metropolitan Police Authority (2005a) the following week, Commissioner Ian Blair explained that development of the 'shoot to kill to protect' policy had not required legislative change and, in his view, 'represented the least worst option' for dealing with suicide terrorism. Giving evidence to the House of Commons Home Affairs Committee (2005) nearly two months later, the Commissioner declared, somewhat cryptically, 'while I am prepared to discuss the policy and must discuss that policy, that does not mean that that policy was necessarily or was not necessarily connected to the death of Mr Menezes' (see further below, p. 41). Sir Ian's predecessor, Lord Stevens, fuelled controversy surrounding the secret development of the policy when he declared on national radio that it had not been discussed with the Metropolitan Police Authority (British Broadcasting Corporation 2005a; Morris 2005). He quickly retracted this comment and eventually, on 29 September 2005, the Kratos policy was officially acknowledged by the Metropolitan Police Authority (2005b) in a statement that its members had been briefed by the Metropolitan Police Service in a closed session in March 2002.[3]

The public interest in knowing why an innocent man could be shot dead in such a calculated way aroused much media attention and raised serious human rights concerns. The United Nations Special Rapporteur on Extra-judicial, Summary and Arbitrary Executions, Philip Alston, wrote to the UK government on 29 July 2005 requesting information about a case that came within his terms of reference as an allegation of excessive use of force by law enforcement officials. In his letter the Special Rapporteur made specific reference to Operation Kratos and statements by the Metropolitan Police Commissioner that 'more people could be shot' as a result of the search for suspected suicide bombers and that the 'shoot-to-kill' policy would remain in force (United Nations 2006: 258–61). Moreover, the death of Jean Charles de Menezes left the counter-suicide terrorism strategy vulnerable to rigorous examination under the UK's obligations as a Contracting State Party to the European Convention on Human Rights. In the case of *McCann* v. *UK* the European Court of Human Rights ruled that the right to life of three Irish Republican Army suspects had been violated when they were shot dead by Special Air Service personnel involved in a counter-terrorism operation. The Court held:

> In keeping with the importance of this provision (art. 2 [the right to life]) in a democratic society, the Court must, in making its assessment, subject deprivations of life to the most careful scrutiny, particularly where deliberate lethal force is used, taking into consideration not only the actions of the agents of the State who actually administer the force but also all the surrounding circumstances including such matters as the planning and control of the actions under examination.
>
> (*McCann* v. *UK* (1995) 21 EHRR 97, at para. 150)

The jurisprudence of the Court quickly developed in this area. By the time of the Stockwell shooting the UK government was obliged to conduct an independent and effective investigation into alleged police violations of the right to life, capable of determining whether the force used was justifiable and identifying and punishing those responsible (*Jordan* v. *UK* (2003) 37 EHRR 2; Smith 2010). Commissioner Blair's primary concern on first hearing of the shooting, within minutes of it taking place, was that under human rights law the deceased's relatives would have access to the investigation. The head of a police service, at the time responsible for an investigation into fifty-two deaths caused by four suicide bombers on 7 July 2005 and a search for at least four suspected suicide bombers whose bombs failed to detonate on 21 July 2005, found the requirement that the relatives of a deceased suspected suicide bomber should have access to an investigation into the circumstances of his death unacceptable (Blair 2009; House of Commons Home Affairs Committee 2005). The Commissioner refused the IPCC, which was responsible for investigating police killings in compliance with the European Convention on Human Rights, access to Stockwell underground station on the morning of 22 July 2005 and wrote to senior government officers in an attempt to prevent the citizen oversight body from conducting an independent investigation into the shooting. Although he did not succeed, the Commissioner delayed the IPCC's investigation into de Menezes's death by five days.

The Commissioner's decision to thwart the IPCC left the police open to criticism on two counts. First, it was sufficient grounds to render the investigation into de Menezes's death a procedural violation of the right to life. In the case of *Ramsahai* v. *The Netherlands* (2007, ECHR 393), the European Court of Human Rights ruled a delay of fifteen hours in the commencement of an independent investigation following a fatal shooting by Dutch police in 1998 was in violation of the obligation to conduct an effective investigation. On the need for independent investigation into alleged violations of the right to life, the Court declared, 'What is at stake here is nothing less than public confidence in the state's monopoly on the use of force' (at para. 325). Second, disclosure of the Commissioner's decision to prevent the IPCC from commencing its investigation into the de Menezes shooting (IPCC 2005), together with leaks from the investigation that challenged accounts given by the police, contributed to widespread public concern that the Metropolitan Police Service was orchestrating a 'cover up' (Tendler and Ford, 2005; Portillo, 2005). Mismanagement of the Stockwell shooting and growing mistrust of the Metropolitan Police Commissioner and senior colleagues eventually led to complaints by members of the de Menezes family and the opening of a second IPCC investigation (IPCC 2007a).

At the same time as the IPCC investigated the Stockwell shooting the Metropolitan Police Service's Assistant Commissioner Central Operations Business Group conducted an operational review of the shoot-to-kill counter-suicide terrorism strategy and an ACPO review was led by the Deputy Chief Constable of Sussex Police. The IPCC (2007b) completed its *Stockwell One* Report into the circumstances surrounding de Menezes's death in January 2006, and an additional Report detailing sixteen operational recommendations, referred to as *Stockwell One B*, was forwarded to the Metropolitan Police Service and Police Authority in March 2006 (neither Report was placed in the public domain until 8 November 2007 when *Stockwell One B* was appended to the *Stockwell One* Report). The Metropolitan Police Service reported on the progress of its review to the Metropolitan Police Authority in February (2006) and ACPO published its review (2006) the following month.

## Operation Kratos

The genealogy of Operation Kratos dates back to the formation of an ACPO-supported Metropolitan Police Service working party led by the Deputy Assistant Commissioner for Specialist Operations (Barbara Wilding) shortly after the al Qaeda attack on the USA on 11 September 2001. Its terms of reference were to:

- conduct research on known suicide bombings worldwide;
- consult and produce a strategy for dealing with suicide terrorism; and
- produce and action an implementation plan.

(ACPO 2006: 4)

Police officers visited countries where law enforcement agencies had considerable experience in combating suicide attacks, including Israel, Sri Lanka and Russia (states regularly singled out for criticism for human rights abuse and undemocratic police practice)[4] and reported back on the modus operandi of suicide bombers and counter-terrorism operations. The research stage of the review revealed, first, that 'the most prevalent type of explosive used by suicide terrorists is extremely sensitive to impact, shock and electrostatic discharge'; second, 'suicide bombers will spontaneously detonate their devices if they believe they have been identified'; and, third, it was held that the existence of 'different legislative, human rights and law enforcement structures' in the UK to the countries visited required different tactical responses (ACPO 2006: 5). This final point reflects the intention of the Metropolitan Police Service and ACPO to distance UK counter-suicide terrorism policy from the human rights abuses associated with the Israeli, Sri Lankan and Russian police (see Steve Swain evidence to the de Menezes inquest, 6 November (Her Majesty's Coroner 2008 and below, p. 44).

On 21 March 2002 the Metropolitan Police Service gave a presentation on its counter-terrorism work to a closed session of the Police Authority. The minutes of the meeting do not give any details of the review and only note that the Authority received a presentation and resolved to receive it (Metropolitan Police Authority 2002). Within days of that meeting the Metropolitan Police held a tabletop exercise codenamed Operation Tavistock which was attended by representatives of the Police Authority, the Home Office, the Police Complaints Authority (precursor to the IPCC), media companies, Her Majesty's Coroner, the Crown Prosecution Service and the Parliamentary Security Committee; lawyers and police officers from other services were also present as observers. Advice was sought from Treasury Counsel on matters relating to:

> the police duty of care to the public, liability of a force for the safety of its officers, the 'self-defence' issue for a police officer shooting a suspected suicide terrorist and the liability of a force for failing to act against a suicide terrorist.
>
> (ACPO 2006: 5)

In the following months, although the Metropolitan Police Service continued to lead, the ACPO Terrorism and Allied Matters Committee's national working group on suicide terrorism took over responsibility for the project. A new policy on the use of lethal force in relation to potential suicide bombers was agreed by ACPO in January 2003: 'Operation Kratos was adopted as national policy and promulgated through the "Terrorism and Allied Matters Committee" of the Association of Chief Police Officers to all Forces around the UK in January 2003'. (Metropolitan Police Authority 2005c: para. 12).

It is interesting to note that when discussing police counter-suicide terrorism strategy in public documents ACPO, unlike the Metropolitan Police Service, did not refer to the Operation Kratos codename[5] in the aftermath of the Stockwell shooting and preferred to cite its own *Manual of Guidance on Police Use of Firearms*[6] as authority for armed operations. Thus, whereas the Metropolitan Police Service has expressly referred to the development of Operation Kratos, ACPO has been far more circumspect about the significance of alterations to police policy. Commenting on its assumption of responsibility for suicide terrorism policy, ACPO asserted:

> The work was taken up for TAM [Terrorism and Allied Matters Committee] by the ACPO Committee on Police Use of Firearms with a view ultimately to update the Police Firearms Manual of Guidance (MOG). The result was a number of relatively minor changes to the MOG:
>
> - That it may not be possible to issue a warning to a suspected suicide terrorist...
> - That while the central body mass is the preferred target area when a shot is absolutely necessary to protect life (to incapacitate as quickly as possible), in dealing with a suspected suicide terrorist the shot may be to the head to negate the possibility of the suspect detonating an explosive device and thereby taking life...
> - That while it is normally the sole decision of the firearms officer whether or not to shoot, in circumstances involving suicide terrorism a shot may have to be fired on the command of a senior officer who alone is in possession of sufficient information to justify use of lethal force.
>
> (ACPO 2006: 6)

In order to overcome the fact that a firearms officer may not possess sufficient information to decide whether to fire a critical (that is, lethal) shot, because of the ease with which a suicide bomber may conceal explosives combined with his or her determination to detonate a device if challenged, counter-terrorism operations of this type are under the command of a 'Designated Senior Officer' appraised of all the relevant intelligence and responsible for issuing the order to shoot (ACPO 2006; Metropolitan Police Authority 2005c).

Journalists quickly became aware of this innovation in counter-suicide terrorism policy and reports appeared in the national press the same month that ACPO disseminated Operation Kratos to national police services. On 18 January 2003 the *Daily Mail*[7] ran an unattributed report under the banner headline 'Shoot to kill, police told':

> [T]he shoot-to-kill policy would involve targeting the central nervous system namely the head. The suspect would die immediately and not be able to use his hands to set off his bomb. The order to shoot would be given by a senior officer.[8]
>
> (Williams 2003)

Before the events of 21 July 2005 police had not anticipated that they would be searching for suspected suicide bombers after the explosive devices they were carrying failed to detonate (Her Majesty's Coroner 2008: 6 November). Shoot-to-kill counter-suicide terrorism tactics had been designed to protect against the risks arising from two foreseeable scenarios: sighting of a suspected suicide bomber reported by a member of the public and intelligence of a planned suicide bombing of a public event. Following the events of 21 July, Metropolitan police officers drew on the experience and knowledge invested in the two existing operational procedures and drafted a tactical options document intended to deal with all contingencies that could arise in the search for the failed suicide bombers. This document provided tactical guidance to Operation Theseus 2 on the morning of 22 July leading up to the shooting of Jean Charles de Menezes (Her Majesty's Coroner 2008: 29 September, 14 October, 6 November). In October 2005 the Metropolitan police reported to the Police Authority that Operation Kratos was a generic title for three tactical options in each of which recourse may be made to the full spectrum of police powers, from stop and search to the deployment of authorised firearms officers. The three options were:

> - Operation Andromeda is designed to deal with the spontaneous sighting by a member of the public of a suspected suicide bomber.
> - Operation Beach is where there is an intelligence-led covert operation to locate and arrest persons suspected of involvement in acts of terrorism.
> - Operation Clydesdale is where intelligence has been received about a suicide attack on a pre-planned event.
>
> (Metropolitan Police Authority 2005c)

## Concealing the substance of Kratos post-Stockwell

The obligation under human rights law to conduct an independent and thorough investigation into all the circumstances surrounding the death of Jean Charles de Menezes effectively negated the two above-mentioned justifications for keeping the details of the shoot-to-kill counter-suicide terrorism strategy secret: that is, *if* the strategy was part of the surrounding circumstances. The Stockwell shooting immediately gave rise to a third, short-term, reason for non-disclosure of the substance of the police counter-suicide terrorism operation pending the conclusion of the IPCC investigation and criminal proceedings. In particular, in order not to prejudice the outcome of the prosecution of the Office of the Commissioner of Police for the Metropolis under the Health and Safety at Work Act 1974 it was held that the degree of publicity generated by disclosure of police tactics would allow the defence to claim that there could not be a fair trial and could cause the contamination of witness evidence (*R (on the application of da Silva)* v. *Director of Public Prosecutions and another* (2006) EWHC 3204 (Admin)).

A fourth and arguably the most important reason why it has been possible for the police to avoid public scrutiny of Operation Kratos, in the longer term, is due to the presentation of consistent police evidence that Kratos was not invoked at Stockwell on that fateful day and acceptance of this narrative by all interested parties with the notable exception of the de Menezes family.[9] Early credibility was given to the collective police account by the IPCC (2007b) which forwarded its *Stockwell One* Investigation Report into the shooting to the Crown Prosecution Service in January 2006. The IPCC stated:

> Neither those in command of Operation Theseus 2 nor those on the ground assert that the shooting of Jean Charles de Menezes was the product of a formal 'Kratos policy' decision. A direct Kratos decision is not advanced by those in Room 1600 [Scotland Yard control room] and the two CO19 [Specialist Firearm Command] officers who shot de Menezes do not suggest that they acted on such a direct instruction.
>
> (IPCC 2007b: 43)

In reading this passage one is reminded of the Metropolitan Police Commissioner Sir Ian Blair's comment to the House of Commons Home Affairs Committee (2005) two months after the Stockwell shooting and his indecisiveness regarding the connection between Kratos and the death of Jean Charles de Menezes (see p. 35 above). The Commissioner's comments and the IPCC's presentation of the evidence indicate that at an early stage in the quest to determine how and why an innocent man died, and who, if anybody at all, should be held accountable, a shoot-to-kill act by police officers was clinically dissected from a shoot-to-kill police policy. In effect, the police evidence as presented by the IPCC justified non-examination of the substantive details of the shoot-to-kill counter-suicide terrorism strategy because the policy was purportedly unconnected to the circumstances surrounding the death of Jean Charles de Menezes. With regard to the lawfulness of Operation Kratos, the IPCC peremptorily concluded in one sentence:

> The IPCC does not regard it as necessary to refer the issue of the legality of such a policy to either the DPP [Director of Public Prosecutions] or the MPA [Metropolitan Police Authority] because it accepts that, if applied in appropriate circumstances, the Operation Kratos policy was lawful.
>
> (IPCC 2007b: 119)

A six-page section of the 133-page *Stockwell One* Report is devoted to Operation Kratos (IPCC 2007b: 40–5) and a further two pages to the police's obligations to protect the right to life (IPCC 2007b: 110–12). The IPCC cites two cases, *McCann* v. *UK* (1995, 21 EHRR 97) and *Osman* v. *UK* ((1998) 29 EHRR 245) in its treatment of the lawfulness of Operation Kratos. The ruling by the European Court of Human Rights in the *Osman* case, that preventive operational measures would be required to protect the right to life if there was a real and imminent risk which the police knew of or ought to have known of, is exclusively relied on by the IPCC in support of the claim 'that a *properly structured* and *properly managed* operation which borrows "KRATOS" strategy and tactics is not unlawful per se'. (emphasis in the original; IPCC 2007b: 112).[10]

Separation of officers' shoot-to-kill actions and shoot-to-kill police policy was strictly maintained throughout all following legal proceedings. In consequence, whereas the lawfulness of police actions has been closely examined, and found wanting in the form of a health and safety conviction of the Metropolitan Police Service and the return of an open verdict by the jury in the coroner's inquest, the lawfulness of the Operation Kratos policy has not been thoroughly tested in the courts. The IPCC inserted a footnote into its *Stockwell One* Report when published after the conclusion of criminal proceedings in November 2007: 'It was accepted by both the defence and the prosecution at the health and safety trial that Kratos was not called' (IPCC 2007b: 121). It is not at all clear why this footnote was retrospectively inserted into the published version of the Report. The prosecution would not seek to establish a Kratos connection as its case relied on police evidence forwarded to the Crown Prosecution Service by the IPCC twenty-two months earlier that the policy was not invoked. Nor would the Metropolitan Police Commissioner in his defence to the health and safety charges go against the evidence of Metropolitan police officers. Moreover, having managed to keep the details of the counter-suicide terrorism strategy out of the public domain for more than two years, the Commissioner would not, then, make them an issue in proceedings. One explanation for the footnote is that, in the court of public opinion, it added weight to police claims that Kratos was not connected to the shooting of Jean Charles de Menezes.

## Conclusion: undemocratic policing

Rather than examine the accountability of individual police officers for their conduct, this chapter raises questions about the accountability of two police institutions, the Metropolitan Police Service and ACPO (Punch 2010), and their lack of openness and transparency in developing and implementing a policy, the Operation Kratos shoot-to-kill counter-suicide terrorism strategy. This policy has not been discussed in Parliament, its lawfulness has not been tested in the courts and the Prime Minister, Home Secretary and Policing Minister have each declined to talk about the subject on the grounds that it was an operational police matter (Kostakopoulou 2008).[11]

The Metropolitan Police Service (2005) and ACPO (2006) have consistently held that it is inaccurate to describe UK police counter-suicide terrorism strategy as a shoot-to-kill policy on three grounds. First, a range of coercive powers are available to protect against a suicide terrorism attack, from stop and search to the use of lethal force. Second, police are accountable to the law for the discharge of firearms, the same as any other member of the public. And, third, police lethal force is only used if absolutely necessary to protect the public. There is a major flaw in this reasoning. If Operation Kratos was not a shoot-to-kill strategy why have the Metropolitan Police Service been so adamant that the shooting of Jean Charles de Menezes was not directly connected to Kratos? Why is it that the police, as a matter of policy, and individual officers in their evidence, did not accept that fundamental mistakes were made in the deployment of Kratos tactics to prevent a suspected suicide bomber from detonating a device on the morning of 22 July 2005? All that would have been required was acknowledgement that instead of officers conducting a stop and search a critical shot was fired at a suspected suicide terrorist. Could it be that the primary concern of the police in thc aftermath of the Stockwell shooting was to protect against a charge that de Menezes had been arbitrarily executed in contravention of the United Nations (1989) Principles on the Effective Prevention and Investigation of Extra-Legal, Arbitrary and Summary Executions? Certainly, the tenor of assertions by the Metropolitan Police Service and ACPO that counter-suicide terrorism operations are intelligence-led and they do not 'shoot first ask questions later' expressly countered the concerns raised by the United Nations Special Rapporteur (see p. 36 above). It is clear that as a consequence of failure to hold their hands up and admit to flaws in Kratos serious questions remain unanswered concerning police use of firearms and accountability to the law – as the inquest jury demonstrated when declining to accept the Metropolitan Police Service's submission that de Menezes was lawfully killed. In short, the claim that the UK police do not operate a shoot-to-kill policy is untenable.

On another level, the refusal of police to divulge details of their counter-suicide terrorism strategy, with the agreement of politicians and judges, was in determined defence of the doctrine of constabulary independence and operational autonomy. The doctrine rests at the heart of police power in the United Kingdom and operational independence undermines democratic principles of accountability and transparency. In the wake of the Stockwell shooting the Metropolitan Police Authority and IPCC made inroads into police operational independence (Smith 2009) and Her Majesty's Inspectorate of Constabulary (2010) has since become a more public-facing regulatory body. Metropolitan Police Commissioner Sir Ian Blair was regularly called to account before the Police Authority and in his autobiography he makes clear that he was uncomfortable with 'a procession of members [of the Metropolitan Police Authority] telling me and my colleagues how awful everything had been' (Blair 2009).

There has not been space in this chapter to examine the evidence presented in criminal and coronial proceedings, yet it is worthy of mention that a retired senior police officer, Steve Swain, who had been instrumental in the development of UK counter-terrorism suicide policy, gave evidence towards the end of the coroner's inquest (Her Majesty's Coroner 2008: 6 November). More than three years after the shooting of Jean Charles de Menezes he gave what is possibly the fullest account that will ever be given of Operation Kratos. Yet two weeks before the shooting, on 8 July 2005, the International Association of Chief Police Officers published two documents on the World Wide Web: Training Key 851 and 852 Suicide (Homicide) Bombers Part I and Part II (Horwitz 2005). The Training Keys examined the profiles of suicide bombers and their common beliefs and explained how police should react to suicide attacks. They gave detailed information of police shoot-to-kill tactics and went over much of the same ground that Steve Swain covered when appearing in the de Menezes inquest. The Training Keys were subsequently removed from the World Wide Web, but not before dissemination of a full critical appraisal of their contents in the New York University School of Law Center for Human Rights and Global Justice's (2006) briefing paper 'Irreversible Consequences: Racial Profiling and Lethal Force in the "War on Terror"'. Withdrawal of the Training Keys has done nothing to further the international cause of democratic policing in much the same way as has the refusal of the UK police to fully account for the development and implementation of their shoot-to-kill counter-terrorism suicide policy.

In their evidence and public statements, all of those connected to the circumstances surrounding the Stockwell shooting and subsequent legal proceedings, from frontline police officers to judges, have been unanimous in their portrayal of the death of Jean Charles de Menezes as a 'tragedy'. It is a sad reflection of the condition of democracy in the United Kingdom that his death has not been equally acknowledged as an injustice caused by counter-terrorism policy.

## Notes

1 I am grateful to Henrietta Hill, Dora Kostakopoulou, Maurice Punch and the editors of this collection for their assistance with this chapter. The usual caveat applies.
2 An open verdict is available in an inquest if the verdicts presented by the coroner are not accepted by the jury. In the inquest into the death of Jean Charles de Menezes the coroner allowed the jury to consider only a verdict of unlawful killing, which the jury rejected (Her Majesty's Coroner 2008).
3 However, the Metropolitan Police Authority did not publish the note of the March 2002 meeting until 17 March 2006 in response to an application under the Freedom of Information Act 2000 (see Metropolitan Police Authority 2006b).
4 See, for example, UN Special Rapporteur on extrajudicial, summary or arbitrary executions annual reports. Online. Available on http://www2.ohchr.org/english/issues/executions/annual.htm (accessed 5 March 2011).
5 However, ACPO's (2006) online publication published on 7 March 2006 is electronically entitled 'Kratos Report Final Version 1.0'.
6 Replaced on 9 November 2009 by the *Manual of Guidance on the Management, Command and Deployment of Armed Officers* (ACPO 2009).
7 The *Daily Telegraph*, 24 January 2003 ran the story the following week (Steele and Sapsted 2003).
8 It was not until the week before the Stockwell shooting, however, that the shoot-to-kill policy was referred to by its Operation Kratos codename: in reports in the London *Evening Standard* (Edwards and Stubbs 2005) and *Sunday Times* (Leppard and Calvert 2005) of the Metropolitan police investigation (codenamed Operation Theseus) into the suicide bombings that left fifty-two people dead on London's transport network on 7 July 2005.
9 See the Jean Charles de Menezes Family Campaign. Online. Available on: http://inquest.justice4jean.org/ (accessed 3 November 2010).
10 'Borrows' in the sense that the existing two Kratos tactical options were adapted to suit the circumstances of a search for failed suicide bombers.
11 A Downing Street spokesman stated that Prime Minister Tony Blair could not recall whether he was informed about the shoot-to-kill policy and it was an operational matter for the police (Morris 2005), and the same stance was maintained by Home Secretary Charles Clarke (House of Commons Home Affairs Committee 2005) and Policing Minister Hazel Blears (Hinsliff 2005).

## References

Association of Chief Police Officers (2005) ACPO – Briefing Note concerning ACPO Firearms Policy and Deadly and Determined Attacks. Online. Available on: www.acpo.police.uk/pressrelease.asp?PR_GUID={661910A9-E2BC-4ECE-BBB3 –7AE87F288C4D} (accessed 3 November 2010).

Association of Chief Police Officers (2006) The UK police service response to the threat posed by suicide terrorism: Review by the Association of Chief Police Officers Police Use of Firearms Committee. Online. Available on: www.acpo.police.uk/asp/policies/Data/ACPO%20(TAM)%20(PUF)%20Review.doc (accessed 3 November 2010).

Association of Chief Police Officers (2009) *Manual of Guidance on the Management, Command and Deployment of Armed Officers*. Online. Available on: www.npia.police.uk/en/docs/MCD_Armed_Officers_Gen3_100709.pdf (accessed 3 November 2010).

Blair, I. (2009) *Policing Controversy*. London: Profile Books.

British Broadcasting Corporation (2005a) *Today Programme*, BBC Radio 4, 19 September 2005. Online. Available on: www.bbc.co.uk/radio4/today/listenagain/listenagain_20050919.shtml (accessed 3 November 2010).

British Broadcasting Corporation (2005b) *Dimbleby Lecture*, delivered 16 November 2005. Online. Available on: http://news.bbc.co.uk/1/hi/uk/4443386.stm (accessed 17 July 2010).

Dixon, B. and Smith, G. (1998) 'Laying down the Law: The Police, the Courts and Legal Accountability', *International Journal of the Sociology of Law* 26, 419–35.

Edwards, R. and Stubbs, F. (2005) 'Shoot to Kill Orders for Terror Squad Marksmen', *London Evening Standard*, 14 July, p. 4.

Her Majesty's Coroner (2008) Coroner's Inquest into the Death of Jean Charles de Menezes: Hearing Transcripts. Online. Available on: http://webarchive.nationalarchives.gov.uk/20090317235546/www.stockwellinquest.org.uk/ (accessed 8 November 2010).

Her Majesty's Inspectorate of Constabulary (2007) *HMIC Review into MPS Implementation of Stockwell 1B Recommendations.* Online. Available on: www.mpa.gov.uk/downloads/scrutinites/stockwell/hmic-response1b.pdf (accessed 3 November 2010).

Her Majesty's Inspectorate of Constabulary (2009) *Stockwell – MPS progress: January 2008–April 2009.* Online. Available on: www.mpa.gov.uk/downloads/scrutinites/stockwell/hmic-mpsprogress.pdf (accessed 23 January 2012).

Her Majesty's Inspectorate of Constabulary (2010) *Her Majesty's Inspectorate of Constabulary in 2009/10: A report on the work of HMIC in the year from 1 April 2009 to 31 March 2010.* Online. Available on. www.hmic.gov.uk/SiteCollectionDocuments/Annual%20Reports/ARP_20101018.pdf (accessed 19 November 2010).

Hinsliff, G. (2005) 'Shoot-to-Kill Anger Grows', *Observer* 31 July, p. 1.

Horwitz, S. (2005) 'Police Chiefs Group Bolsters Policy on Suicide Bombers', *Washington Post*, 4 August 2005. Online. Available on: www.washingtonpost.com/wp-dyn/content/article/2005/08/03/AR2005080301867.html.

House of Commons Home Affairs Committee (2005) Home Affairs Committee publications on the internet: Oral evidence taken before the Home Affairs Committee on 13 September 2005. Online. Available on: www.publications.parliament.uk/pa/cm200506/cmselect/cmhaff/462/5091305.htm (accessed 3 November 2010).

Independent Police Complaints Commission (2005) IPCC Statement: Jean Charles de Menezes, 18 August 2005. Online. Available on: www.ipcc.gov.uk/news/pr180805_stockwell.htm (accessed 3 November 2010).

Independent Police Complaints Commission (2007a) *Stockwell One: Investigation into the Shooting of Jean Charles de Menezes at Stockwell Underground Station on 22 July 2005.* London: IPCC.

Independent Police Complaints Commission (2007b) *Stockwell Two: An Investigation into Complaints about the Metropolitan Police Service's Handling of Public Statements Following the Shooting of Jean Charles de Menezes on 22 July 2005.* London: IPCC.

Independent Police Complaints Commission (2008) IPCC Chair Nick Hardwick comments on Jean Charles de Menezes inquest, 12 December 2008 news release. Online. Available on: www.ipcc.gov.uk/news/pr121208_menezes_inquest.htm (accessed 17 July 2010).

Jackson, R., Murphy, E. and Poynting, S. (2009) 'Terrorism, the State and the Study of Political Terror', in R. Jackson, E. Murphy and S. Poynting (eds) *Contemporary State Terrorism: Theory and Practice.* London: Routledge, pp. 1–9.

Jones, T., Newburn, T. and Smith, D. (1994) *Democracy and Policing.* London: Policy Studies Institute.

Kostakopoulou, D. (2008) 'How to do Things with Security Post 9/11', *Oxford Journal of Legal Studies* 28(2), 317–42.

Leppard, D. and Calvert, J. (2005) 'The Web of Terror', *Sunday Times* 17 July, p. 11.

Lustgarten, L. (1986) *The Governance of the Police.* London: Sweet and Maxwell.

Mansfield, M. (2009) *Memoirs of a Radical Lawyer.* London: Bloomsbury.

Marenin, O. (1998) 'The Goal of Democracy in International Police Assistance Programs', *Policing: An International Journal of Police Strategies & Management* 21(1), 159–77.

Metropolitan Police Authority (2002) Minutes of a Meeting of the Metropolitan Police Authority held on 21 March 2002. Online. Available on: www.mpa.gov.uk/committees/mpa/2002/020321/minutes/ (accessed 3 November 2010).

Metropolitan Police Authority (2005a) Minutes of the Meeting of the Metropolitan Police Authority held on 28 July 2005. Online. Available on: www.mpa.gov.uk/committees/mpa/2005/050728/minutes (accessed 3 November 2010).

Metropolitan Police Authority (2005b) Minutes of the meeting of the Metropolitan Police Authority held on 29 September 2005. Online. Available on: www.mpa.gov.uk/committees/mpa/2005/050929/minutes (accessed 3 November 2010).

Metropolitan Police Authority (2005c) *Suicide Terrorism,* Report presented to the Metropolitan Police Authority on 27 October 2005. Online. Available on: www.mpa.gov.uk/committees/mpa/2005/051027/13.htm?qs=1&qu=kratos&nh=1&sc=1&dr=1&ar=&po=&fo=&lv=&pg=1&hl=1 (accessed 3 November 2010).

Metropolitan Police Authority (2006a) Events of July 2005 – MPS response suicide terrorism – update, 23 February 2006. Online. Available on: www.mpa.gov.uk/committees/mpa/2006/060223/08/ (accessed 2 November 2010).

Metropolitan Police Authority (2006b) Memo to all members of the Metropolitan Police Authority on 8 August 2005 re counter suicide terrorism. Online. Available on: www.mpa.gov.uk/downloads/foi/log/kratos-attach.pdf (accessed 3 November 2010).

Metropolitan Police Authority (2007) MPS Health and Safety Trial Report. Online. Available on: www.mpa.gov.uk/committees/mpa/2007/071122-egm/02/ (accessed 19 November 2010).

Metropolitan Police Authority (2008) *MPA Stockwell Scrutiny.* London: Metropolitan Police Authority.

Metropolitan Police Authority (2009) MPS response to the MPA Stockwell Scrutiny. Online. Available on: www.mpa.gov.uk/committees/sop/2009/090402/09/?qu=menezes&sc=2&ht=1 (accessed 19 November 2010).

Metropolitan Police Service (2005) Operation Kratos. Online. Available on: www.met.police.uk/communities_together/docs/v_05–11–08_srb_anna_de_vries_1_.pdf (accessed 3 November 2010).

Morris, N. (2005) 'Government Ministers "Knew of Shoot-to-Kill Policy Three Years Ago"', *Independent,* 20 September, p. 19.

New York University School of Law Center for Human Rights and Global Justice

(2006) 'Irreversible Consequences: Racial Profiling and Lethal Force in the "war on terror"'. Online. Available on: http://chrgj.org/docs/CHRGJ%20Irreversible%20Consequences%20June%202006.pdf (accessed 19 November 2010).

Portillo, M. (2005) 'Only a Public Inquiry Can Cure the Mess at the Met', *Sunday Times*, 21 August, p. 17.

Punch, M. (2010) *Police Shoot-to-kill: Police Accountability, Firearms and Fatal Force.* Bristol: Policy Press.

Smith, G. (2009) 'Citizen Oversight of Independent Police Services: Bifurcated Accountability, Regulation Creep and Lesson Learning', *Regulation and Governance* 3(4), 422–42.

Smith, G. (2010) 'Every Complaint Matters: Human Rights Commissioner's Opinion concerning Independent and Effective Determination of Complaints against the police', *International Journal of Law, Crime and Justice* 38(2), 59–74.

Steele, J. and Sapsted, D. (2003) 'Rules for Police on Suicide Bombers', *Daily Telegraph*, 25 January 2003. Online. Available on: www.telegraph.co.uk/news/uknews/1420063/Britain-Rules-for-police-on-suicide-bombers.html.

Tendler, S. and R. Ford, (2005) 'Police Chief "Tried to Scupper Inquiry into Tube Shooting"', *The Times*, 18 August, p. 6.

United Nations (1989) Principles on the Effective Prevention and Investigation of Extra-Legal, Arbitrary and Summary Executions (recommended by the Economic and Social Council Res. 1989/66, 24 May 1989). Online. Available on: www2.ohchr.org/english/law/executions.htm (accessed 17 July 2010).

United Nations (2006) Extrajudicial, Summary or Arbitrary Executions: Report of the Special Rapporteur, Philip Alston Addendum: Summary of cases transmitted to Governments and replies received. Online. Available on: www.extrajudicialexecutions.org/application/media/E_CN_4_2006_53_Add_1%202006.pdf (accessed 17 July 2010).

Williams, D. (2003) 'Shoot to Kill, Police Told', *Daily Mail*, 18 January, p. 8.

# 3 British counter-insurgency practice in Northern Ireland in the 1970s – a legitimate response or state terror?

*Paul O'Connor and Alan Brecknell*

> The maximum use should be made of loyal military and para-military local forces.
>
> (UK Ministry of Defence, 1970: 8)

## Introduction

The UK government has portrayed its role in Ireland as that of the neutral broker, the reluctant peacekeeper between two bitterly divided sectarian factions. This 'community relations' or 'two warring factions' explanation for the conflict is pivotal to the British state narrative that the UK has been the victim of a terrorist campaign. Evidence that the state itself used terror or that its relationship to one of the 'factions' was anything but neutral casts doubt on the 'peacekeeper' status that Britain has assumed (Jamieson and McEvoy, 2005).

This chapter will analyse counter-insurgency practice in the 1970s with a focus on locally recruited security forces in the fight against the IRA. Declassified British government documents show knowledge at the highest levels of government of loyalist paramilitary infiltration of the local security forces. Using the Ulster Defence Regiment, the then largest regiment in the British Army, as a case study, the authors will show that successive governments tolerated an illegal and deadly relationship between paramilitaries and security forces as part of a counter-insurgency policy. The result was state terror.

## Loyalist infiltration of the UDR

In the summer of 1975 the British Conservative Party elected Margaret Thatcher as its new leader in opposition, and the Bay City Rollers were top of the British pop charts. In Ireland the Miami Showband still dominated the pop scene and filled venues on both sides of the border. On 31 July, after a concert in the market town of Banbridge, north of the border, five of the six band members set off in their minibus for Dublin in the Irish

Republic. At approximately 2.30 a.m. they were stopped at what appeared to be a military checkpoint some miles north of the border.

The musicians were told to get out of the vehicle and line up along a hedge, and a 'soldier' asked their names and addresses while the bus was searched by other members of the patrol.

It appeared to be a routine checkpoint. In fact two of the 'soldiers' were hiding a bomb inside the minibus. They intended the bomb to go off while the band were travelling on towards Dublin. Had the plan succeeded, no one would have known about the checkpoint.

The premature explosion of the bomb killed two of the 'soldiers'. Other members of the gang opened fire on the musicians lined up on the side of road. Fran O'Toole, Tony Geraghty and Brian McCoy were all killed, and Stephen Travers was seriously injured.

The massacre caused shock waves on the island of Ireland. Concerts were cancelled as bands refused to cross the border. The *Irish Times* reported:

> The British Ambassador, Sir Arthur Galsworthy, was last night summoned to hear the Irish government's strong feelings about the murder of members of the Miami Showband.... The government holds the view that not enough has been done to stop sectarian assassinations and has told the British government so on several occasions in recent months.
>
> (*Irish Times*, 1 August 1975)

In Helsinki, where the Irish and British prime ministers were attending a European summit, the two leaders issued their first ever joint statement condemning a 'terrorist' incident (PRO1;[1] *Irish Times*, 1 August 1975).

The attack was claimed by one of the loyalist paramilitary groups, the Ulster Volunteer Force (UVF), but within days rumours began to circulate that the fake checkpoint also included soldiers of the locally recruited regiment of the British Army, the Ulster Defence Regiment (UDR). This was strenuously denied by official sources in Belfast and London (PRO1). Two of the three people who were eventually prosecuted in respect of the attack were in fact UDR members. In 2011 a fresh official investigation conducted by the Historical Enquiries Team (HET)[2] concluded the attack was 'pre-planned ... and was carried out by a UVF terrorist gang, which included a number of UDR soldiers. Many of the terrorists were dressed in army uniforms similar to those of the UDR' (HET1). Had it been divulged at the time that members of the British Army were involved in the incident, the political ramifications would have been considerable.

This was not a one-off incident. The British government was aware that loyalist paramilitaries had infiltrated the security forces.

Following a second incident less than a month later in which two civilians were taken from their vehicle and murdered at another 'security force' checkpoint on 24 August 1975 (HET2),[3] a senior civil servant admitted in relation to the UDR, 'There are well established doubts about the Regiment's reliability' (PRO2).

The 'well established doubts' were shared at the very highest level of government. In a meeting on 10 September 1975 between Prime Minister Harold Wilson and the leader of the Conservative opposition, Margaret Thatcher, the opposition leader and future Prime Minister was told by the Secretary of State for Northern Ireland,

> Unfortunately there were certain elements in the police who were close to the UVF and who were prepared to hand over information, for instance to Mr Paisley.[4] The Army's judgement was the UDR were heavily infiltrated by extremist Protestants[5] and that in a crisis situation they could not be relied on to be loyal.
>
> (PRO3)

That same month the British government was advised that the Irish Foreign Minister and government was 'alarmed at the degree of influence apparently wielded by the Protestant paramilitary groups and are suspicious that they may have penetrated the RUC[6] (police) and UDR[7]' (PRO1).

By 1975, in other words, both the Prime Minister and the future Prime Minister of a Western parliamentary democracy were aware that the largest regiment in the British Army was 'heavily infiltrated' by right-wing extremists. Was this infiltration frowned upon or did successive governments tolerate an illegal and deadly relationship between paramilitaries and security forces as part of a counter-insurgency policy? This chapter will seek to shed light on this question. To find the answer we first must turn the clock back to 1970 and the creation of the UDR.

## UDR by day – UDA/UVF[8] by night

Following widespread civil unrest in 1969, thousands of refugees from the nationalist/republican community in Northern Ireland fled across the Irish border to camps set up by an ill-prepared Irish Army. They were fleeing attacks from loyalists aided and abetted by the RUC, the Northern Irish police and the Ulster Special Constabulary (also known as the B Specials), a Unionist police auxiliary force that was both feared and hated by the nationalist/republican community.[9]

The arrival of British troops on the streets of Belfast and Derry in August 1969 was initially seen by many in the nationalist/republican community as a welcome sign that the government in London would intervene and protect them from the worst excesses of the regional Unionist government in Belfast.[10]

One of the reforms forced upon a reluctant Unionist government was the disbandment of the B Specials.[11] In its place a new part-time force was to be recruited but under the command structure of the regular British Army, as opposed to the B Specials who were under RUC and therefore Unionist Party control.

The year 1970 also saw the emergence of growing militancy within the nationalist/republican community and a resurgence of the Irish Republican Army (IRA) which had launched periodic but fruitless armed campaigns against the Northern Irish state since its foundation in 1922. In 1970 Brigadier Frank Kitson took over command of the British Army 39th Brigade in Belfast and the surrounding area. In 1971 Kitson published a book titled *Low Intensity Operations – Subversion, Insurgency, Peacekeeping,* based on his experiences as a British officer involved in counter-insurgency campaigns in Malaya, Kenya and Cyprus. As outlined in the land operations manual (Ministry of Defence, 1970), these counter-insurgency campaigns all had in common the use of local military and paramilitary forces, also known as 'pseudo gangs', as an aid in combating guerrilla forces.

In August 1971 internment without trial was introduced and hundreds of 'suspects' were arrested and taken to interrogation centres. The internment operation signposted the growing role of the UDR. Over 3,000 members of the regiment were mobilised as swoops were carried out on what later turned out to be highly questionable intelligence. The introduction of internment in August 1971 saw a dramatic increase in levels of violence which in turn resulted in calls to increase recruitment to the UDR and expand its role.[12]

Publicly the UDR was vaunted as non-sectarian and impartial. Privately the intended role of the regiment was seen somewhat differently. In a meeting with British Prime Minister Edward Heath in the weeks after internment was introduced the Unionist Prime Minister of Northern Ireland, Brian Faulkner, urged the recruitment of UDR units in workplaces such as the Harland and Wolff Shipyard in Belfast as a 'means of avoiding further pressures for the formation of irregular Protestant armed groups' (PRO4). While the two prime ministers were meeting, a civilian member of the UDR Advisory Council[13] was putting his thoughts on paper in regard to the proposal to expand the role of the regiment in counter-insurgency operations (guard duties, search operations, patrols, checkpoints, etc.). In his view, those who would wish to join would include:

> a Men who wish to fight the IRA.
> b Men who wish to fight for the Constitution of N.I. and defend the border.
> c Men who wish to protect their homes and families.
> d Business people in urban areas who desire protection.
> e Men who are frustrated at the state of the community and want to do something about it.
>
> (PRO5)

He went on to admit that the 'majority of groupings aforementioned' are clamouring for a 'third force', and added, 'When it is realised that under paragraph 2a, b and c, we will be largely arming one section of the community, then the operation is fraught with serious political implications' (ibid.).

The British Army's Chief of the General Staff (CGS) visited Belfast on the day before the above memo was written and met with the British Army's General Officer Commanding (GOC) in Northern Ireland and the British Army's Commander of Land Forces (CLF) in Northern Ireland. According to the Secret Minute (PRO6) of the visit, the most senior officer in the British Army was left in no doubt by his own senior staff of the potential for a loyalist 'backlash, the threat of which is very menacing' (emphasis in original document). Though the document does not elaborate, the 'backlash' being referred to is the loyalist response to the growing IRA campaign. In reference to the UDR it was noted: 'We need to capture the imagination of the public and harness their energy while retaining a semblance of the non-sectarian image' (ibid.).

Lest any doubts remained about where the pressure was coming from to expand the regiment, the senior staff member to the CGS noted that he had spent the morning with the GOC, CLF and (MI5) Director of Intelligence (D. Int.)[14] and they were: 'desperately worried about the Protestant backlash and think we underestimate it at Whitehall. (They certainly convinced me that if we do not harness their energies, the Protestants will fight the Republicans and consider themselves right to do so)' (ibid.).

It was becoming clear that it was 'Protestant' (loyalist) energies that must be harnessed. The Unionist Prime Minister's plea to Prime Minister Edward Heath only three days earlier to recruit young men to the UDR who might otherwise join loyalist militias, contrary to the original aims of the Hunt Report, clearly had the backing of senior military figures at Army HQ and the powerful MI5 Director of Intelligence.

The above minute (PRO6) of the CGS visit makes very clear the aim of the military command that locally recruited security forces were to function as a safety valve within the pro-British loyalist community. Moreover, this aim was to become (un)official security policy in the early 1970s. Publicly, of course, the 'semblance of the non-sectarian image' (PRO6) was maintained. This was to lead to the gradual replacement of regular troops with locally recruited forces.[15]

As early as May 1971 the UDR Advisory Council (PRO7) was aware of the slow leakage of Catholics from the regiment. Some 25 per cent of resignations in the first four months of 1971 were of Catholics. Three of the seven UDR Battalions had no Catholic officers while a fourth had one officer. The same statistics showed that over half of all officers were ex-B Specials (115 of a total of 218) (PRO7, Annex 'B'). Later the fear of IRA retribution would deter the majority of potential recruits from the minority community. Five UDR members were killed in 1971, the first during internment.[16] Ryder has highlighted the hostility encountered by many Catholics within the regiment in the lead-up to internment and the anger felt by those recruits who were shocked at the frequent brutality meted out at checkpoints (Ryder, 1991). In the aftermath of internment Catholics resigned in droves in protest at a security policy aimed exclusively at the nationalist/republican population.

As the conflict escalated with the Bloody Sunday massacre in 1972,[17] two apparently contradictory realities faced decision-makers on the security front. The war being waged by the British Army against the IRA depended increasingly on support from the UDR. In rural areas especially, the UDR was seen as the local 'eyes and ears' for British regiments that were on four-month emergency secondments in areas as hostile and unfamiliar as Helmand province is today for NATO forces. In June 1972 the Chief of the General Staff recommended greater use of the UDR (PRO8) to relieve the burden on the regular army. The apparent contradiction, however, was that senior civil servants and British command staff were well aware that the UDR was itself part of the problem. The Chief of General Staff admitted that an 'increase in the UDR's visible presence might help mollify Protestant opinion but at the expense of increased Catholic mistrust. It would be unwise to expect the UDR to have to confront militant Protestants' (ibid.).

If the role of the British Army was truly that of a neutral broker, of a peacekeeping force, then these contradictions might well have caused an agonising reappraisal of security policy. In fact no such reappraisal was necessary since the UDR was vital to security policy precisely *because* it had developed into an *ersatz* loyalist militia.

In the same month Headquarters Northern Ireland (British Army HQ) believed the time was right to consider the future of the regiment now that it was within 15 per cent of its 10,000 man target. In a memo to the Ministry of Defence concerns were raised that 'there would be disappointment amongst the Protestant members of the population at any announcement that the recruiting ceiling was to remain at 10,000. This could lead to men joining a para-military organisation such as the UDA as an alternative to the UDR'.[18] The UDA or Ulster Defence Association[19] was the largest of the loyalist paramilitary groups by June 1972. By the end of that year loyalist paramilitaries had murdered 121 people (PRO9; PRO10; PRO11; PRO21). That British Army HQ should seek to actively recruit extreme loyalists who might otherwise join a paramilitary organisation is in itself an extraordinary admission.

The UDR Advisory Council meeting that June was made aware that weapons being stored at home by UDR soldiers were being 'stolen' at an alarming rate (PRO12). According to the UDR Commander there was 'already some evidence that certain recruits were motivated primarily by the wish to obtain access to arms' (PRO15). The Head of the Defence Secretariat[20] was also well aware of the inherent dangers in expanding the

UDR and commented on the proposal to put UDR patrols into the centre of Belfast thus: 'Moreover the dangers of possible confrontation between members of the UDR and the UDA are also considerable and in some circumstances a heavy strain could well be placed on UDR loyalties' (PRO13).

A meeting of the UDR Advisory Council in August 1972 (PRO14) reported on the massive British Army operation to regain control of urban areas controlled by the IRA, Operation Motorman. The 5,357 UDR soldiers on duty during early August as the British Army moved into the no-go areas was evidence of the increasing reliance of the regular army on the regiment (PRO14).[21] The meeting was informed of a major surge in recruitment as a result of the military operation (the loyalist/Unionist community had been demanding action) and the statistics for August bore this out (PRO14).[22] Those statistics also confirmed that the numbers of Catholics in the regiment had sunk to a new low of 389 men.

The meeting also noted that four high-velocity rifles, one sub-machine gun and two pistols had gone 'missing' since 18 July and there had been a number of media reports of UDA infiltration of the UDR.

Both the military and political authorities were aware that Catholics were leaving the regiment, loyalist paramilitaries were joining and weapons and ammunition were being stolen as a consequence. They were also aware that loyalist paramilitaries were involved in an assassination campaign against Catholic civilians.

## The UDR – a safety valve for loyalist extremism

July and August 1972 were among the deadliest months in over three decades of conflict. On 21 July, or 'Bloody Friday', over twenty-one IRA bombs exploded in Belfast on a single day. Nine people were killed and hundreds were injured. Meanwhile loyalist paramilitaries were killing Catholic civilians at a rate of one every second night in July and August.[23] UDR weapons were 'disappearing' from barracks, vehicles and soldiers' homes and, according to the Ministry of Defence, 'in a number of cases collusion is suspected' (PRO15). It was clear by the middle of 1972 that an illegal and deadly relationship was developing between loyalist paramilitaries and the UDR. The response of the British government and senior military figures is to be found in a series of secret memos and letters between Belfast and London.

On 24 July the Commander of the UDR, Brigadier D.L. Ormerod, sent a memo to all Battalion Commanders on the subject of UDA membership. In stressing the importance of maintaining morale he noted, 'As a principle therefore soldiers are not to be forced into declaring a political allegiance now nor are they to be punished simply for being members of the UDA' (PRO16).

On 31 July Army HQNI wrote to Adjutant General Secretariat at the Ministry of Defence on the subject of UDA membership of the UDR.

> It is inevitable that a part of the Protestant element of a part-time Regiment in Ulster will sympathise with the aims of the UDA; and it is suspected that there are cases where this sympathy is carried to the extent of active membership.
>
> (PRO17)

The HQNI letter went on to suggest that,

> The UDR has to draw a line somewhere between hard-line Protestants who can safely be contained in the UDR, and those who cannot. The UDA is not an illegal organisation, and membership of the UDA is not a military offence under the military laws; it is also a large organisation not all of whose members can be regarded as dangerous extremists. One important (but unspoken) function of the UDR is to channel into a constructive and disciplined direction Protestant energies which might otherwise become disruptive. For these reasons it is felt that it would be counter-productive to discharge a UDR member solely on the grounds that he was a member of the UDA.
>
> I am sure this moderate line towards UDA supporters is the right one in light of the role of the UDA as a safety valve. In my opinion it would be politically unwise to dismiss a member of the UDA from the UDR unless he had committed a military offence; the dismissal of a member of the UDR on lesser grounds could well lead to widespread morale problems particularly in certain areas.
>
> (ibid.)

The ease with which the author[24] of this document moves between UDA and UDR and attributes essentially the same role to both, that of loyalist safety valve, is striking. The memo, though confirming that the vetting process for recruits had been tightened, made clear that membership of both a loyalist paramilitary group and the British Army was not only acceptable but was politically preferable. In the four weeks preceding this letter the UDA had murdered nineteen people.[25]

On 11 September a meeting was held in London of the Gen 79 security committee, a secretive committee comprising Cabinet ministers (including Edward Heath, the British Prime Minister) and senior figures from the military and security services.[26] At the meeting the Prime Minister said that 'the question of members of the UDR who were also associating with the UDA required further consideration. The Secretary of State (for Northern Ireland) should circulate a note indicating what he proposed' (PRO18). Given the extent to which the UDA had been involved in bombings, hijackings, kidnappings, torture and assassinations (Wood, 2006) in the weeks before this meeting, it is extraordinary that the Prime Minister did no more than suggest that the relationship between soldiers and loyalist paramilitaries should be given 'further consideration'. Significantly, the letter confirms that the Prime Minister was aware of loyalist infiltration of the regiment.

The July memo from Army HQ (PRO17) referred to above highlights the role of the *UDR* in channelling Protestant energies. In a memo in November the MoD attributes the same role to the UDA: 'Secondly an important function of the UDA is to channel into a constructive and disciplined direction Protestant energies that might otherwise become disruptive' (PRO19). Most likely this is a Freudian slip, but it may also reflect a very real convergence of the functions of the UDR and the UDA in 'channelling' loyalist energies.

By November 1972 at least 193 UDR rifles, sub-machine guns and pistols had gone missing from UDR stocks along with thousands of rounds of ammunition (PRO20). In one incident in October 1972 armed men carried out a raid on a joint UDR/Territorial Army base in Lurgan in Co. Armagh. They escaped with eighty-five high-velocity rifles and twenty-one sub-machine guns. An army intelligence report on the raid and a subsequent HET[27] report confirmed that the weapons were used in a number of murders and attempted murders attributed to the UDA. According to the confidential army intelligence report, collusion in the raid was thought to be 'highly probable' (PRO21, page 8, para. 12b). As early as the beginning of August the British Army had compiled a list of seventeen incidents of weapons losses for that year alone where collusion was suspected (PRO22).

On 24 November the British Prime Minister was due to meet the Irish Taoiseach Jack Lynch to discuss the UDA among other issues. His officials provided a background brief for the British Prime Minister which explained security force policy towards the UDA. The confidential Army document was classified and designated as too sensitive to be passed in writing below battalion level. The Prime Minister was informed that the RUC had similar instructions.

> Operations against UDA should be directed against their criminal extremist elements whilst making every endeavour to maintain good relations with law abiding citizens in the organisation.
>
> Contact should be maintained at company commander level with the UDA.
>
> Unarmed, locally resident vigilante type patrols should be tolerated provided they did not break the law.
>
> (PRO23)

The official view was that loyalist violence was confined to *criminal extremists*[28] and that this paramilitary organisation, handled correctly, would be a valuable ally in the war against the only real enemy, the IRA. From a British military perspective, both the UDR *and* the UDA had a role to play in combating this threat.

The declassified documents from this period that we have analysed here show an official toleration of loyalist violence and infiltration of the local security forces that is justified with repeated reference to the 'safety valve' function of both the UDR and the UDA.

## Maximum plausible deniability

The theory of 'maximum plausible deniability' (for a discussion, see Campbell, 2000) depends on the defence that a government, institution or individual was unaware of certain information and is therefore not responsible for any wrongdoing revealed by that information. In other words, there is a direct correlation between the extent of knowledge and the level of culpability. This section of the chapter explores in more detail the argument that the British government had knowledge of, and tolerated, an illegal and deadly relationship between loyalist paramilitaries and the UDR. In 1973 the British Army produced a detailed report into the extent of loyalist infiltration of the UDR called 'Subversion in the UDR' (PRO21).[29] The report was written for the Joint Intelligence Committee (JIC) in London and ultimately for No. 10 – Downing Street and the Office of the Prime Minister.

According to the report,

> Since the beginning of the current campaign the best single source of weapons (and the only significant source of modern weapons) for Protestant extremist groups has been the UDR.
>
> There is little doubt that subversion in the UDR has *added significantly* to the weapons and ammunition stocks of Protestant extremist groups.
>
> (PRO21)

The report goes on to suggest that the level of subversion goes well beyond the odd 'bad apple in the barrel' theory: 'It seems likely that a significant proportion (perhaps 5% – in some areas as high as 15%) of UDR soldiers will also be members of the UDA, Vanguard Service Corps, Orange Volunteers or UVF' (ibid.). All those organisations were involved in loyalist paramilitary activities and were, according to the report, receiving weapons training from UDR soldiers. The extent to which the security forces had been subverted was outlined in no uncertain terms notwithstanding the admission that, given the intelligence gaps, the situation might be much worse.

This internal army intelligence report concluded by considering the 'Circumstances In Which Subversion Might Render The UDR (or elements within it) Unreliable' (ibid.). Two political scenarios were 'war gamed' in the report. The first was a possible Unilateral Declaration of Independence (UDI) by loyalist leaders while the second essentially expanded on the same theme and hypothesised wholesale rebellion within the regiment in the event that a Labour government proposed a Council of Ireland or anything perceived to move in the direction of a United Ireland.

The scenarios which 'might render the UDR unreliable' are extremely difficult to reconcile with the overwhelming evidence that the UDR was already unreliable by this stage. Yet despite this evidence the report argued, 'Except in limited circumstances subversion in the UDR has not compromised its ability to carry out its duties' (ibid.). The message to the Prime Minister was clear. Any attempt to introduce a political initiative not supported by loyalists had the potential to provoke a mutiny within the largest regiment in the British Army. Was the intention of the authors to alert the government to this possibility in order that the danger might be averted?

There are a number of clues that suggest otherwise. Nowhere in this intelligence document is there any discussion of what might be done to rid the UDR of paramilitaries: no proposals for an urgent conference at the Ministry of Defence, no major overhaul of the vetting procedures,[30] no Parliamentary Inquiry. No solution is offered to the problem. But the dangers inherent in ridding the regiment of loyalists *are* spelled out. This could lead to a very small regiment indeed, the PM is told, and this at a time when the British military commitment in Ireland had seriously compromised its NATO responsibilities in central Europe.[31]

The second clue concerns the hypothetical discussion of scenarios where the UDR *might* become unreliable. Subversion was already having a real and measurable impact on Catholic civilians who were being murdered at work, on the street and in their homes by loyalist paramilitaries using UDR weapons. Loyalist paramilitaries were quite explicit that their assassination campaign against the civilian population was aimed at forcing an IRA 'surrender' (Edwards, 2009).[32]

The report focused on the potential for mutiny within the armed forces should a future Labour government consider any political initiative that could be interpreted as giving in to the demands of republican 'terrorists'. From the perspective of the military, the weakest link in the war against the IRA was the scenario whereby a Labour government might accede to demands from within its own party for a withdrawal from Ireland. This assessment refers specifically to a Labour government, yet Labour was in opposition when it was written, a telling sign of nervousness within the armed forces.

The final clue lies in subsequent events. Within months it was decided to increase the role of the UDR in intelligence-gathering. The public were not to be told.

## Loyalty in the UDR

On 15 March 1974 the London *Times* ran an article titled 'Ulstermen Establish Subversive Group'. The article alleged that a group of men within the UDR and the RUC had established a subversive organisation, 'For Ulster', and had taken an oath threatening mutiny if the British government moved against loyalists.

In response, a background brief (PRO24)[33] on the regiment was prepared for the Undersecretary of State (Army). According to the brief, a 'number of members of the UDR are associated with Protestant paramilitary organisations'. The brief goes on to highlight the importance of the Regiment and its 'substantial ... contribution to anti-IRA operations'. At paragraph 13b there is a brief mention of a policy decision that was to have far-reaching consequences for the regiment and, ultimately, for loyalist paramilitaries: 'Intelligence gathering: proposals for enhancing the present capability are being prepared for submission to Ministers' (ibid.).

In a further document senior military figures including the Chief of the General Staff (PRO25) had decided that the time was right to increase the role of the UDR in intelligence-gathering. In an April 1974 memo the Vice Chair of the General Staff clarified the proposal which he stated was aimed at gathering:

> intelligence on terrorist activities.... There is no intention of recruiting or encouraging members of the UDR to become informers on subversive elements within the UDR although, as you know, subversion in the UDR is a cause for concern.
>
> (ibid.)

Senior government officials shared this somewhat dubious differentiation between 'terrorists' outside the regiment and 'subversives' within (PRO26).

By the summer of 1975, when the Miami Showband ambush took place, it had been agreed that the regiment was to have an enhanced intelligence-gathering role. The UDR had become an essential element in the long-term security strategy.

Less than a month after the Wilson/Thatcher meeting in September 1975 – where it emerged that the 'Army's judgement was the UDR were heavily infiltrated by extremist Protestants' (PRO3) – a 'Secret UK Eyes only' briefing was sent to the Secretary of State. The briefing, on the subject of UDR security, was from the Head of DS 10, a department within the Ministry of Defence; the security classification meant in effect that this document was not to be shared with local security forces. The document alluded to a number of recent loyalist arms raids where UDR weapons had been stolen, the potential for collusion – 'this might have been the case' – and the general issue of loyalist subversion in the UDR (PRO27). According to the document, an investigation had shown that a 'small number, around 200 spread between the 11 Battalions of the Regiment are thought to have connections however slight with extremist organisations'. Subsequent events in Belfast suggest that this estimate was the tip of the iceberg and the comment made to Mrs Thatcher a month earlier would also confirm this. In reality the problem of subversion was exemplified by the military instruction referred to in the document, a military instruction that had not changed since the creation of the regiment.

> Soldiers in the UDR are already well aware that they will be discharged if their sympathies for the UDA or any similar organisation are strong enough to affect the performance of their military duties or to call into question their future loyalty or complete impartiality.
>
> (PRO27)

The brief response of the Secretary of State to this alarming briefing tells its own story: 'S of S considers that it is very important to foster the UDR's non-sectarian image' (PRO28).

It is important to put the above in context. The largest regiment in the British army was heavily infiltrated by loyalist paramilitaries. The regiment was playing an increasingly vital role in counter-insurgency operations. Its intelligence-gathering capability had been strengthened. The general staff and senior members of the British Cabinet were aware that the regiment had been compromised. In 1974 loyalist paramilitaries, including the UDA, murdered 131 people.[34] Thirty-three people died following car bomb attacks in the Irish Republic in May of that year. An official inquiry headed by an Irish Supreme Court Judge found evidence of collusion between loyalist paramilitaries and members of the UDR and RUC in the attacks.[35] In 1975 loyalists were responsible for a further 121 deaths.[36] According to recent HET reports, a number of these murders were carried out by UDR members.[37]

## Infiltration of the Belfast City Battalion

In February 1978 a series of highly secret meetings were held in Belfast between HQNI, the Intelligence and Security section of the Army, the Director of Security in London and, eventually, the Secretary of State, The meetings concerned an internal investigation into 10 UDR, the Belfast city Battalion of the Regiment. According to the security investigation, 'It seems likely that the Battalion has been infiltrated by the UVF' (PRO29); 'Investigations currently being conducted within 10 UDR are revealing evidence of serious penetration of the battalion by paramilitary organisations' (PRO30).

By 1978, in other words, subversion was still widespread. Given that at least seventy members of the Belfast Battalion had subversive traces according to the internal security investigation into 10 UDR referred to above, then the earlier estimate of 200 across all eleven battalions was clearly an underestimation. Despite concerns of 'serious penetration' of the battalion, this information was withheld from the public and parliament.

It emerged that at least fifteen members of 10 UDR based at Girdwood Barracks in North Belfast were part of a UVF unit which had been in the battalion over a period of years. In this period the Belfast UVF contained a death squad, the Shankill Butchers, who kidnapped, tortured and murdered their victims using butchers' knives. Nineteen people were murdered by this UVF gang (Dillon, 1998). Most of these gruesome murders took place within one square mile of Girdwood Barracks.

## Conclusion: an illegal and deadly relationship

The declassified documents that are available from the 1970s show knowledge at the highest levels of government and the military of loyalist paramilitary infiltration of the UDR. The paper trail of knowledge led to HQNI, the Ministry of Defence, secretaries of state and even prime ministers. The 'safety valve' provided by the UDR was in fact an illegal and deadly relationship with loyalist paramilitaries that fuelled the assassination campaign. The decision to increase the intelligence gathering role of the UDR in effect increased the intelligence-gathering capability of loyalist paramilitaries, as became evident in the 1980s and 1990s.[38] This provided a basis for a range of collusive relationships between the security forces and the paramilitaries.

The evidence does not support the claim that loyalist violence was in any way neutralised through the 'safety valve' of the UDR – the key legitimising claim made to justify tolerance of the UDA presence inside the UDR. The loyalist threat increased as a direct result of a policy which tolerated and encouraged paramilitary involvement in the armed forces. The British government manipulated loyalist paramilitaries as part of a counter-insurgency policy.

The illegal flow of intelligence from the UDR to loyalist paramilitary groups intensified in the 1980s with hundreds of files on alleged republican suspects being provided to the UDA in particular.[39] This in turn led to a significant increase in loyalist assassinations including that of human rights lawyer Pat Finucane.[40]

The UK government has portrayed its role in Ireland as that of the peacekeeper. In fact, the British state relationship with loyalist violence was tolerated to the point of tacit and at times explicit encouragement. The UK government used loyalists to wage a proxy terrorist campaign aimed at making the IRA capitulate. The result was state terror.[41] Loyalist paramilitaries killed over 1,000 people. It remains to be seen how many died as a result of loyalist infiltration of the UDR.

## Postscript

In 1979 then Prime Minister Margaret Thatcher penned some comments for a progress report on Northern Ireland. She urged mention of the 'Volunteer Ulster Defence Regiment (? Is that the name)'. Her officials clearly had difficulty reading her handwriting and the typed version of her comment reads: '(viii) The Prime Minister would also like to see some reference to the valiant work being carried by the Ulster Volunteer Force' (PRO31).

Apparently neither she not her officials were fully cognisant of the difference between the UDR ('? Is that the name'), the largest regiment in the British Army, and the UVF, a loyalist paramilitary group. On this point at least she found herself in agreement with the nationalist/republican community.

## Notes

1 The initials PRO denote that the source is a government document obtained from the UK Government Public Records Office. A full numbered list of documents with PRO references is included below (pp. 66–7).

2 The initials HET denote that the source is a 'Historical Enquiry Team Review Summary Report' of an inquiry conducted by the Police Service of Northern Ireland. The HET is a police unit responsible for reviewing and where possible reinvestigating all conflict-related deaths between 1969 and 1998. Most of the unit (approx. 130 staff) is made up of former detectives from British forces because of concerns that former police officers from Northern Ireland would not gain the confidence of the entire community. A full numbered list of documents with 'HET' references is included below (p. 67).

3 The murders of Sean Farmer and Colm McCartney in Altnamacken, County Armagh. HET Report (on file).

4 See Conflict Archive on the Internet (CAIN) website for a biography of this controversial political and religious figure – http://cain.ulst.ac.uk/othelem/people/biography/ppeople.htm.

5 Terminology is a recognised minefield. The use of the terms Protestant and Catholic is problematic and the authors will usually refer to loyalist/Unionist as opposed to Protestant and nationalist/republican as opposed to Catholic. However, it may be more accurate to use religious labelling in some instances; e.g. we cannot be certain that Catholics who joined the UDR perceived themselves as nationalist or republican and therefore Catholic is more appropriate.

6 Royal Ulster Constabulary, the police force in Northern Ireland between 1922 and 2001.

7 Ministerial brief for Venice meeting, 11–12 September 1975, page 2. These concerns were also being openly discussed in the media. In the wake of the Miami and Altnamacken attacks the *Irish Times* editorialised: 'there is doubt about the Ulster Defence Regiment and evidence, which cannot be ignored … of collusion between the UDR and Loyalist extremists'. The editorial went on to suggest that the UK should revisit an earlier Irish government proposal to invite in UN peacekeeping forces since 'this may at last be a serious policy option', an implicit indictment of British security policies.

8 The CAIN website contains information and source material on 'the Troubles' and politics in Northern Ireland from 1968 to the present. For further information about the UDA and UVF, see http://cain.ulst.ac.uk/othelem/organ/

uorgan.htm. According to the authoritative record of conflict-related deaths, 'Lost Lives', Table 2 – Responsibility for Deaths, the UDA/UFF were responsible for 408 deaths and the UVF/RHC were responsible for 547.

9 See the CAIN website for extensive background on this period: http://cain.ulst.ac.uk/events/index.html.

10 From the foundation of the state of Northern Ireland the regional parliament in Belfast, Stormont, retained control of policing. One party, the Ulster Unionist Party, maintained control of Stormont from 1922 until the regional parliament was prorogued in 1972 when Westminster assumed overall control of policing and all other security matters.

11 A report published in October 1969, the Hunt Report, recommended the disbandment of the Specials and the creation of a new impartial force (Advisory Committee on Police in Northern Ireland 1969).

12 Thirty-one people were killed between January and 9 August when internment was introduced. Another 148 were to die before the year ended. See also McKittrick *et al.* (1999: Table 2 – Responsibility for Deaths).

13 The UDR Advisory Council was made up of civilians and senior British Army officers. The role of the group was to advise the General Office Commanding (GOC) of the British Army on issues concerning the regiment.

14 In 1970 a senior officer in the British internal security service, MI5, was appointed Director of Intelligence in Belfast. See evidence to the Bloody Sunday Tribunal: http://report.bloody-sunday-inquiry.org/evidence/K/KD_0002.pdf.

15 See for instance Ministry of Defence (1970). By the mid-1970s an overt strategy of 'Ulsterisation' was announced which aimed to increase the security role of the locally recruited RUC and UDR and reduce the frontline profile of regular British troops. See http://cain.ulst.ac.uk.

16 See McKittrick *et al.* (1999), according to which 206 members of the UDR or Royal Irish Regiment were killed between 1966 and 1999.

17 See www.bloodysundayinquiry.org.

18 Development of the Ulster Defence Regiment, confidential letter from Headquarters Northern Ireland to Ministry of Defence, 12 June 1972 (on file).

19 The UDA remained legal until 1992 when the British government finally banned the organisation. Government ministers sought to justify the failure to proscribe the group by claiming that it was a smaller terror group within the UDA (the Ulster Freedom Fighters, UFF) which carried out assassinations and bombings. The reality was that the UFF was a flag of convenience for the UDA. See also McKittrick *et al.* (1999), Table 2 – Responsibility for Deaths.

20 The Head of the Defence Secretariat (DS 10) was a senior civil servant tasked with liaising between the military and government ministers and responsible for policy-making and political issues in respect of the British Army role in Northern Ireland. See the evidence of the Head of DS10 to the Bloody Sunday Tribunal: http://report.bloody-sunday-inquiry.org/evidence/K/KS_0003.pdf.

21 See CAIN for background on Operation Motorman http://cain.ulst.ac.uk/events/intern/index.html.

22 In the week ending 2 August there had been 182 applications, of which four were from Catholics; for 9 August there had been 209 applications, of which four were from Catholics. In the week ending 9 August 169 men had applied. One was Catholic. By 16 August 45 Catholics had resigned from the regiment, leaving a total of 389.

23 According to McKittrick *et al.* (1999) between 1 July 1972 and 31 August 1972 loyalists were responsible for 29 deaths, 19 in July and 10 in August.

24 The author of this letter was J.F. Howe who was the Civil Advisor to the General Office Commanding the Army at the time of writing.

25 See above, note 23.

26 Gen 79 was a Cabinet sub-committee established immediately after Bloody Sunday in anticipation of the resumption of direct rule. Its membership included the secretaries of state for Northern Ireland, the Home Office, Defence, and the Foreign and Commonwealth Office, as well as more junior ministers. It was also attended by senior civil servants, the Chief of the General Staff of the armed forces, and by MI5. It was chaired by the Prime Minister.

27 See (HET5) on the death of Henry Cunningham.

28 See 'Note of a Meeting between the Secretary of State and the Ulster Unionist Party at Stormont Castle 12 December 1972' (on file). See also 'Note of a Meeting between the Secretary of State and Sir Patrick McGrory on Wednesday 13 December 1972' (on file). The official denial of the extent of loyalist violence is exemplified in the minutes of a meeting in London in 1974 where an official from the Attorney General's Office asked 'why only Roman Catholics had been interned before 1973'. A Treasury solicitor representative replied that it was the view of the security forces that there was 'no serious Protestant threat in that period that led to death or serious injuries'. In effect the UK government was denying knowledge of 143 assassinations carried out by loyalists during 1971/72. (In so doing it was also misleading the European Court of Human Rights.) 'Note of a Meeting at the Northern Ireland Office, Wednesday 13 November 1974' (on file).

29 The document is available at www.patfinucanecentre.org under the section 'Declassified documents'.

30 The issue of vetting procedures was the subject of constant reviews. A memo dated 20 August 1973 from the Director of Security (Army) to BGS (Int) (Brigadier-General Staff with responsibility for Intelligence) alludes to the 'security vetting process' in the UDR and notes that it was introduced to dispel fears that the UDR would evolve into the B Specials 'in a different guise'. 'Although the injection of the interview has probably been successful as part of the PR exercise, it can have had little effect in improving the value of screening'.

31 According to an internal memo, the British Army on the Rhine (BAOR) had not been able to take part in major NATO exercises between 1971 and 1976 because of its Irish commitments. Confidential Annex to COS 15th Meeting/76 dated 14 September 1976.

32 Edwards (2009: 150) notes, 'Moreover, by carrying out indiscriminate acts loyalist terrorists could also communicate a message to the wider nationalist community that continued IRA violence carried a heavy price'.

33 This brief estimates the strength of the regiment as of March 1974 at 7,908 soldiers in 11 battalions based at 43 permanent bases.

34 McKittrick *et al.* (1999: Table 2 – Responsibility for Deaths).

35 For further information see Justice for the Forgotten's website at www.dublin-monaghanbombings.org/.

36 See above, note 34.

37 For example, UDR members were involved in gun and bomb attacks on the Eagle Bar (HET3) and Clancy's Bar in May 1975 where four people died, in the Miami Showband and Altnamackin ambushes in July and August (see above, notes 2 and 3) and in the gun and bomb attack on Donnelly's Bar (HET4) on 19 December 1975 where three people including the father of one of the authors of this chapter died. HET reports on above incidents on file.

38 For further background on reports and investigations into collusion between paramilitaries and the security forces throughout the conflict, see www.patfinucanecentre.org.

39 See Stevens Inquiry: Overview and recommendations, 17 April 2003, Sir John

Stevens QPM, DL, Commissioner of the Metropolitan Police Service: http://cain.ulst.ac.uk/issues/collusion/stevens3/stevens3summary.htm; British Irish Rights Watch (1999) *Deadly Intelligence: State Involvement in Loyalist Murder in Northern Ireland* (Summary). London: British Irish Rights Watch, http://cain.ulst.ac.uk/issues/violence/birw0299.htm; Amnesty International (2000) United Kingdom – Patrick Finucane's killing: Official collusion and cover-up, 1 February, www.amnesty.org/en/library/asset/EUR45/026/2000/en/83f047ba-dfc0–11dd-8e17–69926d493233/eur450262000en.pdf (accessed 4 September 2011).

40 In January 1988 loyalist paramilitaries received a huge haul of South African weapons. In the six years before the arrival of the weapons loyalist paramilitaries killed 71 people of whom 49 were sectarian/political in nature. In the six years following, from January 1988 to 1 September 1994, loyalists killed 229 people of whom 207 were sectarian/political in nature. See www.madden-finucane.com/patfinucane/archive/pat_finucane/1997–12–21.htm (accessed 4 September 2011).

41 See also Rolston (2006).

## List of Primary Sources Obtained from the UK Government Public Record Office

PRO1 – Additional Brief: Northern Ireland, prepared for ministerial meeting on European political co-operation, Venice, 11–12 September 1975 (on file).

PRO2 – Northern Ireland Office, letter dated 1 September 1975 from B.M. Webster to Mr Bourne (on file).

PRO3 – Note of meeting between the prime minister and Mrs Thatcher on 10 September 1975 (on file).

PRO4 – Ministry of Defence telex to Home Office summarising meeting between the two prime ministers, 7 September 1971 (on file).

PRO5 – Thoughts on the proposed rapid build-up of the UDR, F.G. Guckian, 10 September 1971 (on file).

PRO6 – Loose Minute Secret Perimeter Reference A/BR/20201/MO3 E/88/I 10 September 1971 (on file).

PRO7 – Minutes of the 18th Meeting of the Advisory Council held on Wednesday, 12 May 1971 at 4.00 p.m. (on file).

PRO8 – UDR Duties–Memo from John Howe, Civil Advisor to GOC Northern Ireland, to the Undersecretary of State (US of S) (Army) and to the UDR Steering Committee, 2 June 1972 (on file).

PRO9 – Foreign and Commonwealth Office internal letter to K.C. Thom Esq., Dublin, 7 February 1973.

PRO10 – Letter and accompanying report from J.B. Bourne to PS (Private Secretary)/Secretary of State, reference 'Sectarian Assassinations', 23 May 1975.

PRO11 – Report from B.M. Webster to PS/PUS, reference 'Killings since the beginning of the Ceasefire', August 1975.

PRO12 – Minutes of the 32nd Meeting of the Advisory Council held on Monday, 12 June 1972 at 4.00 p.m. (on file).

PRO13 – Reply from Head of Defence Secretariat, Ministry of Defence, London to Civil Advisor, GOC HQ Lisburn, 21 June 1971 (on file).

PRO14 – Minutes of the 34th Meeting of the Advisory Council held on Wednesday, 17 August 1972 at 4.00 p.m. (on file).

PRO15 – Background Note attached to Loose Minute – Northern Ireland Loss of UDR Weapons from Colonel H.S.L. Dalzell-Payne, to PS/US of S (Army) MoD, 31 July 1972 (on file).

PRO16 – Letter dated 24 July 1972 from Commander UDR – UDR Involvement in UDA (on file).
PRO17 – HQNI letter to Lt. Col. J.L. Pownall OBE, Ag Secretariat MoD Subject UDR – Membership of UDA, 31 July 1972 (on file).
PRO18 – MoD confidential letter MO 19/3A, 29 November 1972, C.V. Roberts regarding the GEN 79 (72) 33rd meeting held on 11 September 1972 (on file).
PRO19 – MoD response, November 1972 (on file).
PRO20 – Oral reply to Parliamentary Question PQ 3141A, 30 November 1972, to Bernadette Devlin MP (on file).
PRO21 – 'Subversion in the UDR' (on file).
PRO22 – Loose Minute to PS. US of S Northern Ireland, Losses of UDR Weapons – Comparison of Losses of Weapons Between Battalions of UDR and Incidents of Suspected Collusion, 1 August 1972. (This memo was for ministerial attention – US of S is the Undersecretary of State or Junior Minister) (on file).
PRO23 – Security Forces and UDA, Background Brief, 23 November 1972 (on file).
PRO24 – Secret Annex A The Ulster Defence Regiment, 19 March 1974, from AUS (GS) to PS/US of S (ARMY) (on file).
PRO25 – Attached minute from Vice-Chief of the General Staff to Undersecretary of State (Army), 17 April 1974 (on file).
PRO26 – Confidential Northern Ireland Office note to A.G. Rucker Esq. Lord President's Office, Privy Council Office, Whitehall, copied to PS/Minister of State; PS/US of S (Army); DUS (ARMY); AUS (GS); Head of DS 10; Head of C2 (AD) 24 June 1974 (on file).
PRO27 – Minute from Head of DS 10 (D.E. Johnston) to Assistant Private Secretary to the Secretary of State, 6 October 1975 (on file).
PRO28 – Note from APS/Secretary of State to Head of DS 10 dated 13 October 1975 (on file).
PRO29 – Letter dated 2 March 1978 titled 'UDR Irregularities', sent to various agencies including the Northern Ireland Office, SoS, the Army and the Legal Department among others (on file).
PRO30 – Brief from a lieutenant-colonel (name illegible) dated 2 March 1978 (D/DINI/2010) (on file).
PRO31 – PM's notes of 13 July 1979 and typed transcript signed M.W. Hopkins Esq., Northern Ireland Office (on file).

## Historical Enquiry Team Review Summary Reports

HET1 – Concerning the Deaths of Anthony Geraghty, Brian McCoy and Francis O'Toole, date of deaths: 31 July 1975.
HET2 – Concerning the Deaths of Colm McCartney and Sean Patrick Farmer, date of deaths: 24 August 1975.
HET3 – Concerning the Death of Frederick George McLoughlin, date of incident, Saturday, 15 May 1976, date of death, Monday, 31 May 1976.
HET4 – Concerning the Deaths of Trevor Brecknell, Michael Francis Donnelly and Patrick Joseph Donnelly, died on 19 December 1975.
HET5 – Concerning the Death of Henry Cunningham, date of death, 9 August 1973.

## References

Advisory Committee on Police in Northern Ireland (1969) *Report of the Advisory Committee on Police in Northern Ireland*, Chairman: Baron Hunt, CBE, DSO,

Presented to Parliament by Command of His Excellency the Governor of Northern Ireland, October 1969, Belfast: HMSO.

Campbell, B. (2000) 'Death Squads: Definition, Problems and Historical Context', in B. Campbell and A. Brenner (eds) *Death Squads in Global Perspective: Murder with Deniability*, London: Macmillan, pp. 1–26.

Dillon, M. (1998) *The Shankill Butchers – a Case Study of Mass Murder*. London: Arrow Books.

Edwards, A. (2009) Abandoning Armed Resistance? The Ulster Volunteer Force as a Case Study of Strategic Terrorism in Northern Ireland, *Studies in Conflict & Terrorism*, vol. 32, no. 2, pp. 146–66.

Jamieson, R. and McEvoy, K. (2005) State Crime by Proxy and Juridical Othering, *British Journal of Criminology*, vol. 45, pp. 504–27.

McKittrick, D., Kelters, S., Feeney, B. and Thornton, C. (1999) *Lost Lives, the Stories of the Men, Women and Children who Died as a Result of the Northern Ireland Troubles*, Edinburgh: Mainstream.

Ministry of Defence (1970) *Land Operations Volume III: Counter-Revolutionary Operations, Part 3 Counter-Insurgency*, London: UK Ministry of Defence. Available at www.scribd.com/doc/28436846/15858-Land-Operations-Volume-III-Part-3.

Rolston, B. (2006) An Effective Mask for Terror' Democracy, Death Squads and Northern Ireland, *Crime, Law & Social Change*, vol. 44, no. 2, pp. 181–203.

Ryder, C. (1991) *The Ulster Defence Regiment: An Instrument of Peace?* London: Methuen.

Walsh, D. (1975) Murders Underline Inadequate Security: British Ambassador Told of Government's Concern, *Irish Times*, 1 August, no. 1.

Wood, I.S. (2006) *Crimes of Loyalty – A History of the UDA*, Edinburgh: Edinburgh University Press.

Wright, P. (1988) *Spycatcher: The Candid Autobiography of a Senior Intelligence Officer*, London: Heinemann.

# 4 Terrorism and justice

## Some useful truisms

*Noam Chomsky**

On a highly controversial topic like the one we turn to now, perhaps it is a good idea to begin with a few simple truths.

The first is that actions are evaluated in terms of the range of likely consequences. A second is the principle of universality; we apply to ourselves the same standards we apply to others, if not more stringent ones. Apart from being the merest truisms, these principles are also the foundation of just war theory, at least any version of it that deserves to be taken seriously. The truisms raise an empirical question: Are they accepted? Investigation will reveal, I believe, that they are rejected almost without exception.

The first truism may merit a word of elaboration. The actual consequences of an action may be highly significant, but they do not bear on the moral evaluation of the action. No one celebrates Khrushchev's success in placing nuclear missiles in Cuba because it did not lead to nuclear war, or condemns the fear-mongers who warned of the threat. Nor do we applaud North Korea's Dear Leader for developing nuclear weapons and providing missile technology to Pakistan, or denounce those who warn of possible consequences because they haven't taken place. An apologist for state violence who took such positions would be regarded as a moral monster or lunatic. That's obvious, until it comes time to apply the same criteria to ourselves. Then the stance of the lunatic and moral monster is taken to be highly honorable, indeed obligatory, and adherence to the truisms is condemned with horror. Let us, nevertheless, accept the truisms for what they are: truisms. And then think about a few crucial current cases to which they apply.

### Truisms and terror

Take 9–11. It is widely argued that the terrorist attacks changed everything dramatically as the world entered a new and frightening "age of terror" – the title of a collection of academic essays by Yale University scholars and others.[1] It is also widely held that the term *terror* is very hard to define. We might ask why the concept of terror should be considered particularly obscure. There are official US government definitions that fall well within the range of clarity of other usages that are regarded as unproblematic. A US Army manual defined *terrorism* as "the calculated use of violence or threat of violence to attain goals that are political, religious, or ideological in nature.... Through intimidation, coercion, or instilling fear." The official US Code gave a more elaborate definition, essentially along the same lines. The British government's definition is similar: "Terrorism is the use, or threat, of action which is violent, damaging or disrupting, and is intended to influence the government or intimidate the public and is for the purpose of advancing a political, religious, or ideological cause.[2] These definitions seem fairly clear. They are close enough to ordinary usage, and are considered appropriate when discussing the terrorism of enemies.

The official US definitions are the ones I have been using in writing about the topic since the Reagan administration came into office in 1981, declaring that a war on terror would be a centerpiece of its foreign policy. The reliance on these definitions is particularly appropriate for our purposes because they were formulated when the first war on terror was declared. But almost no one uses them , and they have been rescinded, replaced by nothing sensible. The reasons do not seem obscure: the official definitions of *terrorism* are virtually the same as the definitions of *counterterror* (sometimes called "low-intensity conflict," or "counterinsurgency"). But counterterror is official US policy, and it plainly will not do to say that the US is officially committed to terrorism.[3]

The US is by no means alone in this practice. It is traditional for states to call their own terrorism "counterterror," even the worst mass murderers: the Nazis, for example. In occupied Europe they claimed to be defending the population and legitimate governments from the partisans, terrorists supported from abroad. That was not entirely false; even the most egregious propaganda rarely is. The partisans were undoubtedly directed from London, and they did engage in terror. The US military had some appreciation of the Nazi perspective: its counterinsurgency doctrine was modeled on Nazi manuals, which were analyzed sympathetically, with the assistance of Wehrmacht officers.[4]

It is this common practice that allows for the conventional thesis that terror is a weapon of the weak. That is true, by definition, if *terror* is restricted to their terrorism. If the doctrinal requirement is lifted, however, we find that, like most weapons, terror is primarily a weapon of the powerful.

Another problem with the official definitions of *terror* is that it follows from them that the US is a leading terrorist state. That much is hardly controversial, at least among those who believe that we should pay some attention to such institutions as the International Court of Justice or the UN Security Council, or mainstream scholarship, as the examples of Nicaragua and Cuba unequivocally reveal. But that conclusion won't do either. So we are left with no sensible definition of *terrorism* – unless we decide to break ranks and use the official definitions that have been abandoned because of their unacceptable consequences.

The official definitions do not answer every question precisely. They do not, for example, draw a sharp boundary between *international terrorism* and *aggression*, or between terror and resistance. These issues have arisen in interesting ways, which have direct bearing on the redeclared war on terror and on today's headlines.

Take the distinction between *terror* and *resistance*. One question that arises is the legitimacy of actions to realize "the right to self-determination, freedom, and independence, as derived from the Charter of the United Nations, of people forcibly deprived of that right ... particularly peoples under colonial and racist regimes and foreign occupation." Do such actions fall under *terror* or *resistance*? The quoted words are from the most forceful denunciation of the crime of terrorism by the UN General Assembly, which stated further that "nothing in the present resolution could in any way prejudice the right" so defined. The resolution was adopted in December 1987, just as officially recognized international terrorism reached its peak. It is obviously important. The vote was 153 to 2 (with a single abstention, Honduras), hence even more important.[5]

The two countries that voted against the resolution were the usual ones. Their reason, they explained at the UN session, was the paragraph just quoted. The phrase "colonial and racist regimes" was understood to refer to their ally, apartheid South Africa. Evidently the US and Israel could not condone resistance to the apartheid regime, particularly when it was led by Mandela's African National Congress, one of the world's "more notorious terrorist groups," as Washington determined at the time. The other phrase, "foreign occupation," was understood to refer to Israel's military occupation, then in its twentieth year. Evidently, resistance could not be condoned in that case either.

The US and Israel were alone in the world in denying that such actions can be legitimate resistance, and declaring them to be terrorism. The US–Israeli stand extends beyond the occupied territories. Thus the US and Israel regard Hezbollah, for example, as one of the leading terrorist organizations in the world, not because of its terrorist acts (which are real) but because it was formed to resist the Israeli occupation of southern Lebanon, and succeeded in driving out the invaders after two decades of defiance of Security Council orders to withdraw. The US even goes so far as to call people "terrorists" if they resist direct US aggression: the South Vietnamese, for example; or recently, the Iraqis.[6]

The public knows nothing about the major UN condemnation of what Reagan called the "evil scourge of terrorism" and its fate by virtue of the usual double veto. To learn about such matters one has to wander into forbidden territory: the historical and documentary record, or marginalized critical literature.

Despite the unclarities, and the sharp divide between US–Israel and the world, the official US definitions of *terror* seem fairly adequate to the purposes at hand.

Let us turn to the belief that 9–11 signaled a sharp change in the course of history. That seems questionable. Nonetheless, something dramatically new and different did happen on that terrible day. The target was not Cuba, or Nicaragua, or Lebanon, or Chechnya, or one of the other traditional victims of international terrorism, but a state with enormous power to shape the future. For the first time, an attack on the rich and powerful countries succeeded on a scale that is, regrettably, not unfamiliar in their traditional domains. Alongside horror at the crime against humanity and sympathy for the victims, commentators outside the ranks of Western privilege often responded to the 9–11 atrocities with a "welcome to the club," particularly in Latin America, where it is not easy to forget the plague of violence and repression that swept through the region from the early 1960s, or its roots.

The plague can in part be traced to a decision by the Kennedy administration in 1962 to change the mission of the Latin American military, effectively, from "hemispheric defense" to "internal security." The effect was a shift from toleration "of the rapacity and cruelty of the Latin American military" to "direct complicity" in their crimes, to support for "the methods of Heinrich Himmler's extermination squads," in the words of Charles Maechling, who led US counterinsurgency and internal defense planning from 1961 to 1966.[7] The perception of the victims is similar. To take one case of unusual current significance, the highly respected president of the Colombian Permanent Committee for Human Rights, Alfredo Vásquez Carrizosa, writes that the Kennedy administration "took great pains to transform our regular armies into counterinsurgency brigades, accepting the new strategy of the death squads," ushering in

> what is known in Latin America as the National Security Doctrine … not defense against an external enemy, but a way to make the military establishment the masters of the game [with] the right to combat the internal enemy … : it is the right to fight and to exterminate social workers, trade unionists, men and women who are not supportive of the establishment, and who are assumed to be communist extremists. And this could mean anyone, including human rights activists such as myself.[8]

The "great pains" to which he refers coincided with the fateful 1962 decision. In that year, Kennedy sent a Special Forces mission to Colombia, led by General William Yarborough. Yarborough advised "paramilitary, sabotage and/or terrorist activities against known communist proponents," to be "employed now … [i]f we have such an apparatus" in place – "we" because there is no need to prevaricate in secret communications.[9] In counterinsurgency doctrine, the phrase "known communist proponents" extends to the categories of "assumed communist extremists" that Vásquez Carrizosa enumerates, a fact well known to Latin Americans, just as they know that the primary victims are the poor and oppressed who are daring to raise their heads.

The National Security Doctrine reached Central America in the 1980s. El Salvador became the leading recipient of US military aid as state terror reached its awful peak. When Congress hampered direct military aid and training by imposing human rights conditions, as in Guatemala after massive government atrocities, surrogates undertook the task.

The victims do not easily forget, though among the powerful, these crimes are subject to the standard "ritual avoidance" of unacceptable facts. Hardly a day passes without examples. Thus, a front-page story in the national press warns that the threat of Al Qaeda is increasing, as it is turning from targets that are "well protected ... to so-called soft targets."[10] The story should at once recall Washington's official instructions to its proxy forces to attack "soft targets" in Nicaragua immediately after it was ordered by the highest international authorities to terminate its terrorist war, and the reaction to these orders.

Whether attacking "soft targets" is right or wrong, terrorism or a noble cause, depends on who is the agent. The practice is routine, and unproblematic once moral truisms have been deemed irrelevant and unwanted facts efficiently "disappeared."

## The art of "disappearing" unwanted facts

One contributor to the Yale volume (Charles Hill) observed that 9–11 opened the second "war on terror," the first having been declared by the Reagan administration twenty years earlier, a rare recognition of reality. And "we won" the first war, Hill reports triumphantly, though the terrorist monster was only wounded, not slain.[11] How "we won" is someone else's department: the Jesuit intellectuals in Central America, the School of the Americas, truth commissions, serious scholarship, activist and solidarity literature, and the memories of the survivors.

We can learn a good deal about the current war on terror by inquiring into the first phase, and how it is now portrayed. One leading academic specialist describes the 1980s as the decade of "state terrorism," of "persistent state involvement, or 'sponsorship', of terrorism, especially by Libya and Iran." The US merely responded with "a 'proactive' stance towards terrorism." Others recommended the methods by which "we won": the operations for which the US was condemned by the World Court and Security Council (absent the veto) are a model for "Nicaragua-like support for the Taliban's adversaries." A prominent historian of the subject, David Rapoport, finds deep roots for the terrorism of Osama bin Laden: in South Vietnam, where "the effectiveness of Vietcong terror against the American Goliath armed with modern technology kindled hopes that the Western heartland was vulnerable too."[12]

The villainy of the terrorists attacking us everywhere is awesome indeed.

Keeping to convention, these analyses portray the US as a benign victim, defending itself from the terror of others: the Vietnamese (in

South Vietnam), the Nicaraguans (in Nicaragua), Libyans and Iranians (if they ever suffered a slight at US hands, it passes unnoticed), and other anti-American forces worldwide. If not everyone in the world shares that perception of history, then they too are "anti-American" and can be safely dismissed.

As discussed earlier, the plague of US-backed state terror that spread through Latin America in the 1960s peaked in Central America in the 1980s, as Reagan's "war on terror" took its deadly toll. Central America was one prime focus of that onslaught. The other was the Mideast/Mediterranean region. Here, too, the contrast between what actually happened and what is portrayed is dramatic and revealing. In this region, the worst single atrocity during the 1980s was the Israeli invasion of Lebanon in 1982, which, like the murderous and destructive Rabin–Peres invasions of 1993 and 1996, had little pretense of self-defense. In the light of crucial Reagan–Clinton support, these operations add to Washington's record of state-supported international terrorism.

The US was directly involved in many other acts of terror in the region, including the three candidates for the prize of most extreme terrorist atrocity of 1985, when terrorism in that region was selected by editors as the lead story of the year: (1) the car bomb outside a mosque in Beirut that killed 80 people (mostly women and girls) and wounded 250 others, timed to explode as people were leaving and traced back to the CIA and British Intelligence; (2) Shimon Peres's bombing of Tunis, killing 75 people, Palestinians and Tunisians, expedited by the US and praised by Secretary of State Shultz, then unanimously condemned by the UN Security Council as an "act of armed aggression" (US abstaining); and (3) Peres's "Iron Fist" operations directed against what the Israeli high command called "terrorist villagers" in occupied Lebanon, reaching new depths of "calculated brutality and arbitrary murder" in the words of a Western diplomat familiar with the area, amply supported by direct coverage, total casualties unknown in accord with the usual conventions.

All these atrocities fall within the category of state-supported international terrorism, if not the more severe war crime of aggression. This accounting excludes many other atrocities, such as the regular kidnappings and killings on the high seas by Israeli naval forces attacking ships in transit between Cyprus and northern Lebanon, with many of those captured brought to Israel and kept in prison without charge as hostages, and numerous other crimes that are not crimes because they were backed by Washington.[13]

In journalism and scholarship on terrorism, 1985 is recognized to be the peak year of Middle East terrorism, but not because of these events; rather, because of two terrorist atrocities in which a single person was murdered, in each case an American.[14]

In the worst of the two terrorist atrocities that passed through the doctrinal filters, a crippled American Jew, Leon Klinghoffer, was brutally murdered during the hijacking of the *Achille Lauro* cruise ship in October 1985 by a Palestinian terrorist group led by Abu Abbas. The murder "seemed to set a standard for remorselessness among terrorists," *New York Times* correspondent John Burns wrote. Burns described Abu Abbas as the "has-been monster" who may "finally have to face a day of reckoning with American Justice" for his role in the crime. One of the heralded achievements of the invasion of Iraq was the capture of Abu Abbas a few months later.[15]

The Klinghoffer murder remains the most vivid and lasting symbol of the ineradicable evil of Arab terrorism and the unanswerable proof that there can be no negotiating with these vermin. The atrocity was very real, and is in no way mitigated by the terrorists' plea that the hijacking was in retaliation for the far more murderous US-backed Israeli terrorist attack on Tunis a week earlier. But the bombing of Tunis does not enter the canon of terrorism because it is subject to the wrong-agent fallacy. It remained unmentioned when Abu Abbas was captured. There would of course be no difficulty in apprehending the "monsters" Shimon Peres and George Shultz, who are far from "has beens," and bringing them to "a day of reckoning with American Justice." But that is beyond unthinkable.

Also efficiently "disappeared" are recent events that bear more than a superficial similarity to the Klinghoffer murder. The reaction was silence when British reporters found the "flattened remains of a wheelchair" in the remnants of the Jenin refugee camp after Sharon's spring 2002 offensive. "It had been utterly crushed, ironed flat as if in a cartoon," they reported: "In the middle of debris lay a broken white flag." A crippled Palestinian, Kemal Zughayer, "was shot dead as he tried to wheel himself up the road. The Israeli tanks must have driven over the body, because when [a friend] found it, one leg and both arms were missing, and the face, he said, had been ripped in two."[16] If even reported in the US, this would have been dismissed as an inadvertent error in the course of justified retaliation. Kemal Zughayer does not deserve to enter the annals of terrorism along with Leon Klinghoffer. His murder was not under the command of a "monster" but a "man of peace," who enjoys a soulful relation with the "man of vision" in the White House.

The basic dynamic at work was outlined 20 years ago by one of Israel's most eminent writers and commentators, Boaz Evron, after an upsurge of settler–IDF [Israeli Defence Forces] violence that caused much consternation in Israel. Evron wrote a sardonic account of how to deal with the lower orders – the "Araboushim" in Israeli slang. Israel should "keep them on a short leash," he wrote, so that they recognize "that the whip is held over their head." As long as not too many people are being visibly killed, then Western humanists will "accept it all peacefully" and even ask, "What is so terrible?"[17]

The guardians of journalistic integrity in the US understand the lesson without Evron's advice. The most prestigious media watchdog, the *Columbia Journalism Review*, gave its cherished "laurel" to the US media for their coverage of Sharon's spring 2002 offensive in Jenin, Nablus, Ramallah, and elsewhere, in the thirty-fifth year of Israel's occupation of the West Bank and Gaza. The recipients earned the laurel, according to the *Review*, for ensuring that scrutiny of the offensive would focus on one cardinal question: Was there a purposeful massacre of hundreds of civilians in the Jenin refugee camp?[18] If not, then civilized people can "accept it all peacefully."

We might try a thought experiment. Suppose that Syria had occupied Israel for 35 years, employing the means and measures of Israel's occupation, and then proceeded further to duplicate Sharon's 2002 offensive: rampaging through Jewish towns, leveling large areas with bulldozers and tanks, keeping the population under siege for weeks without food or water or access to medical care, destroying cultural centers and the institutions of government and archaeological treasures, making it crystal clear to the Yids in every possible way that "the whip is held over their head" – but not slaughtering hundreds of them at once. According to the standards of the "laurel," only an anti-Arab racist would object – and discovery of the scattered parts of a murdered Jewish cripple in a wheelchair crushed by a Syrian tank would merit no notice, let alone stern "American Justice."

Reviewing "the Jenin story," the *Review* berated the British press for "embracing Israel's guilt as established fact" and ridiculed the UN for "preparing an investigation by a team whose political sympathies ensured that its conclusions would be challenged," certainly by the independent thinkers of the *Review*. "Amid all this confounding din," the editors asked, "what was the world to believe?"

Fortunately, all was not lost: "Enter the independent U.S. news media, on a fact-finding mission of their own," which refuted the anti-Israel slanders and revealed that there was "no deliberate, cold-blooded murder of hundreds" at Jenin – in fact, reaching exactly the same conclusions as the disreputable British media (and others), which, however, did not adopt the framework of US–Israeli propaganda as rigidly as the editors of the *Review* demand, and scrutinized the Israeli invasion beyond that single question.

The "independent U.S. media" did not merit the insulting praise of their cheerleader. Careful readers could learn about the crimes that had taken place, though not in the shocking detail presented in the Israeli and European press. And they were carefully protected from the complicity of their own government, in routine fashion.

When the "wrong agents" are implicated in state-supported international terrorism, we sometimes discover that terrorist atrocities are not fully effaced, but rather praised. An instructive case is the country that replaced El Salvador as the leading recipient of US military aid and training: Turkey, where "state terror" was practiced on a massive scale through the Clinton years, relying on US support.[19] I borrow the term *state terror* from the Turkish state minister for human rights, referring to the vast atrocities against Kurds in 1994, and from sociologist Ismail Besikci, returned to prison after publishing his book *State Terror in the Near East,* having already served 15 years for recording Turkish repression of Kurds. As elsewhere, unacceptable facts were "disappeared," but the events did not pass entirely unnoticed. The State Department's *Year 2000* report on Washington's "efforts to combat terrorism" singled out Turkey for its "positive experiences" in combating terror, along with Algeria and Spain, worthy colleagues. This praise was reported without comment in a front-page story in the *New York Times* by its specialist on terrorism. In a leading journal of international affairs, Ambassador Robert Pearson reports that the US "could have no better friend and ally than Turkey" in its efforts "to eliminate terrorism" worldwide, thanks to the "capabilities of [Turkey's] armed forces" demonstrated in their "anti-terror campaign" in the Kurdish southeast.[20] As noted, the voluntary US censorship of Turkish state terror was eased slightly in early 2003 during Turkey's democratic deviation, though the decisive role of the United States remained well concealed.[21]

The considerations just reviewed, a small sample, suggest one simple way to reduce the threat of terror: stop participating in it. That would be a significant contribution to a general "war on terror." Nevertheless, it would not address the category of terror that passes through the doctrinal filters: *their* terror against *us* and our clients, an extremely serious matter, no doubt. Let us put that issue aside for a moment and consider a related domain in which attention to truisms may have some value.

## Truisms and just war theory

The theory of just war has enjoyed a revival in the context of the "new era of humanitarian intervention" and international terrorism. Consider the strongest case put forth: the bombing of Afghanistan, a paradigm example of just war, according to the Western consensus. The respected moral-political philosopher Jean Bethke Elshtain summarizes received opinion fairly accurately when she writes that "nearly everyone, with the exception of absolute pacifists and those who seem to think we should let ourselves be slaughtered with impunity because so many people out there 'hate' us, agrees" that the bombing of Afghanistan was clearly a just war.[22] To mention just one additional example, *New York Times* columnist Bill Keller, now executive editor, remarks that when "America dispatched soldiers in the cause of 'regime change'" in Afghanistan, "the opposition was mostly limited to the people who are reflexively against the American use of power," either timid supporters or "isolationists, the doctrinaire left and the soft-headed types Christopher Hitchens described as people who, 'discovering a viper in the bed of their child, would place the first call to People for the Ethical Treatment of Animals'."[23]

These are empirical statements, so despite the near-unanimity of the declarations, we are entitled to ask whether they are true. Let's ignore the fact that "regime change" was not "the cause" of war in Afghanistan but rather an afterthought late in the game. Were there opponents of the bombing who were not either absolute pacifists or absolute lunatics?

It turns out that there were, and the opponents formed an interesting collection. To begin with, they apparently included the great majority of the population of the world when the bombing was announced. So we discover from an international Gallup poll in late September 2001. The lead question was this: "Once the identity of the terrorists is known, should the American government launch a military attack on the country or countries where the terrorists are based or should the American government seek to extradite the terrorists to stand trial?" Whether such diplomatic means could have succeeded is known only to ideological extremists on both sides; tentative explorations of extradition by the Taliban were instantly rebuffed by Washington, which also refused to provide evidence for its accusations.

World opinion strongly favored diplomatic-judicial measures over military action. In Europe, support for military action ranged from 8 percent in Greece to 29 percent in France. Support was least in Latin America, the region that has the most experience with US intervention: it ranged from 2 percent in Mexico to 11 percent in Colombia and Venezuela. The sole exception was Panama, where only 80 percent preferred peaceful means, 16 percent military attack. Support for strikes that included civilian targets was much less. Even in the two countries polled that supported the use of military force, India and Israel (where the reasons were parochial), considerable majorities opposed such attacks. There was, then, overwhelming opposition to Washington's actual policies, which not only included civilian targets but even turned major urban concentrations into "ghost towns" from the first moment, the press reported.

The Gallup poll was not reported in the US, though it was elsewhere, including Latin America.[24]

Notice that even this very limited support for the bombing was based on a crucial presupposition: that those responsible for 9–11 were known. But they were not, as the government quietly informed us eight months after the bombing. In June 2002, FBI director Robert Mueller testified before a Senate committee, delivering what the press described as some of "his most detailed public comments on the origins of the attacks" of 9–11.[25] Mueller informed the Senate that "investigators *believe* the idea of the Sept. 11 attacks on the World Trade Center and Pentagon came from Al Qaeda leaders in Afghanistan," though the plotting and financing may trace to Germany and the United Arab Emirates. "We *think* the masterminds of it were in Afghanistan, high in the al Qaeda leadership," Mueller said. If the indirect responsibility of Afghanistan could only be surmised in June 2002, it evidently could not have been *known* eight months before, when President Bush ordered the bombing of Afghanistan.

According to the FBI, then, the bombing was a war crime, an act of aggression, based on mere supposition. It also follows directly that there was virtually no detectable world support for the policies actually undertaken, since even the minimal support recorded by polls was based on a presupposition that Washington and London knew to be false.

Perhaps the former director of Human Rights Watch Africa, now a professor of law at Emory University, spoke for many others around the world when he addressed the International Council on Human Rights Policy in Geneva in January 2002, saying that "I am unable to appreciate any moral, political or legal differences between this *jihad* by the United States against those it deems to be its enemies and the *jihad* by Islamic groups against those they deem to be their enemies."[26]

What about Afghan opinion? Information is scanty but not entirely lacking. In late October 2001, after three weeks of intense bombing, 1,000 Afghan leaders gathered in Peshawar, some exiles, some coming from within Afghanistan, all committed to overthrowing the Taliban regime. It was "a rare display of unity among tribal elders, Islamic scholars, fractious politicians, and former guerrilla commanders," the press reported. They had many disagreements but unanimously "urged the US to stop the air raids" and appealed to the international media to call for an end to the "bombing of innocent people." They urged that other means be adopted to overthrow the hated Taliban regime, a goal they believed could be achieved without further death and destruction.

A similar message was conveyed by Afghan opposition leader Abdul Haq, who was highly regarded in Washington and by Afghan President Hamid Karzai. Just before he entered Afghanistan without US support, and was then captured and killed, Haq condemned the bombing then under way and criticized the US for refusing to back his efforts and those of others "to create a revolt within the Taliban." The bombing was "a big setback for these efforts," he said: the US "is trying to show its muscle, score a victory and scare everyone in the world. They don't care about the suffering of the Afghans or how many people we will lose." The prominent Afghan women's organization RAWA, which received some belated recognition when it became ideologically serviceable to express concern about the fate of women in Afghanistan, also bitterly condemned the bombing.[27]

Among other opponents of the bombing were the major aid and relief agencies, deeply concerned over the likely effect on the population, agreeing with academic specialists that the bombing posed a "grave risk" of starvation for millions of people.[28]

In short, the lunatic fringe was not insubstantial.

Let us turn now to the most elementary principle of just war theory, universality. Those who cannot accept this principle should have the decency to keep silent about matters of right and wrong, or just war.

If we can rise to this level, some obvious questions arise: for example, have Cuba and Nicaragua been entitled to set off bombs in Washington, New York, and Miami in self-defense against ongoing terrorist attack? Particularly so when the perpetrators are well known and act with complete impunity, sometimes in brazen defiance of the highest international authorities, so that the cases are far clearer than Afghanistan? If not, why not? Certainly one cannot appeal to the scale of crimes to justify such a stand; the merest look at the factual record bars that move.

If these questions are not answered, just war pronouncements cannot be taken seriously. I have yet to discover a single case where the questions are even raised. That leads to some conclusions that may not be particularly attractive but that might merit attention and self-examination – and serious concern about the long-term implications of the apparent inability to accept the principle of universality that underlies these failures.

Although the critical questions are not answered, or in fact even raised, related issues occasionally do come up, and in a manner that gives some useful insight into the prevailing moral and intellectual culture. The Latin American correspondent of the *New York Times* informs us that Latin American intellectuals have "reflexively accorded ... anti-American leaders immunity to the moral standards applied to other leaders." His evidence is a statement by Latin American intellectuals warning against a post-Iraq invasion of Cuba. He believes a "psychological explanation" may be necessary to account for their failure to adopt "universal moral standards."[29] No psychological explanation seems necessary, however, when he and his associates "reflexively accord" their leaders "immunity to the moral standards" they apply to others: specifically, the moral standards that would call for severe punishment for anyone else who dared to carry out terrorist wars comparable to those that their leaders have conducted against Cuba and Nicaragua....

If the moral orthodoxy of the West accommodates the principle of universality, it follows that Cuba and Nicaragua (in fact, many others) can "justifiably and morally resort to" far greater force against the US government. Uncontroversially, the US terrorist attacks and other illegal actions against Cuba and Nicaragua "interfered with key values in the society attacked," far more dramatically than in the case of 9–11, and were intended to do so. ...

We are entitled to ask why the conclusion cannot even be contemplated (quite properly, of course) and what that implies about the elite intellectual culture.

The conclusions with regard to the principle of universality extend far beyond these cases, including even such minor escapades (by US–UK standards) as Clinton's missile attack on the al-Shifa pharmaceutical plant in Sudan in 1998, which led to "several tens of thousands" of deaths, according to the only reputable estimates we have, estimates consistent with the immediate assessment of Human Rights Watch and later reports of knowledgeable observers.[30] A crime of even a fraction of the scale would elicit fury if the target were the US, Israel, or some other worthy victim, and retaliation of a kind that one hesitates to imagine, which would furthermore be acclaimed as a paradigm example of just war. The principle of proportionality entails that Sudan had every right to carry out massive terror in retaliation, even more so if we adopt the more extreme view that Clinton's missile attack had "appalling consequences for the economy and society" of Sudan,[31] so that the atrocity was much worse than the crimes of 9–11, which were appalling enough but did not have such consequences.

Almost all of the limited commentary on the Sudan bombing keeps to the question of whether the plant was believed to produce chemical weapons. True or false, that has no bearing at all on the crime; specifically, on "the magnitude with which the aggression interfered with key values in the society attacked." Many point out that the resulting deaths were unintended, so that the perpetrators, and those who disregard the consequences of the attack, are not culpable. The argument again illustrates, dramatically, the standard rejection of the principle of universality. We would never accept this stand for a moment with regard to others; many of the atrocities we (rightly) denounce are unintended, though that is considered irrelevant – when the perpetrator is someone other than ourselves. But a much harsher conclusion follows, immediately and unequivocally. The claim that the actions were not criminal can be sustained only on the assumption that the fate of the victims was of no concern to the perpetrators. We cannot seriously doubt that the likely human consequences were understood by US planners; the CIA knew as well as Human Rights Watch and many others that they were destroying the country's major source of pharmaceuticals and veterinary medicines, and what the likely effects would be. And the same conclusions could have been drawn at once, and surely can be now, by anyone who thinks that the effects of our violence on poor Africans might merit some concern. The acts can be excused, then, only on the Hegelian doctrine that Africans are "mere things," whose lives have "no value." Observing the attitudes and practice that prevail, those outside the ranks of Western privilege may draw their own conclusions about the "moral orthodoxy of the West."

## Confronting terror

Let us now restrict the term *terror* – improperly, but in accord with near-universal convention – to the subcategory that passes through the doctrinal filters.

The wars contemplated as part of the redeclared "war on terror" are to go on for a long time. "There's no telling how many wars it will take to secure freedom in the homeland," the president announced.[32] That's fair enough. Potential threats are virtually limitless everywhere, even at home, as the anthrax attack and the failed investigations of it illustrate.

Not only is the "war on terror," as conceived, likely to go on for a long time, but it also did not suddenly become a crucial issue on 9–11. The terrorist attacks of that day were not entirely unexpected, yet another reason to question the widely held belief that 9–11 signaled a sharp change in the course of history. Even readers of newspaper headlines, and surely government planners, were well aware years earlier that atrocities of the 9–11 variety might occur. After all, in 1993, one almost *did* occur. Organizations presumably related to those responsible for 9–11 came perilously close to blowing up the Word Trade Center and killing perhaps tens of thousands of people. It was also known, at once, that they had far more ambitious plans that were barely aborted in time. Even with the hideous consummation of these plans on 9–11, risk assessments did not significantly change.

Prospects of major terrorist atrocities were publicly discussed well before 9–11. And there could have been little doubt of the nature of the radical Islamist terrorist organizations since at least 1981, when elements that formed part of the core of Al Qaeda in later years assassinated President Sadat of Egypt; or a few years later, when groups that may have been loosely related drove US forces out of Beirut, killing hundreds of troops and many civilians in separate attacks. Furthermore, the thinking of those involved in these and other similar actions was reasonably well understood, certainly by the US intelligence agencies that had helped to recruit, train, and arm them from 1980 and continued to work with them even as they were attacking the United States. The Dutch government inquiry into the Srebrenica massacre revealed that while radical Islamists were attempting to blow up the World Trade Center, others from the CIA-formed networks were being flown by the US from Afghanistan to Bosnia, along with Iranian-backed Hezbollah fighters and a substantial supply of arms. They were being brought to support the US side in the Balkan wars, while Israel (along with Ukraine and Greece) was arming the Serbs (possibly with US-supplied arms).[33]

The atrocities of 9–11 serve as a dramatic reminder of what has long been understood: the rich and powerful no longer are assured the near monopoly of violence that has largely prevailed throughout history; and with modern technology, the prospects are horrendous indeed. Though terrorism is rightly feared everywhere and is indeed an intolerable "return to barbarism," it is not surprising that perceptions about its nature differ rather sharply at opposite ends of the guns, a fact that is ignored at their peril by those whom history has accustomed to immunity while they perpetrate terrible crimes, quite apart from the moral cowardice so starkly revealed.

## Notes

* This chapter is extracted from Noam Chomsky's *Hegemony or Survival* (Henry Holt, 2003) and is reproduced with permission.

1 Strobe Talbott and Nayan Chanda, eds., *The Age of Terror: America and the World after September 11* (New York: Basic Books, 2001).

2 For US definitions, see Noam Chomsky, "International Terrorism: Image and

Reality," in Alexander George, ed., *Western State Terrorism* (London: Routledge, 1991) (later reprinted in *Pirates and Emperors, Old and New* (London: Pluto Press, 2002). British definition cited by Mark Curtis, *Web of Deceit* (London: Vintage, 2003), p. 93.

3 On the reformulation of the official definitions, see Scott Atran, "The Genesis of Suicide Terrorism," *Science* 299, no. 5612 (7 March 2003): pp. 1534–9. He notes that the revised definitions still make "no principled distinction between 'terror' as defined by the U.S. Congress and 'counterinsurgency' as allowed in U.S. armed forces manuals," one of the perennial problems in defining *terror* in a doctrinally suitable way.

4 Michael McClintock, *Instruments of Statecraft* (New York: Pantheous 1992), chapter 3.

5 UN Resolution 42/159, 7 December 1987. The State Department identifies 1987 as the peak year of terrorism.

6 For a remarkable illustration concerning Vietnam, see p. 193 of Chomsky, *Hegemony or Survival.* On Iraq, see ABC Middle East correspondent Charles Glass, "I Blame the British," *London Review of Books* 25, no. 8 (17 April 2003). Online at: www.lrb.co.uk/v25/n08/glas01_.html.

7 Charles Maechling, "The Murderous Mind of the Latin Military," *Los Angeles Times,* 18 March 1982.

8 Colombian Human Rights Committee, *Colombia Update* 1, no. 4 (December 1989). See Noam Chomsky, *Deterring Democracy* (New York: Hill and Wang, 1992), pp. 130ff.

9 McClintock, *Instruments of Statecraft,* p. 222.

10 Raymond Bonner, "Southeast Asia Remains Fertile for Al Qaeda," *New York Times,* 28 October 2002, sec. A, p. 1.

11 Talbott and Chanda, *Age of Terror.*

12 Martha Crenshaw, "Why America? The Globalization of Civil War," Ivo H. Daalder and James M. Lindsay, "Nasty, Brutish, and Long: America's War on Terrorism," and David C. Rapoport, "The Fourth Wave: September 11 in the History of Terrorism," *Current History* 100, no. 650 (December 2001): pp. 425–32, pp. 403–9, and pp. 419–25.

13 For details, see Chomsky, *Pirates and Emperors, Old and New,* including the added chapter in the updated edition (2002); George, ed., *Western State Terrorism.* On Clinton-backed Israeli invasions of Lebanon in the 1990s, beyond the illegally occupied southern region, see Noam Chomsky, *Fateful Triangle,* updated edition (New York: South End Press, 1999).

14 Crenshaw, "Why America?".

15 John F. Burns, "Ringleader of '85 Achille Lauro Hijacking Says Killing Wasn't His Fault," *New York Times,* 8 November 2002, sec. A, p. 14.

16 Justin Huggler and Phil Reeves, "Once Upon a Time in Jenin," *Independent* (London), 25 April 2002, pp. 4–7.

17 See Chomsky, *Fateful Triangle,* p. 136.

18 Gloria Cooper, "Darts and Laurels," *Columbia Journalism Review* 41, no. 2 (July–August 2002): pp. 14ff. Online at: http://archives.cjr.org/year/02/4/dartsand-laurels.asp.

19 See p. 52 of *Hegemony or Survival.*

20 Judith Miller, "South Asia Called Major Terror Hub in a Survey by U.S.," *New York Times,* 30 April 2000, sec. 1, p. 1. Robert Pearson, *Fletcher Forum of World Affairs* 26, no.1 (Winter–Spring 2002).

21 See pp. 61–2 of *Hegemony or Survival.*

22 Jean Bethke Elshtain, "A Just War?," *Boston Globe,* 6 October 2002, Ideas section; also see her essay in Ken Booth and Tim Dunne, eds., *Worlds in Collision* (London: Palgrave, 2002). Much of the world will be interested to learn that

the US has never engaged in the practice of "unleashing terrorists" or otherwise threatening or harming civilians.

23 Bill Keller, "The Loyal Opposition," *New York Times,* 24 August 2002, sec. A, p. 13.

24 A media review by Jeff Nygaard found one reference to the Gallup poll, a brief notice in the *Omaha World-Herald* that "completely misrepresented the findings." *Nygaard Notes* 132 (16 November 2001). Online at: www.nygaardnotes.org/issues/nn0132.html. *Envío* (Managua, Nicaragua), October 2001.

25 Walter Pincus, "Mueller Outlines Origin, Funding of Sept. 11 Plot," *Washington Post,* 6 June 2002, sec. A, p. 1, emphases mine.

26 Abdullahi Ahmed An-Na'im, "Upholding International Legality against Islamic and American *Jihad,*" in Booth and Dunne, eds., *Worlds in Collision,* pp. 162–71.

27 Abdul Haq, "US Bombs Are Boosting the Taliban," edited version of 11 October 2001 interview with Anatol Lieven, *Guardian* (London), 2 November 2001, Comment & Analysis, p. 20. Online at: www.guardian.co.uk/waronterror/story/0,1361,585302,00.html. Peshawar gathering: Barry Bearak, "Leaders of the Old Afghanistan Prepare for the New," *New York Times,* 25 October 2001, sec. B, p. 4; Farhan Bokhari and John Thornhill, "Traditional Leaders Call for Peace Jihad," *Financial Times* (London), 25 October 2001, p. 3, and "Afghan Peace Assembly Call," *Financial Times* (London), 26 October 2001, p. 2; John F. Burns, "Afghan Gathering in Pakistan Backs Future Role for King," *New York Times,* 26 October 2001, sec. B, p. 4; Indira A.R. Lakshmanan, "1,000 Afghan Leaders Discuss a New Regime," *Boston Globe,* 25 October 2001, sec. A, p. 24; and "Delegates Demand Bin Laden Leave," *Boston Globe,* 26 October 2001, sec. A, p. 31. To learn about the Revolutionary Association of the Women of Afghanistan (RAWA), go to www.afghanwomensmission.org/index.shtml or http://rawa.fancymarketing.net/index.html. The relevant information was available throughout in independent ("alternative") journals, published and electronic, including ZNet (online at: www.zmag.org). For additional quotes, see "The World after Sept. 11," reprinted in Chomsky, *Pirates and Emperors, Old and New,* chapter 6.

28 See Chomsky, *Hegemony or Survival,* pp. 128–9.

29 Larry Rohter, "In Latin America, the Cult of Revolution Wanes," *New York Times,* Sunday, 18 May 2003, sec. 4 (Week in Review), p. 3.

30 Werner Daum, German ambassador to the Sudan from 1996 to 2000, "Universalism and the West: An Agenda for Understanding," *Harvard International Review* 23, no. 2 (Summer 2001): pp. 19–23. Online at: www.hir.harvard.edu/articles/index.html?id=909. The same estimate is given by Jonathan Belke, regional director of the Near East Foundation, who has field experience in the Sudan, "A Year Later, US Attack on Factory Still Hurts Sudan," *Boston Globe,* 22 August 1999, sec. F, p. 2. Kenneth Roth, executive director of Human Rights Watch, warned at once that the bombing had disrupted assistance to 2.4 million people at risk of starvation and had forced the indefinite postponement of "crucial" relief efforts in places where dozens of people were dying daily; letter to President Clinton, 15 September 1998. Online at: www.hrw.org/press98/sept/sudan915.htm. On these and other assessments and related material, see my *9–11* (New York: Seven Stories Press, 2001), pp. 45ff.

31 Christopher Hitchens, "Knowledge (and Power)," *The Nation* 274, no. 22 (10 June 2002): p. 9. Online at: www.thenation.com/doc.mhtml%3Fi=20020610&s=hitchens.

32 George W. Bush cited in Anthony Shadid, "US Rebuffs Second Iraq Offer on Arms Inspection," *Boston Globe,* 6 August 2002, sec. A, p. 1.

33 Richard J. Aldrich, "America Used Islamists to Arm the Bosnian Muslims," *Guardian* (London), 22 April 2002, Leader, p. 16.

# 5 The great game

*John Pilger**

> To me, I confess that [countries] are pieces on a chessboard upon which is being played out a great game for the domination of the world.
>
> Lord Curzon, Viceroy of India, 1898

> We have 50 per cent of the world's wealth but only 6.3 per cent of its population. In this situation, our real job in the coming period ... is to maintain this position of disparity. To do so, we have to dispense with all sentimentality ... we should cease thinking about human rights, the raising of living standards and democratisation.
>
> George Kennan, US strategic planner, 1948

> This is World War Three.
>
> Thomas Friedman, *New York Times*, 2001

'War is never pleasant', declared the liberal *Independent on Sunday* during the Gulf War in 1991. 'There are certain actions that a civilised society can never contemplate. This carpet bombing is undeniably terrible. But that does not make it wrong'.[1] In another war, in paddy fields not far from Saigon, I watched three ladders curve in the sky, and as each rung reached the ground there was a plume of fire and a sound that welled as thunder over deep valleys, rippling and erupting rather than exploding. These were the bombs of three B-52s flying in formation, unseen above the clouds. Between them they dropped about seventy tons of explosives in what was known as a 'long box' pattern, the military term for carpet bombing. Everything inside a 'box' is presumed destroyed.

When I reached a village within the 'box', the street had been replaced by a crater; people a hundred yards from the point of contact left not even their scorched shadows, which the dead at Hiroshima had left. There were pieces of limbs and the intact bodies of children thrown into the air by the blast; their skin had folded back, like parchment. Strange anxieties crowded the mind: I was worried I might step on somebody and disturb the dying. But they were all dead; instead I slipped on the shank of a water buffalo.

It was experiences such as this that led me to question the nature of power imposed from a distance, not just by those above the clouds, but by impeccable, faraway figures who order the mass killing of people, and by those who justify their crimes by representing the victims as terrorists, or merely as numbers, without names, faces and histories, or as the inevitable casualties of a superior morality.

Thirty years later, the British Defence Secretary, Geoffrey Hoon, told Parliament, 'The use of cluster bombs [in Afghanistan] is entirely appropriate. Against certain targets they are the best and most effective weapons we have'.[2]

I was standing on the veranda of a hospital overlooking Hongai, a coal-mining and fishing town on the shores of beautiful Ha Long Bay in the Gulf of Tonkin, northern Vietnam. Dr Luu Van Hoat estimated that 10 per cent of the town's children were now deaf. 'It was as if a great drum beat in our heads', he said. For three days in June 1972, American fighter-bombers flew fifty-two sorties against Hongai, round the clock. This is believed to be a record. Hongai was bombed, on and off, for six years: one of the heaviest and most concentrated bombings ever inflicted.

The town's other distinction was that it was one of the first targets for what was known then as a 'pellet bomb', the prototype of the cluster bomb. This new weapon discharged hundreds of fragments, many of them shaped like darts. At the only school, which was flattened, I found a letter in the rubble. It was written by a young girl called Nguyen Thi An. 'The children wrote many letters to themselves in those days', said a teacher.

> My name is Nguyen Thi An. I am fifteen years old. This letter comes to you from Hongai where I was born at the foot of the Bai Tho mountain and the murmur of the sea-waves lapping against the shore. I had just done the seventh form in the Cao Thang School. It was a glorious day and my mother had just told me to lay the table. My father had come from his work. [He was a miner.] The next thing I heard the siren and I hurried to the shelter nearby. I could hear the engines of the plane, then the explosions. When the siren went again, I came out. My mother and father were lying there, my brother, Nguyen Si Quan, and my sister, Nguyen Thi Binh, were covered in blood. My sister had pieces of metal in her and so did her doll. She kept shouting, 'Where is mother and father? Where's my doll?' My street, Ha Long Street, has fallen down now. This is the end of my letter.

The street where the Nguyen family lived was hit by the new bombs. According to Dr Luu, the darts entered Thi An's sister, Binh, and continued to move around in her body for several days, causing internal injuries from which she eventually died an agonising death. The darts were of a type of plastic difficult to detect under X-ray; the designers, I later read, had intended this.

The more common form of cluster bombs, known in the United States as Rockeyes, were tested in neighbouring Laos. They exploded into about 160 canisters, or bomblets, half of which lay on the ground until an animal or a person stepped on them, or picked them up, as children often did. They then exploded. Thirty years later, they continue to kill and maim an estimated 20,000 people a year in Laos, a tiny country never at war with America, which was bombed as a sideshow to the destruction of Vietnam and Cambodia. With their lethal longevity, cluster bombs are designed purely for terror, as an 'anti-personnel' weapon, to use the military term.

The day Geoffrey Hoon said that cluster bombs were 'the best and most effective weapons we have', they were dropped on Gardez, a dirt-poor town in Afghanistan that had long fallen to the anti-Taliban forces. The casualty figures are not known. Certainly, seven people in one family of refugees were killed and three were badly injured. They were sheltering in buildings belonging to a United Nations landmine-clearing agency, which was destroyed. This irony went unremarked in the press; cluster bombs are landmines. The crucial difference from those banned under international treaty is that they are dropped from aircraft. At the time of writing, an estimated 70,000 American cluster 'bomblets' lie unexploded in Afghanistan, already the most landmined country in the world.[3]

This is the nature of the 'war against terrorism'. The historical lineage is not in doubt. The same B-52s that destroyed much of Indochina bombed lines of civilians in Afghanistan, fleeing Kunduz. 'I saw twenty dead children on the streets', said Zumeray, a refugee. 'Forty people were killed yesterday alone [of an estimated 150 civilians killed in three days]. Some of them were burned by the bombs, others were crushed by the walls and roofs of their houses when they collapsed from the blast'.[4]

The siege of Kunduz ended in a dirt fort called Qala-i-Jhangi, a name that should resonate in the 'civilised' memory; 'civilised' is a word used a great deal these days. American and British special forces called in American bombers in support of the forces of a Northern Alliance warlord, General Rashid Dostum, an Uzbek faction leader whose reputation for brutality includes chaining men to the tracks of tanks and who has since been appointed deputy defence minister in the new government. The men inside the fort were Taliban prisoners-of-war. They were cluster bombed. Those who survived had oil poured on them and were set alight, or were shot with their hands tied behind their backs, or packed into steel containers and left to die in the heat. Up to 4,000 people were killed in this way.

'Surely, the point about civilisation', wrote a *Guardian* columnist, Isobel Hilton,

> is that it does not descend lightly into terror and barbarism?... The Afghans, we hear, have a bent for savagery and it would be absurd to expect a war in Afghanistan to be fought by Queensberry rules. But

> whose war is this?... Were [the Americans and British] fighting by Dostum's rules or by their own? Or do we no longer bother with the distinction?[5]

Nothing has changed. Not the clusters, which were tested in Vietnam. Not the shock to the liberal conscience when forced to acknowledge the truth that mass murder, 'terror and barbarism' are standard practice on 'our' side: only the technology is different. Not the concealment of true objectives in moral illusions by the richest country on earth using its terrifying military might against the poorest, and in the name of 'civilisation'.

Neither has the disregard for peaceful resolution changed. In 1954, US Secretary of State John Foster Dulles walked out of a Geneva conference because the majority had agreed on democratic elections in Vietnam that would unify the north and south of the country. His action ignited a war that took as many as five million lives.

Similarly, in the aftermath of September 11, 2001, the possibility of a peaceful resolution was sabotaged. The leaders of Pakistan's two Islamic parties said they had negotiated Osama bin Laden's extradition to Pakistan, even though the Americans had supplied no evidence with which to prosecute him for the Twin Towers attack. He was to be held under house arrest in Peshawar. The plan was approved by bin Laden himself and the Taliban leader, Mullah Omah. An international tribunal would then hear evidence and decide whether to try him or hand him over to America. A delegation of Islamic clerics from Pakistan, supporters of the Taliban, met Mullah Omah in Kandahar and told him that Pakistan would be plunged into crisis if Osama bin Laden was not handed over. 'Anyone who is responsible for this act, Osama or not, we will not side with him', said the Taliban Information Minister. 'We told [the Pakistani delegation] to give us proof that he did it, because without that, how can we give him up?' Under pressure from Washington, Pakistan's President Musharraf vetoed the plan, which, said an American official, 'risked a premature collapse of the international effort' to capture bin Laden.

Perhaps we shall never know if the proposal was genuine or might have been successful. When the bombing of Afghanistan began, the US and British governments lied that 'no peaceful alternative was ever on offer'. Tony Blair said, 'There is no diplomacy with bin Laden or the Taliban regime ... There is no compromise possible with such people ... just a choice: defeat it or be defeated by it'. George W. Bush said, 'I gave them a fair chance'.[6]

In the spirit of Lord Curzon's 'great game', the bombing of Afghanistan replaced unwanted tribes with preferred tribes. That both groups, in the vernacular of the modern game, are 'terrorists' is beside the point. The difference is that President Bush calls the present occupiers of Kabul, the Northern Alliance, 'our friends'. These are the same people welcomed with kite-flying in 1992, who then killed an estimated 50,000 in four years of internecine feuding. 'In 1994 alone', reported New York-based Human Rights Watch, 'an estimated 25,000 people were killed in Kabul, most of them civilians, in rocket and artillery attacks. One-third of the city was reduced to rubble'.[7]

Today, having tortured and executed hundreds of prisoners-of-war, as well as looted foreign aid warehouses, the new heroes have quietly re-established their monopoly over the affairs of the nation, as well as the heroin trade. Life is meant to be easier for Afghan women, but the burqa remains, along with most of the Taliban's laws. Only a third of children are educated; of these, less than 3 per cent are girls. Sexual policing thrives; and the much-trumpeted Women's Affairs Minister, Dr Sima Samar, has been disposed of and charged with blasphemy. Fazul Hadi Shinwari, the new Chief Justice of the Supreme Court, has said the Taliban's Sharia punishments will continue, including stoning and amputation.

The president, Hamid Karzai, installed by Washington, rules over a tribal council that is seen by most Afghans as an unrepresentative sham. Karzai is guarded by 46 American Special Forces soldiers and has survived one assassination attempt. His country is stricken, with the arrival of only a fraction of the money promised by its 'liberators' with which, they pledged, to build a civilian infrastructure. The Americans dropped 10,000 tonnes of bombs. The United Nations estimates that between fifty and 100 people are killed or injured every week by unexploded bombs and landmines.[8]

The greater sham is the 'war on terrorism' itself. The search for Osama bin Laden and his cohorts in the mountains of Afghanistan was a circus spectacle. The American goal is, and always was, the control, through vassals, of former Soviet Central Asia, a region rich in oil and minerals and of great strategic importance to competing powers, Russia and China. By February 2002, the United States had established permanent military bases in all the Central Asian republics, and in Afghanistan, whose post-Taliban government is American-approved. 'America will have a continuing interest and presence in Central Asia of a kind that we could not have dreamed of before [September 11]', said Secretary of State Colin Powell.[9] This is just a beginning. The ultimate goal is a far wider American conquest, military and economic, which was planned during the Second World War and which, as Vice-President Cheney says, 'may not end in our lifetimes', or until the United States has positioned itself as gatekeeper of the world's remaining oil and gas.

Once the Taliban had retreated south from Kabul, Cheney and Defense Secretary Rumsfeld made this clear. America was planning action against 'forty to fifty countries'. Somalia, allegedly a 'haven' for the Islamic cult al-Qa'ida, joins Iraq at the top of a list of potential targets. Rumsfeld disclosed that he had asked the Pentagon to 'think the unthinkable', after having rejected its 'post-Afghanistan options' as 'not radical enough'.[10] He did not mention that Somalia and part of the north-western Indian Ocean are a major oil and gas reserve, perhaps as large as the Caspian Sea. There, too, American companies have staked claims and await the imposition of a pro-western regime. There is no evidence that al-Qa'ida has bases in Somalia. The Americans are listening to a clan militia called Rahanwein, supported by and grinding the axe of neighbouring Ethiopia, which has long sought to keep Somalia weak and divided.

September 11 provided Bush's Washington with a remarkable justification. Pakistan's former Foreign Minister, Niaz Naik, was told by American officials in mid-July 2001 that military action against Afghanistan would go ahead by the middle of October.[11] Secretary of State Colin Powell was then travelling in Central Asia, already gathering support for an anti-Afghanistan war 'coalition'. For Washington, the real problem with the Taliban was not their human rights violations; these were irrelevant. At first welcomed by Washington, the Taliban did not have total control of Afghanistan; *mujaheddin* factions held territory in the north. For this reason, to the Americans, the regime lacked 'stability', the control required of all clients.

It was this lack of 'stability' that deterred investors from continuing to finance oil and gas pipelines from the Caspian Sea, whose largely untapped fossil fuels of the Caspian Basin have become central, if not critical, to American planning. In 1998, Dick Cheney, then a consultant on pipelines to several Central Asian republics, told a conference of oil industry executives, 'I cannot think of a time when we have had a region emerge as suddenly to become as strategically significant as the Caspian.'[12]

Western interest in the Caspian goes back to the era when oil was being discovered, and exploited for the first time. Near the end of the nineteenth century, Russia fought to keep John B. Rockefeller's Standard Oil Company out of the Caspian. The journalist John Reed, chronicler of the Russian Revolution, asked an audience at the 1919 People's Congress of the East, in Baku, the capital of Azerbaijan: 'Do you know how they pronounce Baku in the United States? Oil!'

Not only America and the European imperial powers wanted the Caspian oilfields. Hitler, in his invasion of Russia, and before running short of fuel and being defeated at Stalingrad, planned 'to take the saving prize of Caspian resources, and then to drive south for the even greater prize of Persia and Iraq', as a contemporary journalist, John Rees, has pointed out.[13]

For the West, the existence of the Soviet Union barred the way to oil and gas reserves, whose potential excited constant speculation. The largest inland sea was said, perhaps optimistically, to contain a third of the world's oil and gas reserves. The most extensive fields are in Kazakhstan and Azerbaijan, with smaller fields in Turkmenistan and Uzbekistan. Following the demise of the Soviet Union, the United States, Russia, China, France, Britain and Germany have competed in an 'oil rush' reminiscent of the imperial scramble for Africa.

In the 1990s, the United States staked its claim with several demonstrations of its 'global reach', such as the well-publicised deployment of 500 paratroopers from the 82nd Airborne Division in North Carolina to the desert of Kazakhstan. At the time, this was the longest airborne operation in military history and meant to demonstrate, said a Pentagon general, 'there is no nation on the face of the earth that we cannot get to', adding the apparent afterthought that the US was concerned with promoting 'independent, sovereign states that are able to defend themselves'.[14]

President Clinton's Energy Secretary, Bill Richardson, candidly described the former Soviet republics as 'all about America's energy security'. He said, 'We would like to see them reliant on western commercial and political investment in the Caspian, and it's very important to us that the pipeline map and the politics come out right.'[15]

The 'pipeline map' is critical, as the oil and gas are worthless without the means to carry them to deep-water ports. There are three routes a pipeline can go: through Russia, Iran or Afghanistan. For Washington, dependence on Russia is anathema, and Iran is the country America has spent more than twenty years isolating. It was not surprising that, in 1996, when the Taliban took power in Kabul, they found themselves courted by the American oil lobby with its eye on 'one of the great prizes of the twenty-first century', as the *Daily Telegraph* reported.

> Oil industry insiders say the dream of securing a pipeline across Afghanistan is the main reason why Pakistan, a close political ally of America's, has been so supportive of the Taliban, and why America has quietly acquiesced in its conquest of Afghanistan.[16]

Following September 11, 2001, none was more fervent in calling for the overthrow of the Taliban than the *Wall Street Journal*. However, five years earlier, the authentic voice of American capital had struck an entirely different tone. The Taliban, the paper declared, 'are the players most capable of achieving peace in Afghanistan at this moment in history'. Moreover, their success was crucial to secure Afghanistan as a 'prime transshipment route for the export of Central Asia's vast oil, gas and other natural resources'.[17]

Not only were the Taliban welcomed by Washington, Taliban leaders were flown to Texas, then governed by George W. Bush, and entertained in Houston by senior executives of the oil company Unocal (United Oil of California). According to George Monbiot, 'the company suggested paying these barbarians fifteen cents for every thousand cubic feet of gas it pumped through the land they had conquered.'[18] A Clinton administration official commented that Afghanistan would become 'like Saudi Arabia', an oil colony with no democracy and the legal persecution of women. 'We can live with that,' he said.[19]

In 1998, Unocal's Vice-President for International Relations, John J Maresca, told a Congressional inquiry that 'by 2010, western companies could increase oil production to 4.5 million barrels a day, an increase of more than 500 per cent in fifteen years'. He appealed for 'the development of appropriate investment climates in the region'. By this, he meant that 'construction of the pipeline we have proposed across Afghanistan could not begin until a recognised government is in place that has the confidence of governments, lenders and *our company* [emphasis added]'. He made no mention of the barbaric nature of the regime, or of the al-Qa'ida terrorists it was said to entertain.

When Unocal eventually signed a 'memorandum of understanding' to build the pipeline from Turkmenistan to Pakistan via Afghanistan, it did so on behalf of a consortium of Enron, Amoco, British Petroleum, Chevron, Exxon and Mobil. The deal-makers were Dick Cheney, former Defense Secretary and future Vice-President, James Baker, former Secretary of State, and Brent Scowcroft, former National Security Advisor to the President. All had served in the Cabinet of George W. Bush Senior; Cheney and Baker are steeped in the oil industry; Cheney is perhaps the most powerful figure in the White House as I write; and Baker remains highly influential, as of course does Bush Senior, the 'oil man's president'.[20] Peeling the onion of the 'Bush oil and gas junta' reveals Bush Senior as a paid consultant to the bin Laden family through the Carlyle Group, which owns sixty-four companies that specialise in oil and gas, aerospace and weapons. The former president has met the family twice.[21]

The pipeline deal fell through when two American embassies in east Africa were bombed and al-Qa'ida was blamed. The *frisson* between Washington and the Taliban has since been revived with the installation of Hamid Karzai as president, a former employee of a Unocal subsidiary, and the appointment as American Ambassador to Afghanistan of none other than Unocal's John J. Maresca. Post-bombing deals have also been struck with the Caspian's oil republics, all of them sporting appalling human rights records. As the bombing of Afghanistan got under way, Rumsfeld promised 'tens of millions of dollars' to Tajikistan and Uzbekistan, which share 900 miles of border with Afghanistan.[22]

The Russians are not happy with this arrangement, believing the republics will move closer to Moscow as a counterweight to the Americans. Vladimir Putin's collaboration has won favours in Washington, such as the prospect of further strategic arms reductions and the licence to proceed with his own 'war on terrorism' in Chechnya, where an estimated 20,000 people have been killed. The reason why Chechnya is so important to Putin is that it is one of the last available routes for Caspian oil. As the Russians see it, the deal is that they keep Chechnya and the US gets unprecedented 'access' to Central Asia. As American bombers took off for Afghanistan, Putin was being entertained by George W. Bush at his Texas ranch. 'He is my new close friend', said Putin, waving from a golf cart.

The other principal member of the 'coalition against terrorism', China, was the quickest off the mark with its condolences following September 11, 2001. From potential foe to friend in six months, China was rewarded with firm US support for its entry into the World Trade Organisation. Sanctions on the sale of military equipment, imposed following the Tiananmen Square massacre in 1989, have been eased so that the Chinese military can buy parts for American Black Hawk helicopters supplied in the 1980s. The issue of Tibet and multiple Chinese human rights abuses are now, like the human rights abuses of the Taliban in 1996, irrelevant.

Turkey, the only Muslim state in Nato, has been given IMF and World Bank loans on American instructions. The Turkish state's relentless ethnic cleansing of its Kurdish minority is another irrelevance. Pakistan's military dictatorship has been relieved of a western embargo imposed after the testing of nuclear weapons and its IMF and World Bank loans have been 'rescheduled'. The US Senate has rushed through a bill allowing Pakistan to receive emergency military aid. All of this follows an established pattern. The 'coalition' that attacked Iraq in 1991, led by the United States, was also put together with some of the biggest bribes in history.

A new 'world order' is evolving, yet the goals and even the vocabulary of Lord Curzon's day are retained. Following September 11, in his zeal to speak for the president of the United States, Tony Blair came closer to an announcement of real intentions than any British leader since Anthony Eden. Indeed, Blair bears a prime ministerial likeness not to Churchill, his acolytes' favourite, but to Eden, the last of Britannia's *ancien régime*, who attacked Egypt over Suez. In an evangelical speech to the Labour Party Conference soon after September 11, Blair served notice that imperialism's return journey to respectability was under way.

Having sent British forces off to war four times since he came to power in 1997 (Iraq, Yugoslavia, Sierra Leone, Afghanistan), Blair now invoked 'morality' to justify these and future actions. It is one of his favourite words; he once used it eleven times in a speech to a conference on press ownership organised by Rupert Murdoch. The bombing of Yugoslavia was a 'moral crusade', Nato's mission is 'entirely moral', etcetera.

Now hark the Christian gentleman-bomber's vision of a better world for 'the starving, the wretched, the dispossessed, the ignorant, those living in want and squalor, from the deserts of northern Africa to the slums of Gaza to the mountain ranges of Afghanistan'. Hark his 'abiding' concern for the 'human rights of the suffering women of Afghanistan' as he colluded in bombing them and preventing food from reaching their starving children. (On September 16, the *New York Times* reported that Washington 'demanded ... the elimination of truck convoys that provide much of the food and other supplies to Afghanistan's civilian population'. Blair subsequently rejected appeals by the international relief agencies for a pause in the bombing.)

As Frank Furedi reminds us in *The New Ideology of Imperialism*, it is not long ago 'that the moral claims of imperialism were seldom questioned in the west. Imperialism and the global expansion of the western powers were represented in unambiguously positive terms as a major contributor to human civilisation'. The quest went wrong when it was clear that fascism, with all its ideas of racial and cultural superiority, was imperialism too, and the word vanished from academic discourse. In the best Stalinist tradition, imperialism no longer existed.[23]

Since the end of the cold war, a new opportunity has arisen. The economic and political crises in the developing world, largely the result of post-colonialism, such as the blood-letting in the Middle East and the destruction of commodity markets in Africa, now serve as retrospective justification for imperialism. Although the word remains unspeakable, the western intelligentsia, conservatives and liberals alike, boldly echo the preferred euphemism, 'civilisation'. From Italy's Prime Minister Silvio Berlusconi, an ally of crypto-fascists, to the former British liberal editor Harold Evans, the new imperialists share a concept whose true meaning relies on an unexpressed contrast with those who are 'uncivilised', i.e. inferior, and who might challenge the 'values' of the West, specifically its God-given right to control and plunder.

There are many blueprints for the new imperialism, but none as cogent as that of Zbigniew Brzezinski, adviser to several presidents and one of the most influential gurus in Washington, whose 1997 book is said to have biblical authority among the Bush gang and its intelligentsia. In *The Grand Chessboard: American Primacy and its Geostrategic Imperatives,* Brzezinski writes, 'Ever since the continents started interacting politically, some 500 years ago, Eurasia has been the center of world power.'[24]

He defines Eurasia as all the territory east of Germany and Poland, stretching through Russia and China to the Pacific Ocean and including the Middle East and most of the Indian sub-continent. The key to controlling this vast area of the world is Central Asia. Dominance of Turkmenistan, Uzbekistan, Tajikistan and Kyrgyzstan ensures not only new sources of energy and mineral wealth, but a 'guardpost' over American control of the oil of the Persian Gulf.[25] 'What is most important to the history of the world?' wrote Brzezinski. 'The Taliban or the collapse of the Soviet empire? Some stirred up Muslims or the liberation of central Europe...?'[26] The 'stirred-up Muslims' replied on September 11, 2001.

The first priority has been achieved, says Brzezinski. This is the economic subjugation of the former superpower. Once the Soviet Union had collapsed, he writes, the United States looted some $300 billion in Russian assets, destabilising the currency and ensuring that a weakened Russia would have no choice but to look westward to Europe for economic and political revival, rather than south to Central Asia. Brzezinski's analysis dismisses the notion of 'local wars as responses to terrorism'. Rather, they are the beginning of a final conflict leading inexorably to the dissolution of national governments and world domination by the United States.

Nation states will be incorporated in the 'new order', controlled solely by economic interests as dictated by international banks, corporations and ruling elites concerned with the maintenance (by manipulation and war) of their power. 'To put it in a terminology that harkens back to the more brutal age of ancient empires', he writes, 'the three grand imperatives of imperial geostrategy are to prevent collusion and maintain security dependence among the vassals, to keep tributaries pliant and protected, and to keep the barbarians from coming together.'[27]

It may have been easy once to dismiss this as a message from the far right. But Brzezinski is also the mainstream; he was President Carter's National Security Advisor and has been influential with Bush Senior, Clinton and now Bush Junior. His students include Madeleine Albright and John Negroponte, the mastermind of American terror in Central America, now Bush's Ambassador to the United Nations. As US Ambassador to Honduras in the early 1980s, Negroponte oversaw the regime's funding of death squads known as Battalion 3-16, which wiped out the democratic opposition. He administered the CIA's 'Contra' war of terror against neighbouring Nicaragua. A month after the Twin Towers attack, Negroponte wrote to the UN Security Council that 'America's self-defence ... requires further actions with regard to other states'. He was warning the world.[28]

## Notes

* This chapter is extracted from John Pilger's *The New Rulers of the World* (Verso, 2002) and is reproduced with permission.

1 *Independent on Sunday*, February 10, 1991.
2 Press Association, November 2, 2001.
3 BBC News, November 19, 2001.
4 *Independent*, November 19, 2001.
5 *Guardian*, November 29, 2001.
6 *Independent*, September 19, 2001; *Financial Times*, September 20, 2001; *Daily Telegraph*, October 3 and 4, 2001; *The Times*, October 8, 2001.
7 Human Rights Watch, New York, October 6, 2001.
8 'The worst is yet to come', *Socialist Review*, November 2002.
9 *Sydney Morning Herald*, February 11, 2002.
10 *Guardian*, November 15, 2001.
11 BBC World Service, September 18 and 22, 2001.
12 Cited in the *Rock River Times*, Rockford, Ill., October 31–November 6, 2001.
13 John Rees, 'Imperialism: globalisation, the state and war', *International Socialism*, issue 93, p. 13.
14 *US News and World Report*, September 29, 1997.
15 *International Herald Tribune*, November 9, 1998.
16 *Daily Telegraph*, October 11, 1996.
17 Cited by Lance Selfa, *Internationalist Socialist Review*, issue 20, November–December 2001.
18 *Guardian*, October 23, 2001.
19 Ibid.
20 Cited in the *Rock River Times*, October 24–30, 2001.

21 *Wall Street Journal* and Judicial Watch: www.azlan.net/jud-watch.htm.
22 *Guardian,* November 5, 2001.
23 Frank Furedi, *The New Ideology of Imperialism,* London: Pluto Press, 1994, p. 44.
24 Zbigniew Brzezinski, *The Grand Chessboard: American Primacy and its Geostrategic Imperatives*, New York: HarperCollins, 1997, p. xiii.
25 Ibid., p. 53.
26 Ibid., p. 73.
27 Ibid., p. 40.
28 *New York Times,* October 19, 2001.

# 6 One more successful war?

## Tamil diaspora and counter-terrorism after the LTTE

*Vicki Sentas*

> Our successful war should be considered as part of the global campaign against terror.
>
> Defence Secretary, Gotabaya Rajapaksa, 18 September 2009

> The aim of the government now is to seize all assets belonging to the LTTE and eradicate the LTTE from the entire world.
>
> Defence Secretary, Gotabaya Rajapaksa, Government of Sri Lanka 8 October 2009

How does a successful war end? Using the case study of the Sri Lankan conflict, this chapter explores how counter-terrorism creates continuing state violence. The international ban on the Liberation Tigers of Tamil Eelam (LTTE) transformed a conflict in one state into a broader, violent terrain. The Sri Lankan conflict is now a transnational war against the Tamil diaspora that enables the continued repression of political aspirations both in Sri Lanka and abroad.

The Government of Sri Lanka (GoSL) declared the end of the Sinhala–Tamil conflict on 21 May 2009. In its military annihilation of the LTTE, the Sri Lankan military is estimated to have killed tens of thousands of Tamil civilians at the end of the civil war alone.[1] There is credible evidence that the Sri Lankan state was responsible for serious breaches of human rights and international humanitarian law, amounting to crimes against humanity, war crimes and genocide: summary executions of combatants and civilians, enforced disappearances and the deliberate shelling of declared no-fire zones and hospitals (UN 2011). Tens of thousands more people were displaced, and 280,000 Tamils were confined in internment camps across Sri Lanka. Dire conditions in the camps include subjection to severe deprivation of liberty, sexual violence, enforced disappearances, death and serious health problems as a result of deprivation of food, water and sanitation (ICG 2010). Around 12,000 suspected LTTE combatants were detained without charge or trial at the end of the war, many with tenuous links to the LTTE: an estimated 8,000 remained interned as of June 2010 under Emergency Regulations (ICJ 2010).

The LTTE were also responsible for repeated and grave violations of international law during the conflict, including the deliberate targeting of civilians, the forced recruitment of child soldiers, and killing Tamil political opponents (ECCHR 2010). The leadership of the LTTE cannot be charged as they were killed in the last stages of the war. Allegations were levelled by former Sri Lankan General Sarath Fonseka that some LTTE leaders were executed by the Sri Lankan military on the Defence Secretary's orders, despite assurances of their safety on surrender (Jansz 2009).

The material violence of Sri Lanka's 28-year counter-terrorism campaign continues to be reproduced through layers of state denial. At the time of writing, an effective process for peace and reconciliation remains elusive. The GoSL denies that civilians were targeted by the army and mention of war crimes in Sri Lanka is treated as treason against the state. The international community, after doing nothing to intervene in the onslaught which unfolded, called for an independent international inquiry into war crimes committed by the GoSL and the LTTE. Sri Lanka instead set up an internal inquiry in March 2010, the Lessons Learnt and Reconciliation Commission. The Commission's members include those who served as senior government officials during the final years of the war, prompting fears that an impartial and independent account of the truth may be unlikely.

The absence of credible processes to enable truth and transparency is juxtaposed with the continuation of counter-terrorism measures within Sri Lanka, embedding the state of emergency last imposed in 2005. The northern region of Sri Lanka remains a militarised zone. Emergency powers which criminalise political speech are enforced against the media and ordinary people. Counter-terrorism measures have also enabled the colonisation of Tamil territory and culture. In September 2010 it was reported that: 'Homes are being destroyed, people from other regions are resettling the evacuated villages, cultural heritage, as well as religious symbols are intentionally being destroyed, while the Tamil language is disappearing' (ECCHR 2010).

The Sri Lankan campaign against Tamil nationalism continues to rely on the racist annihilation and assimilation of Tamil identity which structured the armed conflict. The repression of Tamil ethnic identity has been central to Sri Lanka's historic practices of terror. The origins of the conflict lie in the systematic institutionalised racism against the Tamil population by the Sinhala majority since independence from Britain in 1948. The racialised violence committed by Sri Lanka over the course of the conflict's history has been well documented, including state-sanctioned ethnic cleansing, pogroms and colonisation of Tamil land to inflict systematic terror on the Tamil people. While the war is often referred to as an 'ethnic conflict' it is more productive to locate the processes which ethnicised a political conflict – that is, the state discourses and mechanisms which 'define and deepen ethnic dividing lines' (Korf 2006: 282).

Sri Lanka's state violence was perpetrated under the guise of counter-terrorism, with the explicit support of western powers for its military campaign against the LTTE. The Prevention of Terrorism Act 1979 was a key mechanism by which the repression of Tamil identity legitimated Sri Lankan state violence as counter-terrorism. In the collective targeting of the Tamil population as terrorist, counter-terrorism measures also instantiated Tamil identity as persecuted 'ethnic' subjectivity. This state of emergency also allowed the LTTE to effect its own suspension of law and its own authoritarian rule in response to the "rogue other" of the repressive Sinhalese state (Korf 2006: 293). Counter-terrorism in Sri Lanka was central to identity formations which were repressed by state violence and produced violence in response. Counter-terrorism created and supported the conditions that now contribute to the continuation of the war.

Post-war repression relies on counter-terrorism both in Sri Lanka and abroad, in an attempt to annihilate Tamil nationalist aspirations. A large number of Tamils fled Sri Lanka as refugees and economic migrants over the last three decades, forming a considerable diaspora in Europe, Canada, the United States and Australia. While Tamil political formations in Sri Lanka appear no longer to make claims for a separate Tamil nation, Tamils in the diaspora maintain campaigns for self-determination and for Sri Lanka to be accountable for genocide. This chapter considers the effects of the banning of the LTTE by western states, proscribed as a terrorist organisation – a key mechanism by which the international community has supported Sri Lankan state terror. My argument is that post-war, global counter-terrorism continues to enact political violence with reference to the Tamil diaspora. Despite the defeat of the LTTE, the targeting of counter-terrorism measures on the Tamil diaspora reiterates the constituent ordering of migrant political identity as 'ethnic violence'. This chapter examines how the processes of identity categorisation deployed through proscription function as a racialised institutional violence against the Tamil diaspora. Proscription laws transform the diaspora into an originary, foundational violence, thereby perpetuating an irresolvable conflict by simultaneously depoliticising Tamil identity and masking Sri Lankan state violence.

## Networks and netwar: diaspora as terrorist threat

Dominant characterisations of the Tamil diaspora reflected in Sri Lankan government approaches to counter-terrorism are iterated in global proscription laws. I argue that through proscription, dominant concepts of diaspora reify 'ethno-political identity', and continue to construct the Tamil diaspora as a foundational, terrorist violence after the LTTE's defeat. In this section I demonstrate how the Tamil diaspora, becomes instantiated as a bounded membership-based group, a characterisation which poorly reflects the social processes within the diaspora and contributes to knowledge systems which underpin the collective criminalisation of Tamil people.

Security analysts have argued that a terrorist network is indistinguishable in form and strategy from a transnational political movement or diaspora network, but for the deployment of violence (Asal *et al.* 2007; Jackson 2006; Arquilla and Ronfeldt 2001). Asal *et al.*, for example, argue that 'the organizational dynamics, tactics, and avenues for communication and coordination are in many ways exactly the same' (2007: 32) Rather than engineered from the top down, networks and recruitment are understood to develop through existing social configurations – relationships, family and friendship affiliations (Sageman 2005; Asal *et al.* 2007: 16; Adamson 2005: 35). The contemporary terrorist network is characterised by weak linkages between 'members', yet is marked by a common, dispersed ideology (Jackson 2006: 242). The network perspective explains transnational constituencies and resources as a new product of the increased mobility of people and ideas. Increased mobilisation across borders by migrants connected to non-state actors is perceived to cause a proliferation of political causes threatening to the state system (Adamson 2005: 33). The major commonalities between transnational advocacy networks and terrorist organisations, therefore, are identified as the diversity of social actors, voluntary patterns of communication, and information sharing and education aimed at leveraging a political cause or legitimacy (Asal *et al.* 2007: 16).

Concepts favoured by security analysts, such as 'netwar' and 'dark networks' (Arquilla and Ronfeldt 2001; Raab and Milward 2003; Milward *et al.* 2006), explicitly locate migrant diasporas as a driver for political violence. Netwar, according to influential research funded by the Rand Corporation (Arquilla and Roufeldt 2001), describes the 'lower-intensity societal level counterpart to cyberwar which rely on both broad networks of resources and support for terrorist, criminals and ethno-nationalists'. Arquilla and Ronfeldt assert that: 'Netwar, the emergent mode of conflict of choice for networked non-state actors, has two faces – and both matter very much' (2001: x). In this register, 'illicit and licit forms of activity' are perceived as equally important counter-terrorism targets due to the success drawn from 'the social basis for cooperation' (2001: ix, x):

> While a network's level of technological sophistication does make a difference – and people do tend to think that netwar depends heavily on technology – the other levels have just as much, *if not more, of an effect on the potential power of a given group.* One key level is the social basis for cooperation among network members. When social ties are strong, building mutual trust and identity, a network's effectiveness is greatly enhanced. *This can be seen most clearly in ethnically based terror, crime, and insurgent groups in which clan ties bind together even the loosest, most dispersed organization.*
>
> (2001: 2, emphasis added)

In the netwar discourse, ethno-political identity and affiliation within a diaspora connected to armed struggle are considered as much a problem as the insurgency itself. In relation to the LTTE, the concept of diaspora is articulated in security scholarship as the creation of an international lobby in receiving countries to extend support for the LTTE's armed insurgency (see, for example, Wayland 2004: 411, 417). In this analysis, the forced migration of Tamil exiles and refugees due to political repression is viewed as an instrumental device to lend support to insurgent causes, providing legitimacy for non-state actors ideologically.

The articulation of diaspora as *the* insurgency apparent in academic analysis is refracted in the discourse and practice of the Sri Lankan state. The GoSL has long characterised the Tamil diaspora as constituting the LTTE's international network, with political lobbying understood as ideological support for the LTTE. The Tamil diaspora has been successful in sustaining the idea of Tamil Eelam. The two-state solution has been pragmatically advocated by both Tamil nationalists vehemently opposed to the LTTE as well as those who are LTTE supporters. The conflation of support for the right to self-determination as constituting political violence to Sri Lankan sovereignty is rooted in counter-insurgency logic. Peaceful protest, manifestations of dissent and anti-state ideology embodied incipient violence, that is, pre-violent and predisposed to violence. Incipient violence marked the beginning of the continuum where radical political thought and non-violent activity were understood as leading to violence against the state (Hocking 1993: 83–5). I argue that two critical aspects of counter-insurgency function in constructing the Tamil diaspora as foundational violence: the idea of 'the front' and the targeting of 'ethnic identity' through its categorisation as incipient violence.

For the GoSL the diaspora constituted a front for the LTTE during the war. Sri Lankan officials use the front to describe those organisations established and controlled by the Tamil diaspora 'but which espouses the objectives/policies of their parent body', the LTTE (Aryasinha 2009). The diaspora's fundraising for diverse aspects of the Tamil cause – humanitarian or political activity and military procurement – is bundled into one category as funding the LTTE. As will be explained shortly, proscription facilitates a legal framework in which the counter-insurgency logic of the front is embedded in the criminal justice system transnationally.

The counter-insurgency approach understands diasporic 'ethnic identity' as incipient violence because these formations maintain strategic and instrumental loyalties to the homeland. In this literature, the succour from victories or the blows of defeats in the insurgency at home are understood to directly contribute to the formation of ethno-national identity (see Wayland 2004: 413–14). In line with the political process of nation-states conjoining ethnicity with terrorism so as to equate ethnicity with violence, 'Tamil Terrorism' (Nadarajah and Sriskandarajah 2005: 91) is the well-established outcome of criminalising political violence as particularly ethnic. In this sense, ethno-political identity is conceived as part of the arsenal of the networked terrorist organisation, and an instrumental tactic to violence. The diaspora network's purpose is understood to foster unified ethnic identity in furtherance of violence. The 'social basis for co-operation' identified by netwar scholars in relation to migrant communities as the glue forming transnational terror networks is an abstracted concept which draws on racialised norms. The subject of extensive critique, the idea of community plays a critical ideological role in the coding of race (Poynting *et al.* 2004: 260). Collectively formed identities are reified as community, constructing commonality and connection along ethnic, racialised and religious lines.

The heterogenous nature of diaspora is sometimes explicitly noted by scholars who nevertheless maintain an instrumental view of migrant dispersal and its relation to armed struggle (see Wayland 2004: 411; Asal *et al.* 2007: 23). Difference is routinely recognised and valued in multicultural societies in order to categorise a hierarchy of desirable/undesirable diasporas. The valuing of difference is also an important technology in how counter-terrorism seeks to regulate diasporic affiliations. For example, since the war Sri Lankan officials have called on Europe to isolate 'pro-LTTE' elements from the 'respected Sri Lankan Tamil expatriate community' (Aryasinha 2010).

Additionally, according to security scholars, liberal freedoms create distinctive ethnic identities and secessionist mobilisations which are not possible in the homeland where there are limits to the expression of identity. Wayland argues that the Tamil diaspora's access to greater political freedoms in liberal democratic states mobilises funds and emotional and political support for the LTTE. Post-migration policies aimed at recognition of cultural difference are considered in this approach to legitimate exploration of Tamil culture, language and identity (2004: 417–18). Consequently, and as will be seen throughout this chapter, it is liberal freedoms enjoyed by migrants that are targeted by counter-terrorism laws.

## The use and abuse of the concept of diaspora

The layered and complex ways in which Tamil diasporas are connected to the political causes of homeland, and the reconfiguration of ethnic identities through transnationalism, are poorly understood in the security framework outlined in the previous section. In practice, the interactions between insurgencies and diasporas do challenge the purported liberal distinction between sociocultural practices and political support for insurgency (Nadarajah and Sriskandarajah 2005: 95).

Tamil ethnic identities have been forged as collective political identities in the context of diverse struggles for self-determination against Sri Lankan state oppression. Transnational Tamil networks provide critical connections where the preservation of identity continues to be tied to struggles against racism and ethnic victimisation, as well as claims to territory, language and cultural rights. The regenerative and productive role of diasporas in demanding recognition of state crimes, and in actively transforming conflicts into negotiated settlements for peace, are foreclosed in the counter-insurgency logic of netwar where the ideology of self-determination is a foundational violence tied to identity.

The ways in which states deploy the politics of diaspora as a categorical structure point to the institutional violence the concept foregrounds. While it is beyond the scope of this chapter to review the extensive literature on diaspora, I draw on the work of anthropologist Rogers Brubaker who argues that the term diaspora has become 'stretched to the point of uselessness' (Brubaker 2005: 3). He notes that the mere involvement of a population in homeland politics or nationalist movements does not give the term any purposeful analytic capacity. Brubaker points to three criteria which characterise definitions of diaspora, and which I argue structure the netwar conception of diaspora. The first and least-contested aspect requires dispersion of an ethnic group across state borders. The second and most controversial component is an orientation to a real or aspirational homeland as a source of value, identity, loyalty and solidarity. Critics point to migrant desires to recreate life in receiving states rather than reifying the homeland as a singular source of identity, especially where there is no intention of returning 'home' (Brubaker 2005: 6). Third, the maintenance of boundaries and the preservation of identity are said to mark the mobilised diaspora within the host society. Identifications can be maintained as a resistance to assimilation or as a consequence of social exclusion (Brubaker 2005: 7). The assumed relation between diaspora and migrant underestimates the connections second- and third-generation Tamils have transnationally. These symbols of so-called 'boundary maintenance' are of particular interest to counter-terrorism policing, identifying the suspect with potential violence. This counter-insurgency view of violence as incipient in ethno-political identity, also extends to civil society organisations. The International Crisis Group, for example, identifies Tamil youth in the diaspora politicised during the war as being at risk of radicalisation (ICG 2010).

Diaspora in netwar and other security discourse is represented as a factual quantifiable entity, as a unified population dispersed across states and readily understood as comprising members of a terrorist network. Diaspora in this register operates as a kind of ethno-cultural fact with which to recognise identity (Brubaker 2005: 10). Moreover, ethnic identity is routinely used to impute membership of diaspora. In contrast, the lived experience of diaspora lends itself to a relational approach whereby diaspora is conceived not as a 'bounded entity' but rather as contingent practices: the strategies, stances or claims used to mobilise collective aspirations (Brubaker 2005). Rather than simply describing a category of the Tamil population living outside Sri Lanka, diaspora as an analytic tool can be used to understand processes of social organisation beyond the nation-state.

Conversely, the realities and lived experiences of diasporas are often considered as an antidote to constructions of identity as fixed. However, as Brubaker states, 'Diaspora can be seen as an alternative to the essentialisation of belonging; but it can also represent a non-territorial form of essentialised belonging' (2005: 12). Identity labels such as Sinhalese versus Tamils, which fix ethnicity, are devices routinely used by both sides to conflicts, albeit with disproportionate effects generated by the abuse of state power (Nadarajah and Sriskandarajah 2005: 90). Diaspora identifications which present or are represented as fixed and knowable are more a strategy than a sociological fact. The ways in which identity congeals and is undoubtedly used by those who make political claims to identity should be understood analytically as related to power, structure and interests rather than being simply cultural.

Interpretations of diaspora as group membership inform how state agencies understand Tamil diaspora as a security problem, and how states identify and interact with Tamil communities in order to disrupt political projects and identifications (for detailed discussion of how western states govern and discipline Tamils through proscription, see Nadarajah 2009; Sentas 2009: chapters 5 and 6). Critical analysis of categorical knowledge structures such as diaspora can reopen the closure performed by state practices. In the following sections I examine terrorist organisation proscription to establish the functioning of diaspora as an identity category which reinscribes diaspora as a violent subjectivity.

## The globalised ban on the LTTE: criminalising the Tamil diaspora

Whereas Sri Lanka proscribed the LTTE in 1978,[2] and the United States in 1997, it was not until the war on terror that globalised legal instruments to ban the LTTE were circulated, enabled primarily through United Nations Security Council Resolution 1371. Most nations enacted terrorist organisation laws empowering the executive to ban non-state actors in armed conflict, in accordance with broad definitions of terrorist organisation that criminalise acts and threats of acts of politically motivated violence. The LTTE were proscribed by the UK in 2001, and by Canada and the EU in 2006.[3]

The common political object of government measures regarding terrorist organizations across states is to remove the sources of legitimacy of non-state actors for their political claims and actions. For example, the Australian Parliament deemed: 'proscription provides a clear statement that Australia rejects the claims to legitimacy of groups that engage in extreme forms of political violence as a means of achieving their political, ideological or religious goals' (PJCIS 2007: 2.39). The explicit aim of the designation of terrorist organisations in Australia is to cut off all ties which legitimate armed resistance movements. The Attorney-General's Department described the intention of the legislation as being to 'stop [ties] from existing in the first place' (PJCIS 2006: 10). The legitimacy diaspora affords to armed struggle, by virtue of its being a people with a shared historical and political culture, is the target of these laws. In the equation between diasporas as sources of legitimacy and acts of armed political conflict, the counter-insurgency logic of netwar discussed above is discernible.

The structure of the legal offences reflects the aim of proscribing the LTTE: to sever international support for its political aims as well as the provision of funding to its military campaign. The legal regime of banning an organisation makes almost any contact, association or affiliation with that organisation illegal. Proscription offences vary across jurisdictions, but it is generally an offence to be a member, provide support (both material and emotional or political support), make financial contributions, provide training to or receive it from the organisation and to associate with the organisation.

The elements of the offences are expansive, drawing on largely undefined terms new to criminal law. The significance of this breadth is that the offences are both as broad, and as specific, as the diverse connections to homeland or armed struggle. The offences seek both to prevent and to incapacitate that which enables political causes to exist. The international ban on the LTTE was not intended to weaken the LTTE militarily but rather to undermine its political project for independence and for the establishment of a separate Tamil state (Nadarajah and Sriskandarajah 2005: 17). By targeting the social basis of diasporic identification, the offences are designed as counter-netwar or counter-insurgency. In its open-ended, discretionary scope, each offence potentially mirrors and captures diverse affiliations and aspirations. No actual involvement in or conspiracy to commit acts of harm within the proscribing state, or anywhere else, is required to constitute an offence. The offences do not penalise *actions* at all, but rather relations and connections, both material and affective. Terrorist organisation offences are targeted not at the actions of guerrillas, but rather at the transnational identifications bound up with and constitutive of ethno-national liberation struggles. The netwar concept of targeting diasporas' 'social basis for co-operation' is discernible in the disruptive logic of these offences. Australian Government justifications for stopping the networks that allow for armed struggle 'to exist in the first place' substitute diverse ethnic sociocultural practices and political support for the violent insurgency itself. It is precisely because diasporic support is non-violent and garners legitimacy that the offences target this conduct.

The emotional and more intangible connections, supports and identifications which proscription offences seek to disrupt are best understood as affects. Sarah Ahmed describes how affect circulates as an economy to materialise social bodies, like the body of the nation: 'In such affective economies, emotions *do things*, and they align individuals with communities – or bodily space with social space – through the very intensity of their attachments' (Ahmed 2004: 119). Affects constitute relationships in the social and material world and it is this accumulation and circulation of diasporic connections which terrorist organisation offences target. In a netwar approach, the affective relations of diaspora bind diaspora to violence, and are anathema to 'national belonging' in the proscribing state.

For example under the UK Terrorism Act 2000, it is a crime to wear or carry any item that would give rise to a reasonable suspicion that you support any proscribed organisation. During demonstrations held by Tamils in London in 2009 against the war, several protesters were arrested but not charged for flying the flag of Tamil Eelam. Metropolitan Police Commissioner Sir Paul Stephenson stated:

> During the last 43 days these pro-LTTE supporters had been there around the clock, waving flags with the Tiger insignia in violation of the UK anti-terrorism laws. In addition they had been creating a cacophony of noise, beating drums and taking over the streets surrounding Big Ben and the Parliament. These actions caused traffic chaos, crippled the transport system and caused untold suffering to the general taxpaying British Public.
>
> (GoSL 2009a)

As these 'untold sufferings to the general taxpaying British Public' demonstrate, proscription offences do not require material violence in order to constitute its subjects as violence. Grief, anger and the desire for justice, which may have connected Tamils globally in demonstrations at the end of the war, congeal in the criminal offence of flag waving.

## Of fronts and sleepers: hiding out in liberal multiculture

After the EU banned the LTTE, the GoSL applied to the European Council on 5 June 2008 to take steps against Tamil diaspora 'front organisations', arguing that such groups 'circumvent the legal provisions of proscription, making a mockery of the EU listing' (Aryasinha 2009). Among the evidence Sri Lanka provided to support the application was a dossier outlining a number of public events held throughout Europe to commemorate Martyrs Day on 27 November every year, on the grounds that it 'propagated the LTTE's terrorist ideology including glorification of terrorism and martyrdom' (Aryasinha 2009). For Sri Lanka, the 'pro-LTTE' diaspora exploits Europe's liberal democracies; this requires that Europe criminalise support for and glorification of terrorism, then protected under the guise of freedom of expression (Aryasinha 2009, 2010). In Sri Lanka in 2010, Emergency Regulations outlawed the commemoration of

Martyrs Day, denying Tamils public, collective remembrance of the war dead. By outlawing grief and remembrance, Sri Lanka continues to eliminate traces of its crimes. Labelling the LTTE terrorist by virtue of its political violence negates the role of the Sri Lankan state in establishing the conditions of conflict. This erasure and forgetting, enabled globally through proscription, is central to Sri Lankan myths of reconciliation, where numerous allegations of atrocities committed by security forces were never investigated during the course of the war and contributed to a cycle of retribution and retaliation.

Despite the military annihilation of the LTTE, the GoSL continues to understand the Tamil diaspora as posing a violent threat to its sovereignty, and as equated to the LTTE's international network. The diaspora is considered heir to the LTTE's international network of financial support and capable of reinvigorating the LTTE (US State Department 2010; GoSL 2009b). In my analysis of Sri Lankan Government statements issued since the end of the war, targeting the Tamil diaspora remains a deliberate foreign policy and counter-terrorism strategy. This policy discourse appears with frequency and urgency now that the LTTE have been militarily defeated and the GoSL seeks to consolidate its victory over the idea of political self-determination for Tamils.

Just before the defeat of the LTTE when all indications of its military annihilation were apparent, Europol hosted a tactical meeting on combating LTTE front organisations on 30–31 March 2009. Sri Lanka described the meeting as the first time extensive attention was given by a broad range of European justice and counter-terror organisations to specifically discussing countering the LTTE in the diaspora (Aryasinha 2009). In his keynote speech, Sri Lankan Ambassador Aryasinha said that although he expected the LTTE would soon be defeated militarily, 'it must be expected that they will continue to mutate and metamorphose abroad'. This teleological approach propagates the idea of diaspora as a deterministic reproduction of violence devoid of political agency – simply the enactment of bounded Tamil ethnic 'groupness'. In what the Ambassador describes as 'the post proscription phase' of the LTTE, it is 'seemingly innocuous pursuits' such as 'humanitarian relief and cultural activities' which finance the LTTE that are the target of proscribing states (Aryasinha 2009). In this logic, the act of banning the LTTE leads to the idea that front organisations will take the LTTE's place and continue its activities.

Shortly after the end of the war, the Sri Lankan authorities announced an international operation to counter Tamil activities in the diaspora in favour of self-determination. On 15 January 2010 President Rajapaksa stated that Sri Lanka was under threat from separatists despite the fact that the LTTE had been militarily crushed (Acharya 2010). The Defence Secretary indicated intelligence gathering abroad was intended to stop LTTE sympathisers from regrouping (GoSL 2010a). Major General Prasad Samarasingha of the Sri Lankan military stated:

> We have won the war in Sri Lanka but internationally the second phase of the war has started.... Not only the forces, but the whole nation, including the people living overseas, must get together and stop this international LTTE propaganda and activities.
>
> (Hodge 2010)

The counter-insurgency strategy of disrupting the diaspora has been central in legitimating domestic Sri Lankan counter-terrorism. The Sri Lankan Prime Minister justified the extension of emergency regulations in Sri Lanka on the grounds that it was necessary to thwart the revival of the LTTE as a result of support by the diaspora through fundraising and political advocacy (Acharya 2010). The state of emergency is justified on the grounds that the activities of the Tamil diaspora are not simply spectral, symbolic violence, but a crisis equivalent to the armed conflict itself. The netwar concept of diaspora has a material effect in Sri Lanka, shoring up the continued state of emergency and state violence against Tamils, including the persecution of journalists for exposing state crimes.

The counter-terrorism expert Rohan Gunaratna gave testimony before the Lessons Learnt and Reconciliation Commission about the importance of dismantling the LTTE's international network, arguing it remained intact today through charity, non-government organisations and non-profit organisations. As before the defeat of the LTTE, the diaspora's violent collective subjectivity resides in its political stances and claims. For Gunaratna, 'LTTE members and sympathisers in charge of propaganda disseminate various misinformation and they carry fabricated stories against the government and the security forces' (GoSL 2010c). Gunaratna's position reflects that of senior Sri Lankan officials and security think-tanks – that the number of civilian deaths was propaganda fabricated by the LTTE and its 'agents abroad' (GoSL 2009b, 2009f; Jayasekara 2009). The official position of the GoSL is that the military destroyed the LTTE 'while liberating civilians without harm', and, according to Prime Minister Wickremanayaske, 'no crimes were committed by the army' (GoSL 2009c, 2009e). The government in September 2009 referred to allegations of war crimes levelled by the international community and the diaspora, as constituting a threat 'as serious as the one posed by the LTTE a year ago' (GoSL 2009d).

Security analysts characterise the diaspora after the defeat of the LTTE as corresponding to rival factions of the LTTE fighting over access to its funds, in reiteration of Sri Lankan intelligence sources (see Acharya 2010; Jayasekara 2009). The conceptual apparatus of identifying diaspora organisations with factions solidifies the idea of the front. It is a knowledge claim cemented by the pseudo-evidence of linking particular organisations with former LTTE advisers or leaders. Yet think-tanks, such as the Institute for Conflict Management, which propose this schema, acknowledge that the diaspora does not have real linkages with so-called LTTE 'survivor groupings' in Sri Lanka (Acharya 2010). Just the aspiration for a Tamil Eelam, in the absence of any evidence of calls in the diaspora for armed conflict, is described as extremist and as grounds on which to criminalise the diaspora. On the basis of the technique of equating political aspirations for self-determination with violence, diaspora organisations such as the British Tamil Forum and the Global Tamil Forum are routinely characterised as LTTE fronts doing the bidding of the LTTE. The International Crisis Group has also argued that the Tamil diaspora will not be able to play a useful role in reconstruction unless it moves away from a separatist stance, which it labels 'pro-LTTE' (ICG 2010).

Political campaigns for self-determination predated the emergence of the LTTE, however. Non-violent political groupings have historically and post-war been at the forefront of Tamil nationalism (Vimalarajah and Cheran 2010). Vimalarajah and Cheran argue that the persistence of Tamil desires for self-determination, despite the end of the LTTE, demand examination of Tamil political agency as a rational response to the material conditions in Sri Lanka which underpins desires for self-determination. Post-LTTE, they argue that transnational Tamil politics has become more dynamic and participatory, and more inclusive of the diversity within the diaspora.

The threat to reactivate terrorist organisation laws in the diaspora also amounts to an institutional denial of the productive role of Tamil politics in conflict transformation. Proscription assists Sri Lanka's representation of the diaspora as having no legitimacy as an advocate for the needs of the Tamils in Sri Lanka (GoSL 2010d) as demands for self-determination are dismissed as the expression of a pro-LTTE faction. This politicisation of the diaspora as embodied violence, territorially disconnected from the 'homeland', has an impact on how Tamils understand their forms of organisation. Writing of a 'vibrant debate' among Tamils about the term 'Tamil diaspora', Vimalarajah and Cheran state:

> There is a growing anxiety within the Tamil diaspora that the term has been re-introduced into the current political discourses concerning Sri Lanka to divide the global Tamils from the Tamils on the island in a sinister move to weaken the political project of the Tamils and de-politicise their cause to a mere humanitarian and development concern. This is a new challenge posed to academics and policy makers in addition to other conceptual challenges pertaining to the term diaspora.
>
> (2010: 8)

The concept of diaspora is used by both the GoSL and proscribing states to counter political claims and affective attachments to self-determination. As an identity category reiterated in law, government discourse and security studies, diaspora is targeted in order to disrupt the politics of transnationalism.

## A new battlefield: post-war criminal prosecutions and the denial of asylum

> When I was asked at a seminar on the LTTE organised by Europol in December 2008, as to what will happen if the LTTE was defeated in Sri Lanka, I remarked, 'It is then that your problem will begin', and in a sense that has come to be true. Since May 18 2009 there has not been a single bullet fired in Sri Lanka on account of terrorism. But when I look around in your part of the world, over the past few months, I see arrests and convictions of LTTE activists taking place at regular intervals.
>
> (Aryasinha 2010)

Sri Lanka's battle with Tamil nationalism has shifted to the diaspora in Europe, the United States, Canada and Australia. In accordance with the desires of the GoSL, proscription of the LTTE continues to be used in order to charge Tamils in the diaspora, in spite of the fact that the proscribed organisation no longer exists. In Germany on 3 March 2010 six Tamils were arrested, of whom three were charged in August 2010 with belonging to a banned organisation and breaking export laws. Those charged are believed to be involved in the German branch of the Tamil Coordinating Committee, long designated a front organisation by the GoSL. The prosecution's case is reported to be that the defendants fundraised for the LTTE (an alleged €3 million between July 2007 and April 2009), and either sent this money to the LTTE or used it on LTTE orders to purchase weapons and other items (*Daily Times* 2010). The Sri Lankan embassy in Germany claimed that the defendants were using blackmail and extortion to raise funds from Tamils in Germany (BBC Sinhala 2010). In April 2010 seven Tamils were arrested in the Netherlands for offences in relation to supporting the LTTE (Aryasinha 2010). Arrests and investigations of Tamils have also been conducted in Denmark, Italy and Norway since the end of the war.

As well as criminal law, immigration law is being used to further a counter-terrorism agenda against diaspora Tamils. Consistent with the netwar rationale, the fact of Tamil migration is understood by government officials in, for example, Canada as an instrumental strategy whereby the LTTE used the refugee system to enlist supporters (GoSL 2010b). Sri Lankan officials argue that Sri Lanka is safe to return to and that according to the Sri Lankan Ambassador to Australia, 'There is no reason for anybody to seek refuge in Australia' (Maley 2010). Since the end of the war, signatories to the Refugee Convention have abrogated their responsibilities, denying refugee status as a counter-terrorism strategy. The Australian Government suspended the processing of any Tamil asylum seekers between April and July 2010 (Neighbour 2010). At least 17 Tamils recognised as genuine refugees were, however, given secret adverse security assessments by the Australian Security Intelligence Organisation (ASIO) (RISE 2011: 6). The reported grounds for the adverse assessment of one refugee was that she was a legal officer who had worked in LTTE-run courts (Neighbour 2010).

United Nations High Commission for Refugees (UNHCR) guidelines state that asylum seekers alleged to have LTTE connections require special consideration for protection due to evidence of continued persecution in Sri Lanka. The UNHCR states: 'LTTE membership is not a sufficient basis in itself to exclude an individual from refugee status, particularly in light of the well-documented practices of forced recruitment, particularly of children' (UNHCR 2010: 12). Proscription, however, creates a presumption that acts of association and support for the LTTE serve as grounds for exclusion from the refugee convention. But the UNHCR cautions against the exclusion of civilians who performed a range of activities and services for the LTTE in areas under former LTTE control (2010: 13). The former legal officer who worked in the LTTE courts – while not excluded from refugee status under the Refugee Convention – remains excluded by intelligence assessments made secret in pursuance of counter-terrorism, in a state of indefinite detention.

## Conclusion: diaspora, banned indefinitely?

This chapter has explored the changing terrain of the Sri Lankan conflict and how it has become a war across the world. Drawing on the banning of the LTTE as a terrorist organisation, I have argued that the key features of global proscription law reflect a counter-insurgency logic which posits non-violent ideological claims to self-determination as incipient violence in two principal ways. First, through the characterisation of diaspora organisations as 'fronts', Tamil political claims are denied their legitimacy and are reinscribed as a deterministic extension of the LTTE's violence. Second, by positioning diasporic claims, affects and positions as group identity or membership, counter-terrorism reifies the idea of ethnic identity as a source of violence, while masking continuing Sri Lankan political violence.

The deployment of the idea of diaspora as a dispersed category of ethnic identity across borders is also apparent in GoSL discourse and in 'netwar' security literature. Unpacking hegemonic approaches to diaspora allows us to understand how transnational political claims to self-determination have become the primary battleground. In targeting collective Tamil political identity, the global proscription regime is an institutional, structural violence which criminalises diaspora politics and affective connections to the idea of Tamil Eelam. The GoSL's war against the diaspora is also used to justify the continued repression of political freedoms in Sri Lanka

Most proscription regimes provide statutory opportunity for an organisation to be delisted if it no longer meets the criteria for listing: that is, if it is no longer engaged in 'terrorist acts'. With Sri Lanka's continuation of its war against Tamil self-determination, it is the Tamil diaspora which primarily constitutes the violent insurgency. International political will for delisting a non-existent entity, while legally possible, is politically unlikely while the diaspora continues to be constructed as representing the originary violence threatening Sri Lankan sovereignty. The netwar logic of diaspora as an incipient violence which structures counter-terrorism turns Tamil ethno-political identity into an irresolvable problem. If the war is to end, this positioning of the Tamil diaspora and the factors which cause and sustain state terror and violence must be addressed.

## Notes

1 The *Report of the United Nations Secretary General's Panel of Experts on Accountability in Sri Lanka* states 'there is still no reliable figure' but concludes that up to 40,000 civilian deaths 'cannot be ruled out' (UN 2011: 42). For a discussion of the evidence base of differing estimations of casualties, see UN (2011: 39–42); ICG (2010: 5–6).
2 Proscription was repealed in order to facilitate peace negotiations in 2002.
3 While Australia did not ban the LTTE under its Criminal Code, the LTTE were listed under the United Nations Charter in 2001 and three Tamils have been prosecuted under this provision (Sentas 2010).

## References

Acharya, A. (2010) 'Sri Lanka and the LTTE: Diaspora Wars', *South Asia Intelligence Review*, 14 June 2010. www.satp.org/satporgtp/sair/Archives/sair8/8_49.htm, accessed 1 March 2011.

Adamson, F. (2005) 'Globalisation, Transnational Political Mobilisation and Networks of Violence', *Cambridge Review of International Affairs*, 18 (1): 31–49.

Ahmed, S. (2004) 'Affective Economies', *Social Text*, 79 (2): 117–39.

Arquilla, J. and D. Ronfeldt, (2001) *Networks and Netwars: The Future of Terror, Crime and Militancy*, Santa Monica, Calif.: Rand Corporation.

Aryasinha, R. (2009) 'Confronting False Dichotomies: The Public Good and the Challenge of Meeting the Terrorist Front Organisation Phenomenon in Europe: Keynote address to Eurojust tactical meeting on LTTE Front Organisations', 30–31 March 2009, The Hague, printed in *The Asian Tribune*, 2 April 2009. www.asiantribune.com/node/16483, accessed 1 March 2011.

Aryasinha, R. (2010) 'Dismantling LTTE's Global Network', Speech given at The 2010 Diplomatic Security Conference on the Terrorism Situation and Trends in the EU, European Corporate Security Association (ECSA) and the Belgian Foreign Ministry, Brussels, 11 May 2010. www.defence.lk/new.asp?fname=20100517_01, accessed 1 March 2011.

Asal, V., B. Nussbaum, and W. Harrington. (2007) 'Terrorism as Transnational Advocacy: An Organizational and Tactical Examination', *Studies in Conflict and Terrorism*, 30: 15–29.

BBC Sinhala (2010) 'LTTE fundraisers' Arrested in Germany', 5 March. www.bbc.co.uk/sinhala/news/story/2010/03/100305_ltte_germany.shtml, accessed 2 March 2011.

Brubaker, R. (2005) 'The "Diaspora" Diaspora', *Ethnic and Racial Studies*, 28 (1): 1–19.

*Daily Times* (2010) 'Germany Charges Suspected Tamil Tigers' Suppliers', 1 September. www.dailytimes.com.pk/default.asp?page=2010%5C09%5C01%5Cstory_1-9-2010_pg20_7, accessed 2 March 2011.

European Centre for Constitutional and Human Rights (ECCHR) (2010) *Study on Criminal Accountability in Sri Lanka as of January 2009*, June, Berlin. www.ecchr.eu/index.php/ecchr-publications.html, accessed 2 March 2011.

Government of Sri Lanka (2009a) 'Pro-LTTE Demos Cost UK Police 8 Million Pounds', 2 June. www.priu.gov.lk/news_update/Current_Affairs/ca200906/20090602pro_ltte_demos_cost_uk_police.htm, accessed 1 March 2011.

Government of Sri Lanka (2009b) 'Sri Lanka Urges EU to Act against LTTE International Network', 20 July. www.priu.gov.lk/news_update/Current_Affairs/ca200907/20090720sl_urges_eu_to_act_against_ltte_international_network.htm, accessed 1 March 2011.

Government of Sri Lanka (2009c) 'LTTE Still Being Promoted – SL Ambassador to US', 3 September. www.priu.gov.lk/news_update/Current_Affairs/ca200909/20090903ltte_still_being_promoted.htm, accessed 1 March 2011.

Government of Sri Lanka (2009d) 'Sri Lanka Targeted for Defeating LTTE Terror – Defence Secretary', 18 September. www.priu.gov.lk/news_update/Current_Affairs/ca200909/20090918sl_targeted_defeating_ltte_terror.htm, accessed 1 March 2011.

Government of Sri Lanka (2009e) 'Resurgence of LTTE Must Be Prevented' – PM to Asia Society, 25 September 2009. www.priu.gov.lk/news_update/Current_Affairs/ca200909/20090925resurgence_of_ltte_must_be_prevented.htm, accessed 1 March 2011.

Government of Sri Lanka (2009f) 'Aim of Government Is Total Eradication of LTTE – Secretary Defence', 8 October. www.priu.gov.lk/news_update/Current_Affairs/ca200910/20091008aim_govt_is_total_eradication_of_ltte_secy_defence.htm, accessed 1 March 2011

Government of Sri Lanka (2010a) 'Strengthening Intelligence Vital to Stop LTTE Regrouping – Defence Secretary', 21 May. www.priu.gov.lk/news_update/Current_Affairs/ca201005/20100521strengthening_intelligence_vital_to_stop_ltte_regrouping.htm, accessed 1 March 2011.

Government of Sri Lanka (2010b) 'LTTE Uses Refugee System to Lure Supporters – Former Canadian HC', 13 August. www.priu.gov.lk/news_update/Current_Affairs/ca201008/20100813ltte_uses_refugee_system.htm, accessed 1 March 2011.

Government of Sri Lanka (2010c) 'LTTE Global Network Remains Intact – Prof. Gunaratne', 5 October. www.priu.gov.lk/news_update/Current_Affairs/ca201010/20101005ltte_global_network_remains_intact.htm, accessed 1 March 2011.

Government of Sri Lanka (2010d) 'Minister Peiris Refutes LTTE Propaganda in London', 21 October. www.priu.gov.lk/news_update/Current_Affairs/ca201010/20101021minister_peiris_refutes_ltte_propaganda_london.htm, accessed 1 March 2011.

Hocking, J. (1993) *Beyond Terrorism: The Development of the Australian Security State*, Sydney: Allen & Unwin.

Hodge, A. (2010) 'Sri Lanka Hunts for Tamil Tigers Operating Overseas', *The*

*Australian*, 14 May. www.theaustralian.com.au/news/world/sri-lanka-hunts-for-tamil-tigers-operating-overseas/story-e6frg6so-1225866298151, accessed 2 March 2011.

International Commission of Jurists (ICJ) (2010) *Beyond Lawful Constraints: Sri Lanka's Mass Detention of LTTE Suspects: ICJ Briefing Note*, September. www.icj.org/default.asp?nodeID=349&sessID=&langage=1&myPage=Legal_Documentation&id=23159, accessed 2 March 2011.

International Crisis Group (ICG) (2010) *The Sri Lankan Tamil Diaspora After the LTTE*, Asia Report No. 186, 23 February. www.crisisgroup.org/en/regions/asia/south-asia/sri-lanka/186-the-sri-lankan-tamil-diaspora-after-the-ltte.aspx, accessed 2 March 2011.

Jackson, B. (2006) 'Groups, Networks or Movements: A Command and Control Driven Approach to Classifying Terrorist Organizations and its Application to Al Qaeda', *Studies in Conflict and Terrorism*, 29: 241–62.

Jansz, F. (2009) '"Gota Ordered Them to Be Shot" – General Sarath Fonseka', *The Sunday Leader*, 13 December. www.thesundayleader.lk/2009/12/13/%E2%80%9Cgota-ordered-them-to-be-shot%E2%80%9D-%E2%80%93-general-sarath-fonseka/, accessed 2 March 2011.

Jayasekara, S. (2009) 'How the LTTE were destroyed', *Asian Conflicts Report*, 6 (June): 4–5.

Korf, B. (2006) 'Who is the Rogue? Discourse, Power and Spatial Politics in Sri Lanka', *Political Geography*, 25 (3): 279–97.

Maley, P. (2010) 'Tamil Asylum-seekers Identified as Tiger terrorists', *The Australian*, 16 August. www.theaustralian.com.au/national-affairs/tamil-asylum-seekers-identified-as-tiger-terrorists/story-fn59niix-1225905600592, accessed 2 March 2011.

Milward, H., P. Kenis and J. Raab (2006) 'Introduction: Towards the Study of Network Control', *International Public Management Journal*, 9 (3): 203–8.

Nadarajah, S. (2009) 'Disciplining the Diaspora: Tamil Self Determination and the Politics of Proscription', in K. Dodds and A. Ingram (eds) *Spaces of Security and Insecurity: New Geographies of the War on Terror*, Farnham Ashgate: 109–30.

Nadarajah, S. and D. Sriskandarajah (2005) 'Liberation Struggle or Terrorism? The Politics of Naming the LTTE', *Third World Quarterly*, 26 (1): 87–100.

Neighbour, S. (2010) 'Tamil Tigers at Front Door', *The Australian*, 16 July.

Parliamentary Joint Committee on Intelligence and Security (PJCIS) (2006) *Hansard Transcripts of Committee Hearings*, Review of Security and Counter Terrorism Legislation, Canberra: Parliament of the Commonwealth of Australia, 1 August.

Parliamentary Joint Committee on Intelligence and Security (PJCIS) (2007) *Inquiry into the Terrorist Organisation Listing Provisions of the Criminal Code Act 1995*, Canberra: Parliament of the Commonwealth of Australia, 20 September.

Poynting, S., G. Noble, P. Tabar, and J. Collins (2004) *Bin Laden in the Suburbs: Criminalising the Arab Other*, Sydney: Sydney Institute of Criminology Series No. 18.

Raab, J. and B. Milward, (2003) 'Dark Networks as Problems', *Journal of Public Administration Research and Theory*, 13 (4): 413–39.

Refugees, Survivors and Ex-Detainees (RISE) (2011) 'Submission in Relation to the Annual Review of the Administration, Expenditure and Financial Circumstances of ASIO, ASIS, DSD, DIO, DIGO and ONA', 27 February. www.aph.gov.au/house/committee/pjcis/adminexp9/sats.htm.

Sageman, M. (2005) *Understanding Terrorist Networks*, Philadelphia: University of Pennsylvania Press.

Sentas, V. (2009) '*Traces of Terror: Counter-terrorism Law and Policing in Australia*', Thesis, Doctor of Philosophy, School of Political and Social Inquiry, Monash University.

Sentas, V. (2010) 'Terrorist Organisation Offences and the LTTE: R v Vinayagamoorthy', *Current Issues in Criminal Justice*, 22 (1): 159–69.

UNHCR (2010) 'UNHCR Eligibility Guidelines for assessing the International Protection Needs of Asylum-Seekers from Sri Lanka', 5 July. www.unhcr.org/refworld/docid/4c31a5b82.html, accessed 2 March 2011.

United Nations (2011) *Report of the Secretary General's Panel of Experts on Accountability in Sri Lanka*, 31 March 2011. www.un.org/News/dh/infocus/Sri_Lanka/POE_Report_Full.pdf, accessed 15 June 2011.

US Department of State (2010) *Country Reports on Terrorism for the Year 2009*, 5 August. www.state.gov/j/ct/rls/crt/2009/index.htm, accessed 2 March 2011.

Vimalarajah, L., and R. Cheran (2010) *Empowering Diasporas: The Politics of Post-war Transnational Tamil Politics*, Occasional Paper No. 31, Berlin: Berghof Peace Support.

Wayland, S. (2004) 'Ethnonationalist Networks and Transnational Opportunities: The Sri Lankan Tamil Diaspora', *Review of International Studies*, 30: 405–26.

# 7 'No permission to shoot in Gaza is necessary'

## Israeli state terror against Palestinians in Gaza during Operation Cast Lead[1]

*Victoria Mason*

### Introduction

The 2009 United Nations (UN) Human Rights Council-mandated Fact-Finding Mission on the Gaza Conflict (herein known as the FFM, and more widely known as the Goldstone Report) found that during the December 2008 to January 2009 Israeli assault on Gaza – codenamed Operation Cast Lead (OCL) – both Israel and Hamas committed gross abuses of international humanitarian law (IHL) and international human rights law (IHRL), amounting in some cases to war crimes and possible crimes against humanity (HRC 2009). This chapter will focus on Israel's actions in the lead-up to, and during, OCL.[2] In exploring the rationale behind the operation, and the violations committed in its course, this chapter will demonstrate that OCL was not a defensive measure of last resort by Israel, but a carefully planned offensive aimed at achieving the continued subjugation of the Gazan population. It will establish that Israel did not fulfil the criteria of either *jus ad bellum* (the right to go to war) or *jus in bello* (just conduct in war). Moreover, this offensive was part of Israel's wider strategy in relation to the Occupied Palestinian Territories (OPTs), encapsulated in the tactic known as the 'Iron Wall'.

The 'Iron Wall' strategy was first devised by Ze'ev Jabotinksy, who is seen as the 'father' of the Israeli right. As Avi Shlaim explains it,

> the Zionist project could only be implemented unilaterally and by military force. The crux … was to enable the Zionist movement to deal with its local opponents from a position of unassailable strength.… Despair was expected to promote pragmatism on the other side.… The Arabs … learnt the hard way that Israel could not be defeated on the battlefield and were compelled to negotiate with it from a position of palpable weakness.
>
> (2010a: 285–6)

The chapter will consider the extent to which the 'Iron Wall' strategy, couched as counter-terrorism, itself constitutes 'state terror'. It will demonstrate that as part of the 'Iron Wall', during OCL Israel applied the so-called '*Dahiye* doctrine', named in relation to the tactics adopted by Israel during the large-scale destruction of the Shia suburbs in southern Beirut during Israel's 2006 war with Hezbollah. *Dahiye* centres on using disproportionate force and causing large-scale destruction and civilian suffering, with the resultant fear being seen to subjugate and coerce civilian support for particular groups. As such, the *Dahiye* doctrine explicitly advocates the use of terror to achieve political aims. The application of *Dahiye* during OLC saw the use of massively disproportionate violence; acts of collective punishment; intentional and indiscriminate attacks on civilians and civilian infrastructure; impeding medical access to the wounded; and wide-scale acts of wanton destruction, intimidation and humiliation. As the FFM notes, OCL

> was a deliberately disproportionate attack designed to punish, humiliate and terrorize a civilian population, radically diminish its local economic capacity both to work and to provide for itself, and to force upon it an ever increasing sense of dependency and vulnerability.
> (HRC 2009: 408)

## OCL: 'the destruction of all means of life'

OCL began on 27 December 2008 with a week-long air attack followed by a ground invasion on 3 January (assisted by continued air operations). By the time the assault ended on 18 January 2009, some 1,400 Palestinians had been killed. Approximately 55 to 70 per cent of the dead were civilians, including 300 children, and at least another 5,400 people were seriously wounded. During the conflict 13 Israelis were killed – 10 of these being soldiers (four by friendly fire) and three civilians (PCATI 2009; HRC 2009; AI 2009). By the time the assault ended, Gaza – which is one of most densely populated areas in the world – had suffered devastating blows to its political, economic and social fabric. Some 25 government buildings, 60 police stations, 34 hospitals and 214 schools were destroyed or severely damaged. United Nations Relief Works Agency (UNRWA) facilities were targeted, as were utilities (such as electricity plants and water and sewage installations) and industrial facilities and factories (including for food production). Eighty per cent of agricultural infrastructure and crops were destroyed (including farms, greenhouses and orchards), with 35,750 livestock and one million poultry killed. There was also extensive destruction of private houses, with 6,400 destroyed and 46,000 damaged, leaving at least 100,000 homeless. Fifty-two mosques and churches were destroyed or severely damaged and property damage was estimated at (US) $1.6 to $1.9 billion (HRC 2009; AI 2009; HRW 2010; *JPS*

2009: 210–11). The FFM characterises the strikes on Gaza's basic infrastructure as 'attacks on the foundations of civilian life' and officials argue that destruction of large areas of farmland represented 'the destruction of all means of life' (HRC 2009: 21; Beaumont 2009). As noted by journalist Peter Beaumont, 'as well as the physical damage done by Israeli bulldozers, bombing and shelling, land has been contaminated by munitions, including white phosphorus, burst sewerage pipes, animal carcasses and even asbestos used in roofing' (2009). There is also concern that depleted uranium was used in Gaza (with potentially catastrophic long-term health implications), with the International Atomic Energy Agency (IAEA) launching an investigation into these allegations in January 2009 (BBC 2009a). UN humanitarian chief John Holmes has said that economic activity in Gaza was set back perhaps by decades (BBC 2009b). As the UN Special Rapporteur on Human Rights in the OPTs, Richard Falk, laments, the brutality of OCL has also left deep mental and emotional scars on Gazans (*Haaretz* 2009). An estimated 96 per cent of Gazans suffer depression as a result of the attack, and at least 25,000 to 50,000 people (including 14,000 to 28,000 children) will require psychological intervention (Save the Children 2009).[3]

Before moving on to a discussion of *jus ad bellum* or *jus in bello*, it is necessary to place OCL within the context of previous Israeli actions in Gaza, and the OPTs more widely. As the FFM notes, OCL came as part of 'a continuum of policies aimed at pursuing Israel's political objectives' in both Gaza and the OPTs as a whole, with many of these policies 'based on' or 'resulting in' violations of IHRL and IHL (HRC 2009: 82). Since 2000, Gazans have endured a range of escalating assaults with Operations: Automatic Gear; Root Canal; Continuous Story; Rainbow; Active Shield; Days of Penitence; King's Court; Orange Iron; Violet Iron; Autumn Wind; Eastern Step; First Rain; Starting All Over Again; Blue Skies; Southern Arrow; Summer Rains; Samson's Pillars; Locked Kindergarten; Autumn Clouds; and Hot Winter (Esposito in *JPS* 2009). OCL was also: 'a culmination of the long process of economic and political isolation imposed on the Gaza Strip by Israel', including the continuing blockade on Gaza (HRC 2009: 82). While purported to be driven by Israel's security concerns after Hamas took control of Gaza in 2007,[4] as the FFM outlines, the primary purpose of the blockade 'was to bring about a situation in which the civilian population would find life so intolerable that they would leave (if that were possible) or turn Hamas out of office, as well as to collectively punish the civilian population' (HRC 2009: 256–7, 404–5). As the FFM outlines, this collective punishment meant severe restrictions:

> [on] basic necessities of life, such as food and medical supplies … fuel, electricity, school items, and repair and construction material … compounded by the withholding of financial and other assistance by

> some donors ... the effects of the prolonged blockade did not spare any aspect of the life of Gazans ... the Gaza economy had been depleted, the health sector beleaguered, the population had been made dependent on humanitarian assistance for survival.... Men, women and children were psychologically suffering from long-standing poverty, insecurity and violence, and enforced confinement in a heavily overcrowded territory.
>
> (HRC 2009: 404–5)

Clear evidence that the blockade's objective is collective punishment was uncovered in late 2010 when the Israeli human rights group the Legal Centre for Freedom of Movement (GISHA) obtained copies of official Israeli documents that detailed Israel's policy of deliberately reducing the amount of basic goods available in the Gaza Strip – a move clearly not driven wholly by security concerns (GISHA 2010). While the Israeli government announced in June 2010, in the wake of the much criticised May 2010 flotilla attack (where Israeli commandos attacked a flotilla seeking to break the siege, killing nine people), that it would 'ease' its illegal blockade of Gaza, a December 2010 report compiled by 21 NGOs confirmed that 'there are few signs of real improvement on the ground' (Amnesty International *et al.* 2010: 3–4).

## OCL: the 'Iron Wall' continues

This brief background to the blockade leads us to examine whether Israel was justified in launching OCL. The major principles of *jus ad bellum*, or 'just war', are generally summarised as: just cause, last resort, right authority, right intention, reasonable hope of success, and proportionality. Given that Israel argued that OCL was justified on the basis of it being a 'just cause' and a measure of 'last resort', I will focus my discussion on these two principles. The issue of *jus ad bellum* is crucial, as most analyses of OCL (including the FFM) have focused on Israel's conduct *during* the war (*jus in bello*), and have not questioned the justifications behind the attack itself.

Israel's position is that OCL was a 'just' war (having the right of defence against aggression – in this case preventing rocket attacks from Gaza in southern Israel), and that there was no other option but military attack (IMFA 2009). Evidence, however, shows that there were a range of alternatives to OCL that had achieved proven results in terms of ending Hamas rocket (and other) attacks on southern Israel. The main example here was the Israeli–Hamas ceasefire between June and November 2008, the chief terms of which were that Hamas would end the firing of rockets into Israel, while Israel would ease the blockade. It was then planned for negotiations to begin over the release of the captive Israeli soldier Gilad Shalit in return for a 'staged release' of 1,000 Palestinians imprisoned in Israel (Esposito in *JPS* 2009: 162–3). While the dominant Israeli narrative is that

Hamas broke the ceasefire, it was actually broken by Israel on 4 November 2008, when Israel launched a raid into Gaza resulting in the deaths of six Hamas members.[5] Prior to this, Hamas had scrupulously adhered to the ceasefire – not firing rockets themselves, and reining in other Palestinian groups (ITIC 2008). Hamas's adherence to the ceasefire was admitted by official Israeli spokesperson Mark Regev (Fuller 2009) and the finer points were discussed in detail by the Israeli Intelligence and Terrorism Information Centre (ITIC), an organisation with close links to the Israeli administration. A December 2008 ITIC report states that the small number of rockets fired into Israel from Gaza during the ceasefire were fired 'by rogue terrorist organizations, in some instance in defiance of Hamas (especially by Fatah and Al-Qaeda supporters)' (ITIC 2008: 2).[6] As a result of Hamas's adherence to the ceasefire, ITIC notes there was a 'marked decrease' in rocket and mortar attacks and 'relative calm in Sderot and the towns and villages near the Gaza Strip' (2008: 6–7).

Looking, however, to Israel's adherence to the ceasefire, while it did allow the entry of some humanitarian aid, the overall blockade was not reduced, and indeed, as Henry Siegman (2009) – former Executive Director of the American Jewish Congress – summarises, Israel only 'tightened ... its throttlehold'. Indeed, as the FFM outlines, imports into Gaza dropped by 30 per cent between September and October 2008 alone (HRC 2009: 68). That it was Israel that undermined the ceasefire is recognised by a range of leading commentators, including the former commander of the Israeli Defence Forces' (IDF) Gaza Division, Shmuel Zakai, who said, in an interview five days before OCL was launched:

> [Israel] could have eased the siege over the Gaza Strip, in such a way that the Palestinians, Hamas, would understand that holding their fire served their interests. But when you create a *tahadiyeh* [minor truce], and the economic pressure on the Strip continues, it's obvious that Hamas will try to reach an improved *tahadiyeh*, and that their way to achieve this, is resumed Qassam fire.
>
> (Burston 2008)

Yet despite Israel's unrelenting blockade, Hamas continued to adhere to the ceasefire until the 4 November Israeli attack. After this attack, Hamas responded by sending a volley of rockets across the border and violence between the two ensued. Yet Hamas attempted to negotiate a new long-term ceasefire, with these efforts confirmed by Shin Bet head Yuval Diskin and former US President Jimmy Carter (*JP* 2008; Beaumont 2009a; Porter 2009). All of these factors seriously undermine Israel's *casus belli* for OCL (Shlaim 2010; Siegman 2009). As ex-Israeli Mossad Director Efraim Halevy outlines: 'If Israel's goal were to remove the threat of rockets from the residents of southern Israel, opening the border crossings would have ensured such quiet for a generation' (in McGreal 2009).

Further undermining the Israeli narrative that OCL was a defensive war of last resort, in December 2008 Israeli *Haaretz* journalist Barak Ravid revealed that 'long-term planning, meticulous intelligence-gathering, secret discussions, visual deception tactics and disinformation' preceded OCL (2008), with evidence suggesting that the assault had been planned for up to two years. As Ilan Pappe reveals, in 2004 Israel built a $45 million 'dummy Arab city' in the Negev:

> this phantom city became a dummy Gaza in the winter of 2006, after Hizbullah fought Israel to a draw in the north, so that the IDF could prepare to fight a 'better war' against Hamas in the south. When the Israeli Chief of General Staff Dan Halutz visited the site after the Lebanon war, he told the press that soldiers 'were preparing for the scenario that will unfold in the dense neighbourhood of Gaza City'.
>
> (Ali *et al.* 2009: 13)

Accounts from IDF soldiers given to the group 'Breaking the Silence' corroborate such claims (BTS 2009). Military planning for the war was also coupled with diplomatic and media strategies – at least six months in the making – to drum up support for, and sell the message of, the attack (McGreal 2009a; Pfeffer 2008; Ravid 2008).

One of the primary stated goals of OCL was to destroy Hamas or substantially weaken it. However, while the operation was driven partly by Hamas's attacks on Israel, leading experts have argued that Israel was also increasingly concerned by a growing international acknowledgement that any settlement of the wider Israeli–Palestinian conflict requires engaging with Hamas (Shlaim 2010a: 367; Carter 2009; Halevy 2010). As Augustus Richard Norton outlines, 'Although neither the US nor Israel is presently prepared to endorse direct contacts with Hamas, many of the most influential policy hands in Washington already acknowledge that ostracising Hamas is a dead end' (2009).[7] Similarly in 2007 a UK parliamentary committee argued that the boycott of Hamas was 'counterproductive' (*Haaretz* 2007).

Although Israel has historically been able to disregard calls to engage with Hamas by dismissing it as a 'terror organisation', since its democratic election Hamas has increasingly been seen as a rational actor that has moderated its policies and tactics (Shlaim 2009: 3). As a plethora of well-informed scholars and commentators have indicated – including ex-US President Jimmy Carter – Hamas is a complex organisation whose ideologies, politics and tactics have shifted and evolved over time (similar to other organisations which have used violence when denied access to political processes and have been regarded as terrorist groups – such as the African National Congress) (Carter 2006; Halevy 2010; Shlaim 2009; Siegman 2009). As former UK Ambassador to the UN Jeremy Greenstock argues, 'It is too easy to describe Hamas simply as a "terror organisation"

... Hamas is a grievance based organisation seeking to end the occupation' (BBC 2009). As such, Hamas has repeatedly sought long-term ceasefires with Israel (and has a record of adhering to such ceasefires), and its leaders have signalled their acceptance of a two-state solution (Shlaim 2009; Chomsky and Pappe 2010). Other Hamas shifts in policy and tactics have included repeated offers to Israel for both sides to agree to end attacks on civilians (Rabbani 2008: 66); dropping its call for the destruction of Israel from its 2006 election manifesto (McGreal 2006); and ending the use of suicide bombings against Israeli civilians in 2006 (Urquhart 2006).[8]

One of the major issues in terms of international perceptions of Hamas since it was elected in 2006 has been its refusal to bow to the three major demands' imposed by Israel, the US and the 'Quartet' that Hamas: recognise Israel's right to exist, honour all previous commitments of the Palestinian Authority, and renounce violence.[9] Hamas has refused to acquiesce to these demands before a Palestinian state is formally created, arguing that to do so would place it in the same untenable situation that Fatah found itself in after Oslo – having given crucial concessions for little political gain. However, Hamas has signalled that it implicitly recognises Israel in repeated statements from figures such as Khaled Meshal – the Damascus-based Hamas politburo chief and head of the movement – along the lines of: 'We are realists ... [and there] is an entity called Israel' but 'realism does not mean that you have to recognize the legitimacy of the occupation' (in Zuhur 2008: 44–5). According to Jonathan Cook, the carte blanche rejection of Hamas – regardless of its shifts in terms of its policies and use of violence – stems from the reality that 'Hamas represents a severe threat to Israel's ambition to crush the Palestinians' long-standing demands for a state in the West Bank and Gaza. Unlike Fatah, its chief Palestinian political rival, Hamas has refused to collude with the Israeli occupation' (Cook 2009). As Cook points out, a long-term truce between Israel and Hamas would be a crucial step towards the creation of a sovereign Palestinian state (2009). As *Haaretz* editor Aluf Benn noted in July 2008 in relation to Hamas's control of Gaza and the Hamas–Israel ceasefire:

> Three years after the disengagement, 15 years after Oslo, Israel faces an independent Palestinian entity with full security and civilian responsibilities for a contiguous area in which there are no Israeli soldiers or settlers.... Finally there is an authentic Palestinian leadership that rose from the grassroots and demonstrates discipline and enforcement abilities.
>
> (2008)

Thus, a number of commentators argue that by breaking the truce with Hamas in November 2008 – thereby provoking it into firing rockets, and providing the pretext for OCL – Israel was attempting to eliminate the possibility of Hamas being seen 'as a legitimate negotiating partner' and to avoid having to make political concessions to the Palestinians (Finkelstein 2009: 6). Hence, as John Mearsheimer points out, Israel once again turned to the 'Iron Wall' strategy, with OCL part of:

> Israel's long-term vision of how it intends to live with millions of Palestinians in its midst ... Israel's leaders remain determined to control all of what used to be known as Mandate Palestine, which includes Gaza and the West Bank. The Palestinians would have limited autonomy in a handful of disconnected and economically crippled enclaves ... Israel would control the borders around them, movement between them, the air above and the water below them. The key to achieving this is to inflict massive pain on the Palestinians so that they come to accept the fact that they are a defeated people and that Israel will be largely responsible for controlling their future.
>
> (2009: 6)

As Shlaim argues, the 'Iron Wall' is pursued by Israel as part of its 'determination to perpetuate the isolation and the de-development of Gaza and deny the Palestinian people a small piece of land – 22% of Mandate-era Palestine, to be precise – on which to live in freedom and dignity' (2010). Such scholars have documented in detail how a long-standing pattern can be discerned whereby Israel has undertaken provocative military action against its opponents when there appeared to be a serious move towards settlement of the Israeli–Palestinian conflict. These moments have included Israel's 1982 invasion of Lebanon (following the PLO's adherence to a ceasefire in Beirut) and Israeli attacks on Hamas targets in 2002 (on the eve of Hamas declaring a truce) (Shlaim 2009a, 2010; Chomsky 2009; Streithorst 2009).

A key part of this 'Iron Wall' policy is Israel's creation of 'deterrence' through the use of disproportionate force (Shlaim 2001; Mearsheimer 2009: 6). As flagged earlier, during the war against Hezbollah, Israel adopted the '*Dahiye* doctrine', which as Mansour explains, emerged from the Israeli notion

> that the necessary restoration of deterrence could be achieved by means other than a decisive battlefield victory ... notably by demonstrating that Israel in the future would not hesitate to target hundreds or even thousands of civilians *as civilians*. Israel's targeting of Gaza civilians and civilian infrastructure was precisely such a demonstration.
>
> (Mansour 2009: 95, original emphasis)

The application of *Dahiye* from the time of the Israel–Hezbollah war is revealed by Gadi Eisenkott, head of Israel's northern command, who argues:

> What happened in the Dahiye Quarter of Beirut in 2006, will happen in every village from which shots are fired on Israel. We will use *disproportionate force* against it and we will cause *immense damage and destruction.* From our point of view *these are not civilian villages but military bases.* This is not a recommendation, this is the plan, and it has already been authorized.
>
> (PCATI 2009: 20, emphasis added)

The strategy outlined by Eisenkott has been further elaborated by other key Israeli figures. Former Israeli National Security Adviser Giora Eiland, for example, argues that in the event of another war with Hezbollah, the aim is not just the defeat of Hezbollah: 'the elimination of the Lebanese military, the destruction of the national infrastructure and intense suffering among the population ... Serious damage to the Republic of Lebanon, the ... destruction of homes and infrastructure, and the suffering of hundreds of thousands of people are consequences that can influence Hizbollah's behaviour more than anything else' (quoted in HRC 2009: 254, emphasis added). In 2008, Gabriel Siboni, a colonel in the reserves, made it clear that *Dahiye* was being employed more widely:

> an updated Israeli security concept regarding Israel's response to rocket and missile threats from Syria, Lebanon, and the Gaza Strip is gradually evolving.... With an outbreak of hostilities, the IDF will need to act ... *with force that is disproportionate to the enemy's actions and the threat it poses.* Such a response aims at inflicting damage and meting out punishment to an extent that will demand long and expensive reconstruction processes.... In Lebanon, attacks should both aim at Hizbollah's military capabilities ... *and the centers of civilian power that support the organization.... This approach is applicable to the Gaza Strip as well.*
>
> (2008: 1–2, emphasis added)

This 'security concept' – targeting civilians instrumentally and collectively punishing them to terrorise them into submission – constitutes a patent policy of state terror. As we will see in the next section, it is clear that *Dahiye* was applied during OCL.

## 'In urban warfare, everyone is your enemy. No innocents'

Following OCL, the FFM and leading international NGOs such as Amnesty International (AI) and Human Rights Watch (HRW) found that Israel committed grave violations of IHL, IHRL and the Geneva Conventions applicable to Israel as an occupying power (HRC 2009; AI 2009; HRW 2009, 2009a, 2009b).[10] As will now be argued, these violations resulted from the *Dahiye* doctrine and a continuation of the 'Iron Wall', and aimed to terrorise the civilians of Gaza into submission (Shlaim 2009a; Chomsky and Pappe 2010; Pilger 2009).

The government of Israel consistently argues that the IDF is the most 'moral' army in the world and took all possible care to protect civilian life during OCL (IMFA 2009).[11] As will be demonstrated, however, the IHL obligations to distinguish at all times between combatants and the civilian population, and to direct attacks only against military targets (summed up as the principles of 'distinction' and 'proportionality'), were seriously violated, amounting, in some cases, to war crimes and possible crimes against humanity (HRC 2009). *Haaretz* journalist Amira Hass (2010) argues that OCL was 'experienced primarily as a war against civilians' while the FFM likewise found that many violations constituted deliberate attacks on civilians. These included point-blank killing of non-combatants (including children); the killing of civilians carrying white flags; attacks on buildings known to be sheltering civilians (and, in some cases, buildings where the IDF had directed people to go); obstructing medical and humanitarian assistance to the wounded (resulting in deaths and extreme trauma); attacks on medical personnel (with at least 16 health workers killed); and the use of human shields (renamed 'Johnnies' during OCL). There was also extensive use of weapons that violate the rule of distinction, such as: white phosphorus (used against hospitals and locations known to be sheltering large numbers of civilians); flechettes (shells packed with 5,000–8,000 metal darts); dense inert metal explosives (DIMES) (causing extensive injuries difficult to treat); a new weapon dispersing sharp-edged metal cubes (that AI calls a version of 'the ball-bearings or nails and bolts which armed groups often pack into crude rockets and suicide bombs'); and the alleged use of depleted uranium (HRC 2009; AI 2009; HRW 2009c; Esposito in *JPS* 2009: 188).

While there is not the space to go into extensive detail about war crimes committed, a few cases are illustrative. One that received worldwide attention was the killing of 21 members of the al-Samouni family when the house the IDF ordered them to assemble in was attacked. Medics were prevented from evacuating the wounded and when they finally reached the area two days later, among the dead and injured they found four small children – too weak to stand up – with the corpses of their mothers (ICRC 2009).[12] There were also numerous civilians shot while carrying white flags, such as the Abd Rabbo children. After IDF messages to leave the area, the family left their house carrying white flags. They saw an IDF tank 10 metres from their door with two soldiers sitting on top eating, and waited for directions from the soldiers. A third soldier then emerged from the tank and shot the children and grandmother. A neighbour – who was an ambulance driver – was prevented from attending to them (alongside being ordered to strip, re-dress, abandon his ambulance and leave the area) (HRC 2009: 173–4).

These attacks on civilians, some clearly deliberate, came alongside the wide-scale destruction of the political, economic and social infrastructure of Gaza. The FFM and leading NGOs found that attacks on the Legislative

Building, prisons, police stations, factories and farms 'constituted deliberate attacks on civilian objects ... unlawfully and wantonly attacked and destroyed without military necessity' (HRC 2009: 416). One attack that clearly demonstrated this was the destruction of the Sawafeary chicken farm (which supplied 10 per cent of Gaza's eggs), whereby IDF bulldozers systematically razed the land, crops and farm machinery and crushed 31,000 chickens inside their coops. Witnesses note how the 'drivers of the tanks would spend hours flattening the chicken coops, sometimes stopping for coffee breaks, before resuming their work' (HRC 2009: 204–5). As one soldier told BTS, the destruction in Gaza 'was incredible. You drive around those neighbourhoods, you can't identify a thing. Not one stone left standing over another. You see plenty of fields, hothouses, orchards, everything devastated. Totally ruined. It's terrible. It's surreal' (BTS 2009: 85).

There was also widespread 'unlawful and wanton' destruction of thousands of private residential houses and water tanks, with soldiers relaying to BTS how they held 'grenade-launching practice' at houses and shot at houses and water tanks 'for the hell of it' (2009: 45, 85). This destruction was accompanied by gratuitous damage and vandalism of homes, including: furniture, appliances and clothes being destroyed; and piles of refuse (including human faeces) being left and faeces smeared on floors, walls, mattresses and belongings. Racist, threatening and intimidating graffiti were also common, with examples including: 'Kahane[13] was right'; 'The Zionist conqueror was here'; 'We're here to annihilate you'; 'Death to the Arabs'; and 'Death will find you soon' (Hass 2009; HRC 2009: 172; BTS 2009: 80, 84, 87, 96, 99–100) As the FFM outlines, the widespread destruction of civilian infrastructure was:

> a deliberate and systematic policy.... It was not carried out because those objects presented a military threat or opportunity, but to make the daily process of living, and dignified living, more difficult for the civilian population ... there appears also to have been an assault on the dignity of the people ... an overall image of humiliation and dehumanization of the Palestinian population.
>
> (HRC 2009: 407)

As this statement illustrates, OCL was clearly instrumental, aiming to send a message beyond the stated target of Hamas to the people of Gaza, that they would be collectively and indiscriminately targeted and punished. The aim and instrumentality of such acts – making the pain for civilians so high that they will be compelled to act against those in control – is a key element of acts of terror (Blakeley 2009; Jackson *et al.* 2009). As Richard Falk (2009) outlines, a key driver of Israeli policy during OCL was 'to teach the people of Gaza a lesson for their support of Hamas'. This motive was similarly recognised by the FFM:

> While the Israeli Government has sought to portray its operations as essentially a response to rocket attacks in the exercise of its right to self-defence, the Mission considers the plan to have been directed, at least in part, at a different target: the people of Gaza as a whole. In this respect, the operations were in furtherance of an overall policy aimed at punishing the Gaza population for its resilience and for its apparent support for Hamas, and possibly with the intent of forcing a change in such support.
>
> (HRC 2009: 406)

## Teaching the people of Gaza 'a lesson': *Dahiye* and state terror during OCL

This instrumental creation of immense suffering of the civilian population as collective punishment points to the 'full implementation' of the *Dahiye* doctrine during OCL (HRC 2009: 257–8). Indeed the adoption of *Dahiye* was clear in statements by leading Israeli political and military figures (PCATI 2009: 28). Just prior to OCL, for example, Prime Minister Ehud Olmert proclaimed that: 'we are stronger; there will be more blood there. We have power, enormous power; we can do things that are devastating' (PCATI 2009: 22). Deputy Prime Minister Eli Yishai went further:

> It [should be] possible to destroy Gaza, so they will understand not to mess with us ... it is a great opportunity to demolish thousands of houses of all the terrorists, so they will think twice before they launch rockets.... In my opinion, they should be razed to the ground, so thousands of houses, tunnels, and industries will be demolished.
>
> (HRC 2009: 256)

Similarly in February 2008, Matan Vilnai, the deputy minister of defence, outlined that the Palestinians 'will bring upon themselves a bigger shoah [Holocaust]' (*Guardian* 2008). The implementation of *Dahiye* was also clear in comments by military figures, such as a comment by a Reserve Major General that 'What we have to do is act systematically and with the aim of punishing all the organisations that are firing the rockets and mortars, *as well as the civilians who are enabling them to fire and hide*' (in Finkelstein 2009: 3, emphasis added). As the FFM concludes, statements by such figures implies that 'disproportionate destruction and creating maximum disruption in the lives of many people ... [is] a legitimate means to achieve military and political goals' and leaves little doubt that the 'disproportionate destruction and violence against civilians' in OCL was 'part of a deliberate policy' (HRC 2009: 257–8).

Further evidence that *Dahiye* was implemented in Gaza is found in comments by one of the main architects of Israel's current military ethics policy – philosopher Asa Kasher. Kasher developed the IDF code of conduct in the mid-1990s, and in 2003 – alongside Amos Yadlin (head of military intelligence until 2010) and a team of IDF legal experts – put together a more wide-ranging document on 'military ethics in fighting terror' (Harel 2009). Kasher argues that the lives of IDF soldiers should not be put in danger to avoid killing civilians who live in the 'vicinity' of terrorists. He further believes that Israel 'does not bear the moral responsibility for properly separating between dangerous individuals and harmless ones' (Kasher 2010). In line with this position, Kasher argues that the 'norms followed by the commanders in Gaza were generally appropriate' (Harel 2009). Kasher claims that while his ethical theories have not been made officially binding by the IDF, they have been adopted in principle by IDF chiefs from the time of Moshe Ya'alon (who was made Chief of Staff in July 2002). Kasher argues that the IDF Chief during OCL – Gabi Ashkenazi – was also 'very familiar' with these principles (Harel 2009).

In the application of *Dahiye*, supported by Kasher's brand of 'ethics in conflict', the rules of engagement during OCL focused on 'the aim to eliminate as far as possible any risk to the lives of the Israeli soldiers' and 'provided for a low threshold for the use of lethal fire against the civilian population' in Gaza (HCR 2009: 180). The resulting permissive rules of engagement are clear in IDF testimonies. As one soldier told BTS:

> everyone who talked to us ... sounded extremely militant, used very fierce language ... our brigade commander ... went so far as to say ... in war, no consideration of civilians was to be taken. You shoot anyone you see ... no humanitarian consideration played any role in the army at present.
>
> (2009: 27)

Another recounted that his battalion commander told him it was better to 'hit an innocent than hesitate to target an enemy.... When you enter a house, the idea is that it contains an enemy.... Rules of engagement here [in Gaza] are different because no permission to shoot is necessary' (BTS 2009: 50–1). A third outlined that he was told: 'In urban warfare, anyone is your enemy. No innocents' (BTS 2009: 20).

We can see from this discussion that OCL was clearly directed beyond the stated target of Hamas, and comprised a deliberate attack on civilians designed to 'teach them a lesson' through terror. As the FFM explains:

> The operations were carefully planned in all their phases. Legal opinions and advice were given throughout the planning stages and at certain operational levels during the campaign. There were almost no mistakes made according to the Government of Israel. It is in these circumstances that the Mission concludes that ... [OCL] was *a deliberately disproportionate attack designed to punish, humiliate and terrorize* a *civilian population,* radically diminish its local economic capacity both to

> work and to provide for itself, and to force upon it an *ever increasing sense of* dependency and *vulnerability*.
>
> (HRC 2009: 407–8, 414, emphasis added)

## Conclusion

Despite the extreme violence and destruction wreaked on Gaza during OCL, it was, as Rashid Khalidi states, 'an astonishingly sanitised war'. This sanitisation resulted partly from the media ban during OCL, which Khalidi argues was an 'effort to remove witnesses from the scene before the crime took place'. Furthermore, in the West:

> in a bizarre attempt at 'balance', the highly inaccurate rocket attacks against Israel and their three civilian victims ... received as much attention as the levelling of Gaza and the killing of more than 1000 Palestinians and the wounding of nearly 5000, most of them civilians.
>
> (Ali *et al.* 2009: 8)

The response of the US government to OCL did not deviate from its well-established support for its key ally, and while concerns about the death toll were raised in Europe, there was no intrinsic questioning of Israel's assertion that OCL was a justified war of self-defence (Greenwald 2009; Baird 2011).

Outrage was palpable in the Arab world, particularly in response to what was seen as the silence and complicity of Arab states, with many regimes 'facing accusations of impotence and even treason' in enormous grassroots demonstrations. Targeted for particular criticism was the silence of Palestinian Authority President Mahmoud Abbas, and Egypt's Hosni Mubarak, who blamed Hamas for OCL and kept Egypt's borders with Gaza tightly sealed during the assault (Khalidi in Ali *et al.* 2009: 6). From the deluge of confidential diplomatic cables recently laid bare by Wikileaks and the so-called Palestine Papers, we now know that both Abbas and Mubarak had advance warning of OCL (Ravid 2010).

As it became clear that gross violations of IHL and IHRL had occurred during OCL, the FFM was tasked with carrying out an independent investigation. From the outset Israel refused to cooperate with the mission, attacked the integrity of its investigation, undertook vicious character attacks on Justice Goldstone (despite his previous Zionist and pro-Israel credentials), and roundly condemned and rejected the findings of the FFM. Furthermore, as has become a common strategy in response to criticism, Israel attempted to rebuff censure of its actions through using the charge of anti-Semitism as a trope to silence anyone who criticised the motive behind, or actions during, OCL (Dugard 2009a; Chomsky and Pappe 2010; Shlaim 2009). Falk (2009) argues that Israel's 'panicked' reaction to the FFM stemmed from the fact that Goldstone could not 'credibly be accused of anti-Israel bias, making it harder to deflect attention from the findings no matter how loud the screaming of "foul play"' and that a 'fair reading' shows the FFM to be balanced and 'eminently mindful of Israel's arguments relating to security', giving Israel 'the benefit of the doubt on some key issues'.

Israel's internal investigations into OCL strongly deny that war crimes occurred and admit only 'operational lapses and errors in the exercise of discretion' (State of Israel 2009, 2010). At the time of writing, of the 400 command investigations conducted by Israel, 52 have been referred for criminal investigation and three cases have been submitted for prosecution. Of these three, two cases have to date resulted in criminal charges (HRC 2011: 6). In the first, a soldier who stole $400 from a Gazan's credit card was jailed for seven and a half months and in the second two soldiers found guilty of using a nine-year-old Palestinian boy as a human shield received suspended three-month sentences and were demoted (HRC 2011: 9–10; BBC 2010).

While the FFM calls for the war crimes and possible crimes against humanity committed during OCL to be addressed, to date Israel's longstanding impunity in regard to its violations of international law has continued. As John Dugard – who has served as a judge on the International Court of Justice, and is a former Special Rapporteur on human rights in the OPTs – reports, the FFM and a plethora of reports by independent NGOs

> support the conclusion that war crimes and crimes against humanity were committed by the IDF in its Operation. Those who dispute this, such as the US House of Representatives, the US government and many European states, have clearly either not read the evidence presented by these reports or have decided that Israel is above the law. I would like to believe that the European States which voted against the Goldstone report in the General Assembly have not read the report but I fear that they have the reports and have decided that the norms of International Humanitarian Law applicable to other states do not apply to Israel.
>
> (Dugard 2009)

Given the state terrorism that Israel planned and perpetrated under the guise of 'counter-terrorism' during OCL – as part of its application of the *Dahiye* doctrine and wider policy of the 'Iron Wall' – it is imperative that the flagrant violations of international law committed during OCL be redressed. In addition to the ever-escalating violence being committed against Gaza, and the OPTs more widely, Israel is openly challenging the basic tenets of IHL – with Kasher positing that 'We in Israel are in a key position in the development of law in this field.... This is gradually being recognized both in the Israeli legal system and abroad.... What we are doing is becoming the law' (in Harel 2009). The grave global consequences that such a position poses should be of concern to us all.

## Post-script: the Goldstone Op-Ed

In April 2011, after the completion of this chapter, Justice Goldstone published an Op-Ed in the *Washington Post* entitled 'Reconsidering the Goldstone Report on Israel and war crimes'. The Op-Ed followed the publication of the March 2011 Report of the UN Human Rights Council Committee of Independent Experts (led by Judge Mary McGowan Davis), which assessed the compliance with international standards of both Israeli and Palestinian investigations of the war in Gaza. In the Op-Ed, Goldstone (2011: 1) argues that 'a lot more' was known about what happened in the Gaza war than when he chaired the FFM and that 'If I had known then what I know now, the Goldstone Report would have been a different document.' Attributing his shift in views, he says that 'investigations published by the Israeli military and recognised in the UN committee's report have established the validity of some of the incidents involving individual soldiers, they also indicate that civilians were not intentionally targeted as a matter of policy' (Goldstone 2011).

It is difficult to ascertain, however, how Goldstone comes to such conclusions on the basis of the McGowan Davis report. For the report raises clear concerns about the investigations carried out by Israel, outlining that 'out of the 36 incidents ... referred to in the committee's previous report, more than one-third remain unresolved or with an unclear status two years after the events' (Human Rights Council 2011: 13). The report also notes that there has been a lack of investigations by Israel concerning 'allegations related to higher level decisions about the design and implementation of the Gaza operation, including those related to the nature, objectives and targets of the Israeli military' (2011: 13–14). The report moreover flags issues concerning the promptness, transparency, independence and impartiality of Israel's investigations. On the last point, for example, the report notes its apprehension regarding the 'dual responsibility' of the Military Advocate General (MAG) in Israel, who is both 'legal advisor to the Chief of Staff and other military authorities and ... supervisor of criminal investigations with the military' (HRC 2011: 12).

The Op-Ed has been seized upon by Israel as a retraction of the key findings of the FFM, with Israeli Prime Minister Netanyahu calling for the FFM to be withdrawn. A debate around what drove Goldstein's Op-Ed ensued in the media, particularly in relation to the fierce pressure applied on Goldstone after the publication of the FFM (including the South African Zionist Federation Chair accusing Goldstone of causing 'irreparable damage to the Jewish people as a whole' and threatening to picket Goldstone's grandson's bar mitzvah). Following the flurry of attention the Op-Ed received, the other three esteemed members of the FFM –

Christine Chinkin (Professor of International Law at the LSE), Desmond Travers (Retired Irish soldier and peace-keeper) and Hina Jilani (a founding member of Pakistan's Human Rights Commission) – published a statement in the *Guardian* newspaper. In it, they make reference to the 'personal attacks and the extraordinary pressure placed on members of the fact-finding mission' and make it absolutely clear that they stand by the findings of the FFM:

> In recent days some articles and comments appearing in the press ... Have misrepresented facts in an attempt to delegitimize the findings of this report and cast doubts on its credibility.... [These] aspersions ... cannot be left unchallenged.... We concur in our view that there is no justification for any demand or expectation for reconsideration of the report as nothing of substance has appeared that would in any way change the context, findings or conclusions of that report with respect to any of the parties to the Gaza conflict.... We firmly stand by [the report's] ... conclusions.... We consider that calls to reconsider or even retract the report, as well as attempts at misrepresenting its nature and purpose, disregard the rights of victims, Palestinian and Israeli, to truth and justice.... Had we given in to pressures from any quarter to sanitise our conclusions, we would be doing a serious injustice.... The report has triggered a process that is still under way and should continue until justice is done and respect for international human rights and humanitarian law by everyone is ensured.
>
> (Jilani *et al.* 2011)

## Notes

1 The author would like to thank Kynan Gentry, Ruth Blakeley, Mary Nazzal-Batayneh and the editors for their feedback on drafts of this chapter.
2 While abuses by Hamas are not the focus of this chapter, for details about war crimes and possible crimes against humanity committed by Hamas, particularly in firing rockets at civilian centres in Israel, see HRC (2009), AI (2009) and HRW (2009b).
3 For a moving account of the mental scars of OCL on one family, see McNeill (2009).
4 The takeover of Gaza came when the democratically elected government of Hamas pre-empted a US-backed Fatah coup (Rose 2008).
5 Israel argues that the raid was aimed at destroying a tunnel that Hamas was building to kidnap Israeli soldiers. Analysts such as Augustus Richard Norton (2009), however, have questioned whether Hamas would have risked the truce in order to kidnap additional soldiers.
6 For a day-by-day account of the ceasefire see *JPS* (2009: 164–8).
7 With key figures such as Richard Haass (US Council on Foreign Relations President) and Martin Indyk (former US Ambassador to Israel) arguing that negotiations excluding Hamas are 'bound to fail' (Norton 2009).
8 Since April 2006 the number of suicide bombings against Israeli civilians has dropped dramatically. Those that have occurred were undertaken by groups

such as Islamic Jihad and the Fatah al-Aqsa Martyrs' Brigades. An April 2008 attack at Kerem Shalom crossing in Gaza was claimed by Hamas; however, this attack was not directed at civilians, but was an attempt to open the crossing.

9 As a number of prominent scholars wryly point out, no such concomitant pressure has been applied to the Israelis to recognise Palestine, renounce violence or abide by past agreements – with the ever-increasing settlement activity in violation of the peace process one example of this (Chomsky and Pappe 2010: 145–69).

10 While Israel removed settlers and troops from Gaza in 2005, it remains the occupying power through its continued control of Gaza's land and sea borders, airspace and control of the economy by virtue of the blockade (HRC 2009: 74).

11 Gaza's size and population density (21 miles by 4 to 7.5 miles with 1.5 million people), the extent of the bombing, the absence of bomb shelters and the sealed borders, meant there was nowhere for people to seek refuge. As John Ging, UNRWA Gaza Director of Operations, stated during the conflict 'There is nowhere safe in Gaza. Everyone here is terrorized' (HRC 2009: 129–30).

12 This case has garnered further attention following the April 2011 publication of an Op-Ed by Justice Goldstein (see Postscript, pp. 131–2, for further details. In the Op-Ed, Goldstone (2011) argues that in relation to the al-Samouni case, 'the shelling of the home was apparently the consequence of an Israeli commander's erroneous interpretation of a drone image, and an Israeli officer is under investigation for having ordered the attack' (2011). He then continues: 'I regret that our fact-finding mission did not have such evidence explaining the circumstances in which we said civilians in Gaza were targeted, because it probably would have influenced our findings about intentionality and war crimes.' However, Goldstone's comments do not reflect the actual findings of the McGowan Davis report, the 2011 UN report which addressed Israeli and Palestinian compliance with international standards in their OCL investigations, the report which apparently sparked Goldstone's Op-Ed. The McGowan Davis report instead outlines that contradictory accounts of the event had been given by IDF involved, including that

> a senior officer … told investigators he was not warned that civilians were at the location. However, some of those civilians had been ordered there by IDF soldiers from that same officer's unit and air force officers reportedly informed him of the possible presence of civilians. Despite allegedly being made aware of this information, the officer apparently approved the air strike.
>
> (HRC 2011: 7-8)

Goldstone's confidence that 'it appears the appropriate process is underway and I am confident that if the officer is found to be negligent, Israel will respond accordingly' is also not shared by the McGowan Davis report, which notes with concern that 'the events may relate both to the actions and decisions of soldiers on the ground and of senior officers located in a war room, as well as to broader issues implicating the rules of engagement and the use of drones'. The report also worryingly outlines that 'there are also reports indicating that the MAG's [Military Advocate General's] decision to investigate was opposed by the then head of IDF Southern Command'. On the basis of such issues, the McGowan Davis report comments that it 'does not have sufficient information to establish the current status of the on-going investigations into the killings' (2011: 7).

13 Meir Kahane founded an ultra-right-wing group banned in Israel for inciting racism.

## References

Ali, T. *et al.* (2009) 'Responses to the War in Gaza', *London Review of Books*, 29 January, www.lrb.co.uk/v31/n02/gaza-writers/responses-to-the-war-in-gaza (accessed 20 February 2009).

Amnesty International (AI) (2009) 'Israel/Gaza: Operation Cast Lead: 22 Days of Death and Destruction', www.amnesty.org/en/library/info/MDE15/015/2009/en (accessed 12 February 2010).

Amnesty International *et al.* (2010) 'Dashed Hopes: Continuation of the Gaza Blockade', 30 November, www.amnesty.org.uk/uploads/documents/doc_21083.pdf (accessed 3 December 2010).

Baird, Brian (2011) 'The US Congress and the Goldstone Report', *The Goldstone Report: the Legacy of the Landmark Investigation of the Gaza Conflict*, ed. Adam Horowitz, Lizzy Ratner and Philip Weiss, New York: Nation Books, pp. 369–74.

BBC News (2009) 'Hamas Diplomacy Is "Hard to See'," 12 January, http://news.bbc.co.uk/today/hi/today/newsid_7823000/7823746.stm (accessed 20 January 2009).

BBC News (2009a) 'Israel to Probe Phosphorus Claims', 21 January, http://news.bbc.co.uk/1/hi/7841999.stm (accessed 23 January 2009).

BBC News (2009b) 'UN "shocked" by Gaza Destruction', 23 January, http://news.bbc.co.uk/go/pr/fr/-/1/hi/world/middle_east/7846625.stm (accessed 25 January 2009).

BBC News (2010) 'Israeli Troops Demoted over Gaza "Human Shield" Boy', 21 November, www.bbc.co.uk/news/world-middle-east-11807152 (accessed 21 November 2010).

Beaumont, P. (2009) 'Gaza Desperately Short of Food after Israel Destroys Farmland', *Guardian*, 1 February, www.guardian.co.uk/world/2009/feb/01/gaza-food-crisis (accessed 16 June 2010).

Beaumont, P. (2009a) 'Israel PM's Family Link to Hamas Peace Bid', *Guardian*, 1 March, www.guardian.co.uk/world/2009/mar/01/israel-hamas-olmert-palestine-shalit (accessed 5 March 2009).

Benn, A. (2008) 'The Legacy of the Tahadiyeh', *Haaretz*, 27 July, www.haaretz.com/misc/article-print-page/the-legacy-of-the-tahadiyeh-1.250498?trailingPath=2.169%2C2.225%2C2.227%2C (accessed 6 June 2009).

Blakeley, R. (2009) *State Terrorism and Neoliberalism: The North in the South*, London: Routledge.

Breaking the Silence (BTS) (2009) 'Soldiers' Testimonies from Operation Cast Lead, Gaza 2009', 15 July, www.shovrimshtika.org/oferet/ENGLISH_oferet.pdf (accessed 30 June 2009).

Burston, B. (2008) 'Can the First Gaza War Be Stopped before It Starts?', *Haaretz*, 22 December, www.haaretz.com/news/can-the-first-gaza-war-be-stopped-before-it-starts-1.260017 (accessed 28 December 2008).

Carter. J. (2006) 'Give Hamas a Chance', *CNN News*, 2 February, http://articles.cnn.com/2006-02-01/world/carter.hamas_1_hamas-leaders-palestinian-parliament-palestinian-elections?_s=PM:WORLD.

Carter, J. (2009) 'An Unnecessary War', *Washington Post*, 8 January, www.washingtonpost.com/wp-dyn/content/story/2009/01/07/ST2009010702803.html (accessed 12 January 2009).

Chomsky, N. (2009) ' "Exterminate all the Brutes": Gaza 2009', 19 January (revised 6 June), www.chomsky.info/articles/20090119.htm (accessed 26 January 2009).

Chomsky, N. and Pappe, I. (2010) *Gaza in Crisis: Reflections on Israel's War Against the Palestinians*, London: Penguin.

Cook, J. (2009) 'The Plot against Gaza', *Przekroj Magazine* (Warsaw), 16 January, www.jkcook.net/Articles2/0365.htm#Top (accessed 20 January 2009).

Dugard, J. (2009) 'Options for the Prosecution of Crimes Arising from Operation Cast Lead', *Middle East Monitor*, 6 December, www.middleeastmonitor.org.uk/downloads/documents/keynote-address-by-professor-john-duggard-to-MEMO-seminar-on-universal-jurisdiction.pdf (accessed 10 December 2010).

Dugard, J. (2009a) 'Two States or Apartheid?', *Huffington Post*, 12 August, www.huffingtonpost.com/john-dugard/post_356_b_258206.html?view=print (accessed 14 September 2009).

Falk, R. (2009) 'Why the Goldstone Report Matters', *Sabah*, 22 September, http://sabbah.biz/mt/archives/2009/09/22/richard-falk-why-the-goldstone-report-matters/ (accessed 23 September 2009).

Finkelstein, N.G. (2009) 'Foiling Another Palestinian "Peace Offensive": Behind the Bloodbath in Gaza', 19 January, www.normanfinkelstein.com/finkelstein-on-gaza-war-massacre/ (accessed 25 January 2009).

Fuller, M. (2009) Interview with Mark Regev, Israel Government Spokesperson, Channel 4, UK, 9 January, www.youtube.com/watch?gl=ES&hl=es&v=N6e-elr-gYL0 (accessed 15 November 2010).

GISHA (Legal Centre for Freedom of Movement) (2010) 'Israel Reveals Documents related to the Gaza Closure Policy', 21 October, www.gisha.org/index.php?intLanguage=2&intItemId=1904&intSiteSN=113 (accessed 15 November 2010).

Goldstone. R. (2011) 'Reconsidering the Goldstone Report on Israel and War Crimes', *Washington Post*, 1 April.

Greenwald, G. (2009) 'Unanimous Consent: When Israel Acts, Congress Applauds. No Debate Required', *The American Conservative*, 26 January, www.amconmag.com/article/2009/jan/26/00014/ (accessed 10 February 2009).

*Guardian* (2008) 'Israeli Minister Warns of Palestinian "holocaust"', *Guardian*, 29 February, www.guardian.co.uk/world/2008/feb/29/israelandthepalestinians1 (accessed 1 January 2010).

*Haaretz* (2007) 'Israeli Ambassador Slams British MPs' Call to End Hamas Boycott', 13 August, www.haaretz.com/misc/article-print-page/israeli-ambassador-slams-british-mps-call-to-end-hamas-boycott-1.227337?trailingPath=2.169%2C2.216%2C (accessed 15 January 2009).

*Haaretz* (2009) 'UN Human Rights Official: Gaza Evokes Memories of Warsaw Ghetto', 24 January, www.haaretz.com/news/un-human-rights-official-gaza-evokes-memories-of-warsaw-ghetto-1.268743 (accessed 24 January 2009).

Halevy, E. (2010) 'Why not Hamas? The Answer to Israel's Strategic Dilemma May Reside in Gaza', *The New Republic*, 26 March, www.tnr.com/print/article/politics/why-not-hamas (accessed 1 April 2010).

Harel, A. (2009) 'The Philosopher who Gave the IDF Moral Justification in Gaza', *Haaretz*, 2 February, www.haaretz.com/print-edition/news/the-philosopher-who-gave-the-idf-moral-justification-in-gaza-1.269527 (accessed 2 February 2009).

Hass, A. (2009) 'Return to Gaza', *London Review of Books*, 26 February, p. 33.

Hass, A. (2010) 'In Gaza, Cast Lead Felt like a War on Civilians', *Haaretz*, 7 July, www.haaretz.com/misc/article-print-page/amira-hass-in-gaza-cast-lead-felt-like-a-war-on-civilians-1.300452?trailingPath=2.169%2C2.225%2C2.226%2C (accessed 7 July 2010).

Human Rights Council (2009) 'Human Rights in Palestine and Other Occupied Arab Territories: Report of the United Nations Fact-Finding Mission on the Gaza Conflict', (more commonly known as the 'Goldstone Report) A/HRC/12/48, 25 September, http://www2.ohchr.org/english/bodies/hrcouncil/docs/12session/A-HRC-12–48.pdf (accessed 26 September 2009).

Human Rights Council (2011) 'Report of the Committee of Independent Experts in International Humanitarian and Human Rights Law Established Pursuant to Council Resolution 13/9', [more commonly known as the McGowan Davis report'] A/HRC/16/24, 18 March 2011 (accessed 2 April 2011).

Human Rights Watch (HRW) (2009) 'Precisely Wrong: Gaza Civilians Killed by Israeli Drone-Launched Missiles', 30 June, www.hrw.org/en/node/84077/section/1 (accessed 1 September 2009).

HRW (2009a) 'Rain of Fire: Israel's Unlawful Use of White Phosphorus in Gaza', 25 March, www.hrw.org/en/reports/2009/03/25/rain-fire (accessed 1 June 2009).

HRW (2009b) 'White Flag Deaths: Killings of Palestinian Civilians during Operation Cast Lead', 13 August, www.hrw.org/en/reports/2009/08/13/white-flag-deaths-0 (accessed 1 September 2009).

HRW (2010) '"I Lost Everything": Israel's Unlawful Destruction of Property During Operation Cast Lead', *Human Rights Watch,* 13 May, www.hrw.org/node/90334 (accessed 4 June 2010).

Intelligence and Terrorism Information Centre at the Israel Intelligence Heritage and Commemoration Centre (ITIC) (2008) 'The Six Months of the Lull Arrangement', December, www.terrorism-info.org.il/malam_multimedia/English/eng_n/pdf/hamas_e017.pdf (accessed 1 April 2009).

International Committee of the Red Cross (ICRC) (2009) 'Gaza: ICRC Demands Urgent Access to Wounded as Israeli Army Fails to Assist Wounded Palestinians', 8 January, www.icrc.org/eng/resources/documents/news-release/palestine-news-080109.htm (accessed 9 January 2009).

Israeli Ministry of Foreign Affairs (IMFA) (2009) 'IDF Operation in Gaza: Cast Lead', 21 January, www.mfa.gov.il/MFA/Terrorism-+Obstacle+to+Peace/Terrorism+and+Islamic+Fundamentalism-/Aerial_strike_weapon_development_center+_Gaza_28-Dec-2008.htm (accessed 1 March 2009).

Jackson, R., Murphy, E. and Poynting S. (eds) (2009) *Contemporary State Terrorism: Theory and Practice,* London: Routledge.

*Jerusalem Post* (*JP*) (2008) 'Hamas Wants Better Terms for Truce', 21 December, www.jpost.com/Home/Article.aspx?id=125429 (accessed 5 January 2009).

Jilani, H., Chinkin, C. and Travers, D. (2011) 'Goldstone Report: Statement issued by members of UN Mission on Gaza War', *Guardian,* 14 April, www.guardian.co.uk/commentisfree/2011/apr/14/goldstone-report-statement-un-gaza (accessed 16 April 2011).

*Journal of Palestine Studies* (*JPS*) (2009) 'Special Focus: Operation Cast Lead', Vol. 38, No. 3, Spring, pp. 1–407.

Kasher, A. (2010) 'A Moral Evaluation of the Gaza War: Operation Cast Lead', *Jerusalem Centre for Public Affairs,* Vol. 9, No. 18, 4 February, www.jcpa.org/JCPA/Templates/ShowPage.asp?DBID=1&LNGID=1&TMID=111&FID=378&PID=0&IID=3345 (accessed 1 November 2010).

McGreal, C. (2006) 'Hamas Drops Call for Destruction of Israel from Manifesto', *Guardian,* 12 January, www.guardian.co.uk/world/2006/jan/12/israel (accessed 1 February 2009).

McGreal, C. (2009) 'Israeli Incursion into Gaza Replays Well-worn Blueprint', *Guardian*, 4 January, www.guardian.co.uk/world/2009/jan/04/israel-gaza-invasion-troops-hamas (accessed 4 January 2009).

McGreal, C. (2009a) 'Why Israel Went to War in Gaza', *Guardian*, 4 January, www.guardian.co.uk/world/2009/jan/04/israel-gaza-hamas-hidden-agenda (accessed 4 January 2009).

McNeill, S. (2009) 'Raed's Story', 9 May, available at: www.gazaspeaks.com/articles/raedstory.pdf (accessed 5 January 2010).

Mansour, C. (2009) 'Reflections on the War in Gaza', *Journal of Palestinian Studies*, Vol. 38, No. 4, pp. 91–5.

Mearsheimer, J. (2009) 'Another War, Another Defeat: Wrecking Gaza Won't Make Israel More Secure', *The American Conservative*, 26 January, www.amconmag.com/article/2009/jan/26/00006/ (accessed 10 February 2009).

Norton, A.R. (2009) 'The Gaza War: Antecedents and Consequences', *Real Instituto Elcano*, ARI 21/2009, 2 March, www.realinstitutoelcano.org/wps/portal/rielcano_eng_/Content?WCM_GLOBAL_CONTEXT=/elcano/elcano_in/zonas_in/mediterranean+arab+world/ari21-2009 (accessed 6 August 2009).

Pfeffer, A. (2008) 'Israel Claims Success in the PR War', *The Jewish Chronicle Online*, 31 December, www.thejc.com/news/israel-news/israel-claims-success-pr-war (accessed 5 January 2009).

Pilger, J. (2009) 'Holocaust Denied: The Lying Silence of Those Who Know', *antiwar.com*, 8 January, www.antiwar.com/pilger/?articleid=14015 (accessed 1 June 2009).

Porter, G. (2009) 'Israel Rejected Hamas Ceasefire Offer in December', *Inter Press Service News Agency*, 9 January, www.ipsnews.net/news.asp?idnews=45350 (accessed 15 January 2009).

Public Committee Against Torture in Israel (PCATI) (2009) 'No Second Thoughts: The Changes in the Israeli Defence Forces' Combat Doctrine in Light of "Operation Cast Lead,"' November, www.stoptorture.org.il/files/no%20second%20thoughts_ENG_WEB.pdf (accessed 6 June 2010).

Rabbani, M. (2008) 'A Hamas Perspective on the Movement's Evolving Role: An Interview with Khalid Mishal: Part 2', *Journal of Palestine Studies*, Vol. 37, No. 4, pp. 59–81.

Ravid, B. (2008) 'Disinformation, Secrecy and Lies: How the Gaza Offensive Came About', *Haaretz*, 27 December, www.haaretz.com/news/disinformation-secrecy-and-lies-how-the-gaza-offensive-came-about-1.260347 (accessed 5 January 2009).

Ravid, B. (2011) 'WikiLeaks Exposé: Israel Tried to Coordinate Gaza War with Abbas', *Haaretz*, 28 November, www.haaretz.com/news/diplomacy-defense/wikileaks-expose-israel-tried-to-coordinate-gaza-war-with-abbas-1.327487.

Rose, D. (2008) 'The Gaza Bombshell', *Vanity Fair*, April, www.vanityfair.com/politics/features/2008/04/gaza200804 (accessed 5 January 2009).

Save the Children (2009) 'Fact Sheet: Children of the Gaza Crisis', 9 February, www.scsmena.org/Alliance%20Gaza%20Child%20Rights%20Fact%20Sheet%209%202%2009.pdf (accessed 29 February 2009).

Shlaim, A. (2001) *The Iron Wall: Israel and the Arab World*, New York: Norton.

Shlaim, A. (2009) 'Captive Nation: How Gaza Became a Palestinian Prison', *The American Conservative*, 26 January, www.amconmag.com/article/2009/jan/26/00009/ (accessed 10 February 2009).

Shlaim, A. (2009a) 'Israel Committing "State Terror" in Gaza Attack, Preventing

Peace," *Democracy Now,* 14 January, www.democracynow.org/2009/1/14/leading_israeli_scholar_avi_shlaim_israel (accessed 1 June 2010).

Shlaim, A. (2010) 'Blair: Gaza's Great Betrayer', *Guardian,* 3 February, www.guardian.co.uk/world/2010/feb/03/gaza-tony-blair-betrayal/print (accessed 3 February 2010).

Shlaim, A. (2010a) *Israel and Palestine: Reappraisals, Revisions, Refutations,* 2nd edition, London: Verso.

Siboni, G. (2008) 'Disproportionate Force: Israel's Concept of Response in Light of the Second Lebanon War', *INSS Insight,* No. 74, 2 October, www.inss.org.il/publications.php?cat=21&incat=&read=2222 (accessed 12 October 2010).

Siegman, H. (2009) 'Israel's Lies', *London Review of Books,* 29 January, pp. 3–4.

State of Israel (2009) 'The Operation in Gaza – Factual and Legal Aspects', 29 July, www.mfa.gov.il/NR/rdonlyres/E89E699D-A435–491B-B2D0–017675DAFEF7/0/GazaOperationwLinks.pdf (accessed 1 September 2009).

State of Israel (2010) 'Gaza Operation Investigations: An Update', January, www.mfa.gov.il/NR/rdonlyres/8E841A98–1755–413D-A1D2–8B30F64022BE/0/GazaOperationInvestigationsUpdate.pdf (accessed 5 February 2010).

Streithorst, T. (2009) 'Operation Cast Ballot: The Political Calculation Behind Olmert's War', *The American Conservative,* 26 January, www.amconmag.com/article/2009/jan/26/00011/ (accessed 10 February 2009).

Urquhart, C. (2006) 'Hamas in Call to End Suicide Bombings', *Guardian,* 9 April, www.guardian.co.uk/world/2006/apr/09/israel (accessed 5 February 2009).

Zuhur, S.D. (2008) 'Hamas and Israel: Conflicting Strategies of Group-Based Politics', Strategic Studies Institute, United States Army War College, 23 December, www.strategicstudiesinstitute.army.mil/pubs/display.cfm?pubID=894 (accessed 5 February 2009).

# 8 Untouchable compradores?

## Colombian state narco-terrorism and the people's struggle for national liberation

*Oliver Villar*

The Uruguayan writer, Eduardo Galeano, recently wrote that 'the experts, known as violentologists, say Colombia is a country in love with death' (Galeano 2009: 351). For more than half a century, the Colombian state has misrepresented itself as a 'democracy', while engaged in a life and death struggle against the landless poor. This chapter concerns a popular struggle in the first Latin American country ever to be subjected to the theatre of modern United States government imperialist anti-guerrilla warfare. It is a struggle with profound political consequences for the struggle of the working class, not just in Colombia but in Latin America and throughout the Third World where US imperialism is also being challenged.

In a period of world history where enemies of the US government can be classified 'terrorists' and armed struggle is considered 'outdated', I will argue that any discussion of political violence in Colombia is incomplete without understanding 'terrorism' and 'counter-terrorism' as the politico-military dimension of contemporary high-intensity class warfare. In Colombia there are principally two armies leading this war. One is the 'special bodies of armed men' of the Colombian state, which include the army, police and paramilitary death squads. The other army is the Revolutionary Armed Forces of Colombia – People's Army (FARC-EP), whose mass base of support is among the landless poor *campesinos*.

The chapter will examine what is essentially a class question: what is 'narco-terrorism'? In doing so it examines why a comprador regime in Bogotá has been able to wage a largely unsuccessful war of terror on FARC with impunity but, more importantly, why the popular struggle has become almost indomitable for both military and ideological campaigns waged by the Colombian state and mainstream analyses. The chapter demonstrates how it is in the political as well as the economic interest of compradores as the national business class of Colombia and their key sponsor the United States that the popular struggle is blamed for their crimes.

## US 'counter-terror' as state terror: origins and objectives

For more than 30 years Colombia has experienced a reign of terror from the Colombian state, combining drug cartels and their anti-guerrilla paramilitary death squads. However, Colombian state terrorism before drugs can be traced to a period in Colombian history known as *La Violencia* (1948–58), when the country's two major parties, the Conservatives and the Liberals, split along political, ideological and regional lines instigating a bloody civil war (Richani 2002). At the centre of this split was Jorge Eliecer Gaitan, a Liberal presidential candidate who promised land reform and an end to oligarchic rule. Gaitan was assassinated on 9 April 1948, a state crime believed to be the first in Colombia organized by the US Central Intelligence Agency (CIA) (Weiner 2008; Idels 2002). The political assassination spurred a major uprising called the *Bogotázo*. Workers and the general population stormed the city, attacking anything which represented the oligarchy. Police stations, government offices and buildings were set alight instigating *La Violencia* (Pearce 1990). Every social institution from the family to the church was affected, hence the generic name Colombians gave it – the Violence.

The Conservative government backed by the military and police drove Liberals and leftists to the countryside where landowners formed paramilitary groups (Richani 2002). Radicalized Liberals and Communists were marked for death. The Conservatives were condemned as *falangistas* in reference to Franco's fascist ideology in Spain, for their sheer brutality and distaste for democracy (Campos *et al.* 1963). In 1949 the Colombian Communist Party (Partido Comunista de Colombia, PCC) called for the 'people's mass self-defence', advancing the revolutionary slogan, 'Reply to the violence of the reactionaries with the organized violence of the masses' (Partido Comunista de Colombia 1960: 93). The mountains of Colombia became the only place where resistance to the state terror could be organized. The PCC played a pivotal role in founding guerrilla camps for self-defence purposes (Pearce 1990). A regime of mass extermination of those in opposition to the government, particularly peasant movements pursuing agrarian reform, was set in motion. This gave rise to a spontaneous guerrilla movement as the masses took action to protect their lives and their property.

By 1958 *La Violencia* had cost the lives of approximately 300,000 Colombians. State terrorism continued through the creation of the *Frente Nacional* (Richani 2002). Washington's Cold War policy of anti-Communism helped to unify the Conservative and Liberal parties through the National Front. It was a united front between Colombia's landowners and the urban bourgeoisie. The basis for this political arrangement was to settle differences between Conservatives and Liberals with alternating presidencies: Alberto Llera Camargo (Liberal) 1958–62; Guillermo Leon Valencia (Conservative) 1962–6; Carlos Lleras Restrepo (Liberal) 1966–70; Misrael Pastrana Borrero (Conservative) 1970–4 (Osterling 1989). This exclusive bourgeois 'democracy' would be sustained with an iron fist until 1974.

The use of clandestine terror units was standard warfare for American counterinsurgency doctrine. General William Yarborough advised the Colombian government in 1962 to create an irregular unit trained to 'execute paramilitary, sabotage and/or terrorist activities against known communist proponents' (McClintock 1992: 222). The historian Greg Grandin (2006) notes that by the early 1960s the civil war between the state and emerging Communist-organized peasant 'republics' was seen as a potentially greater crisis than the one in Vietnam. The peasants, inspired by the Paris Commune in 1871 and the Chinese Revolution in 1949, created Marquetalia, the principal rebel agrarian community, and others in Rio Chiquito, El Pato-Guayabero, and Santa Barbara (Kirk 2003; Arenas 1972).

Marquetalia was the birthplace of US 'counter-terror' policy in Colombia with the use of American-trained death squads (Colby 1996). On 18 May 1964, the state terror campaign sent 16,000 troops (one-third of the Colombian army), accompanied by tanks, helicopters and warplanes supplied by the United States military, to destroy the department of Marquetalia. The PCC and peasant rebels retreated to the agricultural frontiers in Amazonia where the state had a limited presence (Schneider 2000). In the 1960s, US 'counter-terror' in Colombia was merely an extension of anti-guerrilla tactics developed in the Philippines and Guatemala years earlier. The CIA set out to induce fear and terror rather than win political allegiance (Grandin 2006).

The battle for Marquetalia marked a new beginning for the popular struggle in Colombia. The National Front which ruled the country with dictatorial powers secured the surrender of all guerrilla detachments with the exception of those led by the Communists. A general amnesty for all guerrilla fighters was promised which effectively neutralized the Liberal opposition. Contrary to Gaitan's hopes for liberal democracy, Liberal and Conservative parties run by urban and rural 'oligarchies' would maintain their reign of state terror and patronage well into the twenty-first century (Ospina 2008).

The Colombian writer, Antonio Garcia, wrote of the state terror that was unleashed on the defiant *campesinos*:

> We are harvesting the only crop which our 'historic parties' have sown: in this spilling of blood, in these odious crimes, in this unpunished cruelty, is summed up the sense of our party-laden history. Those truly responsible for this blood-letting are not the vulgar *delincuentes* ... [but] the political system which takes them as its instruments.
>
> (Caicedo 1954: 17, my translation)

## The US 'War on Drugs': state terror reorganized

Two years after Marquetalia, the popular insurgency became officially recognized as a guerrilla movement during the Tenth Congress of the

PCC (Gott 1970). *La Violencia* veterans Jacobo Arenas and Manuel Marulanda Velez (Tiro Fijo, Sure Shot) were its co-founders. The official name of the insurgency, Revolutionary Armed Forces of Colombia – People's Army (Fuerzas Armadas Revolucionaria de Colombia – Ejercito del Pueblo, FARC-EP), only became recognized nearly two decades later between 4 and 12 May 1982 during FARC's Seventh Congress proceedings (FARC-EP 2000). Arenas was of proletarian origin and already a member of the PCC when he met Marulanda, a young Liberal peasant leader. Arenas greatly influenced Tiro Fijo politically, and Marulanda joined the PCC, living to become one of history's most extraordinary revolutionary leaders until the old age of 84 (Petras 2008).

Other insurgent groups, the National Liberation Army (ELN), the Popular Liberation Army (EPL), and M-19, initiated operations soon after FARC, thereby intensifying the conflict for the nation's militarists, politicians and comprador bourgeoisie. Between 1970 and 1982 FARC grew from 500 *campesinos* to a peasant army of 3,000 fighters (FARC-EP 2000).

By the 1970s many Latin American countries were ruled by right-wing military juntas intent on combating Communism. At the same time the drug trade began receiving noticeable political and media attention. When President Nixon officially declared the US 'War on Drugs', the Southern Cone, and in particular the drug-linked Argentine military junta of 1976, targeted revolutionary movements throughout the continent with the backing of the notorious *Alianza Anticomunista Argentina* (Argentine Anticommunist Alliance, AAA) (Marshall *et al.* 1987).[1] In the 1970s the CIA offered training to Colombian and other Latin American police officers at its bomb school in Los Fresnos, Texas. The CIA taught a curriculum of 'Terrorist Concepts; Terrorist Devices; Fabrication and Functioning of Devices; Improvised Triggering Devices; Incendiaries; and Assassination Weapons: A Discussion of Various Weapons which may be Used by the Assassin'. The bomb school specialized in bomb making (McClintock 1992: 193).[2] Within a regional counterinsurgency plan against Communist-inspired insurgencies, Colombian 'democracy' adopted its own national counterinsurgency plan, incorporating anti-guerrilla paramilitary death squads linked to the country's emerging drug cartels. CIA assistance played an integral part in the Colombian state security apparatus and counterinsurgency strategy against FARC (Scott 2003).

After Argentina's military defeat in Las Malvinas in 1982, the Argentine connection, together with its links to the drug trade, were replaced by a multiplicity of criminal organizations and right-wing forces working closely with the CIA (Scott and Marshall 1998). The term 'narco-terrorism' became an essential adjunct to the doctrine of national security developed by right-wing Latin American militaries to justify their domestic state terror campaigns against leftist insurgencies. The Colombian state security apparatus, in conjunction with the CIA, had ongoing contacts with this right-wing nexus (Scott 2003). This was declared at the Fourteenth Bilateral

Intelligence Conference of the general staffs of the Argentine and Bolivian armies, held in Buenos Aires in August 1988 (Scott and Marshall 1998). The military leaders echoed President Reagan's warnings two years earlier concerning a 'link between the governments of such Soviet allies as Cuba and Nicaragua and international narcotics trafficking'. For Reagan, 'These twin evils – narcotics trafficking and terrorism', represented the most 'insidious and dangerous threats to the hemisphere' (Scott and Marshall 1998: 23). The military leaders agreed,

> narcoterrorism now constitutes a means of Revolutionary War. The international communist movement uses narcoterrorism as a socio-ideological procedure for provoking social imbalances, eroding community morale, and corrupting and disintegrating Western society, as part of the strategic objective of promoting the new Marxist order.
>
> (Scott and Marshall 1998: 24)

During the Conservative government of Belisario Betancur (1982–86), FARC founded the political party the Patriotic Union (Union Patriotica, UP), as part of the peace negotiations that the guerrillas and sectors of the Colombian left had initiated with the Betancur administration. Five thousand activists and leaders including elected officials, candidates and community organizers of the UP were assassinated. Eight congressmen, 70 councilors, dozens of deputies and mayors and hundreds of trade unionists and peasant leaders were targeted and two of the UP's presidential candidates were assassinated (Dudley 2004; Brittain 2010; Leech 2011). Any illusions of a Colombian parliamentary road to socialism were dashed.

The real face of Colombian bourgeois democracy was revealed through the US 'War on Drugs' to combat FARC. The so-called drug war masked Washington's sponsorship of Colombian state narco-terrorism. The available evidence reveals that the CIA had an ongoing relationship to key Colombian traffickers, dating back at least to the creation of the death squad Death to Kidnappers (Muerte a Sequestradores, MAS) in 1981 (Scott 2003). MAS was originally set up by the Cali Cartel and the Colombian military to retaliate against guerrillas who kidnapped members of the national business class for ransom. MAS targeted the revolutionary left, unionists and other enemies of the state. The Cali traffickers accepted a much larger role for the rising Medellin Cartel of Pablo Escobar Gaviria who would eventually dominate the Colombian cocaine industry (Lee 1998). The CIA worked with Colombian military officers to reorganize Colombia's intelligence network, strengthening pre-existing anti-guerrilla paramilitary death squads with direct links to the drug cartels (Human Rights Watch 1996).

The reorganization of Colombia's intelligence network in the early 1980s groomed the clandestine terror units which had already been created by the US military during the early period of the Cold War. Anti-guerrilla paramilitary death squads linked to the Medellin and Cali drug cartels laid the groundwork for Washington's counterinsurgency plans. The US and Colombian states' use of extreme methods to eliminate FARC went beyond simply national security concerns. They reflected a changing world, where a growing and lucrative drug business penetrated the Colombian system and indeed the entire Western Hemisphere.

## 'Plan Colombia': legitimizing state narco-terrorism

With the fall of the Berlin Wall in 1989, a deceptive debate in the West about the 'evils' and 'failures' of Soviet Communism was used to attack the relevance of revolutionary thought and organization in a post-Cold War world. Despite Western expectations, it did not weaken the popular struggle in Colombia (Petras 2001). In a coordinated effort with state narco-terror in Colombia, an imperialist propaganda assault targeted Marxism through the corporate mass media and political, legal and educational institutions, including the belief and value systems of religious organizations (Fukuyama 1992).

Meanwhile, the emergence of cocaine hydrochloride in the Colombian drug world offered a flourishing business opportunity for traffickers enmeshed in the drug trade. Colombia had been a supplier of marijuana to the US in the 1970s, but what became known as the 'cocaine decade' of the 1980s was a bonanza for the newly formed 'cartels' and especially for those who owned the best land in Colombia (Villar 2007).

Cocaine was unlike any other illegal drug in Colombia. It brought with it wealth, power and political acceptance in the comprador bourgeoisie. It also provided President Reagan with a snowball of American ideologies to attack FARC as 'narco-terrorists'. Prior to the end of the Cold War, Reagan condemned the left-wing Sandinista government in Nicaragua as a base of Soviet influence in Central America and a centre of 'narco-terrorism'. Rachel Ehrenfeld of the American Center for Democracy advanced the spectre of the 'narcoterrorist' in three books where Latin American guerrilla movements (principally in Colombia and Peru) were described as 'narcoterrorists' linked to Cuba and the Soviet Union (Ehrenfeld 1986, 1988, 1990). Ehrenfeld argued that with the demise of the East European Socialist bloc, 'narcoterrorism' replaced the ideological foundations of FARC with alleged links to the drug trade through Colombia's Medellin drug cartel, the Sandinista government and Cuba. Leading US counterinsurgency experts promoted Ehrenfeld's thesis to capitalize on an invented social panic about terrorists and drug traffickers and mobilize support for foreign interventions against leftist regimes in Latin America (Waghelstein 1987).

'Narco-terrorism' encompassed a variety of phenomena: guerrilla movements financed by drugs or taxes on drug traffickers, drug syndicates using terrorist methods to counter the state's law enforcement apparatus, and state-sponsored terrorism associated with drug crimes (Lupsha 1989). Colombia's future President, Alvaro Uribe Velez, represented the last phenomenon when he was a senator of Antioquia, according to a 1991 intelligence report from US Defense Intelligence Agency (DIA) officials in Colombia. Uribe was named one of the 'more important Colombian narco-traffickers contracted by the Colombian narcotics cartels for security, transportation, distribution, collection and enforcement of narcotics operations in both the US and Colombia' (National Security Archive 2004).

Between 1995 and 1997, Uribe helped set up a 'civilian–military force' known as Convivir while governor of Antioquia. This paramilitary force was absorbed by MAS's successor, the United Self-Defence Forces of Colombia (AUC) (Hylton 2006). By the mid-1990s, over 500 existed throughout the country, coercing rural civilians to act as paramilitaries under local military command (Aviles 2006; Tate 2002). Thousands of trade unionists, students and human rights workers were murdered, disappeared or were driven out of the province (Feiling 2004). The creation of 'civilian militias' was endorsed by a RAND study called *Colombian Labyrinth* (Rabasa and Chalk 2001). The American study was instrumental in legitimizing Cold War terror squads linked to the underworld in a more 'inclusive' and civilian-based counterinsurgency strategy. A 'top secret' report from the DIA leaked to the *Washington Post* concluded that FARC could defeat Colombia's military within five years unless the armed forces drastically restructured (Farah 1998).

The 1990s saw a bombardment of anti-FARC propaganda through the services of public relations firms such as the Sawyer/Miller Group, a leading PR company in the United States. Sawyer/Miller helped manufacture the left-wing narco-terrorist conspiracy. The director of Sawyer/Miller's Colombia account explained,

> the main mission is to educate the American media about Colombia, get good coverage, and nurture contacts with journalists, columnists, and think tanks. The message is that there are 'bad' and 'good' people in Colombia and that the government is the good guy.
>
> (Stokes 2005: 147)

The manufacture of consent was done through corporate America and its global power in mass communication to disseminate Colombian government propaganda, with the routine production of pamphlets, letters to editors signed by Colombian officials, and advertisements placed in leading bourgeois newspapers like the *New York Times* and the *Washington Post* (Stokes 2005).

The Reagan–Ehrenfeld message that FARC was a grouping of drug trafficking terrorists was promoted by disregarding the popular insurgency's clear class target and revolutionary objectives. The same distortion was applied to FARC's use of 'kidnapping'. FARC has practised 'retention' since the mid-1970s (Brittain 2010). FARC targets right-wing ideologues, members of the political elite and military, and those with relative wealth. These members of the ruling class remain in custody as prisoners of war until a monetary fee has been paid or a humanitarian prisoner exchange has been honoured. The latter is rarely the case. In the media, POWs held by FARC are misrepresented as 'hostages' who are 'starved', 'mistreated' and regularly 'beaten'. By comparison, according to the Australian organization Peace and Justice for Colombia, there are approximately 10,000 political prisoners incarcerated in Colombian prisons, living in inhumane conditions and subject to torture and rape. They come from backgrounds as diverse as universities, trade unions and armed combat and are collectively punished by being regularly transferred to maximum security sections dominated by paramilitary inmates (Peace and Justice for Colombia 2006).

A major study in 1999 by Colombia's National Planning Department and the Colombian Army estimated that both FARC and the ELN earned twice as much from kidnapping and robbery as from any alleged 'drug trafficking' activities (US Foreign Broadcast Information Service 1999).[3] No more than 2.5 per cent of all coca cultivation is traceable to the insurgents and it is confined only to taxation of the coca plant within Colombia (Wilson 2003). Colombian intelligence reports attribute the 2.5 per cent to 'cocaine exports', when right-wing paramilitary death squads of the AUC (now renamed the 'Black Eagles') control 40 per cent of the cocaine leaving the country (Scott 2003). The rest is monopolized by the Colombia's comprador 'narco-bourgeoisie' (Villar and Cottle 2012).

The legitimization of state narco-terror was finally completed with the official backing of US President Clinton. This was the most ambitious effort by an American president to continue the US commitment to support the Colombian security forces' combat against FARC. In 2000, Clinton authorized a $1.3 billion US package for the 'War on Drugs' titled 'Plan Colombia'. The plan mainly involved military assistance, including helicopters, planes and training, a massive chemical and biological warfare effort, and electronic surveillance technology (Storrs and Serafino 2002; Villar *et al.* 2003). The total budget for the Colombia plan was $7.5 billion to which the Colombian government originally pledged $4 billion, the US$1.3 billion, and the European Union and other countries $2.2 billion. The first formal draft of Plan Colombia was written in English, and the Spanish version only became available months after, when a revised English version was already in place (Livingstone 2003).

Clinton's promotion of 'Plan Colombia' was made easier by the absence of the 'Soviet menace' and the apparent 'destruction' of the drug cartels with the killing of Pablo Escobar in 1993. Carlos Castaño, who led the AUC, set up a vigilante group backed by the Cali cartel called Los Pepes (People Persecuted by Pablo Escobar). An investigation by Amnesty

International in 2001 filed a lawsuit to obtain CIA records on Los Pepes. The report found 'An extremely suspect relationship between the US government and the Castaño family – at a time when the US government was well aware of that family's involvement in paramilitary violence and narcotics trafficking' (Amnesty International 2001).

The CIA's ongoing relationship with anti-guerrilla paramilitary death squads continued under the Clinton presidency. Once Escobar was killed, Pepes was incorporated into the nationwide paramilitary network which accounted for the vast majority of political killings in Colombia (Amnesty International 2001; National Security Archive 2008). 'Plan Colombia' was post-Cold War American ideology and the complete militarization of Colombian society rolled into one. As for the drug war, Colombia's Central Bank estimated that 30 per cent of Colombia's total wealth derived from the cocaine trade (Richani 2002).

The machine for mass extermination of those in opposition to the Colombian government was ready to confront the new century as clandestine narco-terror units graduated into counterinsurgents. Consequently, US-sponsored Colombian state narco-terrorism became responsible for approximately 90 to 95 per cent of human rights violations due to high-intensity class warfare in the country (Brittain 2010).[4] State narco-terror would reach unimaginable proportions with the dramatic events unfolding in two key imperial centres on 11 September 2001.

## Post-11 September and class-based narco-fascism

From the mid-twentieth century, the FARC insurgency intensified the Colombian state's reliance upon both US military assistance and US involvement. By the new millennium, FARC had 18,000 fighters on 60 fronts and had built support bases in the *barrios* across the country that totalled at least 30,000 fighters. Its urban militia members were estimated at between 2,000 and 2,500 in Bogotá alone and between 4,000 and 6,000 in other key cities nationwide (Richani 2002). More recent fieldwork shows that FARC numbered between 40,000 and 50,000 fighters in the mid-2000s (Brittain 2010). These figures certainly represent a large percentage of the Colombian population of whom 68 per cent are poor peasants (Knoester 1998). The strength of the popular insurgency prompted American presidencies since Ronald Reagan's to condemn Latin America's oldest revolutionaries as 'narco-terrorists'. A flourishing cocaine trade with direct links to state terrorism has become acceptable 'counter-terror' policy.

The terrorist attacks of 11 September in New York and Washington DC provided the US and Colombian governments with virtually unrestrained political and military power. The 'War on Drugs' was intensified, the Colombian 'security forces' now being helped to do what they had been doing for more than 30 years. The war on Colombian 'narco-terrorists' became part of the US 'Global War on Terrorism' (GWOT) (Washington Office on Latin America 2004). In 2001 President Bush added $550 million to 'Plan Colombia', renaming it the 'Andean Regional Initiative' – his father George H.W. Bush had originally named it the 'Andean Initiative' (Giordano 2001). Between 1996 and 2001 US military aid to Colombia had increased fifteen-fold from $67 million to $1 billion (Tickner 2003). Bush's 'War on Terror' exposed the raw class character of US imperialism in Colombia and its comprador appendages through their politico-military emphasis on FARC.

The Bush presidency coincided with the rise to power of Alvaro Uribe Velez. He came from a wealthy landowning family and his father, Alberto Uribe Sierra, was subject to an extradition warrant for drug trafficking charges in the United States. This made him a likely target for FARC and he was eventually killed in 1983. Uribe's 'narcopolitics' was developed by his growing up with the children of Fabio Ochoa, three of whom became leading members of Pablo Escobar's Medellin cartel (Contreras and Garavito 2002; Hylton 2006). Uribe's paramilitary connections deterred many from looking into his links to the drug cartels. An exception was *Noticias Uno,* a current affairs programme on the television station Canal Uno. In April 2002 this programme examined alleged links between Uribe and the Medellin cartel. After the reports were aired, unidentified men threatened to kill the investigative journalist, Ignacio Gomez (Feiling 2004).[5]

In 2003 in the context of GWOT, Bush and Uribe intensified the class war with an all-out offensive against FARC titled 'Plan Patriota', which authorized state narco-terror. Uribe's 'democratic security' measures rendered any policy titles of little importance. Uribe's focus on FARC was a continuation, strongly enhanced, of what his predecessor Andres Pastrana (1998–2002) had begun with Clinton's 'Plan Colombia'.

During the Pastrana government, FARC controlled San Vicente Del Caguan, known as the *zona de despeje* or the demilitarized zone (DMZ). The DMZ consisted of five municipalities the size of Switzerland, where tens of thousands of workers and peasants lived and participated in its daily management (Leech 2002). London's *Daily Telegraph* described San Vicente Del Caguan as '"FARClandia", the world's newest country' (Lamb 2000; Novak 1999). To justify invading the DMZ, on 21 February 2002 Pastrana accused FARC of running a lucrative drug trafficking business from San Vicente and of hiding kidnap victims in the zone (Ruth 2002). The town had become a base for peace negotiations initiated by FARC. Under pressure from the United States, Pastrana ordered the Colombian military to invade the zone and the Colombian air force to bomb its communities. FARC's 'independent republic' had been the safest region in all Colombia (Hylton 2006). Anticipating bloodshed for San Vicente's population, FARC ordered residents to evacuate and retreat to nearby mountain jungles where most of the guerrillas were located. Like Marquetalia in 1964, the Colombian military offensive on San Vicente Del Caguan was an attack on FARC's ability to construct an alternative socialist society; it had little to do with 'drug trafficking' or 'terrorism' charges.

President Uribe (2002–10) accelerated the conflict with FARC by means of full US military and intelligence support. In Uribe's Colombia, there was no 'conflict', whereas past presidents including Andres Pastrana had acknowledged that the militant *campesinos* were an inherent part of Colombia's troubled history (Gardner 2000). The official line was that 'narco-terrorists' were trying to overthrow a democratic state. 'If Colombia [did] not have drugs, it would not have terrorists', Uribe said in a speech to the Organization of American States (OAS) Permanent Council (2004).

In October 2002 reports were leaked indicating that United States special operations teams were on 'orders to eliminate all high officers of the FARC', 'scattering those who escape to the remote corners of the Amazon' (Garamone 2004; Gorman 2002). In 2008 FARC was seriously hit when its chief negotiator, Comandante Raul Reyes, and another senior member, Ivan Rios, were murdered. In the same year, the legendary Manuel Marulanda (Tiro Fijo) died of natural causes at the old age of 84. James Brittain (2010) has well documented how despite media claims that the high-profile deaths considerably weakened FARC, causing 'desertions' and 'organizational decay', 'Plan Patriota' prematurely claimed victory over it. In reality, the 'insurgency witnessed combatant growth amidst triumphs over corporate and state interests' (Brittain 2010: 23). FARC's political and military strength is only disputed for ideological reasons. Experts from former US Ambassador to El Salvador Robert White to Colombian historian Herbert Braun have argued that FARC will not and cannot be defeated (Braun 2003; Chernick 2007; Ungerman and Brohy 2003). The popular insurgency marches on in clandestine form.

Regardless of Colombia's revolutionary capacity to defeat US imperialism, a very high price has to be paid to wage a struggle against the 'oligarchy' which Gaitan once opposed. In sharp contrast to the restoration of liberal democracy in Argentina, Uruguay and Chile in the second half of the twentieth century, working-class, radical and leftist parties have been violently repressed in Colombia. Uribe and his successor, Defence Minister Juan Manuel Santos, have cemented the most reactionary and extremist of class forces within the Colombian 'oligarchy'.

Between 2007 and 2008, the worsening human rights situation in Colombia prompted Uribe to extradite top paramilitary leaders to the United States solely on charges of drug trafficking. Salvatore Mancuso, the leader of the former AUC (now 'Black Eagles'), testified, 'I am proof positive of state paramilitarism in Colombia' (Forero 2007). The 'parapolitica' scandal did little to affect the Uribe government. If anything, the scandal exposed a deeply disturbing reality about the country, given the Western media's and politicians' ongoing celebrations of Colombian 'democracy' (Bronstein 2007). It has demonstrated that there is significant support for what can be described as 'narco-fascism' in Colombia.

The extradition of Mancuso and other paramilitary leaders such as Diego Murillo (aka 'Don Berna'), Hernan Giraldo and Rodrigo Tovar (aka 'Jorge 40'), known for his annihilation of *Kankuamo* Indians in the northern Sierra Nevada de Santa Marta mountains, unravelled hidden truths about Colombia. First, the Colombian ruling class maintains its power through mass violence, social exclusion and centralized authority. And second, FARC is not the only target of state narco-terrorism. More unionists are murdered by state narco-terrorism in Colombia than in all the rest of the world combined (Stokes 2005; Leech 2011). Considering that FARC's popular support comes predominantly from the poorest sectors of Colombian society, fascism of any kind cannot exist without significant support for the Uribe–Santos comprador regime. *El Tiempo*'s main shareholders, former Vice-President Francisco Santos and Juan Manuel Santos, explained, 'If the whole county is responsible, then no one is responsible' (cited in Forero 2007).

Responsibility rests with the 'oligarchy's' support base. During Uribe's campaign for the presidency in 2002, his war platform against FARC and the ELN was popular among the middle and upper classes. In rural regions, Uribe's paramilitary connections ensured support for the 'popular' president at gunpoint. Uribe received 53 per cent of the votes with media headlines marking it as a 'landslide' victory (Murillo 2003). According to Rafael Garcia, a former high-level official in Colombia's intelligence agency currently serving 11 years in Colombia for money-laundering among other charges, the 2002 presidential elections were 'massive electoral fraud' as paramilitary groups personally selected the candidates for Congress (Anonymous 2007). In 2006, it was no surprise that Uribe was re-elected with 63 per cent of the vote. Again, it was important to vote, as one local paramilitary informed voters, for the 'one wearing glasses' (Vieira 2008). In the recent 2010 presidential elections, Juan Manuel Santos won too, with 69 per cent of the vote (*Daily Telegraph* 2010).

The middle and upper classes constitute approximately 30 per cent of the population and all opinion polls are conducted by telephone, which explains 'record high' approval ratings. In a country where the majority of the people are poor and do not have access to landlines or mobile phones, the Uribe–Santos regime is clearly totalitarian and the political system strictly based on class lines and a climate of fear (Leech 2002; Taussig 2003). FARC enjoys significantly more backing than is acknowledged by 'Colombian' opinion polls, government officials and the mainstream media (Brittain 2010; Leech 2011).

State narco-terrorism is unpopular in Colombia. The Uribe–Santos regime has effectively replaced the traditional authoritarian oligarchy with a 'democracy' that the United States could not openly support in Argentina, Chile or Central America during Latin America's darkest chapters in recent memory. Unlike the fascism of Adolf Hitler or Benito Mussolini, support for Colombian narco-fascism is not multi-class (Gross 1980). Colombian narco-fascism has surpassed the fascism of Guatemala (200,000) and Argentina (30,000) totalling 250,000 'desaparecidos' in the last two decades (Robles 2011). According to Colombian investigative journalist Azalea Robles, the German model has been applied to systematically reduce these figures with the use of crematory ovens and thousands of mass graves throughout the country. Since 2005, 173,183 political assassinations have been carried out against the Colombian left. Death squads are not only an arm of the state; they appear to enjoy the 'popular' support of the middle and upper classes. They are responsible for the dispossession of 5.2 million peasants and play a major role in linking the 'oligarchy' and the political elite to the multi-billion-dollar cocaine trade (Ospina 2008). According to Salvatore Mancuso, 100 politicians in Colombia's Congress have direct links to right-wing narco-terrorists (Thompson 2008). The growth of and support for narco-fascism have clearly been the product of US imperialism and its 'War on Drugs' and 'War on Terror' post-9/11.

## Conclusion: the untouchables?

An 'untouchable' class of comprador appendages in the service of US imperialism has been left relatively undisturbed by the 'international community'. It has constructed a nationwide secret police network of 1.6 million spies; ruled by presidential decree, suspending all constitutional guarantees; endorsed the forced recruitment of 'civilian militias' across the country; trained and armed approximately 30,000 narco-terror units, allowing the nation to become the largest recipient of US military aid and training in the world after Israel and the Middle East; applauded the official secret police of Juan Manuel Santos, the Security Administrative Department (DAS), which numbers in the tens of thousands; encouraged the development of private militias by landowners, bankers and business leaders involving private security firms numbering over 150,000 assassins; and most disturbingly, it was able to mobilize 1 million fanatical Uribistas against FARC at the height of the 'parapolitica' in the spring of 2008.

The election of Obama in 2008 promised 'change' for US–Latin American relations. In his presidential debate with Republican rival John McCain, Obama stated, 'The history in Colombia right now is that labour leaders have been targeted for assassination on a fairly consistent basis and there have not been prosecutions' (*Los Angeles Times* 2008). But as in George W. Bush's initiative in 2001, Obama has Colombia nearly $600 million, signifying continuing support to its security forces in their fight against 'narco-terrrorism' (Shifter 2010). In 2009 Obama seriously considered establishing seven new US military bases in Colombia to respond to the extraordinary war of liberation waged by FARC. The Obama administration praised the Colombian security forces for murdering FARC Comandante Jorge Briceno (Mono Jojoy) in 2010 and former FARC leader Alfonso Cano in 2011 (Feller 2010; *The Age* 2011).

Colombia has become what Hernando Calvo Ospina (2008) described as a 'laboratory of the extreme right'. Its success or failure will ultimately depend on the will of the 'real country', as Gaitan explained. Since Marquetalia 1964, the people's struggle for national liberation has fearlessly confronted the Anglo-American empire and its political and economic interests, with all its instruments of terror, drugs, lies and genocidal oppression.

## Notes

1 The AAA was an international network which aimed to make Buenos Aires its neo-fascist centre.
2 Citing Office of Public Safety, International Police Academy, syllabus for Course No. 6.
3 The study appeared in Colombia's *El Tiempo* on 17 May, 1999 and was analysed and translated into English by the CIA's FBIS, renamed the Open Source Center in November 2005.
4 It is worth noting that FARC is only one of several organizations categorized as 'guerrillas' by a wide variety of human rights sources.
5 Gomez was awarded the 2002 International Press Freedom Award. Upon his accepting the award, the US press censored his comments: 'The picture of war is getting blurry, and Americans, whose taxes and whose drug consumption fuel this war, should be concerned'.

## References

*The Age* (2011) 'Colombia Urges FARC Talks after Cano Kill', 6 November, online. Available http://news.theage.com.au/breaking-news-world/Colombia-urges-farc-talks-after-cano-kill-20111108-1n1ke.html (accessed 10 November 2011).

Amnesty International (2001) 'President Clinton Must Order Investigation into Allegations of US Collusion with Colombian Death Squads: Amnesty International USA Prepares to Sue CIA, DEA, and Others for Unlawfully Withholding Information About Alleged Collusion', Washington DC, 25 April.

Anonymous (2007) 'Detenidos otros cinco Congresistas por caso de la parapolítica', *La República*, 16 February.

Arenas, J. (1972) *Diario de la Resistencia de Marquetalia*, Bogotá: Abejon Mono.

Aviles, W. (2006) *Global Capitalism, Democracy, and Civil–Mililtary Relations in Colombia*, New York: SUNY.

Braun, H. (2003) *Our Guerrillas, Our Sidewalks: A Journey Into the Violence of Colombia*, New York: Rowman & Littlefield.

Brittain, J.J. (2010) *Revolutionary Social Change in Colombia: The Origin and Direction of the FARC-EP*, New York: Pluto Press.

Bronstein, H. (2007) 'Popularity of Colombia's Uribe up despite Scandal', *Reuters*, 14 February.

Caicedo, D. (1954) *Viento Seco*, Buenos Aires: Editorial Nuestra America.

Campos, M.G.G., O.F. Borda and E.U. Luna. (1963) *La Violencia en Colombia*, Bogotá: Ediciones Tercer Mundo.

Chernick, M.W. (2007) 'FARC-EP: From Liberal Guerillas Marxist Rebels to Post-Cold War Insurgents', in M. Heiberg, B. O'Leary and J. Tirman (eds) *Terror,*

*Insurgency, and the State: Ending Protracted Conflicts*, Philadelphia: University of Pennsylvania Press.

Colby, G. (1996) *Thy Will Be Done: The Conquest of the Amazon, Nelson Rockefeller and Evangelism in the Age of Oil*, New York: HarperCollins.

Contreras, J. and F. Garavito (2002) *Biografía No Autorizada de Álvaro Uribe Vélez: El Señor de las Sombras*, Bogotá: Editorial Oveja Negra.

*Daily Telegraph* (2010) *Colombian Presidential Election: Juan Manuel Santos Wins by Landslide*, 21 June, online. Available on: www.telegraph.co.uk/news/worldnews/southamerica/colombia/7842602/Colombian-presidential-election-Juan-Manuel-Santos-wins-by-landslide.html (accessed 20 October 2010).

Dudley, S. (2004) *Walking Ghosts: Murder and Guerrilla Politics in Colombia*, New York: Routledge.

Ehrenfeld, R. (1986) *Narcoterrorism: The Kremlin Connection*, New York: Heritage Foundation.

Ehrenfeld, R. (1988) *Narcoterrorism and the Cuban Connection*, Miami: Cuban American National Foundation.

Ehrenfeld, R. (1990) *Narcoterrorism*, New York: Basic Books.

Farah, D. (1998) 'Colombian Rebels Seen Winning War; U.S. Study Finds Army Ill-Equipped', *Washington Post*, 10 April.

FARC-EP (2000) *FARC-EP: Historical Outline*, Toronto: International Commission.

Feiling, T. (2004) 'Alvaro Uribe Velez', *New Internationalist*, 1 October.

Feller, B. (2010) 'Obama Praises Colombia in Wake of Rebel's Death', in *Associated Press*, 24 September.

Forero, J. (2007) 'Paramilitary Ties to Elite In Colombia Are Detailed: Commanders Cite State Complicity in Violent Movement', *Washington Post*, 22 May.

Fukuyama, F. (1992) *The End of History and the Last Man*, New York: The Free Press.

Galeano, E. (2009) *Mirrors: Stories of Almost Everyone*, New York: Nation Books.

Garamone, J. (2004) 'Special Operations Part of US–Colombia Plan to Reinforce Success', *American Forces Press Service*, 1 April.

Gardner, D. (2000) 'Losing the Drug War', *Ottawa Citizen*, 23 February.

Giordano, A. (2001) *Bush Ups Ante on Plan Colombia*, online. Available on: www.drugpolicy.org/news/03_13_01plancolombia2.cfm (accessed 18 October 2010).

Gorman, P. (2002) 'Marines Ordered into Colombia: February 2003 is Target Date', *The Narco News Bulletin*, 25 October.

Gott, R. (1970) *Guerrilla Movements in Latin America*, New York: Nelson.

Grandin, G. (2006) *Empire's Workshop: Latin America, the United States, and the Rise of the New Imperialism*, New York: Henry Holt.

Gross, B. (1980) *Friendly Fascism: The New Face of Power in America*, Boston: South End Press.

Human Rights Watch (1996) *Colombia's Killer Networks: The Military–Paramilitary Partnership and the United States*, New York.

Hylton, F. (2006) *Evil Hour in Colombia*, London: Verso.

Idels, M. (2002) *Colombia and the New Latin American Keys to US and Global Lies*, 8 November, online. Available on: www.bluegreenearth.us/archive/article/2002/idels5.html (accessed 11 December 2005).

Kirk, R. (2003) *More Terrible Than Death: Massacres, Drugs and America's War in Colombia*, New York: PublicAffairs.

Knoester, M. (1998) *Washington's Role in Colombian Repression*, online. Available on:

www.zcommunications.org/title-washingtons-role-in-colombian-repression-by-matthew-knoester (accessed 2 July 2010).

Lamb, C. (2000) 'Colombian Rebels Plan for Cocaine War', *Daily Telegraph*, 3 September.

Lee, R.W. (1998) *The White Labyrinth: Cocaine and Political Power*, New Brunswick: Transaction Publishers.

Leech, G.M. (2002) *Killing Peace: Colombia's Conflict and the Failure of U.S. Intervention*, New York: Information Network of the Americas.

Leech, G.M. (2011) *The FARC: The Longest Insurgency*, New York: 2ed Books.

Livingstone, G. (2003) *Inside Colombia: Drugs, Democracy, and War*, New Jersey: Rutgers University Press.

Los Angeles Times. (2008) *Complete Final Debate Transcript: John McCain and Barack Obama*, online. Available on: http://latimesblogs.latimes.com/washington/2008/10/debate-transcri.html (accessed 20 October 2010).

Lupsha, P.A. (1989) 'Towards an Etiology of Drug Trafficking and Insurgent Relations: The Phenomenon of Narco-Terrorism', *International Journal of Comparative and Applied Criminal Justice*, 13: 60–74.

McClintock, M. (1992) *Instruments of Statecraft: U.S. Guerrilla Warfare, Counterinsurgency, and Counterterrorism, 1940–1990*, New York: Pantheon.

Marshall, J., P.D. Scott and J. Hunter (1987) *The Iran–Contra Connection: Secret Teams and Covert Operations in the Reagan Era*, Boston: South End Press.

Murillo, M. (2003) *Colombia and the United States: War, Terrorism, and Destabilization*, New York: Seven Stories Press.

National Security Archive (2004) *US Intelligence Listed Colombian President Uribe Among 'Important Colombian Narco-Traffickers in 1991'*, online. Available on: www.gwu.edu/~nsarchiv/NSAEBB/NSAEBB131/index.htm (accessed 14 October 2010).

National Security Archive (2008) *Colombian Paramilitaries and the United States: 'Unraveling the Pepes Tangled Web'*, online. Available on: www.gwu.edu/~nsarchiv/NSAEBB/NSAEBB243/index.htm (accessed 18 October 2010).

Novak, R.D. (1999) 'Terrorism Close to Home', *Washington Post*, 19 April.

Organization of American States (2004) 'Colombian President Thanks OAS for Unconditional Solidarity, Press Release from the OAS', Washington: Permanent Council.

Ospina, H.C. (2008) *Colombia, Laboratorio de Embrujos: Democracia y Terrorismo de Estado*, Madrid: Ediciones Akal.

Osterling, J.P. (1989) *Democracy in Colombia: Clientelist Politics and Guerrilla Warfare*, Oxford: Transaction.

Partido Comunista de Colombia (1960) *Treinta Años de Lucha del Partido Comunista de Colombia*, Bogotá: Ediciones Paz y Socialismo.

Peace and Justice for Colombia (2006) 'Report on Colombia', Latin america Solidarity Conference, University of Technology, Sydney, 10 October.

Pearce, J. (1990) *Colombia: Inside the Labyrinth*, London: Latin America Bureau (Research and Action) Limited.

Petras, J. (2001) 'The Geopolitics of Plan Colombia', *Monthly Review*, 53: 30–49.

Petras, J. (2008) *Homage to Manuel Marulanda*, online. Available on: http://petras.lahaine.org/articulo.php?p=1736 (accessed 15 October 2010).

Rabasa, A. and P. Chalk (2001) *Colombian Labyrinth: The Synergy of Drugs and Insurgency and Its Implications for Regional Stability*, New York: PublicAffairs.

Richani, N. (2002) *Systems of Violence: The Political Economy of War and Peace in Colombia*, New York: State University of New York Press.
Robles, A. (2011) *250 mil desaparecidos claman justicia, y Falsimedia confunde para seguir desapareciendo la verdad*, online. Available on: www.rebelion.org/noticia.php?id=122896 (accessed 21 March 2011).
Ruth, M. (2002) 'UN Tries to Avert War in Colombia', *Independent*, 13 January.
Schneider, C.L. (2000) 'Violence, Identity and Spaces of Contention in Chile, Argentina and Colombia', *Social Research*, 67: 773–802.
Scott, P.D. (2003) *Drugs, Oil, and War: The United States in Afghanistan, Colombia, and Indochina*, London: Rowman & Littlefield.
Scott, P.D. and J. Marshall (1998) *Cocaine Politics: Drugs, Armies, and the CIA in Central America*, London: University of California Press.
Shifter, M. (2010) 'A Decade of Plan Colombia: Time for a New Approach', *Inter-American Dialogue*, 21 June, online. Available on: www.thedialogue.org/page.cfm?PageID=32&pubID=2407 (accessed 15 Sepember 2010).
Stokes, D. (2005) *America's Other War: Terrorizing Colombia*, New York: Zed Books.
Storrs, L.K. and N.M. Serafino. (2002) 'Andean Regional Initiative (ARI): FY 2002 Assistance for Colombia and Neighbours', Washington DC: Congressional Research Service Report.
Tate, W. (2002) 'Colombia: The Right Gathers Momentum', *NACLA Report on the Americas*, 35: 16–19.
Taussig, M. (2003) *Law in a Lawless Land: Diary of a 'Limpieza' in Colombia*, New York: The New Press.
Thompson, M. (2008) 'The Secret War of Colombia', *Sydney Morning Herald*, 17 August.
Tickner, A.B. (2003) 'Colombia and the United States: From Counternarcotics to Counterterrorism', *Current History*, 102: 77–85.
Ungerman, G. and A. Brohy (2003) 'Plan Colombia: Cashing-in on the Drug War Failure': Free-Will Productions (DVD), documentary.
US Foreign Broadcast Information Service (1999) 'Joint Study Sums Up FARC, ELN Earnings – Document #FTS19990517001601', ed. CIA, Reston, VA.
Vieira, C. (2008) *Mark Him on the Ballot – The One Wearing Glasses*, online. Available on: http://ipsnews.net/news.asp?idnews=42290 (accessed 19 October 2010).
Villar, O. (2007) 'US Narcocolonialism? Colombian Cocaine and Twenty-First Century Imperialism', *Research in Political Economy*, 24: 97–128.
Villar, O. and D. Cottle (2012) *Cocain, Death Squads, and the War on Terror: US Imperialism and Class Struggle in Colombia*, New York: Monthly Review Press.
Villar, O., D. Cottle and A. Keys. (2003) 'The Kill for Drugs Policy? Ecocide in Rural Colombia', Greening Sustainability – XIV Ecopolitics Conference of the Ecopolitics Association of Australasia, RMIT University, Melbourne, 27 November.
Waghelstein, J.D. (1987) 'Latin American Insurgency Status Report', *Military Review*, 47: 42–7.
Washington Office on Latin America. (2004) 'Trends in US Military Programs in Latin America', Washington DC.
Weiner, T. (2008) *Legacy of Ashes: The History of the CIA*, London: Penguin Books.
Wilson, S. (2003) 'Coca Trade Booming Again in Peru: US-Sponsored Eradication Plans Spark Peasant Protests', *Washington Post*, 22 March.

# 9 The criminalization of anti-colonial struggle in Puerto Rico

*José M. Atiles-Osoria*

## Introduction

This chapter analyses the criminalization of anti-colonial struggle in Puerto Rico (henceforth PR) by the United States of North America (henceforth USA), and its security agencies. Broadly, I intend to show that many of the legal and political strategies and the state terrorism implemented in the current 'war on terror' have their foundation in the strategies of colonization and legitimation of colonialism in PR. In that sense it is important to understand that an approach to the colonial conflict between PR and the USA must necessarily take into consideration colonialism's various and multiple forms. As a starting point, this approach should recognize that colonialism represents a complex structure where different narratives, scales of power, legitimacy and violence are expressed and manifested in terms of material, spatial and territorial (geopolitical) entities, as well as in epistemological and existential (biopolitical) forms.

This chapter explores the significance of the concept of the state of exception for understanding colonial 'counter-terrorism'. The state of exception has been traditionally understood as the suspension of the rule of law and certain constitutional guarantees by the sovereign, which has the effect of normalizing an 'emergency situation' (Agamben 2005). When we analyse this phenomenon in the context of colonialism, the state of exception begins to look rather different. On a more political level, which not only refers to the liberal-legal analysis of the suspension of the rule of law, but involves the creation of identities and sub-identities, we can see the legitimation of colonial violence, the overlap or superposition of law on politics and the criminalization of those who oppose the colonial regime.

In that sense Agamben's extensive and otherwise persuasive analysis of the state of exception does not really account for all the contexts in which this concept can be applied, notably contexts where a liberal juridical perspective on rights does not apply. A telling example is the colonial situation with its spaces and subjects that are very different from Western liberal-democratic orders. The colonized cannot stand up for their rights as they have never been holders of rights according to the dynamics of colonialism.

This relationship between colonialism and the state of exception has received little attention in the literature. However, two authors have begun to develop, from different perspectives, an analysis of these forms of control and domination. Their accounts illustrate, to some extent, the relationship between colonialism and the state of exception. On the one hand, Santos (2007) suggests that colonies always exist in a paradigm of appropriation/violence. This paradigm implies that the spaces, epistemologies and ways of life in the colonies are rendered invisible, and that colonial ideologies overlap. The organization of the appropriation of the human, natural and cultural resources of colonized peoples, and the exercise of power manifested through multiple and diverse forms of violence, lead the author to argue that colonies live under a permanent or 'normalized' state of exception (Santos 2007). Thereby, a state of exception should not be understood as merely a legal-political strategy, as I try to show above, but also involves the configuration of the subject and colonized identities as well as the power exercised over them.

On the other hand Venator (2006) argues that the state of exception imposed in PR by the USA is not solely related to the liberal-legal interpretation given in the work of Agamben (2005), but can be used to explain the power strategies used by the USA in the process of colonization and legitimation of colonial violence. From this perspective, then, a 'state of exception' refers not only to the elimination of the rule of law and certain legal guarantees, but can also be understood as a foundation of colonialism.

There is a long academic tradition that deals with colonialism and its violence, through the lens of different experiences and concrete cases. First, the writings of Fanon (1999), then postcolonial theories (Bhabha 1994; Spivak 1999) and now the current studies on 'decoloniality or the decolonial turn' (Grosfoguel 2003, 2007; Mignolo 2005; Quijano 2000) have described features of colonialism such as its relations of violence, racism, discrimination and human rights violations. Likewise, when I speak of repression, state violence and the criminalization of Puerto Rican independence movements, there are a considerable number of authors who have previously tackled the issue. Those include Acosta (1998) and her analysis of the Gag Law; Bosques and Colón (1997) and their research on the violation of freedoms and civil and political rights by the police of PR and its programme/practices of creating secret files and lists of 'subversive people'. There is also their analysis of the political persecution carried out by the US Federal Bureau of Investigation (FBI) and its programme COINTELPRO; Nieves Falcón's (2002, 2009) analytical account of political repression during the first century of US colonialism in PR; and Paralitici's (2004) research on the Puerto Rican independence actors jailed over a century of colonial history of US hegemony.

Following the call made by Jackson (2010: 234) and in the introduction to this book to rethink and redescribe the uses of state terrorism in colonial conflicts, I will develop an analysis of legal structures that have legitimized the practices and uses of violence in the Puerto Rican colonial conflict. To this end, I shall observe and describe one of the micro-histories that denote the complexity of the colonial matrix discussed above. At the same time, I will show how the law has played a central role in the maintenance of these power structures and in the legitimization of state counter-terrorism terrorism and the criminalization of the Puerto Rican independence movements. To achieve this aim, I incorporate an analytical narrative of the state of exception as the foundation of the superstructure or colonial power matrix.

The chapter will argue for an expanded understanding of the state of exception, going beyond the use of this concept by Agamben, Santos and Venator, and opening up new ways of thinking about colonial violence. To this end, the chapter will illustrate how the colonized government of PR, with the complicity of the US government, has implemented various forms of state terrorism. These have also enabled 'paramilitaries' and extreme right-wing groups to exercise terrorist violence against the Puerto Rican independence movement, which has resulted in multi-dimensional colonial conflict.

In order to develop these lines of argument, the chapter is divided into three parts. In the first part, the colonial and political history of PR is described. In the second part, I reflect on the concept of the state of exception, addressing its historical development and implementation in PR. The third part is informed by a twofold purpose. On the one hand, I aim to provide an overview of state terrorism and the criminalization of the independence movements in PR. In so doing, I will show how the laws and practices implemented by the USA and the colonial state of PR criminalize the Puerto Rican anti-colonial movements. On the other hand, I will discuss some of the proposals, epistemological considerations and strategies designed by the Puerto Rican anti-colonial movements to resist US colonialism, the PR colonial government, and right-wing movements in PR.

## 1 Puerto Rico: a brief political and colonial history

PR, a nation without a state, or a colony of the USA, constitutes a particular and interesting case for politics and international law. This Caribbean archipelago[1] was invaded by the USA in 1898, in the historical context of the Spanish–Cuban–US War and as a result of a series of economic, geo-political and colonial-imperialist interests developed in the USA since the mid-nineteenth century (Nieves Falcón 2009). PR, the Philippines and Guam were ceded as spoils of war to the US government under the Treaty of Paris. This treaty was signed after Spain lost the Spanish–Cuban–US

War, ending nearly 400 years of Spanish colonial rule on PR (Nieves Falcón 2009; Rivera Ramos 1996, 2001).

Subsequently, in 1900, under the organic law known as the Foraker Act,[2] and after two years of military rule, a 'civil' government was established in PR (Raffucci 1981). At this time, the territory became a domain of the US Congress under the Territorial Clause,[3] which subjugates the sovereign powers of the Puerto Rican nation to the US legal system. At the same time, and as a result of the judicial decisions and opinions expressed in the Insular Cases (discussed below), the US Supreme Court decided: 'PR belongs to the U.S., but it is not part of it' (Burnett 2005; Rivera Ramos 2001; Venator 2006).[4] This legal and political construction established an area of political and socio-legal indeterminacy, or what might be described as a permanent state of exception (Agamben 2005). In 1917 the Jones Act was passed, and reformed part of the Foraker Act of 1900. One of the few major changes introduced by the Jones Act was the imposition of US citizenship upon Puerto Ricans, despite the opposition of the majority of the population of PR, its political leader, and a good part of US leaders and citizens (Nieves Falcón 2009).

The colonial status of PR takes a new turn in 1950 with the creation of the Commonwealth of PR. The Commonwealth of PR was established as a legal and political category in 1952 under Public Law 600 of 1950 of the US Congress[5] and was presented to the UN in 1953. It is important to stress that since its creation in the late 1960s the UN Committee of Decolonization had been putting pressure on the US to resolve the situation of PR (Gautier and Argüelles 1978). This supposed solution to the Puerto Rican colonial conflict was presented to the UN as a strategy to legitimize the colonization of one of the last territories in Latin America and the Caribbean to remain under direct colonial rule.

The outcome of this strategic manoeuvre was that the particular status of PR was introduced into politics and international law. With the concept of 'Commonwealth', the Caribbean archipelago was transformed into a new form of colony (Rivera Ramos 2001). The category of Commonwealth grants a measure of legal, economic and political power to PR, departing significantly from the classical model of colonialism. Nevertheless, PR did not become a 'post-' or 'neo-colonial' state, or a state liberated from colonialism, since the USA did not transfer sovereignty to the people of PR and its political institutions. In other words, the USA continues to exercise sovereignty in PR, as distinct from the model proposed by neo- and post-colonial theorists who assert that post-colonial states are sovereign states that remain subject to some degree of political, military, cultural and economic intervention or control by the former colonial power (see, for example, Young 2001). By contrast, PR has been locked into the same socio-political-legal situation since 1898, when it was invaded by the USA and a state of exception was imposed to support the colonial administration. With the benefit of historical hindsight it becomes clear that the only thing that changed in 1950 with the imposition of Commonwealth was the name and the ways of legitimizing colonialism. Colonial strategies of control and domination remained basically the same.

These historical-political dimensions have made PR a landmark in contemporary colonialism and one case where US colonial and hegemonic practices could be traced (Rivera Ramos 1998). However, during this colonial period there have been dozens of movements, groups and organizations which have struggled for national independence and have sought to challenge the 'appropriation/violence' paradigm that characterizes the state of exception in existing colonies (Santos 2007). Many of these movements have acted within the law, using electoral strategies; others have acted on the boundary between legality and illegality; yet others have opted for armed struggle as a contingency strategy. This diversity of struggles, counter-hegemonic proposals and anti-colonial ethical discourses has nourished Puerto Rican revolutionary nationalism (González 2006). As we will see in the following sections of this chapter, all these movements have faced various forms of persecution, repression, criminalization and state violence. State violence is a fundamental feature of the socio-legal-political situation in PR, which must be understood primarily as a colonial conflict.

## 2 The state of exception as hegemonic action

As Agamben (2005) has shown, the state of exception is not a new phenomenon as a legal term or strategy. This concept has been used at various historical moments, for example in the Roman Empire, the French Revolution and the Nazi concentration camps. Nowadays, emergency powers have been invoked as part of the 'war on terror' to support US global hegemony. However, Agamben's account falls short when it comes to addressing the implementation of the state of exception in the colonial context.

Rivera Ramos (1996, 2001) has argued that the expansionist project of the US during the nineteeth and twentieth centuries, and its purpose in building a nation-state, were followed by legitimating practices through the law, the creation of alternative legal identities and the incorporation of the rule of law into the colonized territories. The uses of the law as a tool to legitimize the violence involved in colonialism (Atiles-Osoria 2008; Fanon 1999; Foucault 1995; Memmi 1974; Santos 2002) and the configuration of US hegemony in local and global contexts have allowed the development of different constitutional and political entities that enable the sovereign to reach beyond the confines of the nation-state. Law, in other words, is central to the exercise of power through 'empire'. This has not only resulted in the political-juridical legitimation of colonial practices, but has provided legitimacy for the development of repressive policies against counter-hegemonic and anti-colonial actors. This hegemonic effect is clear in the case of Puerto Rican revolutionary nationalism and the current 'war on terror'. These strategies have created a space of 'indistinction' or an indeterminate space, or a set of practices that I have described above as a state of exception.

The state of exception as a narrative or analytical strategy traditionally implies a double rationality: on the one hand, the use of the state of exception has been explained in the light of constitutional law theories, history of law and critical legal theories. On the other hand, the state of exception has been understood as an onto-political category in which forms of biopolitical and geopolitical power bifurcate. On the onto-political terrain of analysis, the state of exception represents a stage for creating identities and sub-identities, spaces and the legitimacy of hegemonic-violent actions over them. Generally speaking, this use of the state of exception as a colonial strategy has involved an overlap of law onto political practices and the criminalization of movements opposed to colonialism.

Recent analyses of 'de-coloniality' or the 'colonial turn' have stressed the juridico-political dimensions of colonial projects. However, the argument developed here is that applying the concept of the state of exception to the process of colonialization means emphasizing both juridico-political and onto-political forms.

Drawing on legal-constitutional studies and the ontological tradition as a starting point, Agamben has defined the state of exception as: 'the notion that during time of war, civil, or otherwise, more generally when the polity is internally or externally threatened by a violent threat, the Sovereign can create a space where the constitution or law may be suspended' (Agamben 2005: 5). Apart from proposing a definition of the concept, Agamben introduces new epistemological lines for understanding the formation of the state of exception as a basis for the creation of identities and subjects:

> In truth, the state of exception is neither external nor internal to the juridical order, and the problem of defining it concerns precisely a threshold or zone of indifference, where inside and outside do not exclude each other but rather blur with each other. The suspension of the norm does not means its abolition, and the zone of anomie that it establishes is not (or at least claims not to be) unrelated to the juridical order.
>
> (Agamben 2005: 23)

Agamben's major contribution can be found in his analysis of Schmitt (2005), which shows how the state of exception can be formed in accordance with the needs of the hegemonic actor. Put simply, the implementation of the state of exception takes place when the sovereign considers that suspension of the rule of law is necessary. Its use is emphasized during states of emergency for the control of 'political violence' or when counter-hegemonic movements appear to be 'endangering national security'. In this sense it could be argued that '[t]he state of exception marks a threshold at which logic and praxis blur with each other and a pure violence without logos claims to realize an enunciation without any real reference' (Agamben 2005: 40).

On the other hand, the extensive analysis that Paye (2008) develops on the creation of anti-terrorist laws like the Patriot Act and thus the end of the rule of law and the establishment of a state of exception in a new kind of dictatorship, shows that in the USA the liberal structures that previously supported the state are being reconfigured (see also Whyte 2008). Thus we face a new paradigm of power and governance where the basic rights promoted by modern liberal thought have been radically replaced by a police state. This transformation has meant that the law, especially exceptionalist law, overlaps with politics and in time has led to an increase in state terrorism caused by anti-terrorist practices.

Other authors such as Venator (2006) describe this paradigm of governance as having existed throughout the history of US expansionism. It is likely that the constitutional development of the USA was influenced by expansionism. According to Venator, the spatial-temporal dimensions created by the expansion of US colonial and violent practices underpin the creation of the American state of exception.

He argues that '[t]he relationship between the state of emergency and the state of exception is premised on the need to create spaces where the law is suspended in order to address the demands imposed by threats stemming from an emergency' (Venator 2006: 23). The author suggests three examples of hegemonic-violent processes or traditions that highlight this phenomenon in the USA:

> The first tradition is one premised on territorial conquest, and more specifically premised on the conquest of indigenous populations of what is now the United States. This tradition is of course different to a tradition of colonization.... A second tradition or doctrine can be discerned from the U.S. position on occupied territories. Ironically, the doctrines developed by the court created a zone of indistinction between the international and the domestic. A third doctrine, as Agamben notes, emerged from efforts to maintain national unity amidst Civil War.
>
> (Venator 2006: 23)

From these three traditions and using the analysis of the Insular Cases, Venator develops especially the second tradition, which proposes that the state of exception is a space of anomie or a space outside international and local law. He considers that territorial expansionism, the process of nation-state building and the creation of identities through colonialism and the law have played a crucial role in the development of a state of exception in PR.

These colonial practices and the eventual construction of laws that legitimized the possession of colonial territories enabled the eventual development of the state of exception as a colonial structure, thus putting PR inside the paradigm of appropriation/violence in which the colonies and 'terrorists' live (Santos 2007: 10). This also sets the parameters for the exceptionality in which the global South lives, not only in the legal terms but also epistemologically, politically and economically.

From this standpoint we may transcend the essentialist analysis that Agamben makes on the juridical formation of the state of exception to consider the state of exception along with other micro-histories. The following discussion will show that the scope of the state of exception in this respect is twofold. On the one hand, it comprises the construction of space and subjects deprived of rights or located at least on a border between legality and illegality. On the other hand, it comprises the practices of criminalization of counter-hegemony.

### *2.1 The Insular Cases as juridical precedents of the state of exception in Puerto Rico*

As noted earlier, the colonial territory of PR was 'acquired' by the USA after its invasion of 1898, and after the subsequent secession by Spain in the same year that came into effect with the Treaty of Paris. This discussion raises various issues in relation to constitutional and political theory and has provoked debates among academic elites in the USA and PR. The Insular Cases come to life in this period, and have traditionally been described as follows:

> The name Insular Case is normally given to a series of nine decisions rendered in 1901. Seven of those cases arose from Puerto Rico, one from Hawaii, and one from the Philippine Islands. However, some authors have extended the name to another set of cases from 1903 to 1914 dealing with the same or related questions and another to a decision handed down in 1922 as well.
>
> (Rivera Ramos 2001: 74–5)

These cases, which have been described as racist law (Rivera Ramos 1996, 2001), tried to normalize the newly acquired territory and to legitimize those actions in terms of its own national constitution. This was done by using the legal precedent set by *Dred Scott* v. *Sandford*,[6] which established that the USA could not colonize and perpetuate its colonization in the new territories (Venator 2006: 31). In that sense, the Insular Cases played a fundamental role in the constitution of the hegemonic-legal interpretation and legitimation of US colonialism in PR.

According to the analysis done by Rivera Ramos, the Insular Cases had four general effects. They

> a) provided an explicit legal justification of the U.S. colonial project in Puerto Rico, b) played a central role in establishing the legal and political subject on which the U.S. Metropolitan State may exercise its power, c) created a discourse within which any discussion of the colonial problem must be conducted, in other words, defined the 'legitimate' discursive framework for the subsequent political struggles on the question of political space in Puerto Rico and the political and legal rights of Puerto Ricans, and d) constructed a context for action that facilitates the generation of a practice that later reproduced the conditions for the realization of the colonial project as a framework for validation of discourse.
>
> (Rivera Ramos 1996: 228)

Likewise, with the Insular Cases and the eventual passage of the Foraker Act of 1900, the colonial territory of PR was placed under the Territorial Clause of the US Congress. These juridical or legal spaces determined the area or ambit that can be controlled as US colonial territory.

This legal framework has supported US rule over the territory of PR for 113 years of colonialism, and it has recently been reinforced by the 'Report from the President's Task Force on Puerto Rico's Status' in 2007, a document that reasserted US hegemony over the Puerto Rican colonial territory and its people.

The Insular Cases and the location of PR within the Territorial Clause provided a legal form for the extra-juridical and extra-political control of space. The political-juridical designation of the state of exception of PR and territories like this space of anomie is summed up by the designation of the people as 'aliens in domestic sense' in terms of constitutional rights (Burnett and Marshall 2001; Rivera Ramos 1996, 2001).[7] This implies that these territories are in an area of juridical-political indistinction which, following Agamben, exist sometimes inside and sometimes outside the constitutional guarantees and procedures of the US rule of law.

As the creators of the jurisprudence and legal space for the 'Puerto Rican case' in the US colonial government and international community, the Insular Cases have not only determined the patterns of action for the territory, but they have also established categories that define what a 'Puerto Rican' is (Rivera Ramos 1996). As a hegemonic actor, the USA has created what in Gramscian terms is called 'common sense' (Gramsci 1971). This common sense has determined the 'legal truth' about the island (Rivera Ramos 1996, 2001), a truth that seeks to legitimize a geopolitical zone that has been identified as unincorporated territory. As this space of political and juridical anomie was created, so was created a separate juridical category for the people of PR, a people who nominally belong to the USA but are not granted all the constitutional guarantees, rights or privileges of US citizenship.

As the USA operates through the imposition of a state of exception on the Puerto Rican territory and on Puerto Ricans, so the exception has become the 'norm' in this space. Movements have been created that highlight or defend their Puerto Rican identity and reject the identity established by the USA. These movements have built counter-hegemonic identities and practices, which, as the following section will illustrate, have subsequently been labelled as a sub-category, identified as vandals, rioters, subversives, terrorists and criminals.

## 3 Law and the criminalization of counter-hegemony

In the colonization of PR, the USA used the law at three different levels or scales. First, the law served as an effective tool in the process of legitimizing the colonial actions according to the USA's own laws and/or to its constitution. That is, the law served as a tool to legitimize the colonization, the possession of the colony and the imposition of the colonial regime. As shown above, it was the legal-political category of the state of exception that underpinned this implementation of the law as a means to conceal the violence that colonialism involves.

Second, law and legal discourses were invoked in the process of legitimizing of US actions before the international community. The USA made use of the various international forums such as the UN and other agencies then created such as the Organization of American States, as field, for legitimizing its colonial actions. A good example of the use of international law was the mobilization of UN member states by the USA to exclude PR from the list of dependent countries in 1953 (Gautier and Argüelles 1978). This legal and diplomatic move worsened the Puerto Rican situation, as the country was effectively excluded from the international community. The USA forced the annual meeting of the UN General Assembly to approve Resolution 748 (VIII),[8] which states that PR obtained the highest level of self-government in 1952 with the constitution of the Commonwealth and therefore did not have to be included on the list of dependent countries.

Third, law and legal discourses were deployed to fight Puerto Rican revolutionary nationalism. At this time, an arbitrary legal framework denied any form of otherness by establishing that anything other than what it had established would be labelled illegitimate, criminal, seditious or simply terrorism.

The implementation of the state of exception, in the forms of the legal-political and onto-politics, have promoted the use of exceptional measures and mobilized extreme forms of state violence in opposition to Puerto Rican revolutionary nationalism. The USA developed two strategies of particular significance: on the one hand, the stigmatization of the counter-hegemonic and anti-colonialist movements as terrorist and the use of juridical-political terms or strategies for their control/extermination; and, on the other hand, the implementation of the 'enemy's criminal law' (Jakobs 2006), exemplified by laws such as the Seditious Conspiracy Act[9] and the Gag Law[10] – legal tools that permit the criminalization of subjects through the local criminal law. Both strategies enable criminalization and the superimposition of law and legal discourse on politics and thus legitimize state violence.

The following section identifies two historical periods in which the USA and colonial government in Puerto Rico used those strategies to mobilize against Puerto Rican revolutionary nationalism.

### *3.1 The construction of the nationalist enemy between 1898 and 1954*

The first historical period in which we can clearly see the mobilization of the state of exception in PR was between 1898 and 1954. In this period, the law served to legitimize and normalize the use of violence embedded in the colonial domination of PR. Once the colonial regime was established, the USA launched a set of actions against the Puerto Rican revolutionary nationalist movement, which at this time was represented by the Puerto Rican Nationalist Party (PRNP) and Pedro Albizu Campos.

A specific legal strategy applied by the USA was the Seditious Conspiracy Act. This Act and other criminal clauses, along with the subsequently created Gag Law, permitted the criminalization under law of the resistance to colonialism. In this way, the uses of law could be exemplified in two moments: on the one hand, the use, for the first time in PR, of the Seditious Conspiracy Act for the incarceration of the Nationalist Party leadership including Albizu Campos in 1936. At this time, the Nationalist Party leadership, comprising its president, Pedro Albizu Campos, Juan Antonio Corretjer and Clement Soto Vélez, were prosecuted for 'conspiracy to overthrow the regime', after two young nationalists executed the PR Insular Police Chief Col. Rigg. The two were seized and taken to police headquarters where they were shot. The police claimed that they were shot trying to escape, but this has now been established as a case of summary execution by the police (González 2006; Rosado 2007).

The Gag Law was passed in 1948, but it was used mainly in 1950 and 1951 after the nationalist uprising. At that time, thousands of independent nationalist and communist militants were prosecuted by the PR colonial government under this law for the simple fact of dissenting against the colonial government or failing to condemn the nationalist uprising and the use of political violence. This law established a felony for the following items:

1 Promoting, advocating, advising or preaching the necessity, desirability or advisability of overthrowing, stopping or destroying the Insular Government, or any of its policies, by means of force or violence.

2 Printing, publishing, editing, moving, selling, distributing or publicly displaying any writing or publication which promotes, advocates, counsels, or preaches the necessity, desirability or advisability of defeating, crippling or destroying the Insular Government.
3 Organizing or helping to organize any society, group or assembly of persons who promote, advocate, advise or preach the abolition or destruction of the Insular Government.

(Acosta 1998: 74)

Those principles allow almost any person or group who opposes colonial rule, or even government policy, to be prosecuted and even jailed.

In this context, the first dossier of 'subversive people' was compiled. Those files or lists of subversive people were used as a strategy of control and intimidation against the independence and nationalist movement. They basically consisted of personal information or data, information on activities, photos, letters and other political information of nationalist, communist and pro-independence militants. It is important to note that these files were established by the colonial government of Puerto Rico in the Internal Security Offices or Bureau, and later on the FBI did the same in the COINTELPRO project.[11]

The literature on the topic (Atiles-Osoria 2008; Bosques and Colón 1997; González 2006; Nieves Falcón 2009; Paralitici 2004; Seijo 1997) has identified a series of events that show how the conflict between the US/PR government and the Puerto Rican anti-colonial movement began to develop and use different strategies of political violence. The first example of political violence took place when the USA and the colonized government of PR initiated a campaign of state terrorism with the Massacre of Río Piedras (1935). In this incident, the Puerto Rican Insular Police assassinated four young nationalists after they had participated in a rally in the Río Piedras Campus of the University of Puerto Rico. The second involved two political assassinations of nationalist militants in 1936 after they tried to execute a high-ranking police officer. This violent strategy was combined with the imprisonment of the leadership of the Nationalist Party (PN) in 1936, convicted of 'conspiracy to overthrow the regime' as described above.

Two important events followed. The first was the Massacre of Ponce (1937). On 21 March 1937, Governor Winship ordered the Mayor of Ponce to withdraw the permission he had granted to the nationalists to hold a demonstration to commemorate the abolition of slavery in PR and to protest against the arrests of the Nationalist Party leadership the previous year. Following the governor's order, the Insular Police tried to stop the demonstration. Thus, while nationalists and in particular the 'Cadet of the Republic'[12] were organizing the march, the Insular Police began shooting participants and spectators. Twenty people were killed, including women and children who were only onlookers. A further 150 people were injured, all of them unarmed (González 2006; Moraza 2001). In addition, two policemen fell caught in police crossfire (González 2006). These extra-legal killings highlight not only the repression and violence of the colonial conflict but also the use of law in hegemonic colonial actions. Nationalists were formally charged with 'opening fire on police and disobeying the orders of the authorities', even though they were unarmed (González 2006; Moraza 2001). However, this legal process ended in acquittals, thanks to extensive research that established the falsity of the allegations against the nationalists (Moraza 2001).

The second important event was the political assassination of a nationalist militant on 25 July 1938, a year after the Massacre of Ponce. A student, Angel Esteban Antorgorgi, killed a senior Insular Police officer, Col. Irrizary, as part of an attempt to execute Governor Winship (González 2006). The Insular Police arrested and killed the young nationalist, whose body then disappeared (Guadalupe 1989; Rosado 2007).

After this period of intense activity, the country fell into a semblance of political calm, not least due to the imprisonment of the leadership of the Nationalist Party. However, the conflict continued in other ways. In 1948, when the leadership of the PN was released, the legal-political and political-military activities began again on both sides.

The high point of those activities came on 30 October 1950 with an uprising by the nationalists. This event comprised a group of targeted attacks against various installations, police stations and symbols of US power in and out of Puerto Rico (Seijo 1997). Places including police stations in the country's major cities such as Arecibo, Mayagüez, Ponce, San Juan and Utuado were attacked. In addition, country towns such as Jayuya, where the revolution began, were taken by the nationalists (González 2006: 31). The revolution had significant repercussions in many areas of national and international affairs. Some examples are: in the aftermath of the uprising, state of exception measures were expanded to target the entire spectrum of the Puerto Rican independence movement. In addition to the assassination of 21 of those involved in the uprising (Seijo 1997), the towns of Jayuya and Utuado, where the confrontations happened, were bombed. These punitive actions were carried out by the US National Guard when most of the nationalists from those villages were already demobilized or in prison. Although the literature on this topic does not specify how many civilians may have died as a result of the bombing, or the damage caused by the bombing, it is not disputed that many people were killed and that the infrastructure of both towns was almost entirely destroyed (González 2006: Seijo 1997).

Martial law was enacted by the Puerto Rican governor, Luis Muñoz Marín, and thousands of supporters of the liberation movement – not necessarily supporters of the armed struggle – were arrested the night after the bombing. Paralitici (2004) has noted that arrests continued for months after the nationalist uprising, which implies that the number of arrests could have reached 2,000. It is important to note that those blanket arrests were made regardless of political ideology. Many who did not even support the armed struggle and nationalist ideology (for example, members of the Puerto Rican Communist Party) and many ordinary Puerto Ricans who had no political affiliation were jailed.

As part of the uprising, on 1 November 1950 two nationalists attacked Blair House, at that time the temporary residence of President Truman. One nationalist was killed and the other was arrested, tried and sentenced to long-term imprisonment. The final event in the confrontation between the colonial state and the nationalists was the attack on the US Congress on 1 March 1954. This action resulted in the death of a member of the Nationalist Party and the imprisonment of many others for a period of 25 years.

Those events are marked by a dual process of action/containment. Each event in the colonial and counter-colonial conflict was followed by the creation of a new criminal category for those who endured colonialism. During the 20-year period described above, nationalists were labelled, first, 'subversive', then 'seditious' and eventually during the 1950s, 'terrorist'. As the preceding overview has demonstrated, those designations corresponded to a range of forms of state violence that existed in an indeterminate zone between the legal and illegal spheres.

The following section examines the most recent period from 1958 to 2010, a period marked by crisis between the 1960s and mid-1980s. The section explores counter-hegemonic resistance during this period within both legal and illegal frameworks.

### *3.2 From the 'new struggle for independence' to the 'war on terror' between 1956 and 2010*

After 1954, the Puerto Rican anti-colonial movement experienced a period of transition and transformation. New strategic forms of struggle for independence emerged within the movement and reshaped it. The movement comprised a range of different organizations and strategies active in the 'legal' (from the point of view of the hegemon) and 'illegal' contexts, as well as in the border or space between the two paradigms, what Santos (2009) called alegality. As a result of this transformation and reconceptualization, this period has been called the New Struggle for Independence (González 2006).

However, these movements also faced ongoing strategies of state criminalization of their struggles, ideology and policies. Also at this time, a variety of new actors were incorporated into US/PR government hegemonic strategies. These included the Commonwealth law enforcement agencies, right-wing movements and Cuban exiles' movements in Puerto Rico.

This period witnessed an intensification of the use of the law by hegemonic and counter-hegemonic actors. On the one hand, as we have seen, hegemonic actors continued to use the law as a strategy to delegitimize and criminalize counter-hegemonic and anti-colonial actors. This involved a major project of law-making, exemplified by anti-terrorist laws, and the renewed use of clauses of sedition, especially against actors engaged in armed struggle. It became common for criminal law to be used against political actors by the US and PR colonial law system. This obscures the political nature of their actions, allowing them to be defined as 'criminals'. Members of the Armed Forces of National Liberation (FALN) in the 1980s conducted a long struggle for recognition as prisoners of war in US jails. Similarly, members of the Puerto Rican Workers Revolutionary Party–Boricua Popular Army–Macheteros (PRTP–EPB–Macheteros) who were arrested in 1985 also fought for recognition of their actions in political terms (Paralitici 2007).

It is therefore important to note that in the period from the 1960s to the 1990s, there were approximately 176 political prisoners in PR and the USA (Paralitici 2004). In a very detailed analysis, Paraliticci (2004) has shown how in the 1960s there were 13 anti-colonial political prisoners and about 30 more anti-colonial actors were waiting to be tried (Paralitici 2004: 218). In the 1970s there was a considerable increase to 98, of whom 23 were imprisoned in the USA (Paralitici 2004: 333), and in the 1980s there were 65 Puerto Rican political prisoners – 33 in PR and 32 in the USA (Paralitici 2004: 398).

These processes of incarceration sought to demobilize the Puerto Rican independence movements through various strategies: first, the use of criminal law to prosecute political prisoners; second, the dispersal of those prisoners to the most remote prisons in the USA and to maximum security prisons in order to fragment the movement physically; and, finally, the imposition of disproportionate sentences.[13]

Another important strategy in the process of demobilization and criminalization of Puerto Rican revolutionary nationalism was the implementation of the Federal Grand Jury. The Federal Grand Jury in the USA and PR is the main forum in which crimes against US federal law are tried, and therefore is a key mechanism for the criminalization of the PR independence movement. Precisely because it is a federal legal mechanism, the anti-colonial movements have refused to recognize its legitimacy, and have shown reluctance to cooperate with legal institutions and legal processes initiated by the US Federal Court in Puerto Rico or elsewhere.

This second period, or the period of the New Struggle for Independence, has witnessed moments of high intensity in armed confrontation. During the decades from 1960 to 1980 there was a substantial increase in violence by the USA, the colonial government and right-wing movements (González 2006; Nieves Falcón 2009), for example the use of explosive devices against Puerto Rican revolutionary nationalists, gun shots at the homes of pro-independence militants, arson attacks on the headquarters of independence parties, and kidnapping (Nieves Falcón 2009). In most cases those acts of state violence were not punished.

Political assassinations included the killing of Antonia Martines Lagares, a University of Puerto Rico student who was killed by a police officer during the university strike in 1970. Others who were assassinated include, in 1976, Santiago Mari Pesquera, the son of the independence leader Juan Mari Bras; Carlos Muñis Valera, a Cuban citizen who supported the Cuban Revolution; and two young, independence activists killed at Cerro Maravilla in 1978, after having been ambushed by an undercover police officer (Pérez Viera 2000; Suárez 2003). In sum, in PR and in the USA, there were about 20 political assassinations in the 1970s (Nieves Falcón 2009).

The passing of the Patriot Act in 2001 marked a new stage in the use of US law. The implementation of the Patriot Act signalled a radical transformation in terms of political persecution and criminalization of the independence movements. At the same time, there has been an intensification in the use of criminal law to prosecute revolutionary nationalists and to deny them recognition as political prisoners. Outstanding examples of these forms of repression and state terrorist violence are the political assassination of Filiberto Ojeda Ríos, leader of the Macheteros, on 23 September 2003, and the later FBI intervention against citizens who were allegedly members of that organization (González 2008). Filiberto Ojeda Ríos's political assassination clearly shows how a state of exception in PR can be implemented as a strategy of state terror. Although this event was investigated by the FBI itself, no one involved has been charged.[14]

The revolutionary nationalist movement also used armed force against US interests during this period: for example, a large number of actions were carried out by CAL[15] (Irizarry 2010) and by MIRA[16] during the 1960s and 1970s (González 2006). Subsequently, between 1970 and 1980, the FALN conducted a series of military-political actions in the USA which highlighted the dimensions of the colonial conflict (González 2006). Finally, the EPB-Macheteros conducted various activities in cooperation with other armed movements, such as FARP[17] and the OVRP.[18] These actions included: the burning of seven fighter jets in the Muñiz Air Base in the late 1980s and the expropriation of a Wells Fargo truck in 1983 (Fernandez 1987; González 2006, 2008). The movement continued the practice of an 'ethics of violence'. As Rodríguez Vásquez (2004) states, this ethical use of violence has been characterized by a refusal to act against civilians and respect for basic service facilities. In this way, the confrontation moves beyond the legal-political and political-military dimensions to become a struggle for epistemic decolonization. In other words, the struggle focuses not only on the decolonization of the territory but also on the creation of other concepts and ways of perceiving the struggle for Puerto Rican independence. These concepts depart from the categories imposed by the hegemonic agent, such as 'terrorists', 'criminals' and 'enemies of society'. This discourse, or use of an ethical conception of the struggle for independence, seeks and tries to highlight the ideologies and strategies that do not affect Puerto Rican citizenship. This implies an attempt to break the 'common sense' created by the hegemonic agent and/or the subcategories devised by the USA to criminalize the independence movements. With this, it seeks to legitimize their struggles at both the local Puerto Rican civil society and the international levels and thus break the state of exception and the violence of colonialism.

## Conclusion

In this chapter I have shown how the state of exception was established in PR, and how it founded a new epistemological category of analysis which offers a new reading of dominant understandings of the dynamics both of colonialism and of the state of exception. A state of exception implemented in the colonies represents the junction between biopolitical forms of power and geopolitics. At the same time, it represents the constitutive category of the legal and political reality of these spaces, as I have shown through analysis of the Insular Cases and the mode of criminalization and state terror that characterized the counter-terrorism strategy.

In addition to the four effects of the Insular Cases identified by Rivera Ramos (1996) and discussed earlier (pp. 163–5), we can now add two more. As the discussion in this chapter has shown: e) the Insular Cases and the long period of colonial rule that followed allowed the use of doctrines and/or legal precedents that create precisely the same logic of indistinction that can be found in the Guantánamo detention camps; f) in addition to the creation of legal identities, the form of colonial rule in PR constructed sub-identities that would facilitate the later criminalization of individuals who engage in counter-hegemonic activities, depoliticizing their political practices.

Thus the state of exception in this field of action creates the identities and sub-identities of colonial subjects. The changing labels applied to nationalists have facilitated criminalization of counter-hegemonic movements and legitimized other forms of coercion and violence. In the most recent period, the label 'terrorism' has facilitated an intensification of those strategies and has enabled the 'criminality' of revolutionary movements to be elided with those nationalist groups who reject a military strategy, thus mobilizing the criminal law against all nationalists.

While the chapter did not develop an extensive study of the concept of state terrorism, it remains clear from the analysis here that this strategy represents one of the most important aspects of the state of exception in PR. The increasing use of criminal law to control the counter-hegemonic actor, under the excuse of the 'leftist' or 'pro-independence terrorist threat' has represented par excellence the forms of biopower and geopower strategies in the colonial context. These uses and abuses of power are detected through the application of different control strategies and harassment of the Puerto Rican nationalist movement. As this chapter has shown, colonial state violence has been characterized by summary executions, imprisonment for extended periods of time, attacks with explosive devices and firearms on the homes and the offices of nationalists and pro-independence militants, kidnapping and political assassinations.

The analysis of these strategies leads me to propose that the legitimization of the state of exception in PR since the end of the nineteenth century established the legal and political precedents that were recently mobilized to create the spaces of indistinction, as in Guantánamo and Iraq. This analysis reasserts the importance of understanding the close connection between 'terrorism', violence and colonialism, and developing new ways of articulating this relationship. In this sense, I have tried to pave the way for a research agenda that opens up new ways of thinking about the relationship between law and resistance in colonial conflicts.[19]

## Notes

1 Composed of the Puerto Rico main island, Vieques, Culebra, Mona Island and other islands and islets.

2 Foraker Act of 12 April 1900 (cap. 191, 31 Stat. 77).

3 US Constitution Article IV-3, Clause 2: This clause established that:

> The Congress shall have Power to dispose of and make all needful Rules and Regulations respecting the Territory or other Property belonging to the United States; and nothing in this Constitution shall be so construed as to Prejudice any Claims of the United States, or of any particular State.
> (www.house.gov/house/Constitution/Constitution.html; (accessed March 2011)

4 The Insular Case that established this decision was *Balzac* v. *People of Porto Rico*, 258 U.S. 298 (1922). This case is in reproduced in several books such as Ramos de Santiago (1985) and also in different internet domains such as http://caselaw.lp.findlaw.com/cgi-bin/getcase.pl?court=us&vol=258&invol=298 (accessed March 2011).

5 Public Law 600, 81st Act of Congress, provides for the organization of a constitutional government by the people of Puerto Rico (3 July 1950, cap. 446, 64 Stat. 314).

6 *Dred Scott* v. *Sandford*, 60 U.S. 393 (1856).

7 This interpretation comes from: *González* v. *Williams*, 192 U.S. 1 (1904) which established that Puerto Ricans were foreigners in terms of immigration, but at the same time were part of the USA. Overall this discussion continued in academia and the political-legal arena until 1917 when the Jones Act imposed US citizenship on Puerto Ricans. However, as I argue in this chapter, Puerto Ricans have never possessed the same constitutional rights as other citizens born on the US mainland.

8 Resolution 748 (VIII) 549 plenary meeting, 27 November 1953: Cessation of the transmission of information under Article 73e of the Chapter in respect to Puerto Rico. Available on: http://daccess-dds-ny.un.org/doc/RESOLUTION/GEN/NR0/086/13/IMG/NR008613.pdf?OpenElement (accessed March 2011).

9 Seditious Conspiracy Act, US Code, Title 18, Part 1, Chapter 115, § 2384. This Act provides that:

> If two or more persons in any State or Territory, or in any place subject to the jurisdiction of the United States, conspire to overthrow, put down, or to

destroy by force the Government of the United States, or to levy war against them, or to oppose by force the authority thereof, or by force to prevent, hinder, or delay the execution of any law of the United States, or by force to seize, take, or possess any property of the United States contrary to the authority thereof, they shall each be fined under this title or imprisoned not more than twenty years, or both.

This law has been widely deployed by the US government against the Nationalist Party and against Puerto Rican revolutionary nationalists from the 1930s to the present (González 2006). Nieves Falcón (2009) notes that this law had not been applied to any US citizen since the US Civil War ended and it was not until the Puerto Rican independence movement gathered strength that the USA resurrected it.

10 Acosta (1998) establishes in her analysis that the Gag Law was a copy of the Smith Act, passed in the USA in the 1940s to prosecute and criminalize 'anti-American activities', or more specifically communist-leftist activities. In Puerto Rico, Law 53 was adopted on 21 May 1948. It is known as the Gag Law, since its aim was to silence the Puerto Ricans' independence movements. Overall, this law provided a 'legal' framework for the criminal prosecution of those who opposed the colonial system. The law remained in force until 1957 when it was abolished.

11 These activities of data collection and making files on every nationalist and pro-independence militant and the compilation of the list of subversive people are known in PR *as Carpetas* (literary folders). I will present more details about this in the next pages of this chapter.

12 The Group of men that symbolically represents the Puerto Rican Republic Army.

13 These aspects of the experience of PR political prisoners in the USA are derived from interviews conducted by the author between March 2010 and March 2011.

14 On this incident and its subsequent investigation by the FBI, see: US Department of Justice, Offices of the General Inpector (2006), 'A Review of the September 2005 Shooting Incident Involving the Federal Bureau of Investigation and Filiberto Ojeda Ríos' (Available at: www.justice.gov/oig/special/s0608/full_report.pdf; (accessed March 2011). From a more critical analysis of events, see the 'Final Report of the Special Commission for the Investigation of the Events Relating to the Death of Filiberto Ojeda Ríos', by the Puerto Rican Bar Association.

15 Armed Commandos of Liberation (Comandos Armados de Liberación).

16 Armed Revolutionist Independence Movement (Movimiento Independentista Revolucionario Armado).

17 Armed Forces of Popular Resistance (Fuerzas Armadas de Resistencia Popular).

18 Organization of Volunteers for the Puerto Rican Revolution (Organización de Voluntarios para la Revolución Puertorriqueña).

19 I would like to express my gratitude to various people who assisted me in the preparation and writing of this chapter. First, I thank the editors of this book, Dr David Whyte and Dr Scott Poynting, for their invitation to join them in this project. Similarly, I would like to thank Gustavo José Rojas Paez for his helpful collaboration in the editing process, and to Dr Michael González Cruz for his comments and support.

## References


Acosta, Ivonne (1998), *La mordaza.* Río Piedras, PR: Edil.

Agamben, Giorgio (1998), *Homo Sacer, El poder y la nuda vida* (trad. Antonio Gimeno Cuspineta). Valencia: Pre-Texto.

Agamben, Giorgio (2005), *State of Exception: Homo Sacer II, 1* (trad. Kelvin Attell). Chicago: University of Chicago.

Atiles-Osoria, José M. (2008), *Colonialismo, estado de excepción y resistencia: La criminalización de la lucha armada en Puerto Rico.* Oñati: IISJ.net.

Bhabha, Homi (1994), *The Location of Culture.* New York: Routledge.

Bosques Pérez, Ramón and José Colón Morera, (eds) (1997), *Las carpetas: Derechos civiles y persecución política en Puerto Rico.* Río Piedras, PR: CIPDC.

Burnett, Christina Duffy (2005), 'United States: American Expansion and Territorial Deannexation', *The University of Chicago Law Review,* 72, 3, pp. 797–879.

Burnett, Christina Duffy and Burke Marshall (2001), *Foreign in a Domestic Sense: Puerto Rico, American Expansion, and the Constitution.* Durham, NC: Duke University Press.

Butler, Judith (2004), *Precarious Life: The Powers of Mourning and Violence.* London: Verso.

Colegio de Abogados de Puerto Rico (2007), *Informe Final de la Comisión especial para investigar los sucesos acontecidos el 23 de septiembre de 2006 en la casa de Filiberto Ojeda Ríos.* San Juan, PR: CAPR.

Fanon, Frantz (1999), *Los condenados de la tierra* (trad. Esteban Montorio). Nafarroa: Txalaparta.

Fernandez, Ronal (1987), *Los Macheteros: The Wells Fargo Robbery and the Violent Struggle for Puerto Rican Independence.* New York: Prentice Hall Press.

Foucault, Michel (1995), *La verdad y las formas jurídicas* (trad. Enrique Lynch). Barcelona: Gedisa.

Gautier Mayoral, Carmen and María del Pilar Arguelles (1978), *Puerto Rico y la ONU.* Río Piedras, PR: Edil.

González Cruz, Michael (2006), *Nacionalismo revolucionario puertorriqueño.* San Juan/Santo Domingo: Isla Negra.

González Cruz, Michael (2008), 'Puerto Rican Revolutionary Nationalism: Filiberto Ojeda Ríos and the Macheteros', *Latin American Perspectives,* 35, pp. 151–65.

Gramsci, Antonio (1971), *Selection From the Prison Notebooks* (trad. Q. Hoare and G. Nowell Smith). London: Lawrence & Wishart.

Grosfoguel, Ramón (2003), *Colonial Subjects: Puerto Ricans in a Global Perspective.* Berkeley, Los Angeles, London: University of California Press.

Grosfoguel, Ramón (2007), 'World System Analysis and Postcolonial Studies: A Call for a Dialogue from the "Coloniality of Power" Approach'. In Revathi Krishnaswamy and John C. Hawley (eds), *The Postcolonial and the Global.* Minneapolis/London: University of Minnesota Press, pp. 94–104.

Guadalupe, Raul (1989), 'Apuntes históricos en torno al movimiento estudiantil en Puerto Rico durante las primeras décadas del presente siglo', *Trinchera* 1, 2, pp. 12–15.

Irizarry Cruz, Lucila (2010), *Cal: Una historia clandestina, (1968–1972).* San Juan, PR: Isla Negra.

Jackson, Richard (2010), 'Contemporary State Terrorism: Towards a New Research Agenda'. In Richard Jackson, Eamon Murphy and Scott Poynting (eds),

*Contemporary State Terrorism: Theory and Practice.* London and New York: Routledge, pp. 228–39.

Jakobs, Günther (2006), *Derecho penal del enemigo* (2nd edn) (trad. Cancio Meliá). Madrid: Editorial Aranzadi.

Memmi, A. (1974), *Retrato del colonizado* (trad. Carlos Rodríguez Sanz). Madrid: Ediciones Eloisa.

Mignolo, Walter D. (2005), *The Idea of Latin America.* Oxford: Blackwell.

Moraza Ortiz, Manuel (2001), *La Masacre de Ponce.* San Juan: Publicaciones Puertorriqueñas.

Nieves Falcón, Luis (2002), *Violation of Human Rights in Puerto Rico by the United States.* San Juan: Ediciones Puerto.

Nieves Falcón, Luis (2009), *Un siglo de represión política en Puerto Rico 1898–1998.* San Juan: Ediciones Puerto.

Paralitici, José Ché (2004), *Sentencia impuesta. 100 años de encarcelamientos por la independencia de Puerto Rico.* San Juan: Ediciones Puerto.

Paralitici, José Ché (2007), *La voz no silenciada, Primera entrevista a Filiberto Ojeda Ríos, 1986.* San Juan: Ediciones Puerto.

Paye, Jean-Claude (2008), *El final del estado de derecho. La lucha antiterrorista: Del Estado de Excepción a la dictadura.* Hondarribia: Editorial Hiru.

Pérez Viera, Edgardo (2000), *El juicio de la historia: Contrainsurgencia y asesinato político en Puerto Rico.* San Juan, PR: Editorial Cultural.

Quijano, Anibal (2000), 'Coloniality of Power, Ethnocentrism, and Latin America', *Nepantla* 1, 3, pp. 533–80.

Raffucci de Garcia, Carmen I. (1981), *El gobierno civil y la Ley Foraker: Antecedentes históricos.* Río Piedras, PR: Universidad de Puerto Rico.

Ramos de Santiago, Carmen (1985), *El desarrollo constitucional de Puerto Rico: Documentos y casos.* Río Piedras, PR: Editorial Universidad de Puerto Rico.

Rivera Ramos, Efrén (1996), 'The Legal Constitution of America Colonialism: The Insular Cases (1902–1922)', *Revista Jurídica de la Universidad de Puerto Rico,* 65, 2, pp. 225–328.

Rivera Ramos, Efrén (1998), *Hegemonía y legitimidad en el Puerto Rico contemporánea.* Barcelona: Institut de Ciències Polítiques i Socials.

Rivera Ramos, Efrén (2001), *The Legal Construction of Identity: The Juridical and Social Legacy of American Colonialism in Puerto Rico.* Washington DC: American Psychological Association.

Rodríguez Vázquez, José Juan (2004), *El sueño que no cesa: La nación deseada en el debate intelectual y político puertorriqueño 1920–1940.* San Juan, PR: Ediciones Callejón.

Rosado, María. (2007), *El nacionalismo y la violencia en la década de 1930.* San Juan, PR: Ediciones Puerto.

Santos, Boaventura de Sousa (2002), *Toward a New Legal Common Sense: Law, Globalization and Emancipation.* London: Butterworth and LexisNexis.

Santos, Boaventura de Sousa (2006), *A Gramática do tempo: Para uma nova cultura política.* Porto: Edições Afrontamiento.

Santos, Boaventura de Sousa (2007), 'Para além do pensamento abissal: Das linhas globais a uma ecologia de saberes', *Revista Crítica de Ciêcias Sociais,* 78, pp. 3–46.

Santos, Boaventura de Sousa (2009), *Sociología jurídica crítica: Para un nuevo sentido común en el derecho.* Madrid and Bogota: Trotta/ILSA.

Schmitt, Carl (2005), *Political Theology* (trad. George Schwab). Chicago: University of Chicago Press.

Seijo Bruno, Miñi (1997), *La insurrección nacionalista en Puerto Rico, 1950.* Rio Piedras, PR: Editorial Edil.

Spivak, Gayatri Chakravorty (1999), *A Critique of Postcolonial Reason: Toward a History of the Vanishing Present.* Cambridge, Mass., and London: Harvard University Press.

Suárez, Manuel (2003), *Two Lynchings on Cerro Maravilla: The Police Murders in Puerto Rico and the Federal Government Cover Up.* San Juan, PR: Instituto de Cultura Puertorriqueña.

Venator Santiago, Charles R. (2006), 'From the Insular Cases to Camp X-Ray: Agamben's State of Exception and United States Territorial Law', *Studies in Law, Politics, and Society*, 39, pp. 15–55.

Whyte, David (2008), 'Market Patriotism and the War on Terror', *Social Justice* 34, 3–4, pp. 111–31.

Young, Robert (2001), *Postcolonialism: An Historical Introduction.* Oxford: Blackwell Publishers.

# 10 The 'war on terror' and Spanish state violence against Basque political dissent

*Pablo Ciocchini and Stéfanie Khoury*

## Introduction

This chapter examines Agamben's concept of the 'state of exception' in the context of the Basque conflict.[1] It will use Agamben's framework to explore the counter-argument made by the Spanish government that its 'war on terror' (in contrast with those of the US and UK) is lawful. The chapter will further explore how current strategies of Spanish state terror are based upon political interventions that draw indiscriminate parallels between the Basque separatist groups Izquierda Abertzale (IA) and Euskadi Ta Azkatazuna (ETA) via the Ley de Partidos (Law on Political Parties, 2002).

## 1 State of exception

Decades before 9/11, since the time of Franco's dictatorship, the fight against terrorism in Spain has been a powerful screen to stimulate patriotism while legitimating the state's imposition of exceptional measures.

The state of exception has not been formally declared since the transition to democracy in Spain at the end of the 1970s. However, the ability to impose exceptional measures has been maintained in the Spanish Constitution.[2] The constitutionally sanctioned exceptional measures refer to the suspension of a series of constitutional guarantees for individuals accused of terrorist crimes. This seems to correspond to what Agamben (2005) argues when he says that the state of exception depends on the suspension of law. According to him, it is located in the critical and ambiguous space between law and politics. The paradox of what can thus be considered a *legal illegality* represents a fundamental limitation of law, and, for the purposes of this chapter, more specifically a limitation on human rights law. Considering the increased use of law to paradoxically deny rights to certain groups of individuals since 2001, Agamben has described the state of exception as 'neither external nor internal to the juridical order. The suspension of the norm does not mean its abolition, and the zone of anomie that it establishes is not (or at least claims not to be) unrelated to the juridical order' (2005: 23). According to Whyte (2009), Agamben interprets the state of exception as something fundamental to state power. It is the very foundation of state sovereignty. As Agamben points out, 'what is at issue in the sovereign exception is not so much the control or neutralisation of an excess as the creation and definition of the very space in which the juridico-political order can have validity' (1998: 19). In this way, the exception is not simply outside the law, but is created by the suspension of law. The sovereign creates the law, determines its suspension thus creating the exception, and so determines the validity of the law regarding the exception.

We use Agamben's theoretical framework in analysing the case of Spanish state violence against Basque separatist organisations because its broadness allows us to relate legal and illegal measures of apparently different natures. Therefore, using Agamben's interpretation of the state of exception we scrutinise the contradictions in the liberal legal framework's suspension of legal provisions that protect human rights while preserving the rule of law. In Agamben's words,

> As if the juridical order contained an essential fracture between the position of the norm and its application, which, in extreme situations, can be filled only by means of the state of exception, that is, by creating a zone in which application is suspended, but the law, as such, remains in force.
>
> (Agamben, 2005: 31)

This emptiness of law relates the direct violence of Spanish police brutality towards Basque detainees to the exclusion of radical Basque separatist groups from any legal participation in the political realm.

We are not arguing that the Spanish state is alone in applying measures such as incommunicado detentions or the banning of political parties since there have been and continue to be examples in other Western countries, not least in the war on terror. However, the scale of the Basque conflict and the efforts of the Spanish state to present itself as fighting terrorism under the rule of law create an opportunity to explore and scrutinise how the liberal democratic states are paradoxically violating human rights through the lawful enforcement of law; and how these human rights violations are constructed as non-violent democratic measures of counterterrorism through the enforcement of legal provisions under due process.

## 2 STOP *estado de excepción*

The Basque conflict is complex and multi-faceted. There are many political parties in the Basque Country (Euskal Herria), and it would be a mistake to aggregate the separatist groups. The PNV (Basque

Nationalist Party) is a Basque nationalist group that has governed for almost 30 years. It has pursued a strong separatist agenda since 2000, promoting a 'referendum' or popular consultation on the right to self-determination and ways to handle the violence of ETA. More radical than the PNV is the IA, which has in many cases made similar demands to ETA (e.g. for a 'free and socialist Basque Country'[3]). Far from being a well-defined political party, IA is a complex association of Basque leftist separatist groups. It has traditionally maintained an ambiguous position on the use of political violence to achieve independence. At the time of writing, March 2011, IA has radically altered its position by condemning any violence to achieve political goals. ETA and IA share the political goal of independence for the Basque Country, and both describe the Spanish state as an *estado de excepción* (state of exception). IA has specifically used the slogan 'STOP *estado de excepción*' as part of its discourse and on the streets (in graffiti and other propaganda) in a strategic attempt to draw a parallel between the present-day situation and Franco's dictatorship, which was marked by numerous official states of exception.[4] IA is thus addressing not only the Basque population but also the international human rights community. Its demand to 'stop the state of exception' is projected beyond the frontiers of Euskal Herria, for example in its petition to the European Court of Human Rights (ECtHR) against violations of human rights by the Spanish state in 2004.

The state of exception in the Basque Country, according to ETA and IA, means the suppression of any political challenge to the integrity of the state under the pretext of the rule of law. This is illustrated by the discretionary banning of political parties, the prohibition of demonstrations by groups linked to the radical left Basque movement, mass imprisonment often resulting in incommunicado detentions, exceptional treatment of Basque political prisoners, disproportionate to inflation of offences when associated with terrorism, and torture by the police. ETA and IA assert that these measures are carried out in a liberal legal framework.

In contrast to the position adopted by IA, the Spanish government speaks of the 'rule of law' and respect for human rights with rhetorical reverence to legitimise its actions. In July 2004, a few months after the Al-Qaeda 9/11 terrorist attack at Atocha station in Madrid and only four months into his term in office, Zapatero defined his strategy in the fight against terrorism. He insisted it would be in strict accordance with the 'rule of law', an approach differing from the United States and Britain:

> The government over which I preside will have as its primary objective to fight tirelessly against terrorism, against any terrorism, against all terrorism! In this battle, we will consecrate all the possible resources

> available to a democratic society [...] I will not make the mistake of proposing restrictions on our system of freedoms for the sake of security. I will not consider initiatives that violate our own legality or that of international legality.
>
> (Zapatero, 2004a, authors' transl.)

Zapatero's discursive line has strictly obeyed pre-existing legality. Under his government, there have been no legal modifications of the previous governments' counter-terrorist framework. Neither emergency legislations nor executive decrees were sanctioned and security forces have operated under the existing legal framework, following orders from judges who investigated terrorist crimes.[5]

Zapatero's claim to fight terrorism under the rule of law must be contextualised within a history of repression and state terror under Franco's dictatorship and during the transition to democracy, to which we now turn.

## 3 Counter-terror as state terror

### *3.1 A history of state terror: Spain's dirty war*

The Franco years were distinguished by decades of repression and brutality inflicted by the government on the populations of the Spanish territory. All dissident groups throughout this period were violently suppressed, leading to uprisings all over Spain. The most famous of those dissident groups is the armed separatist group ETA founded in 1957. The confrontation between ETA and Spanish officials culminated in the 1968 assassination of Police Commissioner Melitón Manzanas,[6] after which Franco declared an official state of exception. The 1970 military trial of the 'Burgos 16', as the accused ETA members became known, was wrought with fabricated evidence and testimonies recovered under duress and torture (Clark, 1979: 181–8). The trial made waves internationally and eventually the death sentences on nine of the accused were reduced to life imprisonment. ETA's assassinations escalated. In 1973, it targeted Luis Carrero Blanco, then Prime Minister of Spain, whose legacy was what Paddy Woodworth (2005) calls the 'first dirty war'. Underground anti-ETA terrorism began in 1975, organised by SECED, a group of Francoist secret service officers (Servicio Central de Documentación) led by Carrero Blanco. He set the blueprints for what became the BVE (Batallón Vasco-Español) – an elusive paramilitary group fighting outside the law but protected by the state – active from 1975 to 1981, almost exclusively in the French Basque Country. The BVE was made up of death squads and mercenaries acting under the orders of members of state security forces (ibid: 67). It was the forerunner to the state terrorist group GAL (Grupos Antiterroristas de Liberación). Until the Socialist electoral victory in 1982, a number of underground anti-ETA, right-wing terrorist groups (e.g. BVE,

Triple A, Grupos Antiterroristas Españoles) killed an estimated 40 *etarras* or suspected ETA collaborators (Maravall, 2003: 285). A report from the Basque government's Office of Victims of Terrorism (Oficina de Víctimas del Terrorismo del Gobierno Vasco) has officially identified 74 acts of terrorism by paramilitary and extreme right-wing groups in the French and Spanish Basque Country from the period 1975–90, resulting in 66 deaths (Aizpeolea, 2010). The murders carried out by these terrorist organisations were imputed to BVE (18), Triple A (8), Grupos Antiterroristas Españoles (6) and GAL (26).

In the two years immediately following Franco's death in 1975, King Juan Carlos pardoned most Basques imprisoned for political crimes committed under the old regime (Encarnación, 2007: 956). The government provided programmes of reintegration for those who renounced affiliation to ETA. Nonetheless, Spain experienced a spike in terrorist activity in 1977. The majority of Basques, including some nationalist political parties such as the PNV, accepted the 1978 democratic Constitution that recognised the Basque Country as an autonomous province, although denied it the possibility of self-determination. Opposed to this constitutional settlement, ETA continued its attacks, and Prime Minister Suárez introduced the first anti-terrorist legislation of the democratic period. Encarnación (ibid) explains how the 1981 Law for the Defence of the Constitution (Ley por la defensa de la Constitucion) broadened the definition of 'terrorism', ultimately expanding the powers of the Guardia Civil to arrest anyone suspected of affiliation with terrorism.[7] This law led to the arrest and eventual conviction of the leadership of the Basque political party Herri Batasuna, commonly accepted as ETA's political wing. The new law on terrorism, mass arrests, an attempted military *coup d'état* by General Tejero, and the continued activity of the BVE were fodder for ETA's ongoing struggle. The dehumanisation of ETA was maintained in the media with commentaries questioning the justice of human rights for terrorists. In his editorial on 23 March 1981, P.J. Ramírez questioned the 'human rights of beasts' in the right-wing journal *Diario 16*:

> A beast is enclosed behind bars thicker than those of prison cells. To achieve this, you first need to play all kinds of tricks and games. If one [beast] dies in the adventure, it is a case of bad luck (or good luck!). ETA's death is our life. There are no human rights when hunting the tiger. When hunting the tiger, he threatens you, and harasses you. You dominate it and if necessary you kill it. Even if 50 *etarras* die in combat, the hands of Spain will continue to be clear of human blood. We will applaud the courageous police who shoot against them [...].
>
> (quoted in M.M., 2006, authors' transl.)

Ramírez justified the dirty war by claiming that the death of a terrorist is inconsequential and any means are therefore acceptable.

The Socialist Party (PSOE) came to power in 1982, in the first democratic elections in Spain since the Civil War. It was, as Woodworth (2002) calls it, the first Spanish government with 'clean hands' in over 50 years, meaning it was the first government without ties to Franco's regime. It did not, however, change its relationship with the military, which remained Francoist. For reasons explained by Woodworth (2005) and Clark (1990), including pressure from the military and fear of another attempted *coup*, Prime Minister González and his Socialist government delegated primary responsibility for counter-terrorism strategy to the military. Although Suárez's government had previously attempted to centralise military information and require reporting to the government through CESID (Centro Superior de Información de la Defensa), there was an almost 'seamless transfer of military autonomy over the issue of counter-terrorism policy' with the creation of GAL (Encarnación, 2007: 963). The purpose of GAL was to carry out covert counter-terrorist measures against ETA using paramilitary action, sanctioned by the government. Continuities with the anti-ETA terrorist groups set up under the Francoist regime and their activities during the new democracy were evident, with members of the BVE becoming members of GAL (Belloch quoted in Maravall, 2003: ftnt 40). Woodworth's interviews with security officials reported the collusion between the paramilitary group and the state: 'Give us the money and cover, and we will clean things up for you. If you give us a free hand, we will finish off ETA in a very short space of time' (2005: 70). This was all the more subversive since the cover of a left-wing party provided even more protection for the military (Encarnación, 2007).

GAL's creation taints the history of democratisation in Spain and represents in the eyes of many Basques a continuation of the Francoist regime. The Socialists expected their relationship with ETA to be different: they had supported regional politics and devolution; they were Socialist and were making a break with Franco's authoritarian regime; they also believed France, also under a Socialist government, would be more likely to extradite ETA members. None of this was true. ETA remained hostile and France was unwilling to enter into the politics of Basque affairs (Woodworth, 2002; Encarnación, 2007). It was widely known that many *etarras* fled to the French Basque Country where they lived openly and freely. González's government had hoped for a rapprochement with their Socialist neighbours in France under the Mitterrand government. However, initially the French were unwilling to cooperate by extraditing presumed terrorists back to Spain. This provoked GAL's illegal attacks on Spanish Basques living in France, beginning with the disappearances of Joxean Lasa and Joxe Zabala in 1983.[8] This initiated a series of killings and kidnappings by GAL in the French Basque Country. These attacks eventually put enough pressure on the French government that by the end of 1984 it had deported 23 *etarras*, including leaders (Irvin, 1999: 197). Along with new legislation – such as Organic Law 8/1984 which confirmed extraordinary police powers and empowered judges to order the detention of presumed terrorists for up to two and a half years without trial – these actions led even moderate Basques to conclude that 'democracy' had not changed the politics of terror used during the Francoist regime. Cynthia Irvin has shown how the new Organic Law authorised judges to ban political parties and other groups led by convicted terrorists and close down newspapers and magazines supporting terrorist aims; and it became a crime for any elected public official to criticise the Spanish nation, its symbols or its flag (ibid). The election of Jacques Chirac to the French presidency in 1986 consolidated Franco-Spanish efforts against ETA and ushered in a new wave of deportations and raids in the French Basque Country.

GAL was responsible for conducting covert operations in the French Basque Country, kidnapping individuals and bringing them across the border into Spain, where they were tortured and sometimes killed. In its five years of terror (1982–87) GAL was responsible for 27 deaths, one-third of which were of individuals with no connection to ETA (Woodworth, 2005: 63). The government's role in the paramilitary group's activities had long been suspected. Judicial investigations into GAL were started in 1988, spearheaded by Judge Baltasar Garzón. Two policemen were indicted and sentenced to life in prison. Having been assured by the government that they would be protected, the police officers kept their silence, but a few years into their sentence they spoke out about GAL and the government. Senior policemen and politicians (including Prime Minister González) were named, highlighting the collusion between government and military (ibid: 64). Although González was eventually removed from the judicial investigation, some commentators have noted that the conviction of some of his senior staff makes his 'political responsibility crystal clear' (ibid: 76).[9] Democracy had not brought the change expected. Although some state officials involved were exposed and convicted during the 1990s, the courts refused to define them as state terrorists. They argued that the defendants were not terrorists because they did not seek to produce 'the alarm or fear specific to terrorism' (Woodworth, 2005: 76). What is more, although the investigation targeted individual's relations with GAL, there was a strategy of denying the connection between GAL and the state, in other words GAL as a state-sponsored terrorist organisation. Woodworth critiques the reluctance of the Spanish courts to fully understand and address the scale and extent of GAL, as well as the government's role in its existence and actions. As he elucidates, the court prosecuted GAL for appalling crimes but resisted using (state) terror as one of the characteristics of its crusade. For this reason, it is also important to contextualise the investigations and to remain critical of the political objectives which played an important role in their materialisation.[10] Nonetheless, the investigations into GAL were important for several reasons: first, for the practical use of the courts against the collusion of government officials and paramilitaries; second, symbolically for providing a platform from which to critique the causal relationship between the state and the many terrorist organisations that existed between 1975 and 1986; and third, to help us think about the connection between the state and terrorism today.

The 1980s counter-terrorist terrorism – terror carried out by the state under the auspices of counter-terrorist measures – has left a profound mark on the perception of the transition to democracy in Spain. It has fuelled propaganda and continued support for ETA by some, and a distrust in 'democracy' and democratic institutions by others. What is clear is that the legislative and political endeavours to demonise *etarras* in the 1980s have not ceased.

The number of suspected *etarras* killed in questionable circumstances or explicitly by the state has decreased since the 1980s, although the dubiousness surrounding some deaths persists. Two individuals, Josu Zabala Salegi in 1997 and José Luis Geresta Mujika in 1999, were found killed by gunshot in questionable circumstances, and later were officially declared to have committed suicide. In 2004 a Basque autonomous police officer shot to kill Arkaitz Otazua, also under unclear circumstances. In April 2009, Jon Anza, an ETA militant and former prisoner, disappeared after boarding a train travelling within France. A month later *Gara*, a Basque pro-independence newspaper, published the hypothesis that Jon Anza had been 'disappeared' and then killed by the Spanish police during an interrogation. In March 2010, almost a year after his disappearance, his body was found in a French hospital in Toulouse. While the Spanish government, backed by the French government, declared that Jon Anza had died of a heart attack, a series of irregularities in the investigation carried out by the French prosecutor lent credence to the assassination theory.

Since 2000, an important debate has been held on the treatment of detainees in Spanish prisons and on the constitutionality of incommunicado detentions, amid allegations of the continued use of torture by the Guardia Civil and other police forces. Moreover, the dangerously close relationship between the executive and the judiciary is a concern that needs to be addressed in any state claiming to be a democracy.

Spanish counter-terrorist measures include incommunicado detentions, the exceptional treatment of Basque political prisoners, and mass detentions; these are now key parts of the repertoire of numerous states around the world in the 'war on terror'. The intensity with which counter-terrorism measures have been enacted and the number of allegations of torture, along with objections raised by the international community, make the Basque Country paradigmatic of state terror. We now scrutinise how these measures are being enforced in the Basque Country.

## 4 State terror under the rule of law

### *4.1 Incommunicado detentions and torture*

The regime of incommunicado detentions in Spain permits a detainee suspected of terrorism-related offences to be held for up to 13 days. Of those 13 days, the first five are spent in police custody. Then an investigating judge decides if the suspect can be held for an additional eight days. The incommunicado regime implies a series of restrictions on the rights of detainees: they cannot designate their own lawyer; instead, the Bar Association appoints a duty lawyer to provide legal assistance. Nor can they consult a lawyer in private. They can neither have their family informed that they have been detained nor tell them where they are held. Furthermore, foreign nationals cannot inform their embassy or consulate. Lastly, detainees can only be examined by a state-appointed doctor, not a doctor of their own choice (Amnesty International, 2009).

Although the Constitution contains emergency measures that authorise the suspension of certain rights in cases of terrorism, the incommunicado regime stands apart. In other words, it is not regulated by the Constitution but is a 'supplementary' suspension of rights. After his visit to Spain, Theo van Boven, former UN Special Rapporteur on the question of torture, stated, 'incommunicado detention may facilitate the perpetration of torture and could in itself amount to a form of cruel, inhuman or degrading treatment' (United Nations, 2004: 11). According to a report by Askatu (2009: 8), a Basque NGO from the IA milieu, there were 390 detentions in the Basque area under Spanish and French control during 2008; 162 of these detentions were under the incommunicado regime, and 90 of them were by the Spanish security forces. While there have been no claims of torture from detainees held by French security forces, 61 detainees of the Spanish security forces have claimed to be survivors of some kind of torture. Of these, only one allegation comes from a detainee who was held under the regular regime – the rest were tortured during incommunicado detention.

The situation in 2009 was regrettably very similar. According to the Coordinadora para la Prevención y Denuncia de la Tortura (CPDT), a coalition of human rights NGOs from all over Spain, there were at least 88 detainees in 2009 under incommunicado detention. Forty-five claim to have suffered torture (CPDT, 2010: 104). Apart from Theo van Boven's cautionary statement, the Spanish regime of incommunicado detention has repeatedly been denounced by local NGOs and the international community, including Amnesty International (2007), Human Rights Watch (2005), the European Committee for the Prevention of Torture and Inhuman or Degrading Treatment or Punishment (Council of Europe, 2007), and van Boven's successor UN Special Rapporteur on torture, Manfred Nowak (United Nations, 2006, 2007, 2010). Despite this, the Spanish state has continued to deny that it commits torture and has refused to abrogate the incommunicado regime. On the contrary, it has argued that this regime is a fundamental instrument in the fight against terrorism, a statement expressly supported by representatives of the main political parties, PSOE and PP. Illustrative of this position is the attitude of the current Basque government which has gone as far as to declare publicly that it will prefer charges against anyone who accuses Basque security forces of committing torture during incommunicado detentions (CPDT, 2010).

This policy of denial led to a condemnation in 2009 by the ECtHR. The ECtHR found against Spain for dismissing without any investigation accusations of police torture made by a Basque detainee under the incommunicado regime in 2002. This prompted the Constitutional Tribunal of Spain to force a criminal judge to reopen a case of torture during incommunicado detention denounced by Sara Majarenas in 2005, which was filed with medical reports confirming the injuries suffered. In 2010 the case of two Basque detainees, Igor Portu and Mattin Sarasola, both severely injured under incommunicado detention in 2008, was finally brought to court. On 30 December 2010 the Court decided in favour of the applicants and convicted four Guardia Civil policemen to up to four and a half years' imprisonment for torturing, insulting and threatening to kill the detained. The other eleven officers indicted in this case were acquitted.

### *4.2 Treatment of detainees in Spanish prisons*

While ETA prisoners have always suffered severe prison conditions, these have nonetheless changed over time. In the mid-1980s, ETA prisoners were placed together in the maximum-security prison Herrera de la Mancha, under a military regime. The purpose was to break their group solidarity by offering better conditions to those who rejected ETA. However, the policy failed in its objectives. In 1987 a radically different approach was taken. Instead of putting all ETA prisoners together, the policy became one of dispersing them throughout the Spanish territory. There has been and continues to be strong opposition from the majority of the Basque population to the policy of prisoners' dispersion. According to Etxerat, a Basque NGO that supports the families of Basque prisoners, there are currently 597 Basque political prisoners scattered in 49 jails in Spain. The average prisoner is held at a distance of 694 kilometres from his/her home. In France where the state is applying a similar policy 151 ETA prisoners are dispersed in 34 jails (Etxerat, 2010: 10).

Responding to critics, the government of Spain argues that the policy is necessary to avoid the concentration of large numbers of ETA members; to break the organisation's control over individual members; to prevent the planning and execution of new crimes by ETA members from within prison; and to protect victims from potential secondary victimisation. Human rights organisations and ETA itself have argued that this measure is an additional punishment (Human Rights Watch, 2005). Theo van Boven (United Nations, 2004) has said dispersal of detainees 'apparently has no grounding in law and is applied arbitrarily'. Additionally, ETA prisoners are held under a special regime called FIES (Ficheros de internos de especial seguimiento, Files of Inmates Under Special Surveillance). The FIES regime consists of a database that designates the most difficult inmates (Rivera Beiras, n.d.). The FIES was introduced through a simple administrative circular by the General Director of Prisons as a regulation under the more general Art. 10 of Prisons Law which mentions a possible need for an exceptional regime for extremely dangerous inmates. Once an inmate is placed under the FIES regime, his/her living conditions deteriorate drastically. For example, under this regime inmates suffer extended periods of isolation: they are only allowed three hours outside their individual cell per day, when they can be with no more than one other person in the prison yard at a time. They are also subjected to daily cell and body searches (Human Rights Watch, 2005). Under the FIES regime the correspondence of prisoners is censored and limited; their phone calls are recorded, and their personal visits are scrutinised by the prison authority (Rivera Beiras, n.d.; Exterat, 2010). Moreover, while the regime of isolation is normally revised every three months, Exterat contends that ETA prisoners remain condemned to it for years. The policy of dispersion and the harsh conditions under the FIES regime have been accompanied by a progressive increment in the length of prison sentences and an extension of the period before parole.

### *4.3 Mass detentions*

In May 1998, Judge Baltasar Garzón from the Audiencia Nacional initiated a series of criminal proceedings against a large number of grassroots organisations, social movements, businesses and media in the Basque Country. These criminal proceedings have become known as the 18/98 case. The case indicted 276 people, of whom 125 were detained. Of these, 102 have subsequently been imprisoned. The relevance of the case is that with his interpretation of the law, Baltasar Garzón radically expanded the range of crimes related to membership of and collaboration with a terrorist organisation. A 'terrorist' could be anyone belonging to an organisation with obscure links to ETA, without any attempt to establish decisive evidence of alleged criminal activity by individuals. In other words, the investigation seeks to prove a suspect's membership of an organisation that can be linked to ETA through documents and public statements indicating a coincidence of political goals (CPDT 2010).

In cases where it was not possible to declare these organisations as terrorist, such as the youth organisations Jarrai, Haika and Segi (because they did not use weapons or explosives), they were simply banned as ETA's collaborators. Their members were sentenced to prison (CPDT, 2010).

Similarly, Gestoras Pro Amnistía – Askatasuna, Basque human rights organisations that worked with ETA prisoners, were also banned because of their political goals. Besides this macro criminal proceeding, other human rights organisations have suffered threats or even formal accusations by the authorities whenever they raise suspicions or accusations of torture by Spanish security forces. The Coordinadora para la Prevención y denuncia de la Tortura (CPDT, 2010) documents nine cases where criminal law was used to intimidate human rights activists in order to obstruct their activity.

## 5 The politics of state terror

### *5.1 Pact of freedoms and against terrorism*

Zapatero describes the terrorist as an 'irrational criminal'. According to Zapatero, terrorist groups 'neither deserve to be recognised as followers of a religion ... nor of a nation or of the people' (Zapatero, 2004b). They are just groups of 'fanatics who are ready to kill to impose their madness through force. Ready to disseminate the seed of evil' (Zapatero, 2004c). Zapatero calls for the 'unity of democrats' against these 'violent fanatics'. It is a unity that 'is the fundamental element in the fight against terrorism' (Zapatero, 2004b). The enemy (ETA and its sympathisers) is the one who uses violence (evil) to impose his/her ideas; the democrat as 'friend' must help in the (good) fight against terrorism. This essential dichotomy between democrats and terrorists, friends and enemies in a state of normalcy was defined by altering the criminal law for terrorist crimes. However, as Agamben points out contemporaneously, 'the enemy is first of all excluded from civil humanity and branded as a criminal; only in a second moment does it become possible and licit to eliminate the enemy by a "police operation"' (2000: 105–6). The process of social and political exclusion was initiated by the signing of the 2000 Pact of Freedoms and Against Terrorism (Pacto por las libertades y contra el terrorismo) by the two main political parties in Spain.[11]

The Pact constituted a bloc of political forces that agreed to give full support to any counter-terrorist measures taken by the government, regardless of which political party was governing. From that moment onwards, in the political realm the dichotomy between democrats and terrorist supporters, friends and enemies, was defined in a process based on the non-critical support for the government that the Pact demanded. This created a grey zone where the line between critiquing state policies against terrorism, being a terrorist supporter, and being a terrorist collaborator and/or a terrorist became increasingly arbitrary and changed according to political circumstances. This political stigmatisation was then translated into law by the enactment of the Ley de Partidos.

### *5.2 Law on political parties*

In June 2002, the Spanish parliament introduced the Ley de Partidos to regulate political parties. This law allowed the suspension and banning of political parties that did not explicitly condemn terrorist attacks. On the basis of this new legislation, on 27 March 2003 the Special Division of the Supreme Court declared Batasuna, the political continuation of Herri Batasuna to be illegal. Batasuna had been subject to criminal investigation since 1998 for its relationship with an armed group. Despite criticism from civil liberties groups, the Spanish Constitutional Court has judged the Ley de Partidos constitutional. The law has greatly intensified the space of indistinction created by the Pact of Freedoms and Against Terrorism, allowing the suppression of political parties even if they have not been qualified as catalysts of criminal activity. Any link with a terrorist organisation (e.g. with people condemned in the past for terrorist crimes who have served their sentences) renders people suspect of supporting terrorism and provides just cause for the banning of an entire political party.[12]

The politicisation of the criminal process was made evident by the suspension of Batasuna's activities by the penal judge only two days after the Spanish parliament initiated the process of banning under the new Ley de Partidos. In view of these events, these words take on new meaning. The Ley de Partidos seemingly incorporates counter-terrorist measures without producing a 'new' law, in accordance with Zapatero's declaration of a different approach from his Anglo-American allies. The law has been used over the past few years to ban several political parties within the spectrum of IA accused of continuing Batasuna's political activities.[13] Interestingly, in the 2007 elections, during negotiations between the Spanish government and ETA, the prohibition was relaxed and applied to only a few candidates, resulting in some political parties related to IA winning seats in many Basque cities and towns; after the failure of the peace negotiations in 2008, these same political parties were then banned. In this way, the Ley de Partidos allows the government to open or close the political arena to IA depending on the circumstances in the Basque Country. The ambiguous and vague definitions of the Ley de Partido project Basque radical separatist parties into a grey or indistinct area where there is a constant normative uncertainty. In so doing, it creates a pervasive uncertainty with regard to inclusion in the sphere of formal political participation.

The grey area created by the Ley de Partidos also affected elected IA members. Those who were elected prior to the banning of their political parties have kept their seats, but they can no longer claim affiliation to their party. Meanwhile, in order to extend the grey area Spanish political groups, with occasional support from the PNV, have presented motions in town halls demanding that elected members of political parties linked to the IA (e.g. Acción Nacionalista Vasca)[14] publicly condemn ETA's attacks and support Spanish policies against terrorism. Although, IA had traditionally refused to condemn ETA's violence, it had not publicly supported it either. Under the pressure of these so-called 'ethical motions', IA's refusal (until recently) to express condemnation was put on a par with publicly expressing support for terrorist acts. These motions were used predominantly to publicly discredit IA, and in one case a motion was used to incriminate a specific member. This occurred in the city of Mondragón, where the mayor, who was a member of IA, refused to subscribe to an 'ethical motion'. This refusal was used as evidence in a criminal case where she was accused of continuing the political activity of a banned party.

In the winter of 2011, IA through its new political party Sortu fulfilled the demands of the Spanish state and condemned violence as a means of attaining political goals, explicitly including this condemnation into its statute. This is happening within the context of ETA's first 'permanent, general and verifiable' ceasefire in its history. Nevertheless, the Spanish state is threatening to ban Sortu, claiming it is a re-creation of Batasuna, and thus has strong links to ETA. This illustrates how the Spanish state continues to operate within the grey zone established by the Ley de Partidos, in which it can alter legal requirements.

## Conclusion: state terror and Spanish rule of law

On the one hand, it could be argued that exceptional measures, have been enforced in the Basque Country ever since Guernica. However, to equate the current Spanish government with Franco's dictatorship, as do the IA discourse and propaganda, is certainly polemical. The degree of repression and the context are without doubt very different. On the other hand, the Spanish state's use of the guise of rule of law to legitimate counter-terrorist measures that violate human rights amounts to a continuation of state terror.

Spain is not alone in enforcing incommunicado regimes, exceptional treatment of prisoners, torture and mass detentions. These are methods widely used by governments all over the world – and this long before the emergence of the 9/11 counter-terrorist legislation. Considering this, Agamben, quoting Walter Benjamin, pointedly declared that the exception is in fact already the rule in liberal democratic governments. The specificity of the Basque scenario is that these measures are being denounced and challenged with an unusual intensity, making visible the state violence otherwise masked by law.

The banning of political parties which have significant popular support – approximately 150,000 votes in the Basque Country – has brought the politics of exclusion to a new level in Spain. The Ley de Partidos lays bare the political function of law, which liberal democracies generally attempt to hide, making the Spanish case especially relevant to the consideration of counter-terror as state terror. The confirmation of the legality of this measure by the European Court of Human Rights in 2009 highlights the limits of liberal law when confronting these violations of human rights.

The recent ceasefire declared by ETA and the condemnation of violence by the IA should negate the arguments supporting the exceptional measures. However, the reaction of the Spanish state has instead been to persist in its use of these measures, continuing mass detentions and the incommunicado regime, prohibiting mass demonstrations, and continuing to deny legality to Basque leftist parties. This illustrates that in Spain the state of exception is in fact not exceptional. The Basque case exemplifies a model of human rights in liberal democracies based on the exclusion rather than integration of paradigms that challenge it.

## Notes

1 Studies of political terrorism provide a good example of how a research field can flourish without even minimal agreement regarding the definition of basic terms (Douglass and Zulaika, 1990: 239).

2 We are referring to Article 55.2 of the Spanish Constitution which says: an organic act may determine the manner and the circumstances in which, on an individual basis and with the necessary participation of the courts and proper parliamentary control, the rights recognised in section 17, subsection 2, and 18, subsections 2 and 3, may be suspended for specific persons in connection with investigations of the activities of armed bands or terrorist groups.

3 See IA press release *Zutik, Euskal Herria* (Stand Up, Basque Country; February 2010): 'Popular Unity will be the focus of all socialist and pro-independence people in all the Basque Country in the coming political activity, so as to develop the democratic process, in mass mobilisation, ideologically and at the institutional level'. See Juaristi's interview with ETA (April 2007) 'It is known that our objective is a free and socialist Basque Country, and that is what we are fighting for' ('Es conocido que nuestro objetivo es una Euskal Herria libre y socialista y que luchamos para lograrlo').

4 Addressing the specific context of the Basque Country, Linstroth suggests there is 'value potential' in exploiting political images and objects; as he observes, political images in the Basque Country 'have become an effective means of communicating a political message and governments are anxious to limit access to this device' (2002: 216).

5 For a detailed analysis of Zapatero's discourse on the fight against terrorism and the rule of law see Van Klink *et al.* (2011: 316–22).

6 Manzanas had the reputation of a sadistic and brutal police officer, known for torturing Basque nationalists (Arrondo, 2008).

7 Terrorism was defined by this new law as 'embracing any attack on the integrity of the Spanish nation', as well as, 'any effort to secure independence of any part of its territory, even if non-violent' (Clark in Encarnación, 2007: 956).

8 It was discovered years later that GAL was responsible for the disappearance of the two young men, whose bodies were identified a decade later buried in quicklime in Alicante (see Woodworth, 2005: 63).

9 The Basque government's Office of Victims of Terrorism highlighted that of the 74 *acts of terrorism* by paramilitary groups during the period 1975–90, only 17 have led to sentences without appeal (Aizneolea, 2010).

10 This is controversial, but worthy of mention. There is empirical evidence that the third democratic electoral victory of the PSOE in 1993 provoked a strong

political reaction in the Partido Popular (hereafter PP), the Spanish conservative party. According to Maravall (2003), the PP set out to destabilise the PSOE and dislodge González, drawing on powerful and wealthy allies from within the media and banking milieu. This is corroborated by an interview with one of the chief organisers of the PP's strategy, Luis María Ansón, published by the *Tiempo* newspaper in 1998 wherein he admits the instrumentality and politically charged aims of the investigations into GAL Maravall suggests, 'this was the difference between the judicial investigation into what had happened, and the political strategy to dislodge the incumbent that judicialised politics as a political weapon' (2003: 287). Moreover, the ensuing trial was to an extent constructed with the objective of isolating the PSOE from the political forum and from the state. There was never a question of state terror but rather an attack on the PSOE for fraud, a differentiation between the state and the political.

11 The two main political parties in Spain are the right wing PP (Partido Popular) and the centre-left PSOE (Partido Socialista Obrero Español). The Pact was Zapatero's idea.

12 Under article 9.3c of the Ley de Partidos a political party may be banned if it:

> regularly includes in its governing bodies or its electoral lists, people convicted for terrorist offences and who have not publicly renounced the ends and means of terrorism; or has a large number of members who also belong to organisations affiliated or related to terrorist or violent entities, unless they have taken action against them leading to their expulsion.
>
> (authors' translation)

13 IA includes a number of political parties or groups affiliated with Basque nationalist and separatist ideology. Their radical left ideological stance embraces a wide spectrum (e.g. Marxist, Socialist, Social Democratic, etc.) and differentiates them from the conservative Basque nationalist party, the PNV (Partido Nacionalista Vasca).

14 The ANV has been linked to ETA as its new political party since Herri Batasuna was disbanded and *Batasuna* was declared illegal. In 2008, Spain's Supreme Court banned the ANV in the Basque region because of its links to armed separatists ETA (Sanz *et al.*, 2008).

## References

Agamben, G. (1998) *Homo Sacer: Sovereign Power and Bare Life.* Stanford, Calif.: Standord University Press.

Agamben, G. (2000) *Means Without End: Notes on Politics,* trans. Binetti, V. and Casarino, C. Minneapolis and London: University of Minnesota Press.

Agamben, G. (2005) *State of Exception,* trans. Attell, K. London: University of Chicago Press.

Aizpeolea, L.R. (2010) 'Las otras victimas', published by Colectivos de Victimas de Terrorismo en el País Vasco, 21 March, available at www.covite.org/covite_articulos.php?lang=es&idNoticia=448&idSeccion=3, accessed on 1 March 2011.

Amnesty International (2007) 'Spain – adding insult to injury: the effective impunity of police officers in cases of torture and other ill-treatment', available at www.amnesty.org/es/library/asset/EUR41/006/2007/en/dom-EUR410062007en.pdf, accessed on 4 March 2011.

Amnesty International (2009) Spain: out of the shadows – time to end incommunicado detention', available at www.amnesty.org/en/library/asset/EUR41/001/

2009/en/d0b49050-4a2d-44c7-9d18-880fe73c65a2/eur410012009eng.pdf, accessed on 3 March 2011.

Arrondo, C. (2008) 'Melitón Manzanas, 40 años después', *Gara*, 2 August 2008, available at www.gara.net/paperezkoa/20080802/89592/es/Meliton-Manzanas-40-anos-despues, accessed on 15 September 2010.

Askatu (Amnistia Eta Askatusuna) (2009) *Represión en Euskal Herria 2008*, available at www.askatu.org/fitxategia_ikusi.php?id_fitxategia=2902, accessed on 29 May 2009.

Clark, R.P. (1979) *The Basques: The Franco Years and Beyond*. Reno: University of Nevada Press.

Clark, R.P. (1990) *Negotiating with ETA: Obstacles to Peace in the Basque Country 1975–1988 (The Basque Series)*. Reno: University of Nevada Press.

Council of Europe, Committee for the Prevention of Torture (2007) Report to the Spanish Government on the Visit to Spain Carried out by the European Committee for the Prevention of Torture and Inhuman or Degrading Treatment or Punishment (CPT), from 12 to 19 December 2005, CPT/Inf 30, available at www.unhcr.org/refworld/docid/46977e4a2.html, accessed on 3 March 2011.

CPDT (2010) *Informe 2009 sobre la tortura en el estado español – versión completa*, available at www.prevenciontortura.org/wp-content/uploads/2010/01/INFORME_CPDT_2009.pdf, accessed on 3 March 2011.

Douglass, W.A. and Zulaika, J. (1990) 'On the interpretation of terrorist violence: ETA and the Basque political process', *Comparative Studies in Society and History*, Vol. 32, No. 2, pp. 238–57.

Encarnación, O.G. (2007) 'Democracy and dirty wars in Spain', *Human Rights Quarterly*, Vol. 29, No. 4, pp. 950–72.

Etxerat (2010) *Dossier sobre la política de dispersion*, available at www.etxerat.info/txostena.php?id_saila=40&lang=es, accessed on 3 March 2011.

Human Rights Watch (2005) 'Setting an example? Counter-terrorism measures in Spain', available at www.hrw.org/en/reports/2005/01/26/setting-example, accessed on 3 March 2011.

Irvin, C.L. (1999) *Militant Nationalism: Between Movement and Party in Ireland and the Basque Country*. Minneapolis: Minnesota University Press.

Izquierda Abertzale (2010) 'Zutik, Euskal Herria', available at www.ezkerabertzalea.info/irakurri.php?id=3344, accessed on 13 September 2010.

Jáuregui, F. and Vega, P. (2007) *Crónica del antifranquismo: 1939–1975, todos los que lucharon por devolver la democracia a España*. Barcelona: Planeta.

Juaristi, J. (2007) 'Entrevista a ETA', *Gara*, available at www.gara.net/paperezkoa/20070408/12123/es/Si/desaparecen/ataques/estamos/dispuestos/asumir/compromisos/firmes/escenario/sin/violencia, accessed on 13 September 2010.

Lasswell, H.D. (1995) 'Propaganda', in R. Jackall (ed.) *Propaganda*, London: Macmillan, pp. 13–26.

Linstroth, J.P. (2002) 'The Basque conflict globally speaking: material culture, media and Basque identity in the wider world', *Oxford Development Studies*, Vol. 30, No. 2, pp. 205–22.

Maravall, J.M. (2003) 'The rule of law as a political weapon', in A. Przeworski and J.M. Maravall (eds) *Democracy and the Rule of Law*. Cambridge: Cambridge University Press, pp. 261–306.

M.M. (2006) 'No hay derechos humanos a la hora de cazar al tigre', *El Plural,* 17 November, available at www.elplural.com/politica/detail.php?id=8003, accessed on 16 September 2010.

Muñoz Conde, F. and García Arán, M. (2004) *Derecho penal: Parte general,* 6th edn, Valencia: Tirant Lo Blanch.

Rivera Beiras (n.d.) La cárcel y el sistema penal (en España y en Europa)', *Revista Pensamiento Penal,* available at www.pensamientopenal.com.ar/index.php?option=com_content&view=article&id=1592:rivera-beiras-inaki–la-carcel-y-el-sistema-penal-en-espana-y-en-europa&catid=110:doctrina&Itemid=86, accessed on 3 March 2011.

Rubio, A. (2010) 'Guardias civiles olvidaron sus armas en Toulouse a los 7 días de morir Anza', in *El Mundo,* 15 March, available at www.elmundo.es/elmundo/2010/03/14/espana/1268597719.html, accessed on 3 March 2011.

Sanz, I., Larraz, T. and Morris, S. (2008) 'Spain's Supreme Court bans Basque party', Reuters, M. Trevelyan (ed.) available at www.reuters.com/article/idUSLG12129420080916, accessed on 8 March 2012.

Stewart, C.J., Smith, C.A. and Denton, Jr., R.E. (1995) 'The persuasive functions of slogans', in R. Jackall (ed.) *Propaganda.* London: Macmillan, pp. 400–23.

United Nations, Office of the High Commissioner for Human Rights (2004) *Report of the Special Rapporteur on the Question of Torture, Theo van Boven: Visit to Spain* (E/Cn.4/2004/56/Add.2), available at http://ap.ohchr.org/documents/alldocs.aspx?doc_id=9123, accessed on 3 March 2011.

United Nations, Economic and Social Council, Civil and Political Rights, Including the Questions of Torture and Detention (2006) Report of the Special Rapporteur on Torture and Other Cruel, Inhuman or Degrading Treatment or Punishment, Manfred Nowak Follow-up to Country Recommendations (E/CN.4/2006/6/Add.2), available at http://www2.ohchr.org/english/bodies/chr/docs/62chr/E.CN.4.2006.6.Add.2.pdf, accessed on 3 March 2011.

United Nations, General Assembly (2007) Implementation of General Assembly Resolution 60/251 of 15 March 2006 Entitled 'Human Rights Council' Promotion and Protection of Human Rights, Report of the Special Rapporteur on Torture and Other Cruel, Inhuman or Degrading Treatment or Punishment, Manfred Nowak, Follow-up to Country Recommendations (A/HRC/4/33/Add.2), available at http://www2.ohchr.org/english/bodies/hrcouncil/4session/reports.htm, accessed on 3 March 2011.

United Nations, General Assembly (2010) Report of the the Special Rapporteur on Torture and Other Cruel, Inhuman or Degrading Treatment or Punishment, Manfred Nowak. Follow-up to the Recommendations (A/HRC/13/39/Add.6), available at http://www2.ohchr.org/english/bodies/hrcouncil/docs/13 session/A.HRC.13.39.Add%206_EFS.pdf, accessed on 3 March 2011.

Van Klink, B., Lembcke, O.W. and Ciocchini, P.L. (2011) 'Symbolic power: political rhetoric in a state of exception', in Ton van Haaften, H. Hanseur, J. de Jong and W. Koetsenriutjer (eds) *Bending Opinion: Essays in Persuasion in the Public Domain.* Leiden: Leiden University Press, pp. 316–22.

Villa, I. (2007) *Historia breve del País Vasco.* Madrid: Sílex.

Whyte, D. (2009) 'Naked labour: putting Agambiu to work', *Australian Feminist Law Journal,* Vol. 31, pp. 57–76.

Woodworth, P. (2002) *Dirty Wars, Clean Hands: ETA, the GAL, and Spanish Democracy.* London: Yale University Press.

Woodworth, P. (2005) 'Using terror Against terrorists: the Spanish Experience', in S. Balfour (ed.) *The Politics of Contemporary Spain*. New York: Routledge, pp. 61–80.

Zapatero, J.L. (2004a) Assumption Speech as President of the Spanish government, Congress of Deputies, 15 April, available at www.congreso.es/public_oficiales/L8/CONG/DS/PL/PL_002.PDF, accessed on 3 March 2011.

Zapatero, J.L. (2004b) Speech delivered in a summer course on 'The fight against terrorism and its limits' of the Complutense University at San Lorenzo del Escorial, 16 July, available at www.la-moncloa.es/Presidente/Intervenciones/Discursos/p1607040.htm, accessed on 3 March 2011.

Zapatero, J.L. (2004c) Statement to the general debate of the United Nations General Assembly, 21 September, available at www.la-moncloa.es/Presidente/Intervenciones/Discursos/p2109041.htm, accessed on 3 March 2011.

# 11 Indonesian state terror in Timor-Leste and West Papua

*Elizabeth Stanley*

This chapter exposes Indonesian counter-terrorism operations in Timor-Leste and West Papua as state terror. It highlights the continua of state terror across time and regions, from physical violations including the killing of civilians, to environmental destruction, to the building of communities of fear and suspicion. In doing so, the chapter illustrates how state terror has enhanced Indonesia's position in the global political, ideological and economic order. In particular, it shows how Indonesian terror strategies have been made acceptable to, and supported by, powerful states and corporations.

Presented here are five features of Indonesian counter-terrorism operations that have maintained terror for those in Timor-Leste and West Papua. First, Indonesia has been able to portray counter-terrorism operations as being focused events while, in reality, state actions have terrorized many civilians; second, through the overt public violation of bodies and landscapes, Indonesian officials have created community terror; third, through discourse control, Indonesia has fed local mistrust and facilitated the denial of terror at local, regional and international levels; fourth, by engaging Timorese and Papuan people in violations, Indonesia has collectivized terror; and, finally, through the lack of legal protection afforded to West Papuans and Timorese, terror has been built through impunity.

Taken together, these strategies have meant that local populations have been terrorized over decades; few Timorese or Papuans have been exempt. Yet this situation has been challenged in myriad ways. At a local level, activists have engaged in campaigns for cultural and social recognition, they have protested at key sites and endured the consequences of calling for independence. Beyond borders, Timorese and Papuan people have engaged with others to raise awareness, employ legal actions and build international support for their cause. They have demonstrated that, even in bleak circumstances, there is scope and appetite for political mobilization and resistance.

## Introducing Timor-Leste and West Papua

Timor-Leste and West Papua have much in common: both are near neighbours of Australia (Timor-Leste is approximately 400 miles from its northwest coast while West Papua is just 155 miles north); both share their islands with other states (Indonesian West Timor and Papua New Guinea (PNG) respectively); both claim a specific ethnic heritage (Malayo-Polynesian and Melanesian); both have significant populations engaged in subsistence living; both accommodate diverse languages (with more than 20 in Timor-Leste and over 125 in West Papua); both have a Christian tradition (Catholicism in Timor-Leste and Protestantism in West Papua); and both, having claimed independence, were subsequently invaded and violently repressed by Indonesia (Banivanua-Mar 2008; Kirsch 2010; Stanley 2009).

West Papua, like Indonesia, was colonized by the Netherlands. The region known as 'West New Guinea' was, however, administered separately by the Dutch and, when Indonesia proclaimed independence in August 1945, it remained under Dutch rule. In 1961, West New Guinea gained independence, established a Parliament and renamed itself 'West Papua' (Tebay 2005). This situation was not to last; by 1962, a US-brokered agreement between the Netherlands and Indonesia gave possession of West Papua to Indonesia, on the proviso that the people would engage in a vote for their future (Banivanua-Mar 2008; Bertrand 2007). By May 1963, Indonesian flags had been raised over the new 'province' and Indonesia passed decrees to 'crack down' on supposed Papuan subversion (Tebay 2005). Popular resistance ensued and, following the establishment of the Free Papua Movement or Organisasi Papua Merdeka (OPM) in the mid-1960s, Papuans pursued self-determination through flag-raising ceremonies as well as 'bow and arrow' guerrilla violence. In response, a number of military operations were undertaken, culminating in Operasi Wibawa (Operation Authority) in 1969, which aimed to 'eradicate the Papuan resistance, tighten security, and consolidate Indonesian administrative authority' (Tebay 2005: 6). The final administrative push to annex the territory came in the same year, with the so-called Act of Free Choice. Under the watchful eye of international observers, Indonesian officials handpicked 1,026 Papuan 'voting representatives' out of a population of over 800,000. These representatives were isolated and 'trained' by the Indonesian military over several weeks. The election, unsurprisingly, heralded a unanimous declaration to join Indonesia. Despite protests from Papuans as well as almost 30 African states on the undemocratic nature of the vote, United Nations (UN) members affirmed the outcome and the US counselled that free elections would be meaningless to such a 'primitive' local population (Bertrand 2007). The province was renamed Irian Jaya and restructured according to Indonesia's political, administrative and military commands. Today, it remains a contested Indonesian province.

The occupation of Timor-Leste occurred from the mid-1970s. In 1974, after centuries of Portuguese colonial rule, Timor-Leste was faced with a short 'strategy' of decolonization. Three local parties contested power but the popular Fretilin (Front for an Independent East Timor) soon emerged as the leader (Taylor 2003). Indonesia, however, had other ideas and commenced Operasi Komodo (Operation Komodo), a campaign of destabilization. This subversion strategy took many forms – Indonesian forces undertook military attacks on border towns near West Timor, solicited international support for integration, gathered intelligence, discredited Fretilin members, strengthened oppositional political parties and encouraged other leaders to stage a coup (Stanley 2009). The subsequent attempted uprising against Fretilin was not successful. In response, Fretilin leaders reaffirmed the independence of Timor-Leste at the UN on 28 November 1975. Nine days later, with military equipment and strategic support from the US, United Kingdom and Australia, among others, the Indonesian government launched a full-scale attack. The subsequent occupation ran until 1999. Following decades of peaceful and violent resistance, including the armed insurgency of Falintil (the military wing of Fretilin), the Timorese people finally secured a referendum: 98.6 per cent of the population turned out to vote in August 1999 and, despite severe intimidation beforehand, almost 80 per cent voted for independence. Over the following month, more than 1,400 individuals were killed, independence supporters were beaten, raped and tortured, three-quarters of the population was displaced, and most buildings and infrastructure were burnt by the military and militias (Stanley 2009). When a UN military force eventually landed, Indonesia retreated and, by May 2002, Timor-Leste gained full independence.

## Overview of terror

The state narratives of 'fighting communists' or 'countering terrorists' have provided political cover for massive human rights violations by the Indonesian state over many years. Historically, they played a part in the official legitimization of US-supported violence undertaken by the Suharto-led regime against the Communist Party of Indonesia (Nairn 1997). During 1965–6, more than 1 million people were murdered for their supposed communist connections (Amnesty 1977). Within Timor-Leste, the Commission for Reception, Truth and Reconciliation (CAVR 2005) estimates that up to 183,000 people were killed during the Indonesian occupation. In West Papua, security forces have killed as many as 200,000 Papuans since 1963 (*Independent* 2009). The Indonesian state has engaged in violence against perceived opponents across regions and time; terror has been made routine rather than exceptional.

Alongside wide-scale killings, Timorese and Papuan people have been systematically ill-treated, arbitrarily detained, raped and tortured

(Banivanua-Mar 2008; Human Rights Watch 2009; Stanley 2009; UN Human Rights Council 2008). These violations, undertaken under the rubric of countering subversive or terrorist forces, have been dovetailed with all kinds of social controls. Indonesian officials have: placed restrictions on group gatherings; imposed curfews; forcibly displaced populations; conducted house and mail searches; monitored cultural events; and refused 'outsider' access to the regions (Hedman 2007; Stanley 2009). Locals have been punished for asserting their own cultural insignia: in West Papua, those who raise the Morning Star flag face arrests and lengthy punishments; in 2005, Filep Karma and Yusuk Pakage received 15 years and 10 years imprisonment respectively (Human Rights Watch 2009).

Indonesian counter-terrorist operations have also ensured that most aspects of life in Timor-Leste and West Papua have been militarized and policed. Together with police and military commands, Kopassus (the elite counter-insurgency force) holds a reputation for unaccountable brutality; they continue to enjoy funding and training from counter-terrorist partners including Australia, the UK and the US (Human Rights Watch 2009; Asian Human Rights Commission 2010). Although forces have now left Timor-Leste, there remain high troop numbers within West Papua (Hedman 2007). Among others, Col. Burhannudin Siagian and Police Chief Timbul Silean, both of whom were indicted for crimes against humanity in Timor-Leste, have found further work in West Papua (Hedman 2007; Tebay 2005).

### *Advanced global capitalism and terror*

There are strong relations between states, capital and corporations. States 'smooth the way' for private capital (McCulloch 2005: x) and as states reconfigure themselves to promote economic relationships, thereby abandoning their 'social investments', they are often progressively linked to repressive strategies towards those who are tarnished as threats (Giroux 2004: 51). Accordingly, the Western acceptance of Indonesia's advance through Timor-Leste and West Papua reflected strategic and political alliances; however, the 'opening up' of these areas to neo-liberal markets presented sizeable opportunities for states and multinational companies. It created fertile ground in which state terror inevitably sustained state, military and corporate profit.

President Suharto's regime (1967–98) actively enticed Western states and corporations to 'do business' with Indonesia. A number of states obliged – Australia has profited handsomely from the major oil and mineral reserves in the Timor Sea (Stanley 2009) and the US and UK have made billions of dollars from sales of weaponry, aircraft and other military support (Chomsky 2000; Taylor 2003). At a corporate level, Texaco, General Electric, Mobil, Chevron, American Express, Merrill Lynch, Goodyear, Caltex, Siemens, AT&T and US Steel, among others, have all enjoyed strong links with the Indonesian government (Jardine 1997; Leith 2002; Nairn 1997; Pilger 2009).

The connections between terror and economy are nowhere more apparent than in West Papua. The region has natural gas reserves (being developed by BP), as well as legal and illegal logging opportunities (Tebay 2005). However, the landscape is dominated by one multinational, Freeport (a joint venture between British/Australian company Rio Tinto and US-based Freeport McMoRan). In 1967, Freeport became the first foreign company to gain access to West Papua (Ballard 2002; Hedman 2007) and the company literally struck gold; West Papua holds the world's largest deposit of gold as well as the world's third largest open-pit copper reserves. The single mining area of Grasberg is estimated to hold reserves worth between $54 and $80 billion (Leith 2002).[1] With Indonesia now holding a 9.36 per cent stake in the company, and with gold and copper prices soaring, the company makes more than $1 million in profit every day (Pilger 2009; Tapol 2009).

Notwithstanding some recent spending for local communities,[2] most profits have been funnelled to Jakarta and further off-shore (Leith 2002). Like Timor-Leste, West Papua remains extremely poor. This is apparent in many indicators – maternal mortality is three times higher than in the rest of Indonesia (Rees *et al.* 2008); rates of HIV/AIDS are high (Rees *et al.* 2008); and the UN Development Programme ranks West Papua as one of the poorest Indonesian provinces, with over 40 per cent living below the national poverty line (UNDP 2005).

This capture of resources is evident 'on the ground' as mine workers and associates enjoy the trappings of Western lives – running water, power, roads, medical support, schooling, telephone systems and recreation facilities (Leith 2002) – that go beyond most Papuan experiences. The issue has intensified with the dramatic growth of (government-sponsored) migration to West Papua. In the wake of rapid demographic change – non-Papuans represented 2.5 per cent of the population in 1960, 4 per cent in 1971, and 41 per cent by 2005 (Chauvel 2007; Rees *et al.* 2008) – locals have struggled to find work. This, together with levels of state violence, has resulted in significant population displacement to PNG (Hedman 2007). As Banivanua-Mar (2008: 591) argues, terror is backed by a campaign of 'resettlement, relocation, and deculturation'.

Protests about Freeport's environmental, social and economic destruction have been met with strong military repression (Chauvel 2007) and the Freeport mine areas are now the most militarized of West Papua (Leith 2002). The military, used to quell protests and provide mine security (which has included the killing of numerous activists), has been amply rewarded by Freeport (Braithwaite *et al.* 2010). Despite past denials, in 2004 the company finally acknowledged that it had paid the Indonesian military $11.4 million over the previous two years (Kirsch 2010). In sum, Indonesia has built global economic, political and strategic alliances over the contested regions of Timor-Leste and West Papua. Strategies of extreme violence against local populations have maintained Indonesian domination while facilitating external state and corporate involvement in resource extraction and military expansionism.

## Counter-terrorism as terror

The experiences of West Papuans and Timorese indicate an Indonesian structure of terror that is defined by colonization, militarization and global capitalism. However, these experiences also demonstrate other continuities in how state terror is practised. This section explores five main features of counter-terrorism operations that have sustained terror: (i) the management of terrorists and state responses; (ii) performative reminders of state power; (iii) the control of discourse; (iv) the engagement of local populations; and (v) the maintenance of impunity.

### *Terror feature (i): the management of terrorists and state responses*

States are well placed to manage a shift to repression. A principal means by which terror is made acceptable to onlookers is through the political management of identities, so that victims of state terror are represented as 'threatening' (or, perhaps, not represented at all). Bauman (1989: 192) argues that state violence is more likely to happen when distancing takes place, for example when we have moral indifference to, or fear of, others. This distancing is often directed to those who allegedly pose political threats. Those identified as terrorists or subversives become the primary targets for control. Indeed, their dangerous, dehumanized status ensures that violence against 'them' in the name of security or democracy becomes widely accepted and wanted; conventional morality disappears (Crelinsten 2003).

These narratives of terrorism provide a moral framework in which state terror can be performed and sustained (Taussig 2002). They create 'punishable categories of people' (Margold 1999). Indonesia has worked hard to portray Timorese and Papuans as communist fanatics, primitives or subversives for whom Indonesian violence may be necessary and unavoidable. Thus, the seven Kopassus officers, who were lightly sentenced for the 2001 state killing of Papuan leader Theys Eluay, were hailed by the Army Chief of Staff, General Ryamizard Ryacudu, as 'Indonesian heroes' for killing a 'rebel' (Hedman 2007). Yet while terrorism narratives provide a legitimizing focus to Indonesian actions, they do not represent what occurs on the ground.

There is a common perception that counter-terrorism operations will be focused, intelligence-led and measured. In reality this is not the case and, in West Papua and Timor-Leste, those most affected by counter-terrorism strategies have been civilians. In West Papua, the OPM is labelled as an illegal separatist movement by Indonesian authorities and, in consequence, Indonesia has declared West Papua a military operation zone. The military have engaged in numerous raids to quell or eradicate suspected separatists (Tebay 2005). Invariably, sweeping operations and house-to-house searches on perceived OPM villages do not discriminate 'between ordinary villagers and OPM activists and supporters' (Chauvel 2007: 49; Hedman 2007). So all Papuans face arbitrary arrest, torture, execution-style killings, cluster bombs and aerial bombardment by elite Kopassus soldiers (Hernawan 2009). In a 2009 study of 393 cases of torture, only two involved OPM members; instead, most were rural farmers (Hernawan 2009). In November 2010, leaked Kopassus reports indicated that those surveilled and intimidated by security forces are church leaders, journalists, lawyers, students and members of indigenous political groups. Moreover, Kopassus detailed that civilians were specifically targeted because they engaged the 'outside world' with their arguments for freedom and human rights (Asian Human Rights Commission 2010).

This civilianization of terror-fuelled counter-terrorism was also evident in Timor-Leste; there, victims of torture were just as likely to be civilians: women, children, elderly people, students, teachers or local government officials. Indeed, civilians 'became a substitute for punishment' when political activists 'could not be captured' (CAVR 2005: Chapter 7.4.377). Given the realities of such routine human rights abuses against civilians, the discourse of counter-terrorism becomes crucial in building official legitimacy. Counter-terrorism strategies are made to appear to be necessary and focused responses while, in truth, terror is socialized.

### *Terror feature (ii): performative reminders of state power*

The victimization of civilians by Indonesian state officials has increased terror within communities. However, terror is also intensified through communicative practices. That is, Indonesian terror is also performed and inscribed in things – bodies, landscapes, everyday objects – that provide a social memory of the power and violence of the state. Indonesian counter-terrorism strategies have spread fear and violence in ways that reiterate daily terror for local people (Ballard 2002; Margold 1999).

The most obvious sense of performative terror is linked to the public brutalization and killing of individuals. Testimonies from Timor-Leste show that victims would be tortured and then made to walk through the village where family and friends would be forced to watch their suffering and, often, eventual killing (Stanley 2009). In West Papua, campaigners detail stories of individuals being cruelly tortured to death; once dead, relatives and neighbours have been forced to drink their loved one's blood or eat their body parts (Tebay 2005). Reports abound of mutilated bodies being suspended in prominent places in the village; sometimes bodies are left 'on display filled with sticks, cabbages and leaves' (Banivanua-Mar

2008: 591; Ballard 2002; Hernawan 2009). In Timor-Leste, bodies would be left with messages attached to them in blood or paint and paper (Stanley 2009).

Through these events, the bodies – regularly of local leaders or people who have social or cultural significance – become part of a larger strategy of terror. The dehumanization and public agony of victims create fear in that no 'body' is exempt from state violence; anyone could be the next victim. The deliberate enactment of terror sends a message of the state's willingness to employ brutal violence as well as a warning to local people about the risks of political engagement (Rothenberg 2003). In addition, the deliberate display of bodies underpins a collective memory of shared terror that will 'shape survivors' actions for years to come' (Nolin Hanlon and Shankar 2000: 278).

The sight of violence can be an instrument of terror. However, the site of repression also has significance in its repetition of terror over time (Ballard 2002). Local populations can traverse their landscapes and point out where torture happened, where bodies were thrown or where mass graves are located in places where any markers have been erased. In some locations, such as near the Freeport mines in West Papua, the military have marked their insignia across the landscape by painting skulls weeping blood and bearing the Kopassus red beret on cliff faces and boulders. The meaning in this case is clear: it is an 'unmistakable warning of the fate of those who resist the army' (Ballard 2002: 20). These are geographic spaces of terror, and subsequent spatial fear can direct social engagement, stories and movements over decades.

### *Terror feature (iii): the control of discourse*

Sending messages through public events and spaces is an efficient means of communicating terror. However, terror also depends on the management of everyday talk. In West Papua and Timor-Leste, Indonesian authorities created suspicion about interactions through the establishment of intelligence groups. For instance, in Timor-Leste, the Indonesian military built a strong system of intelligence gatherers and informers. So-called 'Civil Defence Force' members could be found in every area and they worked as spies, monitoring and informing on fellow villagers (CAVR 2005). Similarly, in West Papua, Kopassus directs a 'small army' of agents from all walks of life, who receive payment to inform on the activities and whereabouts of suspected 'enemies' (Asian Human Rights Commission 2010).

These intelligence networks have militarized and controlled communities; their actions have fortified an atmosphere of suspicion and fear as every encounter becomes potentially threatening. Local people would not always know who could or could not be trusted. During the author's research in Timor-Leste, many torture survivors noted that their initial arrest was the result of being reported by another Timorese (Stanley 2009). In this context, simple conversations – especially those that highlight political beliefs or intentions – are transformed by the possibility that neighbours or family members might pass information on to authorities (Rothenberg 2003). Everyday 'talk' is distorted by the need for individuals to protect themselves and not give too much away, or to demonstrate their allegiance to state powers, or to gain further knowledge by uncovering suspected informant links. With Indonesian informants penetrating all aspects of life, what is said, or left unsaid, may easily lead to arrest, torture or worse. In this respect, common exchanges are infused with the terror of potential harm and death.

Thus Indonesian counter-terrorism strategies have ensured that daily talk and interactions are distorted by politicized terror. Yet these approaches have also merged with cultural responses. One aspect of West Papuan and Timorese life – the centrality of rumour as a response to state violence – illustrates this well. For instance, rumours about where bodies were taken can serve to confront state discourse: to make local concerns explicit; to acknowledge loss; and, to spread social and political truths without implicating anyone (Kirsch 2002). Yet rumours have also been problematic in that they contribute to the expression of terror. For example, in West Papua and Timor-Leste, rumours could create misinformation on who was a spy or a threat; and they could create worries about the whereabouts or intentions of Indonesian security officials (Kirsch 2002; Stanley 2009). In these ways, rumours increased local fears and they even instigated violence by creating confusion (Stanley 2009). In the sharing of terror-fuelled stories, locals have run the risk of transferring and reproducing 'the mark of terror into the community' (Hernawan 2009: 4).

Still, the alternative to sharing stories is silence. Silence can operate at local levels as individuals find that they are unable to talk about their terrifying experiences and fear. Talking may also require a language that people do not have and it can make terror real. Silence can be, then, a survival strategy (Stanley 2004).[3] Of course, for the Indonesian authorities, silence on state terror is a preferred option. Indonesia has been careful to deny and minimize its involvement in state violence even when terror has been openly performed. For example, in response to the 2010 killing of social justice reporter Ardiansyah Matra'is – who was found naked, beaten and tethered to a tree in West Papua – the local police bluntly claimed it was a case of suicide. Even when faced with irrefutable facts, Indonesian officials consistently argue that any violence has now stopped, perpetrators have been disciplined and terrorists' actions meant that there was no other option (Stanley 2009).

Such silencing techniques have dovetailed with a silencing of the media that sustains the conditions for terror. The nature and extent of state-led terror in Timor-Leste and West Papua have been missing from most international reporting, perhaps because this would undermine the nexus between mainstream media, global economy and political power (Pilger 1992). As the reporting of the 'Santa Cruz massacre'[4] exemplified, revealing violence to British, North American and Australasian viewers, while highlighting the political and economic support of their respective governments to Indonesia, makes it difficult for external states to ignore the conditions and relationships that make terror possible. Yet these moments are rare, and made more difficult by Indonesia's actions to stop journalists from entering these regions, and through their intimidation and killing of reporters.[5] In turn, mainstream media have relied heavily on Indonesian misrepresentations (Chomsky 1996). The true terror in Timor-Leste and West Papua has often been ignored; instead, Indonesian propaganda that has focused on the denigration of communism, the 'backwardness' of local populations, the developmental 'good' provided by the Indonesian government, and the threat of terrorism has found a ready home (Cabral 2000). As a consequence, terror through talk and silence is spread through global, national and local networks.

### *Terror feature (iv): the engagement of local populations*

It is clear that local populations can play a part in the perpetuation of terror. However, locals can also undertake a more direct involvement in terrifying actions through their engagement as militia members or military officials. Within West Papua, this has been relatively unusual as most violence has been conducted by the police and security forces (Hernawan 2010). Yet over recent years, Indonesian defence forces have increased the recruitment, training, arming, financing and directing of militia forces in the region (Banivanua-Mar 2008).

In Timor-Leste, local people were engaged throughout violent institutions and groups. Timorese worked within the Indonesian Army (mostly in the lower ranks) and they also participated in 'ninja' gangs and militias that were established, trained and funded by the Indonesian military. In the early 1990s, local 'ninja' gangs engaged in 'death squad operations', undertaking raids on suspected subversives (CAVR 2005). By the late 1990s, millions of dollars had been channelled to the militias to 'encourage' Timorese votes for Indonesian control and, thereafter, to punish those who supported independence (CAVR 2005).

The Indonesian military was central to the formation and training of militia groups in Timor-Leste (CAVR 2005). Militia commanders were given recruitment targets for each village and received a salary to mobilize, manage and retain local members. Robinson (2001: 277) notes that many individuals joined militias 'under duress'. Those who refused to join had their homes and families attacked. Some 'refusers' were detained for up to four months, tortured and threatened with further terrors (CAVR 2005: Chapter 7.4.563). Nonetheless, some Timorese joined the militias 'freely'

– to earn money, to enact revenge for Fretilin-led violence in the 1970s, to gain power through the carrying of arms or to show support to the regime in which their family had done well (Stanley 2009).

The engagement of local populations in terror has reflected strategies of collusion as well as coercion. At a ground level, the use of militias and informers is socially disintegrative as they undermine collective cohesion; they rip apart the fabric of stable communities (Nolin Hanlon and Shankar 2000). The use of locals also provides a means by which Indonesian officials may distance themselves from terrifying violations, hide their affiliations and avoid international scrutiny, while presenting the idea that they are a neutral force in volatile areas (Robinson 2001).

### *Terror feature (v): the maintenance of impunity*

The silencing of violations, as well as the use of militia members, has contributed to the lack of accountability of Indonesian officials. All but the most sensational violence in West Papua and Timor-Leste has been invisible, and most violence has just been regarded as acceptable within the 'normative political, economic and moral structures' (Banivanua-Mar 2008: 596).

Part of the problem is that West Papua and Timor-Leste (until the late 1990s when the independence movement gained international support) have struggled to attract international attention. The travel restrictions imposed on academics, journalists, human rights workers and diplomats have not assisted the exposure of the political and social conditions of these regions (Kirsch 2010). In addition, the UN as well as European, North American and Australasian states have been reticent to challenge Indonesia, or multinational companies, on their involvement in violence. Any public shaming of Indonesia, or changes to trade or aid agreements, has been short-lived (Kirsch 2010). In the current 'war on terror', counterterrorism measures – whether terrorizing or otherwise – trump other considerations in aid, trade or development decisions (Tujan *et al.* 2004); at a global level, this is a framework in which violations are more likely to occur.

Terror is maintained through the limited political challenge to Indonesia. However, it is also bolstered through the ways in which the impunity of perpetrators is accepted by external powers. For example, despite several UN proclamations that those responsible for violations in Timor-Leste would be brought to account, Indonesian officials have not been threatened by legal accountability. The Indonesian court established to deal with serious violators brought twelve individuals to trial and convicted just one Timorese militia member. In Dili, the UN's Special Panels that were mandated to deal with serious crimes also convicted Timorese militia members (see Stanley 2009). These outcomes – the consequences of limited resources and investment in courts, the lack of political support to compel attendance by Indonesian violators, and the continued dominance of strategic, economic and political interests over questions of 'justice' – have given the appearance of 'doing justice' while doing very little. The constraints imposed by the UN and key powerful states meant that, while a narrative of tackling state terror was propelled, impunity was assured. Many indicted Indonesians have since been promoted and moved to other 'problematic' areas such as West Papua (Stanley 2009).

Overall, this policy of impunity towards state officials is a form of invisible terror which begins to take on a life of its own (Nolin Hanlon and Shankar 2000). For victims, the removal of legal protection increases terror as it says that their violation 'does not matter' and that it could happen again; for perpetrators, impunity provides global legitimacy for terrifying strategies; and, the limitation on justice implicates bystanders as accomplices in terror. In summary, the law, global politics and 'justice' initiatives have served to consolidate Indonesia's political power, and make state violence acceptable.

## Resistance to the techniques of terror

Some writers (notably Taussig 2002) have argued that repressive states embed a 'culture of terror' in which civilians can be incapacitated in such a way that they see no world beyond terror. The experiences of torture, mass killings, 'disappearances' and other violent acts can make resistance very difficult (Taussig 2002). Yet the term 'culture of terror' is, as Margold (1999) argues, inflationary. It implies 'that terror and fear are totalizing conditions that orchestrate all the rhythms of daily life' (Margold 1999: 64). Thus, the idea downplays other possibilities such as agency and resistance.

Given the features of terrifying counter-terrorism operations within West Papua and Timor-Leste, it is instructive that local populations have engaged in directed forms of political struggle. Among other things, Papuans and Timorese have: worked against official representations of local populations; established structures to deal with trauma and enhance community support; contested state and corporate destruction of the environment; reasserted control over indigenous languages, norms and values; and rallied locals to fight for independence (Kirsch 2010; Stanley 2009; Tebay 2005). They have also asserted themselves against the five techniques of terror detailed above.

First, those resisting have continued to work against state narratives of terrorism and counter-terrorism by exposing the civilianization of terror. For instance, both the footage of the Santa Cruz massacre in Timor-Leste as well as the October 2010 video release of two tortured West Papuan priests proved the civilian status of victims (West Papua Media 2010). The recent exposure of Kopassus documents also clarifies the regime's own targeting of civilians in West Papua. In releasing this kind of evidence, resisters confirm the mythical basis of Indonesian claims to be fighting terrorists and they exemplify how gross violence is discursively legitimized to secure political power.

More difficult to resist may be the second technique – to work against the deliberate acts of terror on bodies and across the landscape. In Timor-Leste, local people acted to reassert their 'ownership' of places where serious violations had openly taken place. By placing stones or small crosses at sites of violence, Timorese created social spaces of memory out of places of horror. In West Papua, indigenous populations have responded in comparable ways, by ignoring state graffiti across the landscape and by focusing upon their own connection with the land. For example, the Amungme people are emboldened by their 'privileged access to the meaning of the land and the knowledge of its names' (Ballard 2002: 23). By emphasizing their own cultural traditions, the Amungme downplay the imagery perpetuated by the state and it subsequently fails to recreate terror among locals.

The third technique, of silencing terror or distorting talk, has faced continued opposition. Beyond the attempts by locals to reassert cultural traditions (noted above) or to constrain intelligence networks (noted below), Timorese and Papuans have worked hard to engage the UN and international media in their plight, and they understand the importance of international 'buy in' to their resistance. For Timor-Leste, international acknowledgement and action propelled the independence movement to success in the late 1990s. For West Papuans, actions to expose terror have continued over decades. In 1984–5, activists coordinated the mass exodus of more than 10,000 West Papuans across the border into PNG, in a bid to generate international support (Banivanua-Mar 2008; Chauvel 2007). In January 2006, an organized group of 43 Papuans sought political asylum in Australia. Arriving by outrigger canoe and flying the Morning Star flag, their claims of violence and terror were accepted; all were granted refugee status and Indonesia withdrew its ambassador from Australia in protest (Braithwaite *et al.* 2010; Gordon 2006). Through such actions that have subverted mainstream silencing and provided a counter to Indonesian narratives, external states have been confronted and made to engage with the Papuan 'problem'.

The fourth technique, of involving local populations in terror, has also faced opposition. For instance, the high numbers of Timorese who were recruited as informants did not always behave in ways to benefit the repressive regime. Informants were regularly disloyal, and would give over false information to Indonesian officials while passing on strategic details to independence fighters. Despite extensive networks and resource-backing, Indonesian security forces struggled to control local people (Stanley 2009). In West Papua, relatively few indigenous people have been involved in violent activities. While oppositional violence was a key tactic for OPM activists, particularly during the 1960s and 1970s, Papuans have fought for independence through non-violent means such as rallies, symbolic flag-raisings, land occupations, restoring indigenous names to the landscape and facilitating local alliances through the 2009 'Papua National Consensus' that has rejected violence, discrimination and marginalization (Leith 2002; Papua National Consensus 2009). In these ways, Papuans have maintained an embracing political focus to their strategies of resistance and embedded a strong collective fight against their domination.

Finally, the fifth technique of impunity has provoked lasting opposition. In Timor-Leste, activists continue vocal campaigns for the prosecution of senior Indonesian officials (Stanley 2009) and Papuans have also used the law to assert their rights. Protesting against Freeport's occupation and the destruction of their local environment, the Amungme people have launched a number of legal actions (Ballard 2002; Leith 2002). In 1996, they filed a $6 billion lawsuit against Freeport McMoRan in New Orleans. The case, which argued that mining operations were connected to violations, was dismissed as the court ruled that there was no demonstrable link between the company and the Indonesian military (Kirsch 2010). Undeterred, and with new evidence of corporate–military coordination, the Amungme Tribal Council filed a 2009 lawsuit against Freeport and the Indonesian government in Jakarta (Tapol 2009). Overall, the limits placed on justice have not been accepted by Timorese and Papuan people. Through continued legal action, they have highlighted the connections between Indonesia, corporations and external states, and established how economic expansion and resource capture have sustained violence against civilians. In confronting this terror, they have delegitimized the nature and basis of political, economic and strategic relations in their regions.

Of course, to eradicate state-led terror in West Papua there has to be a benign change within the Indonesian leadership. This is a possibility; after all, states are not homogenous entities and there can be progressive shifts. For instance, the so-called 'Papuan Spring' – in which the Morning Star flag was made acceptable and some Papuan demands were accommodated – occurred within the 1999–2001 presidency of the late Abdurrahman Wahid who was removed by a dissatisfied military and parliamentarians (Hedman 2007). Similarly, the independence would never have been granted to Timor-Leste without the leadership of President B.J. Habibie (the reformer who replaced Suharto in May 1998). Notwithstanding the importance of structural relations and social conditions, regime change can be advanced by collectivities of individuals and small groups.

Nevertheless, international attention and interventions are also required. The position in Timor-Leste, for instance, was supported through a range of practical, ideological, strategic and economic actions by external states and international financial institutions as well as grassroots activists (Stanley 2009). When international bodies and external states withdrew their support to Indonesia, they made repression in

Timor-Leste untenable. Whether this will occur for West Papua, at a time when Indonesia is feted for its stance in the 'war on terror', is yet to be seen.

In summary, the Indonesian approach to counter-terrorism has ensured that human rights interests have been supplanted by corporate agendas that pursue strategic, economic and ideological control at any cost. In the face of perceived threats to national security or resource capitalization, Indonesian terror has been deemed acceptable at regional and global levels. Indonesian actions have involved ad hoc violence, public suffering and intimidation, discourse control, local involvement and limits on legal protection. These have embedded terror within local populations, yet, despite the fear that has ensued, Papuan and Timorese people have not been 'complete victims'. They have struggled, often in the most terrible circumstances, to create resistant actions that strike at the heart of this state oppression. Indeed, ongoing violence to the people and environment has resulted in an intensified commitment to oppose state terror. In the case of Timor-Leste, this struggle eventually resulted in the removal of Indonesian brutality, while, for West Papua, the fight continues.

## Notes

1 All dollar figures in this chapter refer to the US currency.

2 The amount provided to local Amungme and Kamoro villagers is somewhat contested – from an initial $250,000 with an extra $100,000 on an annual basis (Perlez 2006) to an initial $2.5 million with an extra $1 million annually (FCX 2010).

3 While individuals may remain silent, their bodies can illustrate trauma. Individuals who accommodate themselves to terror can endure ulcers, irritability, panic attacks, nightmares, bowel problems and mental health problems. These are the physical manifestations of terror in which the 'chaos one feels becomes infused throughout the body' (Green 2002: 311).

4 On 12 November 1991, approximately 270 people were shot or beaten to death by Indonesian soldiers in a Dili cemetery. The unprovoked brutality of this event was filmed and broadcast around the world. Its exposure presented a landmark shift in terms of resisting violence in Timor-Leste; it galvanized local and international populations.

5 For instance, the 'Balibo Five' were killed on 16 October 1975 by Indonesian troops as they attempted to report on the Indonesian incursion into Timor-Leste. Remarkably, the journalists' governments (Australia, New Zealand and Britain) downplayed the event and made no challenge to Indonesia about the killings (Jolliffe 2009). After decades of campaigning, an NSW coroner held a 2007 inquest into the death of one journalist, Brian Peters, and concluded that the five were killed deliberately by Indonesian special forces to stop them reporting the Indonesian invasion (Pinch 2007).

## References

Amnesty (1977) *Indonesia* London: Amnesty International.

Asian Human Rights Commission (2010) *Files show Kopassus Targets Papuan Churches,* Press Release, www.pacific.scoop.co.nz, accessed on 16 November 2010.

Ballard, C. (2002) 'The Signature of Terror: Violence, Memory, and Landscape at

Freeport' in David, B. and Wilson, M. (eds) *Inscribed Landscapes: Marking and Making Place.* Honolulu: University of Hawai'i Press, pp. 13–26.

Banivanua-Mar, T. (2008) '"A Thousand Miles of Cannibal Lands": Imagining away Genocide in the Re-Colonization of West Papua', *Journal of Genocide Research*, Vol. 10, No. 4, pp. 583–602.

Bauman, Z. (1989) *Modernity and the Holocaust.* Cambridge: Polity Press.

Bertrand, J. (2007) 'Papua and Indonesian Nationalisms: Can they be Reconciled?', in Hedman E. (ed.) *Dynamics of Conflict and Displacement in Papua, Indonesia*, Refugee Studies Centre Working Paper No 42. Oxford: Department of International Development, pp. 16–31.

Braithwaite, J., Cookson, M., Braithwaite, V. and Dunn, L. (2010) *Anomie and Violence: Reconciliation in Indonesian Peacebuilding.* Canberra: ANU E-Press.

Cabral, E. (2000) 'The Indonesian Propaganda War against East Timor', in Hainsworth, P. and McCloskey, S. (eds) *The East Timor Question: The Struggle for Independence from Indonesia.* London: I.B. Tauris, pp. 69–84.

CAVR, Comissão de Acolhimento, Verdade e Reconciliacão de Timor-Leste (2005) *Chega! The Report of the Commission for Reception, Truth and Reconciliation in Timor-Leste.* Dili: CAVR.

Chauvel, R. (2007) 'Refuge, Displacement and Dispossession' in Hedman, E. (ed.) *Dynamics of Conflict and Displacement in Papua, Indonesia*, Refugee Studies Centre Working Paper No. 42. Oxford: Department of International Development, pp. 32–56.

Chomsky, N. (1996) *Powers and Prospects: Reflections on Human Nature and the Social Order.* London: Pluto Press.

Chomsky, N. (2000) *A New Generation Draws the Line: Kosovo, East Timor and the Standards of the West.* London: Verso.

Crelinsten, R.D. (2003) 'The World of Torture: A Constructed Reality', *Theoretical Criminology*, Vol. 7, No. 3, pp. 293–318.

FCX, Freeport McMoRan Copper and Gold (2010) *History*, www.fcx.com/company/history.htm, accessed on 28 September 2010.

Giroux, H. (2004) *The Terror of Neoliberalism: Authoritarianism and the Eclipse of Democracy.* Boulder, Colo.: Paradigm Publishers.

Gordon, M. (2006) 'Refugee Child Ignites Indonesia Tensions', *The Age*, 18 April 2006, www.theage.com.au/news/national/storm-over-refugee-child/2006/04/17/1145126055980.html, accessed on 24 January 2012.

Green, L. (2002) 'Fear as a Way of Life', in Hinton, A. (ed.) *Genocide: An Anthropological Reader.* Oxford: Blackwell, pp. 307–33.

Hedman, E. (2007) 'Papua: The Last Frontier for Democratization, Demilitarization and Decentralization in Indonesia', in Hedman, E. (ed.) *Dynamics of Conflict and Displacement in Papua, Indonesia.* Refugee Studies Centre Working Paper No. 42, Oxford: Department of International Development, pp. 6–15.

Hernawan, B.J. (2009) *Terror, Resistance and Trauma in Papua (Indonesia).* Australian National University, Centre for International Governance and Justice, Issues Paper 14, December 2009.

Hernawan, B.J. (2010) 'Torture as a Spectacle: The Genealogy and Logic of Torture in West Papua, Indonesia', Talk given at Victoria University of Wellington, 17 November 2010.

Human Rights Watch (2009) *'What Did I Do Wrong?' Papuans in Merauke Face Abuses by Indonesian Special Forces.* New York: Human Rights Watch.

*Independent* (2009) 'Bows, Arrows and a Dream of Liberation', *Independent*, 14 August 2009.

Jardine, M. (1997) 'Introduction' in Pinto C and Jardine M (1997) *East Timor's Unfinished Struggle: Inside the Timorese Resistance.* Boston: South End Press, pp. 1–25.

Jolliffe, J. (2009) *Balibo.* Melbourne: Scribe Publications.

Kirsch, S. (2002) 'Rumour and Other Narratives of Political Violence in West Papua', *Critique of Anthropology*, Vol. 22, No. 1, pp. 53–79.

Kirsch, S. (2010) 'Ethnographic Representation and the Politics of Violence in West Papua', *Critique of Anthropology*, Vol. 30, No. 1, pp. 3–22.

Leith, D. (2002) 'Freeport and the Suharto Regime, 1965–1998', *The Contemporary Pacific*, Vol. 14, No. 1, pp. 69–100.

McCulloch, J. (2005) '(In)security in the Age of Globalisation: Human Precariousness in the Move from Welfare to Warfare State', *Just Policy: A Journal of Australian Social Policy*, Vol. 37, pp. 18–23.

Margold, J.A. (1999) 'From "Cultures of Fear and Terror" to the Normalization of Violence: An Ethnographic Case', *Critique of Anthropology*, Vol. 19, No. 1, pp. 63–88.

Nairn, A. (1997) 'Foreword', in Pinto, C. and Jardine, M. (1997) *East Timor's Unfinished Struggle: Inside the Timorese Resistance.* Boston: South End Press, pp. xii–xxv.

Nolin Hanlon, C. and F. Shankar, (2000) 'Gendered Spaces of Terror and Assault: The Testimonio of REMHI and the Commission for Historical Clarification in Guatemala', *Gender, Place and Culture*, Vol. 7, No. 3, pp. 265–86.

Papua National Consensus (2009) *Papua National Consensus*, www.etan.org/issues/wpapua/0905papconsensus.htm, accessed on 28 April 2010.

Perlez, J. (2006) 'The Papuans say, This Land and its Ores are Ours', *New York Times*, Letter from Indonesia, 5 April 2006.

Pilger, J. (1992) *Distant Voices.* London: Vintage.

Pilger, J. (2009) 'Let the Bird of Paradise Go Free', *New Statesman*, 12 November 2009.

Pinch, D. (2007) *Inquest into the Death of Brian Raymond Peters, Magistrate Dorelle Pinch, Coroner.* www.etan.org/etanpdf/2007/Peterssinquest1.pdf, accessed on 20 February 2011.

Rees, S.J., Van de Pas, R., Silove, D. and Kareth, M. (2008) 'Health and Human Security in West Papua', *Medical Journal of Australia*, Vol. 189, No. 11/12, pp. 641–3.

Robinson, G. (2001) 'People's War: Militias in East Timor and Indonesia', *South East Asia Research*, Vol. 9, No. 3, pp. 271–318.

Rothenberg, D. (2003) '"What We have Seen has been Terrible": Public Presentational Torture and the Communicative Logic of State Terror', *Albany Law Review*, Vol. 67, No. 2, pp. 465–99.

Stanley, E. (2004) 'Torture, Silence and Recognition', *Current Issues in Criminal Justice*, Vol. 16, No. 1, pp. 5–25.

Stanley, E. (2009) *Torture, Truth and Justice: The Case of Timor-Leste.* London: Routledge.

Tapol (2009) *Tapol Supports Amungme People's Lawsuit Against Freeport*, Statement 20 July 2009, www.tapol.gn.apc.org, accessed on 13 May 2010.

Taussig, M. (2002) 'Culture of Terror – Space of Death: Roger Casement's Putumayo Report and the Explanation of Torture' in Hinton, A.L. (ed.) *Genocide: An Anthropological Reader.* Oxford: Blackwell, pp. 164–91.

Taylor, J. (2003) '"Encirclement and Annihilation" The Indonesian Occupation of East Timor', in Gellately, R. and Kiernan, B. (eds) *The Specter of Genocide.* Cambridge: Cambridge University Press, pp. 163–85.

Tebay, N. (2005) *West Papua: The Struggle for Peace with Justice.* London: Catholic Institute for International Relations.

Tujan, A., Gaughran, A. and Mollett, H. (2004) 'Development and the "Global War on Terror"', *Race and Class,* Vol. 46, No. 1, pp. 53–74.

UNDP (2005) *Broadening Opportunities: Assessing the Needs of Papua,* http://undp.or.id/factsheets/fs_ciu_papua.pdf, accessed on 30 September 2010.

UN Human Rights Council (2008) *Report of the Special Representative of the Secretary-General on the Situation of Human Rights Defenders, Ms Hina Jilani, Addendum: Mission to Indonesia,* A/HRC/7/28/Add.2, accessed on 28 January 2008.

West Papua Media (2010) *Video Released of Torture Killings by Indonesia Forces,* www.pacific.scoop.co.nz, accessed on 18 October 2010.

# 12 Al Qaeda in the West, for the West

*Jeremy H. Keenan*[1]

## Introduction

Since 9/11, the global war on terror (GWOT) has been used by the US to further expand and entrench its global imperial interests, while its allies, often nothing more in the developing world than the authoritarian elites of regional proxy powers, have used the empowerment given to them by their alliance in the GWOT to increase their own repression and control over subordinate and often minority populations.

One of the best examples of this process is seen in the way in which the GWOT was launched, and has been subsequently 'developed', in North Africa and the Sahel. Indeed, as this chapter reveals, the regional North African Al Qaeda franchise, known as Al Qaeda in the Islamic Maghreb (AQIM), is not just 'in the West' (as the word Maghreb means in Arabic),[2] but 'for the West'. Moreover, the way in which 'terrorism', mostly 'state terrorism', has been 'fabricated' and 'imagined' in the region has not only resulted in the US government's initial and false portrayal of the region as a 'Terror Zone' becoming a self-fulfilling prophecy, but it raises serious issues and questions about the so-called 'Arab Spring'.

The repressive authoritarianism of all North Africa's regimes, as well as most of those of the Middle East, has, since 9/11, been underpinned by the GWOT: the 'war' on political Islam, Al Qaeda and almost all else that has stood up to and opposed the new imperial order. And yet, in the uprisings that have swept most of North Africa and the Middle East since the beginning of 2011, Al Qaeda and Islamists have been noticeable by their absence. Much of the alleged Al Qaeda activity in these countries has, in fact, had nothing to do with Al Qaeda or political Islam, but has been fabricated state terrorism used to justify the GWOT and the further crack-down on minorities, civil society movements and almost all forms of legitimate opposition. It is because the West's intelligence services have been so trapped in their ideological cul-de-sac of the GWOT and its Islamist and Al Qaeda 'bogeymen' that the US, France, the UK, Italy and the rest were all caught flat-footed by the recent Arab uprisings.

Indeed, one fundamental question that hangs over the 'Arab Spring' is the extent to which it is a reaction to the entire GWOT syndrome. The uprisings that began in early 2011 in almost every Arab country are attempts by their peoples to rid their countries of their ruthless authoritarian and repressive regimes, which, without exception, have become increasingly repressive since 9/11 in the knowledge that they have the backing of the West. As Yasmin Ryan wrote when discussing the question of the relationship between the GWOT and the 'Arab Spring':

> All of North Africa's leaders, have been complicit with the West: acting as its torturers, buying its arms and patrolling the Mediterranean Sea to stem the tides of young people desperate to flee their homelands. All were partners in the CIA's controversial 'extraordinary rendition programme' and Libya has been a pro-active partner in a secretive Rome–Tripoli deal, signed in 2009, to intercept boats carrying migrants. In return for the sea patrols, Italy pledged to pay Libya $7bn over 20 years.
>
> (Ryan 2011)

As one Algerian remarked to me in 2005: 'Now they [the *mukhabarat* (police state)] have the Americans behind them, they have become even bigger bullies' (Keenan 2012).

## The role of the Pentagon in the creation of an African 'zone of terror'

The creation of AQIM in the Sahara–Sahel region has gone through two distinct phases: the initial implanting of terrorism into the Sahara–Sahel, and then the actual creation of AQIM in the region. The first of these phases began in 2002, the second in 2006.

To understand how and why the 'West', or, to be more precise, the US, implanted terrorism in the Sahara–Sahel, we need to step back for a moment and consider why Africa, and the Sahara–Sahel in particular, became of such importance in US foreign policy in the years immediately following 9/11.

The US's growing interest in Africa, reflected in the establishment of AFRICOM as a fully unified combat command on 1 October, 2008, did not come about overnight, but was, as AFRICOM's website told us at the time, 'the culmination of a 10-year thought process within the Department of Defense.'[3] This specific 'thought process' by the Pentagon dates from 1997, a landmark year in contemporary US history for two related reasons. First, it saw the founding of the neoconservatives' 'Project for the New American Century' (PNAC 1997). Second, it saw US dependency on foreign oil reaching the psychologically critical 50 per cent. The threat posed to national security by the latter development was not lost on the 'neocons'. They made it an election issue in 2000, with George W. Bush pledging to make energy security a top priority.

One of the new President's first executive decisions on taking office was to establish a National Energy Policy Development (NEPD) Group under the chairmanship of his Vice-President, Dick Cheney. The Cheney Report was published in May 2001 (*National Energy Policy* 2001). Its findings were stark: between 1991 and 2000, Americans had used 17 per cent more energy than in the previous decade, while domestic energy production had risen by only 2.3 per cent. It projected that US energy consumption by 2020 would increase by about 32 per cent, with the oil share remaining at around 40 per cent, more than a quarter of the world's total consumption (Keenan 2009: 116–31).

With Saudi Arabian oil output appearing to plateau and possibly even decline, along with the security risk posed by dependency on oil from the Gulf region, the Cheney Report singled out sub-Saharan Africa as the key source of future US oil supplies. It forecast that by 2015, 25 per cent of US imported oil would come from the Gulf of Guinea. Some subsequent forecasts have put this figure at 35 per cent.[4]

While the crisis engendered by the 9/11 terrorist attacks on the US may have diverted public concern and attention away from the Cheney Report, neither Congress nor the Pentagon, which was now effectively driving US foreign policy, had relegated it to the archives. In January 2002, Ed Royce, the Republican Chairman of the House of Representatives' Africa subcommittee, called for African oil to 'be treated as a priority for US national security post 9/11' (Institute for Advanced Strategic and Political Studies 2002). In April, US Deputy Assistant Secretary of Defense for African Affairs Michael Westphal stressed that 'Africa matters to the United States', pointing out that Africa was already supplying 14 per cent of US oil imports and had the potential to increase that amount substantially over the next decade (Westphal 2002). In June, US Assistant Secretary of State for Africa Walter Kansteiner told a Nigerian audience that 'African oil is of strategic national interest to us' and that 'it will increase and become very important as we go forward' (Akosah-Sarpong 2002: 10).[5] At a Washington conference on US national security interests in April 2004, Acting Assistant Secretary of State for African Affairs Charles Snyder commented:

> It used to be a kind of cruel joke twenty years ago when some of us tried to pretend Africa might rise to the level of a strategic interest, but thanks to the oil deposits we're finding every day in and near Africa, I can say with a straight face 30 per cent of our oil will come from there, and I promise you it is a strategic interest.
>
> (Snyder 2004)

The events of 9/11 constituted the PNAC's 'second Pearl Harbor'. It presented the neocons, who now effectively controlled the Pentagon, under the hierarchy of Donald Rumsfeld, Paul Wolfowitz and Douglas Feith, and many of the other high reaches of the US administration, with the opportunity that they sought. The launch of a GWOT was seen as providing the ideological means of securing the militarization of those regions, such as Africa, that US imperial interests required. Indeed, the Bush administration had already defined African oil as a 'strategic national interest' and thus a resource that the US might choose military force to control (Volman 2003). Thus, rather than acknowledge that US military intervention in Africa was about resource control, the Bush administration was able to use the pretext of the GWOT for justifying its militarization of Africa and securing access to and control over its oil.[6]

However, launching the GWOT in Africa was tricky, as most of the continent, especially sub-Saharan Africa, had hitherto scarcely suffered the atrocities of terrorism in the conventional sense and as it has come to be recognized in the context of the post-9/11 GWOT.[7] The continent's few terrorist incidents, apart from those perpetrated by many of its more repressive regimes against their own peoples, had been confined predominantly to its periphery: the Mediterranean littoral of the Maghreb, East Africa and debatably Somalia[8] – places that were a long way from the oil-rich, West African countries surrounding the Gulf of Guinea.

I have described in great detail elsewhere (Keenan 2009, 2012) how the US administration and its key ally, Algeria, overcame the problem posed by the lack of terrorism in Africa by fabricating it. The US colluded with Algeria's secret military service, the Département du renseignement et de la sécurité (DRS). One result of this collusion was the abduction of 32 European tourists in the Algerian Sahara in February–March 2003. The 'official' story is that the tourists were captured and held hostage by Islamic extremists belonging to the Groupe salafiste pour la prédication et le combat (GSPC). The truth is that the leader of the 'terrorists', whose *nom de guerre* was El Para,[9] was a DRS agent.[10] Through this and a number of subsequent fabricated incidents in the northern Sahel regions of Mali, Niger and Chad during the course of 2003–4, the Bush administration was able to justify the launch of a Sahara–Sahelian front, or what became known as a 'second front', in the GWOT in Africa.[11]

In 2002, a plan was presented to the US Defense Secretary, Donald Rumsfeld, by his Defense Science Board.[12] Excerpts of the DSB's 'Summer Study on Special Operations and Joint Forces in Support of Countering Terrorism' were revealed on 16 August 2002, with Pamela Hess (2002), William Arkin (2002) and David Isenberg (2002) (among others) publishing further details and analysis of the plan. The DSB recommended the creation of a 'Proactive, Preemptive Operations Group (P2OG)', a covert organization which would carry out secret missions to 'stimulate reactions' among terrorist groups by provoking them into undertaking violent acts that would expose them to 'counterattack' by US forces, along with other operations which, through the US military penetration of terrorist groups and the recruitment of local peoples, would dupe them into conducting 'combat operations, or even terrorist activities' (Floyd 2002; Ahmed 2009).

The P2OG Programme raises huge questions about all terrorist actions since 2002, including the GWOT's Sahara–Sahel front. Nafeez Ahmed (2009), in an article on the P2OG programme, reports that the US investigative journalist Seymour Hersh (2005) was told by a Pentagon adviser that the Algerian (El Para) operation was a pilot for the new Pentagon covert P2OG programme. The timing of the developments between Washington and the Algerian Sahara are significant. The P2OG programme 'leak' came two weeks after Marion E. (Spike) Bowman (2002), Deputy General Counsel for the FBI, presented crucial evidence to the Senate Select Committee on Intelligence in regard to proposed amendments concerning the Foreign Intelligence Surveillance Act. Until Bowman's evidence, the US intelligence community was anxious about working too closely with their Algerian counterparts for fear that they would pass sensitive information to Palestinian organizations. However, Bowman's statement, in which he presented the background and nature of what the FBI called the 'International Jihad Movement', dispelled many of the anxieties about collaborating with the Algerians by showing how close Algeria was to the US in its fight against Al Qaeda and terrorism.

The first attempt to fabricate terrorism in the Sahara–Sahel region was not El Para's operation in 2003, but a similar attempt by alleged Islamists to hijack and abduct four Swiss tourists on 18 October, 2002, near Arak in southern Algeria. The operation, however, was botched and the tourists escaped (Keenan 2009: 172–4).[13] There is no evidence that the US was directly involved in this first attempt at abducting western tourists, although it is difficult to imagine, in the light of the close 'post-Bowman' relationship between US and Algerian intelligence services, that the US could have been unaware of the Arak operation.

Before the abduction of the 32 tourists in early 2003, there had been no terrorism in the conventional meaning of the term[14] anywhere in this part of the Sahara–Sahel region. However, by May, with the 32 European hostages making global news headlines, EUCOM's commander, General James (Jim) Jones,[15] was speaking of 'large ungoverned areas across Africa that are clearly the new routes of narco trafficking, terrorist training and hotbeds of instability'.[16] Indeed, even before the hostages had been released, the Bush administration, in line with General Jones's remarks, had designated the Sahara as a new front in the GWOT. Bush referred to El Para as 'Bin Laden's man in the Sahel', while EUCOM's deputy commander, General Wald, described the Sahara as a 'Swamp of Terror', a 'terrorist infestation', which 'we need to drain' (Powell 2004). More than anything else, it was this abduction of the 32 Europeans, effectively an act of state terrorism, that enabled the US to launch this new, fabricated Saharan–Sahelian front in the GWOT and so both create and underpin the ideological conditions for Washington's militarization of those major parts of Africa that were strategically important to it.[17]

President Bush's Pan-Sahel Initiative (PSI) rolled into action on 10 January 2004 with the disembarkation in Nouakchott, capital of Mauritania, of a US 'anti-terror team' of 500 US troops. US Deputy Undersecretary of State Pamela Bridgewater, in Nouakchott to oversee what locals called the 'American invasion', confirmed that these troops would work in Mauritania and Mali, while 400 US Rangers would be deployed into the Chad–Niger border regions the following week, along with Los Angeles-based defence contractors Pacific Architects and Engineers.

The US immediately portrayed Africa's new terrorist threat as having spread across the wastelands of the Sahel, from Mauritania in the west, through the little-known desert lands of Mali, Niger and southern Algeria, to the Tibesti Mountains of Chad, with beyond them Sudan, Somalia and, across the waters, the 'Talibanized' lands of Afghanistan. Shortly after El Para's alleged escapades across the Sahel, western intelligence and diplomatic sources were claiming to be finding the fingerprints of this newly fabricated terrorist threat everywhere. It took only a few days after the Madrid train bombings (11 March 2004) for western intelligence-security services to link falsely that atrocity to Al Qaeda groups lurking deep in the Sahara and to issue warnings that Al Qaeda bases hidden in the world's largest desert could launch terrorist attacks on Europe (Colonel Victor Nelson cited by Fisher-Thompson 2004; General Charles Wald cited by Miles 2004). In 2005, the US expanded the PSI into the Trans-Saharan Counter-Terrorism Initiative (TSCTI), raising the number of countries involved from four (Mauritania, Mali, Niger and Chad) to nine with the inclusion of Senegal, Nigeria, Morocco, Algeria and Tunisia. This enabled Washington to link together two of Africa's main oil- and gas-producing countries, Algeria and Nigeria, along with seven neighbouring Saharan–Sahelian states, into a military security arrangement whose architecture, as Steven Ellis (2006) highlighted, 'was American'.

## Phase 2: from the fabrication of 'terrorism' to the creation of AQIM

The opening of a 'Sahara–Sahelian' front in the GWOT played a key role in enabling the US to justify and legitimize its growing presence in Africa, especially as manifest in the ultimate establishment of AFRICOM in 2008. However, by 2006 the US and its allies, notably Algeria, were beginning to face a problem. This was that, in spite of the interminable barrage of US–Algerian-generated propaganda and disinformation about 'terrorism' in the Sahara–Sahel, the notion of the GWOT was not gaining much traction within the Sahara–Sahel region itself.

There were two main reasons for this. One was that the local populations, mostly Tuareg, knew that there was no 'real' terrorism in the area and had always suspected their governments, especially Algeria, of being in some way involved in the El Para 'affair'. Second, all the governments of the region, without exception, were using the justification provided by the GWOT to crack down on all forms of legitimate political opposition, civil society organizations, ethnic minorities, etc. Again, as most of the region's population were aware of this strategy, they were not willing to present their governments, with the exception of a few incidents, with too many opportunities to use violence against them.[18]

The circumstances which provided the opportunity for the US and its Algerian ally to revamp the GWOT in the Sahara–Sahel and which led up to the rebranding of the GSPC as AQIM emerged in Mali in early 2006 (Keenan 2012).

Libya's leader, Mouamar Gadhafi, had seen renewed discontent among Mali's Tuareg in early 2006 as an opportunity to expand Libyan influence into Mali. He accordingly opened a consulate in Kidal, the administrative centre of Mali's northern Tuareg region, with the promise of massive financial aid. This was anathema to Algeria, which regarded Kidal as being within its sphere of influence (Keenan 2012).

The Algerians and Americans were fully appraised of this situation and saw the possibilities of a Tuareg 'rebellion' as the means of achieving their respective goals. A Tuareg rebellion could be blamed on Libya, thus discrediting it and driving it from the region, while Washington could use it to revamp its GWOT in the region (Keenan 2012).[19]

In preparation for such an anticipated opportunity, three US transporters airlifted on 15–16 February some 100 US Special Forces, their dogs and communications equipment from what is now AFRICOM's headquarters at Stuttgart to the new, Halliburton-built base at Tamanrasset in southern Algeria. Both the US State Department and the US Ambassador to Algeria are adamant that they were not informed by the Pentagon of this covert operation (Keenan 2012).

The trigger for their incursion into Mali came on 10 April. The occasion was Gadhafi's address to the *mawlid*[20] ceremony in Timbuktu in which he launched his idea of a 'Greater Saharan' state (Keenan 2012: Chapter 5). He envisaged a day when the Tuareg of Mali, Niger, Mauritania and Algeria would form a federation with Libya as its base. Taken to its logical conclusion, such a 'state' would necessitate the breakaway of much of northern Mali and northern Niger, part of Mauritania and a large part of southern Algeria. For Algeria, Gadhafi's speech was highly inflammatory and provoked it to take action in Mali. Algeria's plan, implemented in collusion with its US allies, was two-pronged. First, its DRS did a deal with the local Tuareg political leader in the Kidal region of northern Mali, Iyad ag Aghaly, to support a Tuareg rebellion. The rebellion, as Algeria foresaw, would be blamed on Gadhafi who would be forced to withdraw from the region. The second part of the deal was that the Tuareg, in exchange for Algeria's negotiation of favourable peace terms with the Mali government and some additional financial inducement, would help the US and Algerians in their GWOT. The precise words of the deal were: 'We [Algeria] are ready to help you achieve what you want, but on the condition that you help us fight the GSPC in the Tuareg Malian Sahara' (Keenan 2012).

The US Special Forces from Tamanrasset, along with their Algerian allies, crossed into Mali to give backing to the Tuareg rebels, who, at dawn on 23 May, raced into Kidal and Ménaka in 4WDs and trucks mounted with machine-guns. After looting the armouries, killing two soldiers and taking 20 hostage, the rebels withdrew to their bases in the Tigharghar Mountains between Kidal and the Algerian border. Algeria took responsibility for quartering the rebels in Tigharghar and managing on their behalf the long drawn-out peace talks. A number of US Special Forces remained in the area.

Algeria achieved its immediate regional objective of discrediting Gadhafi and ousting him from the region. But once the dust had settled, it was pay-back time. In September, the Algerians, working in concert with the US, called in their favour. Algeria instructed and paid Iyad ag Aghaly a considerable sum of money to organize an attack on an alleged GSPC 'terrorist' in northern Mali.[21]

There were two engagements. In September, Tuareg, having been given coordinates by the Algerians, attacked an alleged band of GSPC[22] near the Mali–Algerian border, with the outcome being inconclusive. A month later, a 'reprisal' attack against Tuareg at Arouane, near Timbuktu, resulted in five Tuareg being killed, two wounded and two taken hostage.

The international media, prompted and facilitated by the US government, gave the two incidents huge coverage, with the US reporting that Iyad ag Aghaly's 'Democratic Alliance for Change', as the 23 May rebel movement called itself, had actively thrown itself into the GWOT. The Alliance spokesman told Reuters that 'Our Democratic Alliance handles security in the region and we chase out those who are not from there, that's the position we've taken to control the zone'. This was the language that Washington wanted to hear: its GWOT was now firmly embedded in the Sahara with the Tuareg tribes, as the US called them, being on the right side.

The two skirmishes laid the basis for much of the US–Algerian propaganda that has surrounded the post-2006 establishment of AQIM in the Sahel. At the time of these incidents, many Tuareg who did not know about the deal between the DRS and Iyad ag Aghaly told me that the Araouane attack had been undertaken by GSPC *repentis* (repentants).[23] These were GSPC 'terrorists' who had accepted the Algerian government's amnesty. In early 2006, Tuareg in southern Algeria came across several[24] such *repentis* in the Mali and Niger border regions and believe they had been sent into Algeria's extreme south by the DRS to 'cause trouble'.

With *repentis* in place and the deal between Mali's Tuareg and the DRS accomplished, all that remained was to rebrand the hitherto insignificant GSPC with the Al Qaeda franchise.

## The structure and organization of AQIM in the Sahara–Sahel[25]

AQIM is, in effect, the Algerian GSPC under a new name. The name change was planned during 2006, probably in conjunction with the contrived 'Tuareg–GSPC' clashes described above, and formally announced in January 2007, with huge publicity in the US, Algerian and other western media. AQIM is structured into three 'components': the 'real' AQIM, AQIM *katibat* (brigades) that have been created by the DRS, and AQIM *katibat* that have been infiltrated by the DRS.

The 'real' AQIM, which is active around Algiers, its immediate hinterland and the Kabyle region to the east of the capital, is frequently quoted by the Algerian security forces as numbering around 600. The extent of its infiltration is uncertain, although it is generally believed that most of its *katibat* are probably subject to some degree of infiltration by the DRS.

AQIM in the Sahara–Sahel is very different from that in the north, being a hybrid of *katibat* that have been both 'created' and 'infiltrated' by the DRS. AQIM's two main emirs in the Sahel are Abdelhamid abou Zaïd and Yahia Djouadi, both of whom have several aliases. Both are associated with the DRS, and can effectively be regarded as 'DRS agents'. Abdelhamid, for example, was El Para's main 'lieutenant' in the fabricated 2003 operation. He also managed the entire Malian end of that operation because of his greater familiarity with the Sahel regions. Yahia Djouadi is also believed to have been involved in the 2003 operation, although his alias at the time is uncertain. The core of Abdelhamid's *katibat* would appear to be the 'regrouped' *repentis* described above, joined by a loose collection of 'Islamists' drawn mostly from Mauritania and Mali. They have also attracted a few local bandits and criminals. Yahia Djouadi's group may also contain some of these Algerian *salafistes* at its core, but has probably recruited more young Islamists from within Mauritania.[26]

The strength of AQIM in the Sahel is not known. Between its creation in 2006/7 and 2008/9, most estimates put it at around 200. Since then, estimates have risen to around 400, although local recruitment has almost certainly increased since the disastrous Franco-Mauritanian military raids into Mali on 22 July (Keenan 2012).

## The 'Al Qaeda' attack on Djanet airport

After the 'creation' of AQIM in 2006/7, it remained something of a 'phantom', but still the subject of extensive US and Algerian disinformation and propaganda. One reason for this AQIM inactivity in the Sahel was that both northern Niger and northern Mali, from early 2007 onwards, became the terrain of new Tuareg rebellions which had nothing to do with Algeria's GSPC/AQIM. Without any 'real' terrorism in the region, the governments there, all beneficiaries of Washington's TSCTI, referred to the Tuareg rebels as 'terrorists' and 'drugs traffickers', or, in the case of at least one Washington analyst, 'putative terrorists' (Keenan 2012). Indeed, the strength of AQIM in the Sahara–Sahel during these years is not known, although most estimates put it at around 200 or less. Not until the resumption of western hostage-taking in 2008 did estimates of AQIM's numbers creep up to nearer 400. Even though 'terrorism' in the region was virtually non-existent during the two years following the AQIM branding, the impression was being given to the world by both Algeria and the US that this new branch of Al Qaeda was posing a dangerous threat to the Sahel, north-west Africa as a whole and even Europe.

In fact, if we take the Tuareg rebellions out of the picture, the only AQIM incident in the entire Algeria–Niger–Mali nexus during the two years following the creation of AQIM was the attack on Djanet airport on 8 November, 2007. The 'incident' occurred at 4 a.m., when, according to Algerian security sources, about ten terrorists in three off-road vehicles fired on Djanet airport with rocket-propelled grenades and machine-guns. Algerian media reports, all sourced to the security services, gave quite contradictory accounts of what had happened. Some said that the attackers damaged an Air Algérie plane; others that two helicopters and a military aircraft had been hit. Accounts of the terrorists' 'escape' were equally confused. Some said the attackers escaped across the border into Niger; others that the terrorists had all been caught and killed by an army helicopter-based operation. The security forces subsequently issued a statement saying that the 'terrorists' had been identified as coming from Al Qaeda training camps in northern Mali affiliated to AQIM. The same report said that the attackers had been targeting oil facilities in the region, and that they knew this because they had infiltrated the attackers' training camps.

The reports, issued by Algeria's security forces and widely published through the US and international media, were false. Aside from there being no oil facilities in the Djanet region, the attackers were not AQIM terrorists but Tuareg youths (mostly teenagers) from Djanet itself. The youths' very amateurish attack had been intended as a demonstration of sympathy for the Tuareg rebels in Niger and a protest against the Algerian authorities in Djanet. Reports (Sahara Focus 2007: 4, 2008: 1) on the truth of what happened at Djanet were ignored by western 'security services', which generally preferred to give maximum media coverage to explaining how the Djanet attack demonstrated the increased threat being presented in the Sahara–Sahel by AQIM, and that the terrorist organization's recent rebranding as an Al Qaeda franchise reflected its increasing 'internationalization' and 'reach'.[27]

The Djanet 'incident' demonstrates quite unequivocally how both Algeria and its western allies were continuing to use 'fabricated', or in this case 'fictitious', terrorism for their own respective agendas. For the US, Djanet was used to demonstrate the expansion of Al Qaeda across the

Sahara–Sahel, thus providing further justification for AFRICOM. For Algeria, the Djanet 'lie' diverted international attention from the escalating internal unrest against the country's thoroughly corrupt and repressive regime, and provided further justification for its repressive 'security' policies and militarization of the extreme south.

The current Algerian regime came to power in 1992 through a military *coup d'état,* having annulled national legislative elections which would have brought to power the first democratically elected Islamist government in the Arab world. Following the so-called 'civil war' of the 1990s,[28] during which some 200,000 Algerians lost their lives, there has been an almost continuous escalation of social and political unrest against the regime which most Algerians regard as wholly illegitimate and corrupt. During the last decade, the government has used a battery of legislation and actions (frequently 'illegal') in the name of 'counter-terrorism' to crush this unrest by increasingly repressive means.

In the country's extreme south,[29] the regime has used the GWOT and its close alliance with the US to justify both the increased militarization of the region and the repression of its local, predominantly Tuareg, population. The demonstration of local youths against the government in Djanet in November 2007 was just one of many anti-government demonstrations that have broken out, often repeatedly, in almost every town in the country in the last few years. In 2010, for example, the police were called out, usually in riot gear, to over 11,000 incidents of public unrest.[30] Since the Djanet incident, which the government used to 'prove' the threat of Al Qaeda in the region, it has increasingly been using the pretext of counter-terrorism to quell any possible dissent and to almost entirely destroy the local Tuaregs' main cash business, namely tourism. The Tuareg believe the government is taking this action against them because of 'jealousy'[31] and because it is planning to destroy much of the cultural heritage of the region's two tourist-oriented national parks for mineral extraction.[32]

## The resumption of hostage-taking

Even though the Djanet incident had nothing to do with AQIM, it was extremely convenient for Algeria and the West, coming as it did just three months before what was portrayed in the local and western media as AQIM's resumption of taking westerners hostage.[33] Four westerners were taken hostage in 2008: two Austrian tourists were abducted in Tunisia in February and two Canadian UN diplomats were seized in Niger in December. Although attributed to AQIM, both abductions were almost certainly acts of 'state terrorism'.

The two Austrians were abducted by Abdelhamid abou Zaïd, almost certainly at the behest of the DRS. The DRS's purpose was to save Algeria from potential embarrassment. Switzerland was demanding that Algeria 'produce' El Para and allow Swiss investigators to interview him with regard to the four Swiss taken hostage in 2003 (Keenan 2009). The investigating magistrate was suspicious of El Para and was not prepared to sign off on the case until he had questioned him. However, with a five-year statute of limitations, Algeria only had to keep El Para out of the way for a few more weeks. The plan was that the hostage-takers would demand the release of El Para from an Algerian prison. This effectively ruled El Para 'off limits' and gave Algeria a justifiable reason to defer the Swiss demand until after the imminent expiry of the statute of limitations. In the meantime, Abou Zaïd took the two Austrians to Mali,[34] a journey which, as one Algerian security official confided to me, would have been extremely difficult without DRS 'protection'.[35]

The two UN diplomats had arrived in Niger on 11 December 2008 as the UN Secretary-General's Special Envoy (and assistant). Their task was to assess possibilities for a peaceful outcome to the Tuareg rebellion. Niger's President and Minister of Interior, both now deposed in a coup, were desperate to stop the envoy visiting the Tuareg regions where the government was committing acts of genocide. Evidence indicates that the two diplomats were seized by thugs associated with the Interior Ministry and 'passed up' to AQIM.[36]

In the case of these four hostages, as well as that of a Frenchman kidnapped a few months later, 'communications' were sent to General Mohamed Mediène, head of the DRS, explaining, or perhaps 'warning', that in the event of their death detailed information covering the DRS's relationship with AQIM would be released to the international media.[37]

During 2009, a further 10 westerners[38] were taken hostage, leading Richard Barrett, a former British intelligence official and the UN's highest ranking official responsible for monitoring the activities of Al Qaeda and the Taliban, to say in November that while attacks by Al Qaeda and its operatives were decreasing in many parts of the world, the situation was worsening in North Africa. One of the westerners taken hostage in 2009 was an Englishman, Edwin Dyer, who was abducted, along with three other tourists, in January and executed by Abdelhamid abou Zaïd on 30 May.

Barrett's statement was extraordinary in that all major western intelligence services, most notably the American, British and Canadian, and almost certainly the French, had received information that all these hostages had finished up in the hands of emirs who were all either known to be or strongly suspected of being associated with the DRS.

## 'At the heart of AQIM is the DRS'

The clearest evidence of the DRS's orchestration of AQIM at the time of Dyer's death came from Colonel Lemana Ould Cheikh (often referred to as Lemana Ould Bou), a senior officer in Mali's state security service. The Colonel had been playing the dangerous game of double agent between

Mali's State Security and AQIM. In an interview with the local media in Timbuktu just after Dyer's death and just before his own assassination, he was reported as saying: 'At the heart of AQIM is the DRS' (Keenan 2011). Thus, when the Malian security forces detained three members of AQIM in the week or so following Dyer's death, AQIM realized it had been double-crossed. Lemana Ould Cheikh, the obvious suspect, was assassinated almost immediately in his home in Timbuktu. His death was reported as another AQIM act of terrorism.

We are thus left with the unanswered questions: was Barrett's statement based simply on media reports that were (and still are) ultimately mostly sourced to the security services, and which therefore unwittingly reproduce disinformation, such as that on the Djanet incident? Was he, as the UN's officer responsible for monitoring Al Qaeda, specifically fed disinformation by the intelligence services? Or was he aware of and thus complicit in both the fabrication and exaggeration of terrorism in the region?

## Conclusion: the creation of a self-fulfilling prophecy

By the beginning of 2010, it was evident that AQIM had established itself as a significant organization in the Sahel, especially in northern Mali where it was effectively 'protected' by elements within both Algerian and Malian security institutions. It was also evident that AQIM was taking on a life of its own, as an economic attraction for local communities that had been left impoverished by the collapse of the tourism industry and almost three years of rebellion, and in recruiting young Islamists from within the region, mostly from Mauritania, when the regimes had been using the pretext of the GWOT to crack down on Islamism.

In spite of AQIM's growing regional activity and the security threat that it posed, it was still under the effective control of Algeria's DRS, Washington's proxy in the region. Even if that was not the case, as Algeria would no doubt argue, AQIM could easily have been wiped out by one cross-border intervention by Algeria's powerful military forces – for which Mali had given permission. That has not been attempted, in spite of AQIM's modest numbers, estimated by the CIA and other such sources at around 300–400, and its predominant location in northern Mali close to the Algerian border.

The US strategy is broadly twofold. At one level, it is giving its blessing to its key ally in the GWOT and its proxy power in the region, Algeria. Washington knows that the Algerian regime, well proven as 'eradicators' in Algeria's 'Dirty War' of the 1990s, will fight Islamism and that it has the resolve and military wherewithal to do so. In exchange, and also for its own regional security interests, the US is discreetly endorsing Algeria's hegemonic designs over the western half of the Sahel, one of the world's richest mineral resource zones. At a second but related level, the US wants a modicum of 'terror' in the region, particularly terror that is of minimal threat to US interests (and ideal if directed at Europe!), as it provides 'proof' of the 'terrorist' threat to Africa, which the Pentagon and other institutions of US imperial power have been articulating in grossly exaggerated form since the P2OG strategy of 2002 as the justification for Washington's militaristic policy towards the continent and the role of AFRICOM.

Maintaining this balance between a 'sufficient' amount of terrorism to create the insecurity and instability required to enable Algeria to fulfil its designs without precipitating external intervention has been the driver behind Algeria's orchestration of AQIM in the Sahel. Increasingly, however, the West, notably the US and France, has been discussing the need to intervene in the region to rid it of AQIM and 're-secure' its huge potential wealth in the form of its mineral resources, notably but not exclusively uranium. Further direct US intervention in the region is now deemed highly unlikely for several reasons. France, however, with its huge dependence on Niger for uranium energy resources, could easily be tempted.

Indeed, a fundamental problem for Algeria's hegemonic designs in the Sahel is the presence, albeit limited, and influence of France, the former colonial power, in the region. Weakening the influence of France, and perhaps even engineering its withdrawal, is a prerequisite for Algeria's own expansion in the region. Neither is such an outcome antithetical to US policy, which would not be averse to a diminution of French influence in the region.

After eight years of largely fabricated and fictitious 'terrorism', the Sahel has finally become Washington's self-fulfilled prophecy. The 'Terror Zone' that the US military marked across the Sahel region on its maps of Africa in 2003, dramatically altering, if not ruining, the lives of most of the region's inhabitants, is now a reality.

What will happen? Only one thing is certain. Western invention, in one form or another, is now imminent. At its meeting in Luxembourg on 25 October, 2010, the EU's Foreign Affairs Council placed the Sahel at the top of its agenda and instructed the Commission to draw up a strategy on the region for the beginning of 2011.

## Notes

1 Jeremy Keenan first worked as an anthropologist amongst the Tuareg of the Cenral Sahara from 1964 to 1972. He returned in 1999 and has worked continuously in and with the people of the region since then, especially on the problems associated with the GWOT and 'state terrorism'. His work now covers the whole of north-west Africa and underpins his parallel work as a 'reporter' and consultant on political risk and security in North Africa, the Sahara and Sahel. In addition to his several books and academic papers on the region, he is the author and editor of Menas's *Sahara Focus* (quarterly) and *Algeria: Politics and Security* (weekly). He is also a regular (monthly) contributor to Al Jazeera. and

the sole author of the report commissioned by the European Commission in late 2010, entitled: *Study on Political Islam in the Sahel and Neighbouring Countries.*

2 Maghreb is the Arabic word for west and refers specifically to the western region of North Africa.

3 See www.africom.mil/AboutAFRICOM.asp/. Since then, Africa's strategic importance to the US has undergone several reappraisals as a result of the US's increased awareness of its own energy crisis, the post-9/11 GWOT and the rapid growth of China's economic investment in Africa.

4 In 2002, sub-Saharan Africa was already supplying 14 per cent of US oil imports; by 2006, the US imported 22 per cent of its oil from Africa, and by 2007 the country was importing more crude oil from Africa than the Persian Gulf (US Dept of Energy 2007).

5 Five years later, following the announcement of AFRICOM, EUCOM commander General Bantz Craddock told journalists in Washington that '[When] you look at West Africa and the Gulf of Guinea, it becomes more focused because of the energy situation', with the result that protecting energy assets 'obviously [*sic*] is out in front'. (National Intelligence Council, 'External Relations and Africa', discussion paper, 16 March 2004, at www.dni.gov/nic/PDF_GIF_2020_Support/2004_03_16_papers/external_relations.pdf (10 May 2007). Ryan Henry, the Principal Deputy Under Secretary of Defense for Policy, told journalists at a Foreign Press Center briefing in Washington on June 2007 that the new US African Command 'is about resources, specifically oil, specifically the oil in the Gulf of Guinea and that's what this command is about.'

6 While the main reason why Africa has become of such strategic importance to the US is oil, US policy towards Africa cannot be reduced to or explained solely by America's increasingly serious energy crisis. Africa has much else to offer the US. For instance, besides oil, the US is dependent on Africa for many other raw materials such as manganese (for steel production), cobalt and chrome, both vital for alloys especially in aeronautics, vanadium, metals in the platinum group, antimony, gold, fluorspar, germanium, industrial diamonds and many other lesser-known materials such as columbite-tantalite (coltan for short), a key component in everything from mobile phones and computer chips to stereos and VCRs (Keenan 2009: 127–9). Other reasons for US policy towards Africa in the Bush era, notably the role of the 'religious right' and military and intelligence 'turf wars', are discussed in Keenan (2009).

7 By 'conventional', I mean that terrorism is the threatened or employed use of violence against civilian targets for political objectives.

8 In 1993, 18 US soldiers were killed in Mogadishu in an incident which some 'terrorism analysts' now attribute to 'Islamic terrorists'. In 1998, some 200 people were killed when US embassies were bombed in Nairobi and Dar es Salaam. In 2002, a hotel was bombed in Mombasa, allegedly by Al Qaeda 'terrorists' and two surface-to-air missiles were fired at an Israel-bound airliner. Northern Algeria has been subjected to both Islamist and state terrorism since the early 1990s, while there have been incidents in Morocco (bombings in Casablanca on 16 May 2003) and Tunisia (el-Ghriba synagogue, April 2002).

9 El Para was his *nom de guerre,* from his time in the elite parachutist regiment. His proper name is allegedly Saifi Am[m]ari. His many aliases include El (Al) Para (Bara), Abderezak, Abou (Abu) Haidara, Ammane Abu Haidra, Abderezak Zaimeche, Abdul Razzaq, Abdul Rasak, Abdalrazak, al Ammari Al Arussi, El Ourassi and further combinations and alternative spellings of these. It is believed that he may have trained at Fort Bragg, as an elite 'green beret', in 1994–96 (Keenan 2009). A detailed account and critique of the 'official version', which is promoted in an estimated 6,000 media articles and reports of one sort or another, is given in Keenan (2009).

10 El Para's relationship with the DRS is documented at some length in Keenan (2009) with more 'follow-up' data and evidence in Keenan (2012).

11 In his State of the Union address of 29 January 2002, President Bush spoke of the expansion of the war on terror to new fronts. Since then, the term 'front', and especially the term 'second front', have become almost synonymous with the attempt to globalize the GWOT. Afghanistan is usually understood to be the first front. The term 'second front' has been applied at one time or another to most parts of the world, including South-East Asia, Iraq, Latin America in the context of the election of left-wing presidents in Brazil and Ecuador, Colombia in terms of the FARC campaign and, since 2003, the Sahara. In the latter case the 'first' front is sometimes understood to be the Horn of Africa and East Africa. See, for example, Pyne (2002); Clays (2003).

12 The plan derived from the 1962, post-Bay of Pigs, Northwoods Project. This project was published online in a more complete form by the National Security Archive on 30 April 2001: 'Pentagon Proposed Pretexts for Cuba Invasion in 1962', *National Security Archive*, 30 April 2001.

13 Evidence for this is that both I and Tuareg with whom I was working at the time were in the vicinity of the hijack. Between us, we were able to interview the tourists concerned, the local police and the local gendarmes who eventually caught the 'terrorists' and who then released them on the orders of Algeria's DRS commander in Tamanrasset (Southern Algeria).

14 See Note 6.

15 Later to become President Obama's National Security Advisor (NSA), before stepping down in October 2010.

16 *World Tribune*, 6 May 2003; *New York Times*, 4 July 2003. EUCOM's second-in-command, air-force General Charles Wald described these groups as 'similar to al-Qaeda, but not as sophisticated or with the same reach, but the same objectives. They're bad people, and we need to keep an eye on that' (*New York Times*, 4 July 2003).

17 General Jones envisaged a new concept of US military basing in Africa. With Cold War-style bases containing large numbers of US forces neither militarily appropriate nor politically feasible, General Jones was planning a far more flexible facilitative arrangement which would enable the US military to deploy quickly, as and when required, through what he called a 'family of bases'. These would include 'forward-operating bases', or what he called 'lilypads', perhaps with an airfield nearby, that could house up to 3,000–5,000 troops, and 'forward-operating locations', which would be lightly equipped bases where Special Forces, marines or possibly an infantry rifle platoon or company could land and build up as the mission required (Schmitt 2003).

18 For details of this strategy, see Keenan (2012). The main incidents in this strategy include the attempts by the Niger government in 2004 to provoke the Tuareg to take up arms, the alleged 'terrorist' attack on the Lemgheity garrison in northern Mauritania in 2005 and the Tamanrasset riots of 2005.

19 See especially, Keenan, J. 'Putting the GWOT back on track', Chapter 5 in Keenan (2012).

20 The Prophet's birthday.

21 This whole episode has been documented in detail in Chapter 5 of *The Dying Sahara* (Keenan 2012; see note 19 above). There is no other published account of the episode, which both the US and Algeria have tried to suppress. However, the main Tuareg fighter in the engagements, Sidi Mohamed ag Acherif, aka 'Merzouk', was assassinated by AQIM on 11 August 2010. A remarkable obituary and comments, written by local people, and giving much insight into these events, can be found on www.kidal.info in the pages immediately after 11 August 2010.

22 The target was allegedly Mokhtar ben Mokhtar, an Algerian 'smuggler', with questionable links to the GSPC/AQIM.

23 This information was given to me by Tuareg informants with whom I was working in that part of the Sahara at that time. The *repentis* to whom these informants referred were particularly noticeable in the villages of western Ahaggar, such as Tit, Abalessa and Silet, as well as around the Bordj Mokhtar–In Hallil border zone between Mali and Algeria.

24 The precise number is not known. Tuareg described finding a few groups numbering about 'two or three'. The total number is therefore unlikely to have been more than a few dozen.

25 The information on the structure and organization of AQIM in this chapter is based largely on my own continuous and detailed fieldwork in and on Algeria and the Sahel since the start of (and preceding) the GWOT. It also draws on a network of informants in all countries of the region and within certain Algerian state structures. There is no reliable study of AQIM. Most of the hundreds of reports and articles that have been written on it are heavily based on sources which rely ultimately on DRS disinformation. Undertaking research into AQIM, because of its close links with the DRS, is obviously not only very difficult, if not impossible, but is impeded further by the fact that the DRS has close relationships with UK, French and US counter-terrorism agencies, which are part of the 'disinformation' process. The UK, for example, not only works very closely with the DRS, but is involved in assisting in its supply of materials and training (Keenan 2011). Some corroborative information on the DRS and its activities can be found on the websites of the Rachad Movement (www.rachad.org/) and Algeria Watch (www.algeria-watch.de/francais.htm). Regular reports on AQIM's activities are published on a subscription only basis by Menas (www.menas.co.uk/home.aspx) in its weekly publication *Algeria: Politics and Security* and its quarterly publication *Sahara Focus*. The most comprehensive documentation of AQIM in the Sahara–Sahel is found in my two volumes: *The Dark Sahara* (2009) and *The Dying Sahara* (2012). Several other reports that I have written on AQIM in the Sahara–Sahel have not been published. I refer, in particular, to a detail analysis provided as an Appendix to my report to the European Union entitled *Political Islam in the Sahel and Neighbouring Countries*' (December 2010. HTSPE Ltd. Funded by the EU. Project Number 2010/245936).

26 A third *katibat* is believed to centre on Mokhtar ben Mokhtar (MBM), an independent 'businessman', who has waged his own war against Algeria since the late 1990s. Details of MBM and his activities are given in Keenan (2009, 2012). His relationship to both GSPC/AQIM and the DRS can be best described as 'freelance'.

27 An official at the British FCO responded to my *Sahara Focus* (Menas) report by saying: 'The Algerians reported that there was a terrorist attack on Djanet airport. Therefore it is a fact' (Keenan 2012). The truth and the accuracy of the *Sahara Focus* (Menas) report was revealed three years later, when a DRS 'journalist', Selima Tlemçani (2010), inadvertently reported both the head of the regional government and the Tuareg Supreme Chief as confirming my account of events.

28 More aptly known as the 'Dirty War', as a result of the Algerian military's responsibility for the massacre of thousands of innocent civilians supposedly killed by 'Islamists'.

29 Notably in the provinces (*wilayat*)) of Tamanrasset and Illizi and the towns of Tamanrasset and Djanet.

30 That is a demonstration of one sort or another almost every half hour.

31 Tourists, who are mostly westerners, tend to shun 'Arab' in preference for

Tuareg tourism agencies. With a few exceptions, it is only the Tuareg who really know the region, its flora, fauna, especially camels which are used by tourists, and its rich cultural heritage.

32 The two national parks of the Tassili-n-Ajjer and Ahaggar have been flagged up internationally by UNESCO and numerous other world cultural and environmental organizations. The Tassili is a World Heritage Site. However, the parks, especially Ahaggar, are rich in uranium, gold and many other minerals. Although, the Tuareg hold internationally recognized indigenous land rights over the region, these are not recognized in practice by the regime. Thus, clearing the region of tourism and hence Tuareg business-environmental interests by the use of counter-terrorism measures is effectively a means of land dispossession. Those who have spoken out against such land dispossession and the destruction of their cultural domain and heritage are being subjected to increasing harassment and repression, which in most cases takes the form of trying to destroy their businesses and associated economic livelihoods.

33 No westerners had been taken hostage since El Para's operation in 2003.

34 On 10 March, two–three weeks after the abduction, Al Jazeera announced that the two Austrians were being held by AQIM. The same day, the Austrian government received information that the hostages had been taken to Mali. This was corroborated by the identification of vegetation in a photograph that the hostage-takers had posted on Islamist websites.

35 Much of the information that I received about this kidnapping was the result of being a negotiator of the hostages' release.

36 This information was given to me by the Niger Tuareg rebels who the Niger government immediately accused of undertaking the kidnapping and who subsequently undertook their own investigations. I also received similar information from other informants in Niamey.

37 Details of these communications are published in Keenan (2012).

38 Two Swiss, one German, one British, three Spanish, one French and two Italians. In 2010, a further six French + one Malagasy and one Togolese were abducted. In 2011, to date, two Frenchmen have been killed in a botched French army rescue attempt and one Italian tourist has been kidnapped. By June 2011, four French and one Italian were still in captivity.

## References

Ahmed, N.M., 2009. 'Our terrorists', *New Internationalist*, October, 17–20.

Akosah-Sarpong, Kofi, 2002. 'Washington eyes Africa's oil', *West Africa*, No. 4354, 2–8 December 2002.

Arkin, W.M., 2002. 'The secret war: frustrated by intelligence failures, the Defense Department is dramatically expanding its "black world" of covert operations', *Los Angeles Times*, 27 October. Available online at http://web.archive.org/web/20021031092436/www.latimes.com/la-op-arkin27oct27001451,0,7355676.story/.

Bowman, M.E., 2002. Statement to Senate Select Committee on Intelligence, 31 July. Available online at www.fas.org/irp/congress/2002_hr/073102bowman.html/, accessed 29 January 2012.

Clays, M.M., 2003. The interagency process and America's second front in the Global War on Terrorism (Reference: Operation ENDURING FREEDOM (OEF) Philippines). April, Accession No: ADA424995. Defence Technical Information Center.

Ellis, S., 2006. 'The pan-Sahel initiative', *African Affairs,* Vol. 103, No. 412, 459–64.

Fisher-Thompson, J., 2004. *US–African Partnership Helps Counter Terrorists in Sahel Region: New Maghreb Co-operation Central to Pan-Sahel Initiative.* Washington File, 23 March. Washington, DC: US Department of State Information Service.

Floyd, C., 2002. 'Into the dark: the Pentagon plan to promote terrorist attacks', *Counterpunch,* 1 November. Available online at www.counterpunch.org/floyd 1101.html/.

Hersh, S., 2005. 'The coming wars: what the Pentagon can now do in secret', *The New Yorker,* 24 January. Available online at www.newyorker.com/archive/ 2005/01/24/050124fa_fact#ixzz0gr8isUqf, accessed 29 January 2012.

Hess, P., 2002. 'Panel wants $7bn elite counter-terror unit', *United Press International,* 26 September. Available online at http://bailey83221.livejournal. com/107138.html/.

Institute for Advanced Strategic & Political Studies, 2002. 'African oil: a priority of U.S. national security and African development', Symposium Proceedings, 25 January. Washington, DC: Institute for Advanced Strategic & Political Studies.

Isenberg, D., 2002. '"P2OG" allows Pentagon to fight dirty', *Asia Times Online,* 5 November. Available online at www.atimes.com/atimes/Middle_East/DK05Ak 02.html/, accessed 29 January 2012.

Keenan, J., 2009. *The Dark Sahara: America's War on Terror in Africa.* London, Pluto.

Keenan, J., 2011. 'UK in North Africa: myths and contradictions', *Al Jazeera.net Briefing.* Available online at http://english.aljazeera.net/indepth/briefings/ 2011/04/20114151412468260 5.html, accessed 29 January 2012.

Keenan, J., 2012. *The Dying Sahara: U.S. Imperialism and Terror in Africa.* London, Pluto (forthcoming).

Miles, D., 2004. "US must confront terrorism in Africa, General says', 16 June. Washington, DC: US American Forces Press Service, US Department of Defense.

*National Energy Policy,* 2001. Report of the National Energy Policy Development Group, May [Cheney Report]. Available online at www.ne.doe.gov/pdfFiles/ NationalEnergyPolicy.pdf, accessed 29 January 2012.

Powell, S.M., 2004. 'Swamp of terror in the Sahara', *Air Force Magazine,* 87 (11), Available online at www.airforce-magazine.com/magazineArchive/Pages/2004/ November%202004/1104sahara.aspa, accessed 29 January 2012.

Project for the New American Century (PNAC), 1997. Statement of principles. Available online at www.newamericancentury.org/, accessed 29 January 2012.

Pyne, D., 2002. 'The new second front in the War against Terrorism', *American Partisan,* 19 December. Available online at www.american-partisan.com/cols/2002/ pyne/qtr4/1219.htm, accessed 29 January 2012.

Ryan, Y., 'Anti-terrorism and uprisings', *Al Jazeera,* 25 February 2011. Available online at http://english.aljazeera.net/indepth/features/2011/02/201121310169 828350.html, accessed 29 January 2012.

*Sahara Focus,* 2007. No 4. Menas, London. Available online at www.menas.co.uk.

*Sahara Focus,* 2008. No 1. Menas, London. Available online at www.menas.co.uk.

Schmitt, E., 2003. 'Threats and responses: expanding U.S. presence; Pentagon seeking new access pacts for Africa bases', *New York Times,* 5 July. Available online at www.nytimes.com/2003/07/05/world/threats-responses-expanding-us-presence-pentagon-seeking-new-access-pacts-for.html/, accessed 29 January 2012.

Snyder, C., 2004. 'U.S. promotes development and governance in Africa to counter terrorism – State Dept. official outlines key programs that bind continent to America', U.S. State Department Press Release, 16 April 2004.

Tlemçani, Selima, 2010. 'La région de Tamanrasset sous haute pression', *El Watan* (Algeria), 12 October. Available online at www.djazairess.com/fr/elwatan/294300, accessed 29 January 2012.

US Department of Energy, Energy Information Administration, 2007. *US Imports by Country of Origin.* Available online at http://tonto.eia.doe.gov/dnav/pet/pet_move_impcus_a2_nus_ep00_im0_mbblpd_a.htm, accessed 29 January 2012.

Volman, D., 2003. 'The Bush administration and African oil: the security implications of US energy policy', *Review of African Political Economy*, 30 (98), 573–84.

Westphal, Michael A. Department of Defense, 2002. *DoD News Briefing* – News Transcript, 2 April. Available online at www.defense.gov, accessed 29 January 2012.

# Conclusion

## Reconnecting the asymmetries of political violence

*Scott Poynting and David Whyte*

Collectively the chapters in this book show very clearly that a primary purpose of the political violence of the state is to devalue, undermine and ultimately eradicate, the political legitimacy of those that resist state power. The causes and the actions of insurgent sub-state political violence are represented as a technical problem, devoid of politics, motivated by irrationality, barbarism and evil. 'Bringing politics back in', the book has therefore shown, entails a focus on both state and counter-state political violence, and indeed the connections between the two.

During the final stages of our putting this book together, US Navy Seals unlawfully entered Pakistan and assassinated Osama Bin Laden. His body was quickly and without discussion disposed of at sea. The questionable criminality of this act was barely remarked on, such is the obfuscatory power of 'war on terror' rhetoric. This has perhaps never been made clearer than in the documentary on the killing of Bin Laden approved by the White House that was aired globally in the days leading up to the tenth anniversary of the September 2001 attacks on the twin towers and the Pentagon.[1] Interviews with Barack Obama and other key White House and US military figures revealed how little justification the architects of state political violence now need for their actions. In this documentary, the US President, along with some of his most senior officials, proudly boasted of their role in this state assassination, an assassination that took the lives of not only the US's chief suspect for the September 2001 attacks on Washington and New York, but also the lives of the people who were said to be 'guarding' him, and their families. This massacre was openly admitted by the President of the US in an interview in which he revealed that his only worry had been that the killing spree might be halted and the US would be discovered by Pakistani authorities before the assassination was complete. Whether Bin Laden would in a court of law have been proven guilty of the crime with which he was publicly accused is doubtful, since, as Chomsky (2011) has noted in the wake of this assassination:

> There is much talk of Bin Laden's 'confession', but that was a boast, not a confession, with as much credibility as my 'confession' that I won

> the Boston marathon. The boast tells us a lot about his character, but nothing about his responsibility for what he regarded as a great achievement, for which he wanted to take credit.

Whether Bin Laden was really guilty or not was not the concern of the US government. If there is an undeniable truth here, it is the historical legacy that, as Chomsky shows (ibid.), the US has long assassinated its opponents – without reference to the rule of law. State assassination is nothing more or less than a technique of power mongering. Like all other empires before it, the US has committed unlawful assassinations with mechanical regularity.

Yet it is precisely this sort of state assassination, imperial exceptionalism, and ultimately utter impunity that motivate many of those sympathetic to Bin Laden in the region where this crime was committed. Portrayed as backward, tribal, uncivilised and all the other pejoratives of orientalism that have served empires here for centuries, their resistance is eminently political. Its violent repression is equally political.

The contributions to this book together make this conclusion irresistible. For in these contributions we can only understand state political violence and sub-state political violence as based upon real, material conditions with their own very concrete histories; often involving struggles for self-determination and struggles against expropriation and exploitation. They are all, in some way, asymmetries of political violence.[2]

A series of four 'themes' emerge from these chapters as they endeavour to uncover and rediscover the material origins of those asymmetries of political violence. The first three of those themes identify the purpose or utility of state political violence:

1 the use of sub-state groups as a proxy for covert operations;
2 the use of political violence as a strategy to neutralise political opposition;
3 the use of political violence as a strategy to pre-empt political opposition.

A fourth theme identifies the centrality of the political and legal mechanisms that ensure impunity for state political violence.

The conclusion now turns to draw out in more detail some of the common threads of those four themes that are woven through the contributions to this book.

In the first of those themes, our contributors reveal some surprising connections between the 'state' and the groups it ostensibly seeks to control as 'terrorists'. Such connections are commonly understood in the counter-terrorism literature as ideological or as 'coincidences of interests'. Yet here we have evidence of military-strategic alliances being made between state military forces and groups that those forces are ostensibly opposed to. Villar's analysis of the motivations and political advantages for the Colombian government in its war against FARC shows how a solidarity between the Colombian state and far right terrorist groups has been germinated both ideologically and militarily. His chapter shows how in Colombia in the 1990s, paramilitary forces engaged by the state conducted thousands of murders, disappearances and expulsions of trade unionists, students and human rights activists. O'Connor and Brecknell's contribution documents not only how loyalist paramilitaries in Northern Ireland in the 1970s infiltrated and operated within the British Army, but how this was tacitly supported and clandestinely approved at the highest level of government. This wilful blindness on the part of at least two British prime ministers can only be understood as part of the long-term military strategy. This relationship of solidarity between 'state terrorist' and 'non-state terrorist' takes on a different dimension in Keenan's contribution which raises questions about the role of the US and Algerian state in the fabrication of 'terrorist' groups that are ostensibly their enemies. The arguments of this chapter have been given weight by recent events in the region that have become known as the 'Arab Spring' of 2011. The collusion of both US and Algerian states in setting up fake 'terrorist' groups and activities in the Sahara–Sahel region have acted as a pretext for realising strategic military and geo-economic aims. Just as in Afghanistan in the 1980s, the strategy has boomeranged, with the staged prophecy of Al Qaeda in this part of Africa fast becoming a self-fulfilling reality.

A second theme that we can identify cutting across all chapters is that counter-insurgency strategies are being used not merely to neutralise militarised opposition, but to expand the range of governments' legitimate political targets. Thus we find in all of the cases discussed in this book that the legitimate targets of states' counter-insurgency measures are expanded well beyond armed opposition to include a range of movements and organisations of civil society engaged in non-violent oppositional politics, from human rights activists, to students, trade unionists and independence movement activists. Purported anti-terror measures, that is to say, are deployed to suppress lawful oppositional politics and cultural resistance. Stanley reveals how the Indonesian counter-insurgency military force, Kopassus, is shown in its own documents to have recorded that in West Papua, 'civilians were specifically targeted because they engaged the "outside world" with their arguments for freedom and human rights'. For Atiles-Osoria, the counter-terrorism waged by the US government and Puerto Rican administration has historically used political violence and extreme forms of judicial intervention indiscriminately against armed and non-armed groups alike. The aim has been to eradicate political opposition to the colonial government of Puerto Rico. The Spanish 'war on terror', as Ciocchini and Khoury show, has facilitated a war on left-wing politics and has similarly expanded a continuum of state violence against a broad spectrum of government oppponents.

A third and related theme that we find cutting across the contributions in this book is that the violence of counter-insurgency is deployed pre-emptively against the populations who are not necessarily mobilised against governments, but are identified in some way as a *potential* threat. This pre-emptive political targeting is developed irrespective of any real involvement in counter-insurgency in such theatres. The strategy of spreading fear and terror in those communities is not an unintended consequence, as Miller and Sabir's chapter shows, but serves as a deliberate and planned part of the strategy. Similarly, Stanley's 'communities of fear and suspicion' are used to expand the continuum of state violence. Sentas has traced in this volume how the proscription of the LTTE under anti-terror laws in the US, Canada, EU nations and Australia at the behest of the Sri Lankan government is at the root of the conditions that enabled genocidal policies to be authorised and carried out in Sri Lanka, and the criminalising of whole diasporic Sri Lankan Tamil communities within Western countries. Criminalisation thus becomes a key element of the depoliticisation of struggle, which in turn legitimates state violence by naming and disciplining its 'enemies' (who just happen to be the voices of resistance to its violence).

The fourth theme that we have highlighted as shared among the contributions to this book is that of the stark impunity of the agents of the state perpetrating political violence, notwithstanding demonstrable illegality. The blatancy of the state crimes involved, and the virtual untouchability of the perpetrators, often add to their potential to terrorise and to deliver collective punishment. An extra-judicial killing by the state in the course of counter-terrorism may in itself arguably not be a terrorist act, as in the case of the British police's execution of the unarmed and innocent Jean Charles de Menezes on the London Underground in July 2005. Nevertheless, as Smith points out in carefully detailing the lack of democratic oversight of the deadly 'shoot to kill' policies and the active cover-up by various arms of the state, the entrenchment and unquestionability of state political violence have far-reaching and enduring consequences.

As we write this conclusion, the British Ministry of Defence announced its apology for the unlawful killing by one of its soldiers of the innocent and unarmed civilian Billy McKavanagh, shot in the back in Belfast on 11 August 1971, and the pistol-whipping, hooding and beating with rifle butts and batons meted out to his two distraught and bereaved companions, Pat and Teddy Rooney (Bowcott 2011). The killer was identified, but was found in the official report to have made an honest mistake; there was apparently never any official investigation into the torture, and its perpetrators are not identifiable. It is not merely history that is repeated in this instance, but this type of impunity is evident in each of the cases dealt with in this book. The global reproduction of state impunity means that geography and history repeat the same patterns across time and place. In each of our chapters, impunity for extreme violence acts as an ever-present underlying context and intensifies the terror of its victims who see in institutionalised impunity the unrestrained character of state violence.

The parallels between the strategies of violent counter-terrorism pursued by states in the various cases in this book are no coincidence. In the context of the 'global war on terror', this should be obvious. Yet the sharing of torture manuals, and the anti-terror 'policy laundering', did not begin after the demolition of the twin towers on 9/11, nor has it finished with the dumping of Osama Bin Laden's body in the ocean. We have contended that the violent counter-insurgency of the fading British empire during post-war decolonisation, and that of the succeeding US-led one, have amounted to 'empire terrorism', with the sharing, cooperating, refining and perhaps even normalisation of its methods that we have delineated. The chapter by Chomsky reproduced in this volume makes this abundantly clear. From the Vietnam war to the Iraq wars, those who 'resist direct US aggression' are defined as terrorists and subjected to the full panoply of counter-terrorism technique. The 'counter-terrorism' can be pre-emptive: Chomsky reminds us that the US mounted a counter-insurgency intervention by special forces in Colombia in 1962, the forerunner of similar 'paramilitary, sabotage and/or terrorist activities' (General Yarborough did not mince words) that was to be repeated in El Salvador in the 1980s, then Guatemala, then Nicaragua, where Washington sent the Contras to attack 'soft targets'. Yet Washington's terror in Central America could never be countennced as terrorism; only the 'known communists' were the terrorists. The transition from Cold War to 'clash of civilisations' rhetoric saw the 'known communists' increasingly replaced by 'Islamic fundamentalists'.

Pilger's chapter likewise traces the technology of empire terror against civilians, from the carpet bombing in Vietnam from unseen B52s 'above the clouds' to the use of the same method by the same empire (alongside some of the same client state allies) two decades later in Iraq and a decade on in Afghanistan and once more in Iraq from 2003. The 'cluster bombs' deployed in Indochina were the progenitors of those in Afghanistan lauded by Defence Secretary Geoffrey Hoon, as Pilger has documented, and used recently in more advanced plastic non-exrayable form by Israel in Gaza, as detailed in Mason's chapter. Cluster bombs are now banned according to international humanitarian law, under the Convention on Cluster Munitions 2008. Following Pilger's lead about unseen weapons deployed at a distance in the name of 'civilisation' against civilians labelled as terrorists, we should right now be asking questions about the criminality of empires (rather than merely states, since not only the US but minor 'special relationship' partners such as the UK and Australia are also involved in their deployment) using 'drones' for extrajudicial killings.

Pilger's big picture of the 'Great Game' provides us with a salutary political-economic explanation of the 'war on terror', and it has little to do with the 'sham' of extending civilisation and democracy.

The chapters in this book collectively break down the hegemonic myths that support this sham. As this struggle for hegemony over understandings of the purpose of state violence is played out, it produces a fundamental contradiction. Governments also need to retain political integrity. They need to provide some plausible justification or narrative for their strategies. And it is in the struggle to defend those narratives that governments remain vulnerable (Whyte 2010). The hegemonic eradication of politics is not something that can be achieved without some risk to the political justifications for the political violence of states. To apply the term first used by the CIA in this context, political repression always carries a risk of blowback.

While this book was being put together, the backlash against the criminalisation of the whole spectrum of left/separatist groups in the Basque Country by the Spanish government resulted in the successful regrouping of the left and its widespread popular support in the Basque Country in the 2011 local elections. Moreover, in every country involved in the 'Arab Spring' of 2011, the violence of the state was experienced as both a motivation for the uprisings and a means of suppressing them. Tunisia looks forward to imminent democratic elections, which are by no means a forgone conclusion. Egypt is still firmly in the grip of a military regime that has the imprimatur of the US, that imprisons without trial and tortures, but which is not unchallenged. Bahrain has seen its uprising cruelly crushed by its own state, with the abetment of Saudi Arabia, the scenes at the Pearl Roundabout reminiscent of Tiananmen Square. Yemen is in violent flux. Libya is in the aftermath of civil war; the control of its oil has always been crucial, and will likely be the object of further political violence. Syria is also in turmoil, but the western allies, unlike in Libya, are here keeping on the side of 'stability'. In each of these cases, we have recently seen the same type of phenomena delineated in this book: connections between the state and terrorist groups, counter-terrorism expanding the state's legitimate targets, pre-emptive 'counter-terrorism' against oppositional groups in civil society, and structural impunity for the perpetrators of state political violence.

As this book comes to a conclusion, we read media reports of documents coming to light in the Libyan civil war, demonstrating the US and British states' facilitation of unlawful 'rendition' to Libya, and their collaboration, in the name of countering Al Qaeda, in interrogation under torture by Gaddafi's regime of a number of victims associated with the anti-Gaddafi Libyan Islamic Fighting Group. These included Abdul Hakim Belhaj, who became military commander of the anti-Gaddafi rebels in Tripoli in 2011, and thus an ally (Cobain and Chulov 2011).

Make no mistake: the 'war on terror' is a political project. It is one that relies upon the willed coordination across the political classes of collaborator nations, and upon some popular consent within subject populations. The prospect of a war on terror that could ever wholly eradicate politics is unimaginable. As a project it could never remain unopposed. And this is where the contributions to this book are important. For each contribution enables us to see how the asymmetries of political violence are based upon real, material conditions. The examples of political violence outlined by each of the contributions have their own histories and they have their own very specific reasons. Most of all, each of them can be understood as a political struggle around concrete issues, often involving movements for self-determination and struggles against expropriation and exploitation, and the state suppression of that which is irreducibly political. For this reason, they describe struggles of political violence that on either side are never reducible to 'terrorism'.

## Notes

1 *Bin Laden: Shoot to Kill*, produced by Nutopia and aired in the UK on Channel 4, 7 September 2011.
2 By 'asymmetries' we mean that they are not equally weighted or equivalent. On the other hand, we recognise that they are intimately connected. The resources upon which state political violence can draw, whether measured in terms of its personnel and technical capacity, resources of sovereign political power or information resources upon which its propaganda can be built, almost always place states in an advantageous position in counter-terrorism and counter-insurgency struggles.

## References

Bowcott, O. (2011) 'MoD says sorry for 1971 army killing in Belfast', *Guardian*, 1 November, p. 15.
Chomsky, N. (2011) '9/11: was there an alternative?', *Al Jazeera online*, 7 September, available online at: www.aljazeera.com/indepth/opinion/2011/09/20119775453842191.html, accessed 10 November 2011.
Cobain, I. and Chulov, M. (2011) 'Gaddafi's secret link to UK rendition', *Guardian*, 5 September, pp. 1–2.
Whyte, D. (2010) 'Dismantling the reasons of state', *Criminal Justice Matters*, December, vol. 82, pp. 4–5.

# Index

*9780415748094*

An environmentally friendly book printed and bound in England by www.printondemand-worldwide.com

PEFC/16-33-415

PEFC Certified

This product is from sustainably managed forests and controlled sources

www.pefc.org

This book is made of chain-of-custody materials; FSC materials for the cover and PEFC materials for the text pages.

- CO - 234/156/14 - PB - 9780415748094